Students with
Severe Disabilities

Students with Severe Disabilities: Current Perspectives and Practices

RICHARD W. BRIMER
Southern Illinois University at Edwardsville

 Mayfield Publishing Company
Mountain View, California
London • Toronto

Copyright © 1990 by Mayfield Publishing Company

Library of Congress Cataloging-in-Publication Data
Brimer, Richard W.
   Students with severe disabilities : current perspectives and practices / Richard W. Brimer.
     p. cm.
   Includes bibliographical references.
   ISBN 0-87484-783-4
   1. Handicapped—Education. 2. Behavioral assessment.
3. Handicapped—Services for. I. Title.
LC4015.B726   1990
371.9—dc20   89-13646
                                               CIP

Manufactured in the United States of America
10 9 8 7 6 5 4 3 2 1

Mayfield Publishing Company
1240 Villa Street
Mountain View, California 94041

Sponsoring editor, Franklin C. Graham; developmental editor, Kathleen Engleberg; manuscript editor, Zipporah Collins; text and cover designer, Wendy Calmenson; production management, The Book Company. The text was set in 10/12 ITC New Baskerville by Interactive Composition, and printed on 50# Finch Opaque by R.R. Donnelley.

This book is dedicated to HAM and to my Itards

Brief Contents

CONTENTS

PART THREE: ADMINISTRATIVE CONCERNS

PART FOUR: NEW DIRECTIONS FOR SERVING PERSONS WITH SEVERE DISABILITIES

PREFACE

This is a book about students with severe disabilities. It seeks to explain the education of these students in terms of facts and concepts and through case studies and examples, not simply by discussing genes, stereotypic behaviors, echolalia, and schooling. It is designed as a problems and characteristics textbook for students in preservice training programs and as a guide for direct service practitioners now educating, training, and working with persons with severe disabilities. Its purpose is to inform, and perhaps arouse, readers, to help them understand the point Pinel made more than a century and half ago: persons with severe disabilities are ordinary human beings.

First, theory, research, and state-of-the-art practices are presented, to provide the soundest possible base of information on students with severe disabilities. Then, an effort is made to tie the theory and research to concrete reality, for readers are unlikely to value or remember such knowledge otherwise. The intent is not to force facts onto readers, but to stimulate their curiosity and intellectual interest, to engage them in ways that encourage learning and understanding. Finally, the controversies surrounding services to persons with severe disabilities are discussed frankly.

The general aim of this book is to increase both cognitive and affective understanding of students with severe disabilities. Both kinds of understanding are needed for thorough insight into the needs, nature, and abilities of the students.

A variety of perspectives—normalization, integration, personal, familial, and educational—form the structural backbone of the book. The first chapter reviews how our ancestors treated persons with disabilities. It then analyzes some of the previous definitions of such persons and proposes a working definition of them.

The text then proceeds to Part One, which examines the categories in the severely disabled cluster. Chapter 2 looks at students with severe and profound mental retardation; chapter 3 examines those with severe and profound behavior disorders; chapter 4 those with severe and profound physical disabilities; and chapter 5 those with multiple disabilities, highlighting students with both visual and hearing impairments. While the characteristics of each disability are thoroughly described, the approach is emphatically humanistic, describing how individuals are affected by the disability and some of the adaptations they must make in daily living. Each chapter concludes with a case study that illuminates the cumulative effects of the disability on the child and how the child is affected by external factors.

Part Two analyzes behavioral concerns of students with severe disabilities, including school and community integration, communication skills, social-personal traits, generalization and maintenance problems, and vocational and employment concerns. The central approach is the educability hypothesis. We are beyond asking if it is possible to educate these students; now we must concentrate our efforts on developing and enhancing their education. For instance, we know that school integration is beneficial for students with and without disabilities. It is already being practiced in many schools. Students with severe disabilities are presently employed in some remunerative, competitive work sites. Students with severe disabilities are already exhibiting appropriate social and personal skills and forming friendships with their nondisabled classmates in some schools. Now we must extend those models to all settings and students.

Part Three analyzes the person with severe disabilities from a life-cycle perspective. Chapter 11 describes the family of the child with severe disabilities from two viewpoints—the effects of the child on the family unit and the effects of the family on the child. The next three chapters deal with schooling. Chapter 12 reports on nontraditional preschool programs, chapter 13 describes curricular and instructional modifications of regular school programs, and chapter 14 discusses adult and community programs. The basic theme is that instruction must be practical, be tailored to the community in which the student lives, be appropriate to the student's chronological age, and take place in natural settings. It makes little sense to teach a student in the classroom how to ride a bus or eat in a fast food restaurant if these skills are not generalized and used in the student's neighborhood or community.

Part Four looks at future developments. Chapter 15 describes the present and future impact of advocates in providing services for persons with severe disabilities. Chapter 16 examines changing perspectives in serving students with severe disabilities and what tomorrow may bring in services for them.

The book as a whole is rooted in the belief that students without disabilities and students with severe disabilities must be viewed as points along a continuum rather than as poles of a dichotomy. Students with severe disabilities should not be regarded as deviant and strange or as helpless and dependent, afflicted with absolute and unalterable conditions; rather, they need to be approached as unique, valuable, and capable persons.

Acknowledgments

Every book represents the efforts of many persons, and this volume is no exception. Countless professionals have provided help and advice, freely giving their time without any expectation of reward or compensation. They have offered ideas, insights, and thoughts. They have taught me compassion and understanding. For these gifts, I shall always be grateful; because of them, I am proud to say that I am a special educator.

There are some whose help and assistance I must acknowledge particularly. For their insight and support, I wish to thank Lynda Atherton, Barb Chatman, Judy Schultzenhofer, and Ruthanna Bryant. For providing years of critical analysis that helped to shape my philosophy, I thank and acknowledge Donna Bishop, Shelly Ryan, Sue Rouse, Marilyn Chandler, and Reuben Altman. For critically reviewing earlier drafts of the text I thank David Feldman, Mary Falvey, Joseph Justen, and Sandy Alper.

I wish especially to thank Frank Graham of Mayfield Publishing Company. Without his extreme patience and understanding, his confidence and encouragement, this book could not have been written.

I sincerely thank all who helped in this endeavor.

CHAPTER 1

Perspectives in Serving Persons with Severe Disabilities: Yesterday and Today

(Courtesy of Houghton Mifflin Company.)

If today we saw a man standing on a street corner flagellating himself with a leather whip, what would happen? A concerned bystander would probably call the police, who would take the man to an emergency treatment center. Yet, when the bubonic plague was devastating Europe during the fourteenth century, such flagellants stood in marketplaces beating themselves with frenzy to atone for the sins that presumedly had provoked God to send the Black Death. These medieval flagellants were regarded with reverence by the people whose villages they visited on their penitential travels.

If today we saw members of a religious sect standing on a street corner, dressed in flowing robes, and espousing a direct revelation from God, what would happen? Even though they might not be accepted and welcomed, these religious individuals would not likely cause great concern to either bystanders or the police. Yet the Massachusetts Bay Colony banished Anne Hutchinson because she claimed to have experienced a direct revelation from God.

Such different reactions can be easily explained. Medieval society could understand trances and passionate self-sacrifices much more than it could comprehend germs, bacteria, and disease. Conversely, the scientific rationalism of twentieth-century society considers self-flagellation a mental disturbance and plague a disease carried by rats rather than evidence of divine wrath. The conventions of the seventeenth-century Puritan society prohibited the thought that God would communicate directly to a woman; therefore, Anne Hutchinson was psychotic or worse. Modern society is more accepting of religious diversity and deviance.

The way in which differences, including disabilities, are defined changes with time and depends on social conventions and values designating what we can and cannot do, where, when, and with whom. These values and norms control much of our existence, from far-reaching decisions to prosaic daily routines. The rather common area of personal dress is regulated not only by climatic and weather conditions but also by social conventions about appropriate dress. For instance, wearing jeans and a chambray shirt is fine for a picnic or around the house, but it is not the appropriate apparel for a seminar or a symphony concert. If a man wears a tuxedo to a formal, candlelit dinner party, his attire is considered the epitome of good taste. If he wears a tuxedo to the center-field bleachers at a ball game, his virility or even his sanity may be questioned; he is expected to wear something closer to a polo shirt and twill pants. Conversely if he wears a polo shirt and twill pants to a formal dinner at the governor's mansion he will be considered either very daring or very ignorant.

The pressures to conform to society's values and norms influence every aspect of our existence. To a person from another culture, such "dress codes" may seem strange and unnecessarily complicated, but an adult socialized in this culture takes the unwritten rules about clothing for granted.

PERSONS WITH SEVERE DISABILITIES: A SHORT HISTORY

How today's society defines, explains, and relates to persons with severe disabilities is the result of trial and error by previous generations coming to grips with such persons. This section presents a brief history of society's attitudes toward and treatment of persons with severe disabilities.

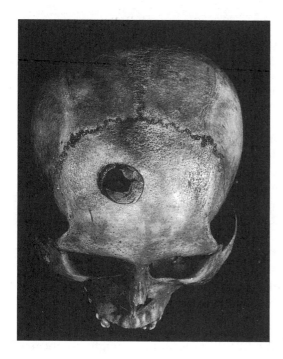

FIGURE 1.1

The technique of trephining involved chipping a hole in the person's skull through which the evil spirit might escape. This skull shows that some individuals actually survived this "operation." The bone had time to heal considerably before the person died.

(FROM: Neg. No. 283258, photo by L. Bierwert; courtesy Department of Library Services, American Museum of Natural History.)

Early Human Society: The Rise of Demonology

Just as ancient peoples attributed all changes—life and death, sunshine and storm, good harvest and famine—to the action of supernatural forces, so persons with disabilities were seen as possessed by spirits. Archaeological evidence indicates that Stone Age people dealt with these spirits in a rather direct way. Using a crude surgical technique called trephining, they chipped a circular hole, or trephine, into the skull of the possessed person to allow the evil spirit to escape. Surprisingly, certain skulls found in China and Peru show healing around the trephine, indicating that some of our ancestors actually survived this operation (Zilboorg & Henry, 1941). Nevertheless, in most primitive societies, children with severe disabilities did not survive infancy because the tribes permitted infanticide (Hewett & Forness, 1977).

The idea that disabilities were due to invasion of the body by an evil spirit endured for many centuries and in many cultures. References to possession are found in the ancient records of the Chinese, the Egyptians, the Greeks, the Hebrews, and the early Christians.

The Greeks: The Birth of Rationalism

As early as the sixth century B.C., the Greeks began to turn away from mythology toward a belief in rationalism, the idea that human reason is equal to the task of understanding nature. Persons with severe disabilities were, for the first time in history, studied as a natural rather than a supernatural phenomenon.

This innovation occurred largely because of one man, the Greek physician Hippocrates, who drew heavily on the work of his teacher, Empedocles.

Hippocrates developed the first naturalistic or organic theory attributing disabilities to physiological factors. He undertook the novel task of observing cases and recording his observations as objectively as possible. He also devised treatments more humane than any used earlier. Hippocrates often moved patients into his home to watch and care for them properly (Calhoun, Acocella, & Goldstein, 1977). Through his efforts, retreats were established to habilitate persons with disabilities through rest, exercise, music, and other therapeutic activities.

Not all Greece adopted an enlightened, Hippocratic treatment of persons with disabilities, however. In Sparta, for example, ruthless eugenics was practiced. Infants who appeared defective were thrown from a cliff to die (Durant, 1966). Even during Hippocrates' time, in Athens deformed infants were left in large earthenware vessels near a temple where they would perish from either exposure or animal attack (Durant, 1954).

With the rise of Rome, the Hippocratic approach continued for a few more centuries. The Greek physicians Asclepiades, Soranus, and Galen, practicing in Rome, expanded on the organic theories of Hippocrates (Zilboorg & Henry, 1941). Nevertheless, the Romans permitted the father to expose to death or abandon any child who was deformed. Well-to-do Romans might accept persons with severe mental retardation into their homes to function as buffoons or objects of amusement at social gatherings (Wallin, 1955). The Roman emperor Commodus periodically gathered individuals with physical disabilities to use for bow and arrow target practice (Durant, 1944).

With the fall of Rome to the barbarians in the fifth century, the Hippocratic philosophy gave way to a resurgence of ancient superstition. Demonology was reborn and quietly but warmly received by the new Christian church.

The Middle Ages and Renaissance: A Return to Demonology

In the Middle Ages, religion was the foundation for all actions, from artistic achievements to abuse of persons with disabilities. The naturalistic philosophy of the ancient Greeks, which looked to the vicissitudes of human life for the causes of disabilities, was eclipsed by Christian supernaturalism, the belief that all things were explained by divine will and were beyond human understanding (Wallin, 1955; Zilboorg & Henry, 1941).

Rationalism was replaced by demonology. Disabilities were considered a punishment for a sin, often of a sexual nature. It was held that persons with disabilities were demonically possessed (Kirtley, 1975). In the early Middle Ages, the possessed were generally subjected to mild exorcisms, but as time passed and theological doctrine was refined, treatments became harsher: The possessed were starved, dunked in boiling water, chained, and flogged. Belief in demons and faith in exorcistic treatments were by no means confined to the ignorant and violent. The wise and mild-mannered Sir Thomas More wrote to a friend, "I caused him to be taken by the constables and bound to a tree in the street before the whole town, and there striped [whipped] him until he waxed wearily. Verily, God be thanked" (cited in Deutsch, 1949, p. 13).

Ironically, this dark period in the treatment of persons with disabilities spans the three centuries of the Renaissance, venerated as the rebirth of ancient wisdom. It is conservatively estimated that from 1450 to 1700, some 100,000 people were executed as witches. During the 1800s, 20,000 witches were put to death in Scotland alone. Throughout Europe, the hunting down of witches became a day-to-day social and religious duty. Neighbors reported neighbors, priests their parishioners, parents their children, and children their parents. Everyone was suspect. The best defense was to show a pious zeal in reporting others (Zilboorg & Henry, 1941).

The Eighteenth and Nineteenth Centuries: A Return to Rationalism

Early in the fifteenth century, the first hospitals for persons with severe disabilities were founded in Moslem Spain. In the following decades, Christian Europe and America followed the Moslem example and opened hospitals in many major cities. However, the dreadful conditions persons with disabilities endured in such hospitals made a quick death as a witch seem almost merciful. In the first hospital founded in Christian Europe, St. Mary of Bethlehem in London, the patients lay howling in chains, and the curious public could buy tickets to watch them "perform." (Eventually, a contraction of the hospital's name, Bedlam, became a synonym for any noisy, chaotic place.) In these hospitals, patients were chained, caged, starved, preyed upon by rats, and forced to lie naked in their own excrement while being displayed for the amusement of the public (Foucault, 1965). In Vienna, the architects of a new hospital created an ingenious structure called the Lunatic's Tower to house persons with disabilities along the outer walls of a cylinder so that they could be viewed better by passers-by (Calhoun, Acocella, & Goldstein, 1977).

The first change in this treatment came in the late eighteenth century, through the work of Phillippe Pinel, chief physician at La Bicetre, a large hospital in Paris, during the French Revolution. Imbued with the spirit of liberty, equality, and fraternity, Pinel was aghast at the conditions in the two Parisian hospitals for persons with disabilities. At La Bicetre, for instance:

> The unfortunate whose entire furniture consisted of this straw pallet, lying with his head, feet, and body pressed against the wall, could not enjoy sleep without being soaked by the water that trickled from that mass of stone. As for the cells of La Salpetriere, what made the place more miserable and often more fatal, was that in the winter, when the waters of the Seine rose, those cells situated at the level of the sewers became not only more unhealthy, but worse still, a refuge for a swarm of huge rats, which during the night attacked the unfortunates confined there and bit them wherever they could reach them; madwomen have been found with feet, hands, and faces torn by bites which are often dangerous and from which several have died [cited in Foucault, 1965, pp. 70–71].

FIGURE 1.2

Pinel believed that persons with disabilities were ordinary human beings and to treat them as animals not only was inhumane but also obstructed treatment.

(FROM: Robert Fleury, *Pinel Freeing Mental Patients at Salpetriere Hospital, Paris 1796.* © Belzeaux/ Rapho-Photo Researchers, Inc. Courtesy of Bruce Roberts from Rapho-Photo Researchers, Inc.)

Pinel made a simple point: Individuals with disabilities were ordinary human beings, and to treat them as animals not only was inhumane but also obstructed treatment. He convinced the French revolutionary government to allow him to unchain a group of patients, many of whom had not seen the light of day for thirty or forty years (Zilboorg & Henry, 1941). He replaced the foul dungeons with airy, sunny rooms. He did away with violent treatments and initiated humane, gentle procedures (Selling, 1940; Zilboorg & Henry, 1941).

The same year that Pinel was instituting the first reforms at La Bicetre, a Quaker tea merchant named William Tuke was attempting similar reforms in northern England. Aroused by the abominable conditions in which persons with disabilities lived and died, Tuke devoted his life to reform. Tuke was convinced that the most therapeutic environment for persons with disabilities would be a quiet and supportive religious setting. He moved a group of such individuals to a peaceful rural estate, called the York Retreat. There they talked out their problems, worked, prayed, rested, took walks in the country, and received wholesome and dignified care from Tuke's fellow Quakers. Not only did the York Retreat serve as a model for half of the facilities built in the United States before 1824, but also Tuke's close contact with the American Quakers gave him more influence than Pinel in introducing his therapeutic treatment, called *moral management,* to the United States (Dain, 1964; Zilboorg & Henry, 1941).

The job of extending these reforms was taken up by a Boston school-teacher named Dorothea Dix. At the age of 40, Dix took a job teaching Sunday School in a prison and encountered the gruesome conditions suffered by persons with disabilities. Soon she was traveling across the country visiting squalid jails, poorhouses, and almshouses, and lecturing state legislatures on their duty to the forgotten inhabitants of these institutions (Deutsch, 1949). Paradoxically, Dix's reforms contributed to the decline of moral management. She impressed on the public the need to hospitalize individuals with disabilities. The new hospitals became overcrowded almost immediately, obliterating the calm, tranquil atmosphere necessary for moral management (Foucault, 1965).

Perhaps the biggest influence on the treatment of persons with severe disabilities, indeed on all special education, was the work of **Jean Marc Gaspard Itard**. Itard's story begins in the forest of Aveyron in southern France in 1799 where a "wild boy" of 11 or 12 was seized by hunters. The boy had apparently lived most of his life as a primitive forest creature. He was like an animal in appearance and behavior: naked, dirty, scared, and unable to speak. He selected food by smell. He did not respond to the sound of a pistol fired behind him but did respond to the fall of a nut from a tree. His sense of touch did not appear to discriminate between hot and cold. He was brought to the National Institute for Deaf Mutes in Paris, where his presence elicited much interest and curiosity.[1] Convinced that with proper training the boy would become normal, Itard obtained permission to care for and work with the boy, whom he named Victor. Nevertheless, leading authorities, including Pinel, considered the boy a "hopeless idiot" and saw little to be gained by Itard's efforts (Itard, 1932; Pritchard, 1963).

Over a five-year period of intensive training, Itard made great advances with Victor, but with the onset of puberty, Victor became violent and eventually uncontrollable. Itard ended his experiment and put Victor in the care of a kindly governess, with whom he resided until his death at age 40.[2]

Itard was bitterly disappointed over his failure to make Victor normal. Nevertheless, his accomplishments were instrumental in stimulating the instruction of persons with disabilities throughout Europe and the United States. He firmly believed and demonstrated that persons with disabilities could learn and improve (Doll, 1962). In his work with Victor, Itard applied sound pedagogical principles to the problems of learning; his techniques are used today in the education of students with disabilities and in early childhood education. Itard's efforts to educate Victor also served as a beacon for Sequin, Montessori, Decroly, Descoeudres, and other followers in the education of individuals with disabilities (Kirk & Johnson, 1951).

The Twentieth Century: The Struggle for Reform

As the United States entered the twentieth century, the predominant service delivery system for persons with disabilities was institution placement. Yet some people wanted to educate students with disabilities in the communities in which they lived. This had been done in Germany since 1860 and by 1900 was firmly established throughout that country. In the United States, the first community-based special class for students with disabilities was established in Boston shortly after the Civil War. By the second decade of the twentieth century, however, less than a dozen cities had public school classes for students with disabilities (Doll, 1962; Wallin, 1955). The vast majority of these programs were intended for children with below-average intelligence and mild disabilities; those with moderate, severe, and profound disabilities were institutionalized or hidden away.

Community-based special classes were founded on optimism and dedication. These feelings changed to pessimism and discouragement when teachers found they were unable to cure students with disabilities. The few classes in operation closed, and the children more often than not were put in state institutions.

Still some spoke against institutionalization. In a speech at the national convention of the National Education Association, Dr. Alexander Graham Bell recommended that programs for children with disabilities should become "annexed to the public school system receiving special instruction from special teachers who shall be able to give instruction to little children . . . without sending them away from their homes or from the ordinary companions with whom they are associated" (cited in Gearheart, 1980, p. 9).

Public school exclusion was based on existing law and in many quarters was considered legal, appropriate, and pedagogically sound. Several states had statutes excluding children with physical and mental disabilities from school attendance. It was widely believed that these children were "depressing" and no adequate instructional program could be or had to be provided for them.

A partial rationale for such statutes is given by a 1919 ruling of the Wisconsin Supreme Court: "The right of a child of school age to attend the public schools of the state cannot be insisted upon, when its presence therein is harmful to the best interests of the school" (*Beattie v. Board of Education of Antigo* (1919), p. 153). Lawyers for Merritt Beattie, the child in question, showed that he was not a physical threat, was mentally normal, and could compete academically with the other pupils. The major argument by the school system was that Merritt's cerebral palsy produced "a depressing and nauseating effect upon the teachers and school children; that by reason of his physical condition he takes an undue portion of the teacher's time and attention, distracts the attention of the other pupils and interferes generally with the discipline and progress of the school" (p. 154).

Excluding students with disabilities from public school extended well into the 1950s. Then changes in society, government, and education markedly influenced the outlook for individuals with disabilities. In the 1950s, the civil rights movement gained momentum as blacks demanded equality in education, equal treatment, and equal access to public places. Their social activism was marked by lobbying activities, sit-ins, and boycotts. A few years later, the parents of children with disabilities adopted the same techniques to obtain equality in education, equal treatment, and equal access to public places for their children. Like the blacks, when their civil rights were denied, these parents and advocacy groups looked to the government to redress their grievances.

In the 1960s, a number of parent groups increased pressure at state and federal levels. The election of John F. Kennedy to the presidency heralded a major upswing in professional involvement in this advocacy (Gallagher, Forsythe, Ringelheim, & Weintraub, 1975). Under Presidents Kennedy and Johnson, a number of landmark laws were passed to provide broad federal assistance to persons with disabilities. Other federal programs were modified to fill the needs of individuals with disabilities.

The 1970s were characterized by child advocacy and litigation. Child advocacy programs went beyond protecting the human and civil rights of children and adults with disabilities (Gallagher, 1975; Koocher, 1976). Despite the greater availability of special classes in the public schools, some parents still had difficulty obtaining necessary services for their children, especially those with severe disabilities. Certain exclusionary policies still restricted public school attendance. Parents, guardians, and other supporters of children with disabilities joined in challenging the courts and state legislatures to guarantee every child the right to equal educational opportunities.

Under the Fourteenth Amendment of the Constitution (which guarantees equal protection), these advocacy groups argued, every child has the right to a public education. In 1972, a landmark court decision adopted this stand. In a class action, *Pennsylvania Association for Retarded Children (PARC) v. Pennsylvania* (1972), the plaintiffs represented an estimated 14,000 mentally retarded children excluded from educational opportunities (Brimer & Barudin, 1981). The court ruled that all children, even those with profound retardation, were entitled to a free, appropriate public education. A few months later, in *Mills v. Board of Education of the District of Columbia,* another class action concerning children with various disabilities, the court stipulated that no child was to be excluded from receiving "a publicly supported education consistent with his needs and ability to benefit therefrom" (cited in Weintraub & Abeson, 1974, p. 548).

Despite these decisions, parents of children with severe disabilities often found that appropriate special education classes were filled, or more often just not available. Parents, educators, and interested legislators vigorously lobbied for a vital piece of legislation designed to end this inequality. Late in 1975, President Ford signed one of the most comprehensive provisions enacted for children and youth with disabilities, the Education for All Handicapped Children Act of 1975 (PL 94–142). It set forth "as national policy the proposition that education must be extended to all persons with disabilities as their fundamental right" (Brenton, 1974, p. 6) and guaranteed a free and appropriate public education to *all* children with disabilities. Under this law, children with severe disabilities were a high-priority, targeted population.

While the *PARC* and *Mills* cases were restructuring public school services for students with disabilities, *Wyatt v. Stickney* (1972) and its appellate cases, *Wyatt v. Aderholt* (1974) and *Wyatt v. Ireland* (1979), were reforming state institutions for children and adults with mental retardation and behavior disorders. The federal district court ruled that persons with mental retardation were being deprived of their right to individual treatment that would give them a realistic opportunity for habilitation while fostering their entry into society. The judge described the institution in question as a human warehouse steeped in an atmosphere of deprivation and abuse. The decision mandated that appropriate training and education programs occur in a therapeutic environment (Hardman, Drew, & Egan, 1987).

Current Treatment: Normalization

If a single word could describe the current direction of services for persons with severe disabilities, it would be **normalization**. Nirje (1969) described normalization as "making available to the mentally retarded patterns and conditions of everyday life which are as close as possible to norms and patterns of the mainstream of society" (p. 181). This represents a significant departure in policy from just a few years ago, when services were likely to stress the differences between persons with severe disabilities and persons without disabilities and therefore were likely to be delivered segregated from society.

The concept of normalization was first proposed by Neils Bank-Mikkelsen, director of Danish services for persons with mental retardation. He wanted "to create an existence for the mentally retarded [that was] as close to normal living conditions as possible" (Bank-Mikkelsen, 1980, p. 56), and he was instrumental in incorporating this principle into the 1959 Danish law governing services for such persons. The first systematic description of normalization did not occur until almost a decade later, by the executive director of the Swedish Association for Retarded Children, Bengt Nirje. Nirje's highly influential article emphasized that normalization gives a person the opportunity to undergo the normal experiences in life. A few years later, Wolf Wolfensberger published a text "North Americanizing" this Scandinavian principle, to incorpo-

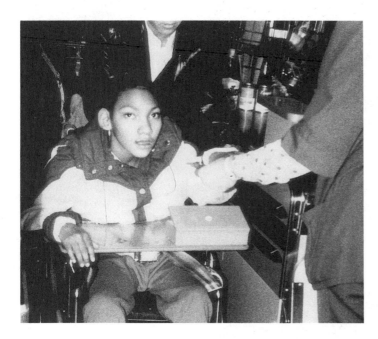

FIGURE 1.3

The principle of normalization suggests that students with severe disabilities be provided with training in their home communities.

(Courtesy of Barbara Chatman.)

rate it into service delivery systems in the United States and Canada. Wolfensberger emphasized that the appropriateness and the desirability of services, facilities, and programs need to be analyzed in relation to the norms of the person's home community (Wolfensberger, 1980).

One example of normalization is **deinstitutionalization**. This means getting persons with severe disabilities out of large, impersonal institutions and back into their home communities. Recent experience has demonstrated that formerly institutionalized individuals often can be much happier and more productive in small, homelike residences, where their life-style resembles everyone else's to a greater degree. Many professionals are urging that all persons with severe disabilities now in institutions be placed in homelike community residences and that institutions no longer accept as residents persons with disabilities.

A second example of normalization is the **mainstreaming** movement in public education. Many children with severe disabilities who used to be placed in special schools segregated from the mainstream are now provided with special services in the same buildings and ideally in the same classrooms as children of their chronological age. Like the trend toward deinstitutionalization, this movement represents a change in outlook from emphasizing differences toward stressing that persons with severe disabilities are not so different from those whom people consider normal.

FIGURE 1.4

With appropriate training, persons with severe disabilities can lead happy and productive lives in their communities.

(FROM: Sailor, Wayne and Guess, Doug, *Severely Handicapped Students: An Instructional Design* © 1983, Houghton Mifflin Company.)

DEFINITIONS OF PERSONS WITH SEVERE DISABILITIES

Even from today's perspective, the formulation of a simple, straightforward definition of severe disabilities is not easy. First, the term embraces not a single condition or neurological entity, but rather a great heterogeneity of **etiologies** and symptomatic conditions. Unlike the definitions of mental retardation, visual disabilities, or hearing disabilities, which are based on two or three exclusionary dimensions, the definition of persons with severe disabilities has to be fairly open. Second, many individuals not only have a primary disabling condition (e.g., mental retardation) but also have one or several secondary conditions (e.g., cerebral palsy, visual disabilities, and hearing disabilities). Some persons with severe disabilities have two conditions that each would not merit the classification alone but do justify it when both conditions occur together (for instance, deafness and blindness).

The Evolution of Contemporary Definitions

Historically, children with severe disabilities were excluded from public school attendance because it was felt that most were nonambulatory, were incapable of basic self-care, were unable to communicate basic needs and wants, and manifested deviant, destructive, or antisocial behavior. Many early definitions of students with severe disabilities therefore argued against the criteria of exclusion. Typical of early definitions is the one proposed by Abt Associates (1974):

> severely handicapped children and youth were functionally defined as those persons age 21 and under who are either mentally retarded, emotionally disturbed, deaf-blind, or multiply handicapped and who exhibit *two or more* of the following behaviors with a degree of regularity: [1] self-mutilation behaviors such as head banging, body scratching, hair pulling, etc. which may result in danger to oneself; [2] ritualistic behaviors such as rocking, pacing, autistic-like behavior, etc. which do not involve danger to oneself; [3] self-stimulation behaviors such as masturbation, stroking, patting, etc. for a total of more than one hour of a waking day; [4] failure to attend to even the most pronounced social stimuli, including failure to respond to invitations from peers or adults, or loss of contact with reality; [5] lack of self-care skills such as toilet training, self-feeding, self-dressing and grooming, etc.; [6] lack of verbal communication skills; and [7] lack of physical mobility including confinement to bed, inability to find one's way around the institution or facility, etc. [p. v].

Early definitions like this one describe the population in categorical terms and then list characteristics typical of persons with severe disabilities. Serious drawbacks to such definitions are lack of precision in defining the parameters, such as "a degree of regularity," "failure to respond to invitations from peers or adults," or "lack of physical mobility."

Recognizing the problems of previous definitions, Justen (1976) proposed a definition taking an educational perspective. This "second generation" definition attempted to describe the population in positive, behavioral terms:

> The "severely handicapped" refers to those individuals age 21 and younger who are functioning at a general development level of half or less than the level which would be expected on the basis of chronological age and who manifest learning and/or behavior problems of such a magnitude and significance that they require extensive structure in learning situations if their education needs are to be well served [p. 5].

Two parts of this definition merit explanation. First, the phrase "general developmental level" refers to an individual's performance in the combined areas of intellectual, social, motor, and adaptive behaviors. The developmental level in each area need not be less than half of that expected on the basis of chronological age, but the combined or overall level must be. Second, Justen did not specify the learning and behavior problems that would require extensive restructuring of the classroom environment, but he suggested the seven behaviors cited by Abt Associates as good criteria for his definition.

Under Justen's definition, an individual must meet both criteria. For example, a child with Down syndrome who had an IQ of 50 might have an overall developmental level less than half that expected on the basis of chronological age but probably would not require extensive restructuring of the learning environment. A child with a visual disability might require the restructuring but probably would have an overall developmental level above half of the expected level. A child with both Down syndrome and a visual impairment would probably fulfill both criteria for the severe disabilities classification.

Sailor and his associates also attempted to define persons with severe disabilities from an educational perspective, but following a *service-need* philosophy. Typical of the service-need definitions is the following proposed by Sailor and Haring (1977):

> A child should be assigned to a program for the severely/multiply handicapped according to whether the primary service needs of the child are *basic* or academic. . . . If the diagnosis and assessment process determines that a child with multiple handicaps needs *academic* instruction, that child should *not* be referred to the severely/multiply handicapped program. If the child's service need is basic *skill development,* the referral to the severely/multiply handicapped program *is* appropriate [p. 68].

Service-need definitions are noncategorical, that is, they focus on the fact that, regardless of the disabling condition, persons with severe disabilities are unable to perform basic skills, and therefore the educational program developed for them should alleviate these weaknesses. These definitions raise an important but subtle issue: By dividing the field into two basic programs, they promote service delivery that would integrate all children with severe disabilities into the educational and social mainstream. However, these definitions have two problems that also weakened Justen's definition: they are limited to the school-age population and they are prescriptive instead of definitive.

These early definitions should not be dismissed as inconsequential. They represent significant attempts by the profession to define a diverse, heterogeneous population, and they provide a firm foundation upon which present definitions are based.

A Working Definition

Since the previous definitions fail to identify the population with severe disabilities clearly and inclusively, the following definition is proposed:

> **Persons with severe disabilities have a very significant functional discrepancy in:** (1) general developmental abilities, (2) caring and looking after themselves, (3)

THE FAMILY CIRCUS®   **By Bil Keane**

Copyright 1987
Cowles Syndicate, Inc. .

"You have to learn numbers so
you can telephone people."

FIGURE 1.5

Even Dolly realizes that functional skills are learned faster than nonfunctional skills.

(Courtesy of King Features.)

expressing thoughts, ideas, and feelings, (4) responding to environmental stimuli, and (5) interacting socially with chronological-age peers.

The first important element of this definition is the phrase *very significant functional discrepancy.* The discrepancy standard is interpreted according to Justen's criterion of "half or less than the level that would be expected on the basis of chronological age." Intertwined with the discrepancy standard is the functional standard, which is the variance between the skills the individual has and those he or she must use in order to function in his or her environment. In other words, each of the five components in the definition would be examined to determine the variance of the individual's functional skills analyzed according to Justen's criterion. To be classified as severely disabled, then, an individual must have functional skills half or less than the level expected on the basis of chronological age.

Functional skills are the skills that *must* be performed for the individual if he or she cannot perform them personally. In other words, they are the skills necessary to sustain and enrich life. Stacking one block on top of another is not a functional skill, since it is not a life-sustaining or life-enriching skill. But, if a person cannot dress, bathe, or groom himself or herself, then someone must do these tasks for the person to sustain and enrich life.

A few examples may clarify the functional discrepancy standard. If a 30-year-old woman with disabilities selects and purchases her food, prepares it, and feeds herself, she would not be considered severely disabled. If she could not do these tasks, she may be judged severely disabled since she is unable to perform life-sustaining skills. Suppose a 15-year-old girl can brush the hair on a doll or a mannequin to an acceptable standard but cannot brush her own hair. She might be considered severely disabled, since brushing the hair on a doll or a mannequin is not a functional skill, but brushing her own hair is.

The other important elements of this definition are the five component skills. *General developmental abilities* refers to an individual's performance in the combined areas of intellectual, social, motor, mobility, self-direction, adaptive behaviors, and possibly independent living and economic self-sufficiency. While the functional level in each area (e.g., motor) need not be less than one-half of the level expected on the basis of chronological age, the combined or overall level must be.

Caring and looking after oneself includes the typical self-care tasks (feeding, toileting, dressing, grooming, etc.), recognizing and avoiding dangerous situations, and behaving in a safe manner (for example, not getting in a car with a stranger, not drinking unknown substances, and seeking aid for an injury).

Expressing thoughts, ideas, and feelings includes various methods of expression (speech, manual sign language, communication boards, and yes or no responses to questions). There are two key aspects: (1) the individual must in some way initiate conversations, and (2) the individual must express thoughts, ideas, and feelings so that someone who does not know the individual can understand what is being communicated. The mode of communication is not important for classifying a person as severely disabled; for instance, a nonverbal individual who uses a communication board to fulfill the two qualifications would not be considered severely disabled on that basis.

Responding to environmental stimuli refers to an individual's performance on a variety of environment-specific tasks, such as starting to eat when food is placed in front of him or her, turning on a light when entering a dark room, or pulling up the blankets on the bed when cold. If the individual has a sensory or physical impairment, the environmental stimuli must be detectable, that is, if the individual is visually impaired, the environmental stimuli must be nonvisual.

Interacting socially with chronological-age peers can be considered part of the first component, but as the fifth component it emphasizes social *interaction* skills rather than social behaviors. Specifically, the first component covers such skills as the elimination of self-stimulatory behaviors, the elimination of disruptive behaviors, and the care of personal belongings. The core of the fifth component is skills needed to get along with other people, for instance, developing relationships with others, accepting criticism, cooperating in activities, and respecting the rights of others.

There are both construct and philosophical advantages to this definition. Probably its greatest advantage is its emphasis on functionality, so that individuals with severe disabilities are no longer identified based on nonfunctional developmental timetables, but rather by a comparison of the skills they need in the environment and the skills they have acquired. This accentuates the principle of normalization, the integration of persons with severe disabilities into regular classrooms and into society in general.

Second, the definition is flexible. An individual could be classified as severely disabled at one stage of life and not severely disabled at another. For instance, a child might exhibit some very significant functional discrepancies during the school years, but upon leaving school might live in the community and be employed in a competitive, remunerative job. Such a person would be classified as severely disabled for only the school years. Or an individual with multiple disabilities (e.g., deafness and blindness) might still not be classified as severely disabled if his or her functional skills are appropriate for the environments in which he or she lives. Helen Keller, in this definition, unlike most definitions, would not be considered severely disabled.

Current Estimates of the Prevalence of Severe Disabilities

How many people may be classified as severely disabled? Nobody knows for sure. The most obvious way to determine the number of persons would be to go across the country, knocking on every door, or on a representative sampling of doors, asking if anyone who lived within that house was severely disabled. But the cost, time, and potential social consequences of doing this privately are prohibitive. So researchers have been forced to estimate the number. Because many factors can bias such estimates, current appraisals range from 0.15 percent to 2.0 percent of the general population (Abramowicz & Richardson, 1975; Brown, Wilcox, et al., 1977; Dollar & Brooks, 1980).

One obvious factor that can bias estimates is the definition of persons with severe disabilities. The broader the definition, the higher the prevalence figures. For example, if the definition required evidence of multiple disabling conditions, the prevalence rate would be reduced. Conversely, if the category is defined simply as an inability to read a specified list of fifty words, to compute simple addition problems, and to write one's name by age 9, the prevalence rate would be greatly enlarged.

Environmental events can also affect prevalence rates. Specifically, metabolic disorders, chromosomal abnormalities, infectious diseases, toxic absorptions, and Rh hemolytic disease vary from one sampling period to the next (Comptroller General of the United States, 1977). For instance, the rubella epidemic of 1964–1965 led to a significant increase in the prevalence of persons with severe disabilities.

Prevalence is also affected by age. It is commonly reported that persons with severe disabilities tend to be identified at or shortly after birth and that prevalence begins to drop after age 25 because of a higher mortality rate. These perceptions are somewhat supported by research. Approximately three-fourths of all children with severe disabilities that stem from congenital disorders are identified at or shortly after birth; the remainder are not identified until after they enter school. The prevalence rate actually begins to drop in adolescence, and sometime after age 25 this decrease accelerates (Abramowicz & Richardson, 1975; Tarjan, Wright, Eyman, & Keeran, 1973).

There are more males than females in programs serving children and adults with learning and behavioral problems. Severe disabilities too strike more males than females. Male:female ratio estimates vary from 7:1 (Lyons & Powers, 1963) to 4:3 (Abramowicz & Richardson, 1975). The ratio most frequently cited is 5:1 (Hingtgen & Bryson, 1972; Morse, 1975; Paluszny, 1979; Ritvo & Freeman, 1977). Two explanations have been suggested for the higher male rate. First, there is a greater frequency of sex-linked recessive conditions in males. Many mental retardation syndromes are either male sex-linked or are more common in males than females. Second, it is generally accepted that the male infant is more delicate and vulnerable to illnesses and injury than the female infant. For instance, the larger size of the male infant may make him more susceptible to injury, especially during birth.

What proportion of individuals in the general population, then, are classified as severely disabled? It must be emphasized that any figure is open to debate and is at best an educated guess. With this in mind, the most accurate appraisal of the prevalence rate for persons with severe disabilities appears to be approximately 1.6 percent of the general population (Brown, Wilcox, et al., 1977).

Conclusion

One truism that should be apparent from the historical survey of severe disabilities is that the field is dynamic and evolving. Over the past decade, we have seen an expansion of services to persons with severe disabilities; growing public awareness of and concern over the rights, access, and treatment of persons with severe disabilities; parental demands for educational and therapeutic services for their children; advances in the training of professionals who treat and serve persons with severe disabilities; and court and statutory mandates for more appropriate and adequate services.

Even with these advances, persons with severe disabilities are still denied participation in the social, economic, personal, and political life-styles offered to persons without disabilities. Society's discriminatory practices are evinced by the lack of access to buildings and community resources, the lack of equality in educational practices, the lack of opportunities in employment, and most disheartening, an open rejection by the nondisabled majority. Society's perception of people with disabilities as people not entitled to equal rights continues to be an immense problem.

SUMMARY   1. The way in which differences, including disabilities, are defined changes with time and depends on social conventions, values, and norms.

2. Ancient peoples believed that individuals with disabilities were possessed by supernatural forces.

3. The Greek physician Hippocrates applied rational, humane treatments and scientific methods to persons with disabilities. But persons with disabilities were often killed or treated inhumanely in the Greek and Roman Empires.

4. In the Middle Ages and the Renaissance, the Catholic Church considered that disabling conditions were punishments for sins. Persons with disabilities were considered possessed by demons or bewitched and were treated by exorcism.

5. In the sixteenth and seventeenth centuries, hospitals for the disabled were founded in the major cities of Europe and America, but conditions in them were dreadful.

6. Pinel and Tuke struggled to reform the hospitals. They instituted moral management, which stressed that persons with disabilities were ordinary human beings and should be treated with dignity. Successful hospitals soon became too crowded for moral management.

7. During the eighteenth and nineteenth centuries, professionals began to educate children, youth, and adults with disabilities. The first and most influential of these educators was Itard, who worked with a feral child.

8. Well into the twentieth century, students with disabilities were typically excluded from public schools.

9. In the late 1950s and early 1960s, parents of children with disabilities formed advocacy groups to lobby for federal and state laws to assist children and adults with disabilities. In the Kennedy and Johnson administrations there was a major upswing in services for and public awareness of persons with disabilities.

10. In the early 1970s landmark court decisions clearly established the right of every child to a free and appropriate public education.

11. *The Education for All Handicapped Children Act of 1975* established that all children with disabilities have the right to an education commensurate with their needs and abilities. Under this law, students with severe disabilities were a high-priority, targeted population.

12. The current trend in services is normalization, an attempt to make the lives of persons with severe disabilities as much like others' as possible. It is exemplified by the mainstreaming and deinstitutionalization movements.

13. The category *severe disabilities* refers to a great heterogeneity of etiological and symptomatic conditions.

14. Many early definitions, such as the one by Abt Associates, described the population in categorical terms and then listed typical characteristics.

15. Justen proposed a definition centered on two components: (1) individuals functioning at a general development level of half or less than that expected on the basis of chronological age, and (2) individuals who exhibit significant learning and/or behavior problems that require an extensive restructuring of the classroom environment.

16. Sailor and his associates proposed a service-need definition, excluding those who needed only academic instruction and including those who needed skill development instruction.

17. Our current proposed definition stresses significant functional discrepancy (half or less than the expected level) in: (1) general developmental abilities, (2) caring and looking after oneself, (3) expressing thoughts, ideas, and feelings, (4) responding to environmental stimuli, and (5) interacting socially with chronological-age peers.

18. Prevalence estimates are affected by the definition adopted, age, gender, and environmental events. The best estimate is currently approximately 1.6 percent of the general population.

NOTES

[1]Since the time of Romulus and Remus, there has been great interest in wolf or feral children, apparently lost or abandoned to the forest or jungle by their families at an early age, yet who survived among wild animals—perhaps actually raised by the animals as their own (see Dennis, 1951). Rudyard Kipling, in *The Jungle Book,* wrote about a man-cub, named Mowgli, who was adopted by a wolf family in the jungle of India. Probably the most famous fictional feral child is Tarzan Clayton. He and his parents were abandoned by mutineers on the west coast of Africa. After the death of his parents, Tarzan was adopted and reared by Kala, a she-ape of the tribe of Kerchak.

[2]Itard's work with Victor is shown in a film entitled *The Wild Boy of Aveyron.* A physical examination of Victor revealed a scar across his throat, which evidently had been made by a knife when the boy was much younger. It was hypothesized that Victor had been unwanted by his family, who took him to the forest, slit his throat, and left him to die. A more recent discovery of a so-called ape-boy occurred near Lake Tanganyiki in Africa (see *People,* February 9, 1976). This 4-year-old was found climbing the trees with a band of apes.

CHAPTER 2

Persons with Severe and Profound Mental Retardation

(Courtesy of Bancroft School, Haddonfield, NJ.)

DEFINING MENTAL RETARDATION

Professionals have long debated the definitions and classification systems of mental retardation. Subtle distinctions in a person's socialization skills, knowledge of the environment, or capacity to learn may determine not only classification as mentally retarded but also the level within that classification.

Definitions and IQ score cutoffs vary. Some individuals clearly have some disability but it is unclear whether the disability is mild or moderate. Others will be classified as mentally retarded no matter what definition is used. Members of this subgroup are often deficient in communication skills, self-care skills, socialization skills, and motor skills. They are the primary subject of this chapter. However, the definition we use must be appropriate for all subgroups with mental retardation as well as distinguishing those not truly mentally retarded from those who are. Among many proposed definitions, the most widely accepted is the one commissioned by the American Association on Mental Retardation (AAMR): "mental retardation refers to significantly sub-average general intellectual functioning existing concurrently with deficits in adaptive behavior and manifested during the developmental period" (Grossman, 1983, p. 1).

The first major element of this definition is the phrase *significantly subaverage general intellectual functioning*. General intellectual functioning is defined by the results obtained on one or more individually administered, standardized tests of general intelligence. Significantly subaverage is conceptualized as a score of 70 or below. However, the IQ score is intended only as a guide; it could extend to 75, if clinical evidence shows that the individual's impaired adaptive behavior is due to deficits in reasoning and judgment. By adopting a maximum IQ score of 70 and stating that it could nevertheless be as high as 75, Grossman and his associates intend to correct the misconception that previous AAMR definitions set a precise score and that individuals who scored higher were not mentally retarded while those who scored lower were (Grossman, 1973, 1977; Heber, 1961). The 1983 definition reflects the position that individuals should be classified according to need, not solely according to IQ score.

The second element of the definition is *existing concurrently with deficits in adaptive behavior*. According to Grossman, adaptive behavior is "the effectiveness or degree with which individuals meet the standards of personal independence and social responsibility expected for age and cultural group" (p. 1). Existing concurrently means that the person must exhibit impairments in both adaptive behavior and general intellectual functioning.

The third key element is the phrase *manifested during the developmental period*. The condition must be identified between birth and the 18th birthday. All three criteria must be met before a person is classified as mentally retarded.

A more optimistic, although less precise, definition of mental retardation was offered by Gold (1980) as an outgrowth of his Try Another Way System:

> The mentally retarded person is characterized by the training process required for him or her to learn, and not by limitations in what he or she can learn. The height of a retarded person's level of functioning is determined by the availability of training technology and the amount of resources society is willing to allocate and not by significant limitations in biological potential [p. 5].

FIGURE 2.1

This young woman with mental retardation has learned to use a communication notebook to order a meal at a restaurant.

(Courtesy of Crestwood Company.)

A central concept in Gold's definition is a balanced relationship between learner and trainer based on mutual respect. Both parties have a responsibility to adapt to the situation and to each other in the learning process and their human relationship. The trainer evaluates the skills the learner will need to know to perform a certain task and then trains the learner to perform that task.

CLASSIFYING PERSONS WITH MENTAL RETARDATION

Once persons with mental retardation have been distinguished from persons without mental retardation, classification problems are not over. Individuals with mental retardation constitute an extremely heterogeneous group. Some appear and behave somewhat like persons without mental retardation in almost every aspect. Some appear dramatically different; for instance, they are unable to ambulate, communicate, and meet their basic needs. Within the mentally retarded category, there is a variability in virtually every attribute, including mental ability.

The major reason for defining mental retardation is to determine which individuals need specific services. Yet the services needed vary enormously. The problem, therefore, is to establish subcategories that arrange the mentally retarded population into more homogeneous clusters.

Probably the two most widely used classification methods are the Grossman (1983) AAMR classification system and the educational classification system. The system proposed by Grossman and his associates consists of four levels of mental retardation: (1) mild, (2) moderate, (3) severe, and (4) profound. According to the AAMR classification manual, individuals with mild mental retardation have IQ scores from 50 or 55 to 70 or 75; their mental age is approximately one-half to three-fourths of their chronological age. Persons with moderate mental retardation have IQ scores from 35 or 40 to 50

TABLE 2.1

Terminology and Levels of Mental Retardation in the Two Major
Classification Schemes

	Classification Scheme	
IQ Score	AAMD (Grossman, 1983)	Educational (cited by Smith, 1971)
100 90 80		[Former borderline category]
70 60	Mild	Educable
50 40 30	Moderate	Trainable
20	Severe	Custodial or dependent
10 0	Profound	

or 55; their mental ages are approximately one-third to one-half of their chronological age. Persons with severe mental retardation have IQ scores from 20 or 25 to 35 or 40; their mental ages range from approximately one-third to one-fifth of their chronological age. Individuals with profound mental retardation have IQ scores of 20 or 25 and lower; their mental age is equal to or less than one-fifth of their chronological age.

The educational classification scheme is divided into four levels of mental retardation: (1) borderline, (2) educable, (3) trainable, and (4) custodial or dependent. Because of the negative connotations of the first and last labels, most educators have now completely dropped the first level and refer to the last level as severe and profound or simply severe.[1] Persons with educable mental retardation have IQ scores from 50 or 55 to 70 or 75. Individuals with trainable mental retardation have IQ scores from 25 or 30 to 50 or 55. Persons with severe mental retardation have IQ scores of 25 or 30 or lower. Table 2.1 compares the two classification systems.

Many states use a "hybrid" system, such as educable, trainable, and severe/profound or simply severe. In most cases the IQ scores for severe mental retardation are 35 to 40 and below.

PREVALENCE OF PERSONS WITH MENTAL RETARDATION

The variables described in chapter 1 affecting the prevalence rate of severe disabilities likewise play a role in mental retardation. While many figures are cited in the research, the ones most consistently mentioned for overall mental retardation are approximately 3 percent of the school-age population and from 1 to 2 percent of the pre-school-age and post-school-age populations (MacMillan, 1982; Mercer, 1970, 1973; Robbins, Mercer, & Meyers, 1967; Tarjan, Wright, Eyman, & Keeran, 1973). The variation in these rates is largely a factor of identification efforts made by schools. That is, until age 5 or 6, children with mild or even moderate mental retardation may fall within the developmental standards of normalcy. Likewise, persons with mild and some with moderate mental retardation may again become assimilated into society upon graduating from school.

The prevalence of persons with severe mental retardation shows less age variation, because such persons are likely to be identified before, during, and after the school years. Tarjan, Wright, Eyman, and Keeran (1973) estimated the prevalence of severe mental retardation at 0.5 percent. Their research was based on a theoretical distribution. Abramowicz and Richardson (1975) reviewed twenty-seven community studies and determined that a best approximation of the "true" prevalence rate was 0.3 to 0.5 percent. They concluded that prevalence of severe mental retardation in the general population was 0.4 percent.

ORGANIC FACTORS

From the time of conception, a child develops and is nurtured, first within the mother, then within the family, and finally within the total culture. In a few decades, the child becomes a mature adult. The miracle of development follows specifications and a timetable that are a joint product of the individual's biological inheritance and the environment in which he or she lives. In view of the complexity of the process, the possibilities of serious errors during development are almost infinite. Fortunately, only a small percentage of children are born with disabilities, and the vast majority of those who are healthy at birth develop normally to maturity.

A small proportion of children never have the slightest chance of developing along the same timetable as most do. They are destined to become mentally retarded from almost the moment of conception. Individuals with **Down syndrome**, for instance, possess "extra" genetic material, usually in the twenty-first chromosome, which inevitably produces mental retardation. In other children, genetic factors cause damage only in combination with specific environmental factors. A child with galactosemia, for example, will be

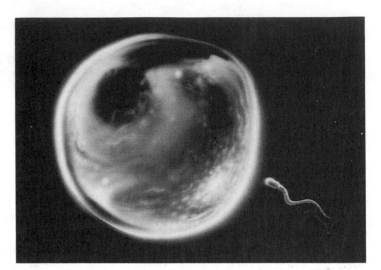

FIGURE 2.2

The basic unit of life is the cell, and it is within the living cell that all new life arises. In the central portion is the nucleus, which contains chromatin, the genetic material.

(Courtesy of Rob Wood of Stansbury, Ronsaville, Wood, Inc.)

damaged by toxic metabolic by-products only if he or she is fed milk, since this hereditary defect is an inability to properly metabolize the galactose in milk. Other genetic processes are much subtler, but investigators are approaching the unanswered questions about human heredity with a much broader and more sophisticated perspective than ever before.

The number of newly recognized causes of mental retardation is increasing rapidly. As new syndromes, **teratogens** (agents producing abnormalities), and biochemical disorders are discovered, it becomes increasingly difficult to determine etiology (causation). The sources of brain disorders may be genetic and chromosomal defects, nutritional and metabolic defects, skull and brain defects, or environmental defects (Grossman, 1983).

Genetic and Chromosomal Disorders

Impressive advances in genetic research during the past decade have revealed much about the mechanisms by which chromosomes and genes influence or determine mental retardation. Before examining the genetic basis of Down syndrome, galactosemia, and other types of genetic disorders this section explores how genetic transmission works.

The basic unit of life is the **cell**, and it is within the living cell that all new life arises. The central portion of all cells is the **nucleus**; it contains the genetic material, called **chromatin**. During the complex process by which genes from the parents join at conception, the chromatin forms threadlike bodies called **chromosomes**. Within the chromosomes are **genes**, which contain the chemical codes that direct all cell functions. Specifically, genes are blueprints for the

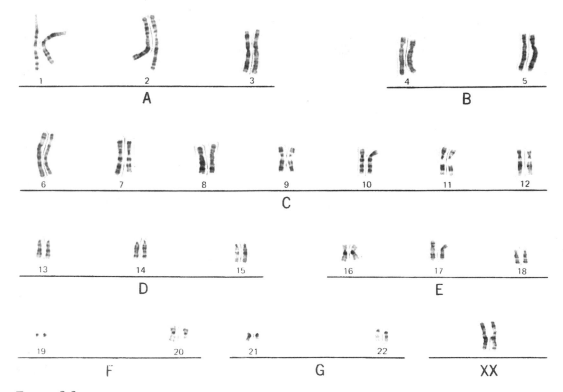

FIGURE 2.3

The Karyotype (set of chromosomes) of a Normal Female

(Reprinted by permission of Roger L. Ladda, Chief of the Division of Genetics, Pennsylvania State University College of Medicine, The Milton S. Hershey Medical Center, Hershey, Pennsylvania.)

assembly and regulation of proteins, the building blocks of our bodies. Each of the approximately 50,000 genes is responsible for a code for a specific sequence of amino acids that the body assembles to form a protein. If even the smallest part of this amino acid chain is altered, the entire protein can malfunction (Anderson, 1985; Baskin, 1984; Plomin, DeFries, & McClearn, 1980; Rensberger, 1984).

Human body cells contain forty-six chromosomes arranged in twenty-three pairs. Twenty-two pairs are called **autosomes,** with each chromosome being a duplicate of the other. One pair is the sex chromosomes, which are duplicated in the female (XX) but not in the male (XY). Figure 2.3 shows the pairs of chromosomes found in the nucleus of a normal cell. Typically, they are referred to by the numbers 1 through 22, from the largest to the smallest autosomes, with pair 23 determining sex.

The chromosomes are not perfectly stable, intact entities; they wax and wane in a rhythm determined by the rate of cell division. Sometimes parts of chromosomes are broken off; as a result, there may be "extra" or "missing" chromosomes in descendant cells. In many cases, the individual born with extra or missing chromosomes becomes mentally retarded.

Dominant and recessive genes. In the **heterozygotic** situation, when the two genes from the parents indicate different traits (e.g., different eye colors), only one trait will be manifested. It is described as **dominant.** A dominant gene determines that trait (e.g., eye color) regardless of its partner. Other genes are called **recessive.** A recessive gene donated by one parent will not determine a trait unless it is matched by the same recessive gene from the other parent. Hence recessive genes have less chance of being manifested.

If both parents contribute various combinations of dominant and recessive genes that might cause mental retardation, what are the probabilities that the offspring will be affected? Figure 2.4 shows the child's chances of inheriting a disorder from a dominant gene from one parent or from recessive genes from both parents. If the trait is dominant and one parent possesses it, there is a 50-percent risk that each child will manifest the defect. If the trait is recessive and both parents carry the harmful gene as well as a nonharmful gene, each child has a 25-percent chance of manifesting the defect, a 25-percent chance of not inheriting the harmful gene, and a 50-percent chance of receiving one harmful and one nonharmful gene, thus becoming a carrier of the condition but not manifesting it.

Autosomal dominant traits are carried as dominant genes in the first twenty-two pairs of chromosomes and may be manifested in one or both parents. Autosomal dominant traits that involve mental retardation are relatively uncommon but do exist. Examples include tuberous sclerosis, neurofibromatosis, Sturge-Weber syndrome, myotonic dystrophy, Apert syndrome, Albright hereditary osteodystrophy, Marfan syndrome, craniofacial dysostosis, and Huntington chorea.[2]

Autosomal recessive traits are those that neither parent manifests but both carry recessively. These are more common causes of mental retardation than autosomal dominant traits. For the offspring to manifest the trait, both parents must have the defective gene. Conditions associated with mental retardation transmitted by autosomal recessive genes include hyperglycinemia, Lignac-Fanconi syndrome, maple syrup urine disease, phenylketonuria, hyperphenylalaninemia, galactosemia, Tay-Sachs disease, Niemann-Pick disease, Laurence-Moon-Biedel syndrome, Hurler disease, Pompe disease, Wilson disease, Morquio syndrome, metachromatic leukodystrophy, and some forms of microcephaly.

Sex-linked characteristics. The sex chromosomes can also create conditions that result in mental retardation. For daughters, dominant and recessive

Dominant Inheritance

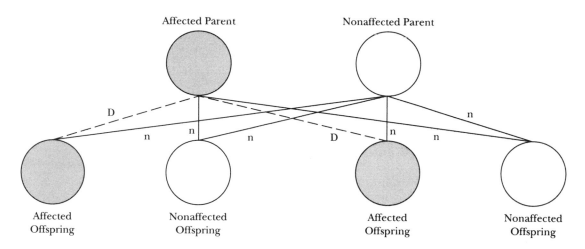

Each child has a 50-percent chance of inheriting the D (dominant faulty) gene and a 50-percent chance of inheriting the n (nonaffected) gene from the affected parent.

Recessive Inheritance

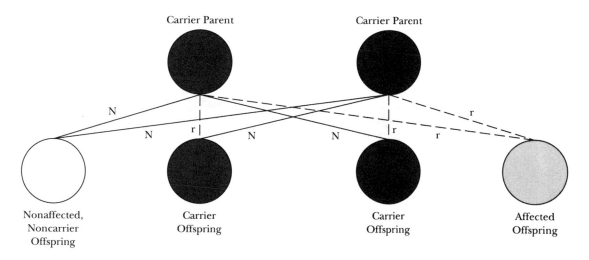

Each child has a 25-percent chance of inheriting two recessive faulty genes that may cause a serious defect; a 25-percent chance of inheriting two nonaffected genes and thus being unaffected; and a 50-percent chance of inheriting one nonaffected and one recessive and thus being a carrier like both parents.

FIGURE 2.4

The Probabilities of the Offspring Being Affected through Dominant and Recessive Autosomal Genes

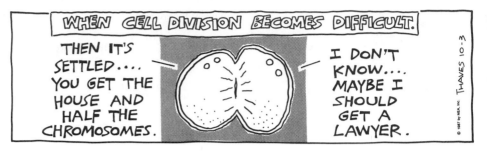

FIGURE 2.5

(Reprinted by permission by NEA, Inc.)

conditions follow the same laws of inheritance as they do for the other twenty-two chromosome pairs. Since a female has two sex chromosomes with a full complement of genes, the recessive gene she inherits from one parent can manifest itself only if she inherits a matching recessive gene from the other parent, an uncommon situation. This is not the case with sons. The Y chromosome is essentially barren of genes, its principal funtion being to establish the sex of the child. The X chromosome carries other genetic information. Thus, if a son inherits a defective gene from his mother on the X chromosome, the trait will be manifested, since the Y chromosome has no gene to counteract the trait. The two X chromosomes thus tend to protect females from recessive genetic disorders transmitted through the sex chromosome. Sex-linked conditions are found far more often in males than in females.

Among the sex-linked conditions associated with mental retardation are Renpenning syndrome, Lesch-Nyhan syndrome, Hunter syndrome, Lowe disease, Turner syndrome, Klinefelter syndrome, and Duchenne type muscular dystrophy. Figure 2.6 illustrates the probabilities of the offspring being affected through sex-linked inheritance. Notice that the example is for a recessive trait and that the odds differ according to the sex of the offspring.

Many of these conditions may cease to exist in the early twenty-first century. A quiet revolution in medicine called **gene therapy** is happening. Physicians should be able to treat many disorders by replacing a defective gene with a normal gene in the patient's cells. In Lesch-Nyhan syndrome, for example, a single gene fails to produce an essential enzyme with a tongue-twisting name—hypoxanthine guanine phosphoribosyltransferase, or HPRT. The absence of HPRT cripples one of the basic biochemical cycles of cells and creates a buildup of uric acid waste, which then causes body degeneration (Anderson, 1985). Gene therapy would insert a normal gene into the appropriate cells, and the disease would be not just treated but cured!

Is this rosy picture really possible in the next decade or so? Probably, for a number of diseases. Researchers now insert foreign genes into animals and get the genes to function. The first successful gene therapy in a mammal was reported in 1984. And scientists can identify the traits controlled by at least 2,000 genes (Anderson, 1985; Baskin, 1984).

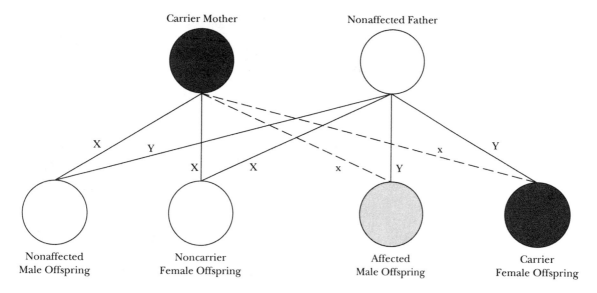

Each *male* child has a 50-percent risk of inheriting the faulty x and manifesting the disorder and a 50-percent risk of inheriting a nonaffected X. Each *female* child has a 50-percent risk of inheriting one faulty x and becoming a carrier and a 50-percent chance of inheriting no faulty gene.

FIGURE 2.6

The Probabilities of the Offspring Being Affected through a Recessive Sex-Linked Gene

Aberrant chromosomes. Aberrant chromosomes have unusual numbers or structures. Aberrations occur in autosomes and sex chromosomes. One of the most common aberrations is called **trisomy:** Improper cell division producing three matching chromosomes instead of the normal two. Down syndrome, for instance, is known as *trisomy 21,* since a person with the syndrome invariably has three twenty-first chromosomes. Figure 2.7 shows the **karyotype** (set of chromosomes) of a person with Down syndrome.

There are basically two ways in which aberrant chromosomes may occur: nondisjunction and translocation. **Nondisjunction aberrations** happen even before conception. Before they combine, the egg and the sperm must duplicate themselves and divide into equivalent pairs. Later, the chromosomes "reshuffle" between the pairs to form a germ cell. If during the reshuffling process in the egg cell two chromosomes fail to separate, they migrate to the same pole in the germ cell. Then when this cell combines with the sperm cell, there will be three chromosomes in that position instead of two. Figure 2.8 shows how nondisjunction in the formation of an egg gets passed along after conception as cells divide. Among the nondisjunction aberrations that can result in mental retardation are Down syndrome, Edward syndrome, and Patau syndrome.

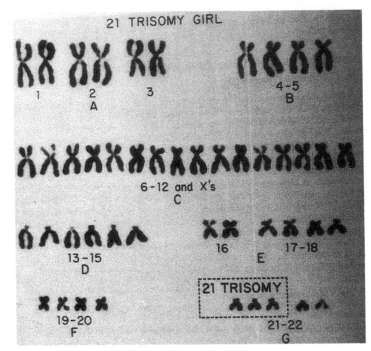

FIGURE 2.7

The Karyotype of a Female with Down Syndrome

(Adapted by permission from *The Child With Down's Syndrome (Mongolism)* by D. Smith and A. Wilson, 1973, Philadelphia: Saunders.)

One type of nondisjunction chromosomal abnormality, **mosaicism,** occurs after conception. As the egg begins to divide, one new cell receives forty-seven chromosomes while the other receives only forty-five, instead of each receiving forty-six. One cell has trisomy and the other monosomy. The latter cell dies, leaving only the cell with three chromosomes to continue dividing. If this error occurs in the first cell division, all the body cells will have trisomy, and the newborn will resemble children in whom the error occurred before conception. However, if the faulty distribution occurs during the second cell division, two of the new cells will be normal, one will have trisomy and one will have monosomy and die. As division continues, the mosaic individual has some normal and some trisomy cells, producing unusual consequences, depending on which parts of the body get the trisomy cells. The disorders that occur from nondisjunction abnormalities may also arise from mosaicism, but most individuals with mosaicism evince milder forms than those in whom disjunction occurred before conception (Bunker et al., 1972).

In **translocation aberrations** all or part of one chromosome attaches (actually fuses) itself mistakenly to another chromosome, either its partner or one of a different pair. This can happen to any chromosome, but pairs 13, 14, 15, 21, and 22 are most commonly involved, since they are located near the end rather than in the middle of the nucleus (see figure 2.3). In the majority of cases

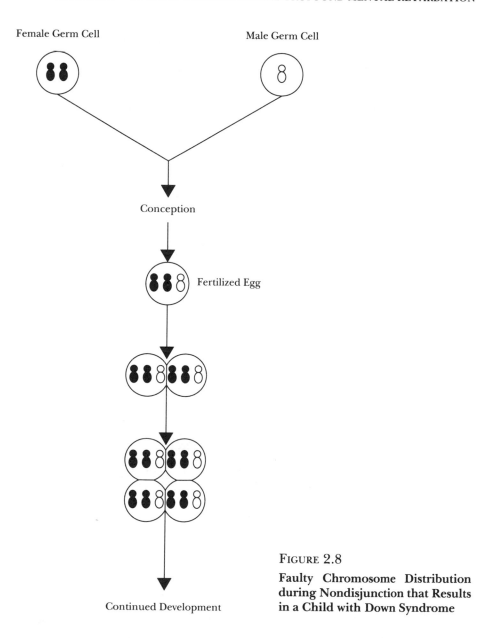

FIGURE 2.8

**Faulty Chromosome Distribution
during Nondisjunction that Results
in a Child with Down Syndrome**

chromosomal material detaches from chromosome 21 or 22 and attaches to
chromosome 13, 14, or 15, either during formation of the egg or sperm or in
the first cell division after conception. This type of chromosomal aberration
may be inherited. In approximately one-third of the cases of translocation, one
parent carried the abnormal gene pattern, and passed it along to the offspring.

Translocation chromosomal abnormalities resulting in mental retardation include DeGrouchy syndrome, cri du chat syndrome, Prader-Willi syndrome, and Williams syndrome.

Nutritional and Metabolic Disorders

In nutritional and metabolic disorders, abnormal genes cause faulty formation of enzymes essential for metabolism. Since proteins, carbohydrates, or lipids cannot then be processed and converted to a useful substance, the nonmetabolized enzymes accumulate, often in the cells. In most cases, little or no damage occurs during the prenatal period because the mother's body accomplishes the metabolic process for the embryo and fetus,[3] providing the essential enzymes. After birth, however, either the nonmetabolized substances accumulate to toxic levels or damage occurs because proteins, carbohydrates, or lipids needed for normal functioning are absent. Both result in damage to the central nervous system, producing mental retardation and other neurological impairments.

Nonmetabolized substances may be detected in the infant with the Guthrie inhibition assay test. Treatment then is: (1) dietary restriction of the nonmetabolized substances, (2) an artificial supply of the missing enzyme so that normal metabolism takes place, or (3) ingestion of biochemicals to break down the toxic, nonmetabolized substances into harmless forms. Many nutritional and metabolic disorders are genetically transmitted through autosomal recessive genes. That is, both parents must be carriers for the offspring to manifest the disorder. Even then, the newborn has only a 25-percent chance of being affected.

Nutritional and metabolic disorders are classified according to the type of enzyme that causes the disability. For instance, *carbohydrate disorders* interfere with the body's ability to metabolize glucose, fructose, glycogen, and other carbohydrates. Disorders resulting in mental retardation include galactosemia, hypoglycemia, fructosemia, glycogenosis, and Unverricht-Lafora disease. *Amino acid disorders* affect the body's ability to convert amino acids into useful proteins. Conditions resulting in mental retardation from these include phenylketonuria, Hartnup syndrome, histidinemia, cystinuria, iminoglycinuria, homocystinuria, Lowe disease, and maple syrup urine disease. *Lipid disorders* include a large group of anomalies that result in increased lipid content in tissues or serum. Those that result in mental retardation include Hurler disease, Jansky-Bielschowsky disease, Batten-Spielmeyer-Vogt disease, Kufs disease, Niemann-Pick disease, Fabry disease, Hunter syndrome, Tay-Sachs disease, Sanfilippo syndrome, and Gaucher disease.

Three other types of metabolic disorders—endocrine, nucleotide, and mineral—are less prevalent. *Endocrine disorders* include conditions associated with abnormal functioning of glands, such as the pituitary, pineal, thyroid, parathyroid, pancreas, adrenal, testicle, and ovary. Disorders that result in mental retardation are congenital cretinism, goitrous cretinism, hypoparathyroidism, and nephrogenic diabetes insipidus. *Nucleotide disorders* include defects in the metabolism of purines and pyrimidines. These disorders are caused by the inability to metabolize the pentose sugars ribose and deoxyribose, which, with phosphoric and nucleic acids, form the fundamental structural units of the genes. Nucleotide disorders that can result in mental retardation include orotic aciduria, xanthinuria, and destructive hyperuricemia. *Mineral disorders* are associated with anomalies in the metabolism of metallic ions. Those resulting in mental retardation include Wilson disease, idiopathic hypercalcemia, and pseudohypoparathyroidism.

Skull and Brain Disorders

There are several congenital and adventitious disorders of the skull and brain that apparently result from a wide variety of causes. For instance, microcephaly may be caused by autosomal recessive genes, prenatal factors (e.g., massive irradiation or maternal alcohol consumption), perinatal factors (e.g., anoxia or injury during birth), postnatal factors (e.g., child abuse), or other disabilities (e.g., phenylketonuria or Down syndrome).

There are two main anomalies of the skull and brain: microcephaly and hydrocephaly. In **microcephaly** the head is smaller than normal and out of proportion with the rest of the body. For an adult, the head must be seventeen inches or less; for a 2-year-old, it must be fifteen inches or less; and for a 6-month-old, it must be thirteen inches or less. **Hydrocephaly** is an increased volume of cerebrospinal fluid within the skull, which ordinarily produces enlargement of the cranium, often to a globular shape. To keep enlargement from happening, a shunt is usually inserted into the cranium. Other craniofacial anomalies include Patau syndrome, de Lange syndrome, macrocephaly, Crouzon disease, Apert syndrome, craniostenosis, Rubinstein-Taybi syndrome, Laurence-Moon-Biedel syndrome, Williams syndrome, and hydranencephaly.

Environmental Disorders

Many factors other than genetics can negatively influence development of the fetus and result in severe mental retardation. Some factors definitely cause certain birth defects; others are suspected of causing defects, but research has not yet confirmed a cause-and-effect relationship. Many of these sources of mental retardation can easily be avoided or at least decreased by concerted effort.

High on the list of prominent environmental factors is poisoning. It has been known to cause mental retardation for well over four decades. Poisoning can come from a variety of sources. Wilson (1973) examined the effects of drugs on the fetus and reported that aspirin, phenobarbital, quinine, insulin, female sex hormones, heroin, morphine, alcohol, cocaine, tar and nicotine, and sulfonamides increase the probability of mental retardation either directly or indirectly. For instance, the nicotine and tar from cigarettes restrict the flow of oxygen to the fetus, indirectly causing anoxia. Statistics reveal that 40 to 60 percent of children born to alcoholic mothers have an increased probability of being born with mental retardation (Baroff, 1986; Landesman-Dwyer, Ragozin, & Little, 1981).

Air and water pollutants, such as lead inhaled from automobile emissions, have also been linked to increased incidence of mental retardation. The Comptroller General's Report (1977) estimated that over 600,000 children have elevated lead-blood levels that are causing brain damage, sensory defects, and psychomotor disabilities. The ingestion of fish caught in mercury-contaminated waters has been linked to mental retardation and cerebral palsy for well over three decades. Professionals are just beginning to examine other pollutants, such as nuclear radiation and toxic chemicals. From preliminary results, it appears that nuclear and chemical pollution may be even more hazardous than either lead or mercury pollution (Comptroller General, 1977; Sells & Bennett, 1977). Asbestos, chlorines, fluorides, and nickel have also been linked to severe mental retardation.

Another environmental factor is Rh hemolytic disease. This can largely be prevented by identifying women with Rh negative blood who give birth to Rh positive children. After each pregnancy, the mother is given immunoglobulin to prevent her from developing antigens. Although the extent of the problem is not known, apparently it is widespread. Yet only five states monitor for Rh hemolytic disease, seven require premarital blood typing, and six have special programs for reporting immunoglobulin use. The tragedy about Rh hemolytic disease is that about 2,000 children become mentally retarded every year needlessly (Comptroller General, 1977).

A variety of maternal infections can likewise cause mental retardation: rubella, rubeola, syphilis, meningitis, encephalitis, toxoplasmosis, infectious hepatitis, and influenza (Sever, 1970). These conditions can be prevented or dramatically reduced through immunization, prenatal examinations, and other hygienic methods, but only a handful of states presently use comprehensive prenatal examinations and other preventive or palliative approaches.

Of the factors associated with low mental performance, malnutrition in the mother and the child has been suggested as a major cause. The independent role of malnutrition is not yet fully understood because most evidence comes from animal research. A classical study on the effects of malnutrition was conducted by Richmond and Tarjan (1977) on three groups of rhesus monkeys. The first group was given a well-balanced diet, the second an impoverished diet, and the third an impoverished diet supplemented with synthetic protein, RNA, and DNA. The monkeys in the first and third groups behaved similarly, but those in the second group behaved significantly below the other two groups. Subsequently all three groups were given a well-balanced diet, yet

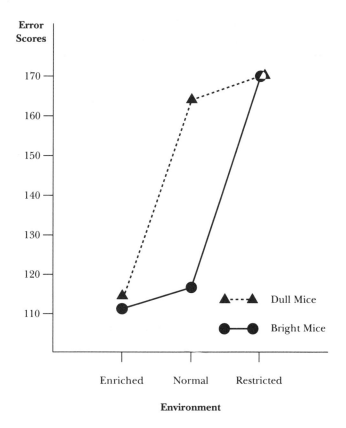

FIGURE 2.9

Mean Error Scores of Bright and Dull Mice Raised in Enriched, Normal, and Restricted Environments

(Derived from "Effects of Enriched and Restricted Early Environments on the Learning Ability of Bright and Dull Rats" by R. Cooper and J. Zubek, 1958, *Canadian Journal of Psychology, 12,* 159–164.)

offspring of the second group had smaller brains and reductions in the number and size of electrical impulses from the brain. The effects of synthetic protein, RNA, and DNA have been substantiated with flatworms and mice. Thus general malnutrition may not be as damaging as protein deficiency.

The long-term effects of acute malnutrition are well substantiated. Studies have indicated that malnourished children are shorter, are less intelligent, do academic tasks less well, have motor coordination problems, and are less competent socially than their classmates (Hoorweg & Stanfeld, 1972; Richardson, Birch, Grabic, & Yoder, 1972).

For many years, it has been known that mental retardation is closely associated with poverty and lower socioeconomic status. In a very early study demonstrating this relationship, Cooper and Zubek (1958) raised *bright* and *dull* mice in three environments, labeled *restricted, normal,* and *enriched* according to the degree of sensory stimulation. The mice were then evaluated on an intellectual task. As figure 2.9 shows, the bright and dull mice raised in the restricted environment performed equally poorly. The dull mice raised in the enriched environment performed almost as well as the bright mice raised in the enriched environment and a little better than the bright mice raised in the normal environment. The greatest difference occurred in the normal environment. Noting that intelligence and environment interact, the researchers concluded that early stimulation has a direct effect on intelligence. This conclusion has been substantiated in a number of studies on children and adolescents (Baltes & Reese, 1984; Horowitz, 1980; Lazar & Darlington, 1982; Mussen, Conger, Kagan, & Huston, 1984; Ramey & Baker-Ward, 1982; Ramey & MacPhee, 1985; Ramey, Yeates, & Short, 1984).

Poverty and low socioeconomic status can combine with other factors to have an adverse effect. Shonkoff (1982) found that low-socioeconomic-status children carried a disproportionate burden of biological vulnerability, largely related to health risks. Regardless of their genetic potential, these children were subjected to a variety of brain-damaging influences throughout their development, which had potential negative impacts on their functioning. Malnutrition, lead poisoning, fetal alcohol syndrome, and other factors that can cause severe mental retardation occurred with greater frequency among the poor. Birch and Gussow (1970) commented that "almost every complication of pregnancy, labor, delivery, and the perinatal period which is potentially damaging to children is excessively prevalent among the economically depressed populations" (p. 46). It is increasingly recognized that many of these environmental factors combine to the detriment of the child. A potentially damaging influence (e.g., malnutrition or lead toxicity) combined with environmental limitations (e.g., restricted stimulation) can and often does affect a child's cognitive functioning (Sameroff & Chandler, 1975).

CHARACTERISTICS OF PERSONS WITH MENTAL RETARDATION

We have always been aware that some children learn more quickly than others and that some learn less efficiently and therefore have difficulty meeting the demands placed on them. This is true of persons with mild, moderate, and severe mental retardation. The latter not only have learning and memory problems but also have residual complications of these cognitive limitations, such as communication, self-care, and social skill limitations that interfere with their ability to interact in society. For instance, if a girl takes a toy from a boy with severe mental retardation, and the boy wants it back, how is he likely to retrieve it? A boy of average intelligence would probably ask for it back, but the boy with severe mental retardation generally has severe communication problems and is likely to grab it or even knock the girl down.

Because persons with severe mental retardation have difficulty learning the skills they need to participate fully in society, they are often isolated. This isolation is a "secondary" difficulty which exacerbates their inability to acquire information as efficiently as age-mates. This section will examine many of these "secondary" problems of persons with severe mental retardation.

Communication Development

The ability to express thoughts and feelings clearly and concisely is often accepted as a sign of intelligence, probably because of the role the brain plays in communication. It is the brain, for instance, that receives symbols, decodes them, associates and stores their meaning according to some internal lexicon, and generates a response. It is not surprising, then, that language skills and intellectual development are closely related. Since the original Stanford-Binet Intelligence Scales were published, researchers have used the size and complexity of a person's native vocabulary as one of the best predictors of generic intelligence.

Therefore, we would expect persons with mental retardation, particularly severe mental retardation, to have communication problems. Over half the persons with mental retardation and three-fourths with severe retardation do have severe speech and language problems (Garcia & DeHaven, 1974; President's Commission on Mental Retardation, 1975; Reich, 1978). Many with severe mental retardation also have hearing losses, which both impair their reception of language and impede their development of expression.

Even this does not tell the whole story of communication problems in persons with severe mental retardation. Their vocabulary is often quite small. It is not uncommon for them to have a receptive vocabulary of less than one hundred words and an expressive vocabulary of less than twenty-five. Obviously this limits the manner in which such individuals can manipulate their environment. To complicate this, many have such severe articulation disorders that only people in frequent contact with them can understand what they are attempting to say. Many individuals with severe mental retardation have semantic and syntax problems that further disrupt their communications. Their typical sentence may be two or three words. Some individuals with severe mental retardation have no speech at all and must communicate through manual sign language, communication boards, and electronic communication devices. Finally, there are even some individuals who can communicate only through *yes* and *no* gestures. To communicate with them, a person must ask questions that can be answered either yes or no.

The type of communication an individual with severe mental retardation uses to express needs, thoughts, and feelings varies from one individual to another and may vary from one stage of a person's life to another. Teachers need to know a variety of communication methods to match the functional needs of the student at the time. These include speech, formal manual sign language, informal manual sign language, computer-augmented speech, electronic communication devices, Premack symbols, Blissymbols, rebus symbols, gestures, pictures, and yes and no indications. (These communication methods are discussed in greater detail in chapter 7.) Since the goal of educating persons with severe mental retardation is their successful integration into society, the communication method selected must foster, not hinder, integration. Thus, the optimum method is speech, and the trainer should help the individual come as close to oral speech as possible.

Social and Emotional Development

Many positive social and emotional characteristics correlate very highly with intelligence. Thus individuals with mental retardation are likely to do poorly in social situations. Such intellectual traits as short attention span, dependence on others, lack of confidence, low frustration tolerance, immature behavior, poor expressive skills, and general expectations of failure have fallout effects in social situations. Many individuals with severe mental retardation also are aggressive, are self-abusive, and lack self-care skills, which hinder their social interactions with others.

It is apparent that many persons with mental retardation also have emotional disturbances. Although the extent of the problem is not clear, it is thought to be substantial. Polloway, Epstein, and Cullinan (1985) summarized a variety of research studies indicating that persons with severe mental retardation exhibit neurotic and psychotic behavior patterns. Many are hospitalized for emotional disturbances, and others are in prisons or other correctional institutions. After analyzing a number of research studies, Balthazar and Stevens (1975) concluded that "there is a relatively high predisposition for emotional disturbance among the mentally retarded" (p. 9).

The parents' child-rearing techniques may hinder their children's development of social skills. For instance, Matson and DiLorenzo (1986) report that many parents are abusive and neglectful, provide minimal intellectual stimulation, engage in limited oral communication, and provide nonnutritious meals for their children. This is true whether the retardation is mild, moderate, or severe (Rie & Rie, 1980; Shonkoff, 1972). In a series of classical studies, Harlow (1964) and his colleagues analyzed the effects of parental deprivation on the development of social skills in monkeys. They found that extreme parental deprivation led to severe disruption in social behavior. Animals deprived of their parents throughout the first year of life showed a severe lack of social skills, which could never be remediated; animals isolated from their parents for two years were totally deficient in social skills and exhibited stereotypic, bizarre, and self-destructive behavior. While Harlow's studies should not be uniformly applied to persons with severe mental retardation, they strongly suggest that the parental deprivation experienced by many such persons has a detrimental effect on their development of social skills.

It should not be concluded that individuals with severe mental retardation will never develop appropriate social skills. This certainly is not the case! Some have been taught sophisticated social skills through self-management techniques (Brimer, 1985; Browder & Shapiro, 1985; Gardner, Clees, & Cole, 1983; Morrow & Presswood, 1984). And it has been repeatedly demonstrated that they can maintain and generalize such skills in new situations (Donnellan,

FIGURE 2.10

The infant monkeys in the Harlow experiments were subjected to various levels of parental deprivation. This infant monkey was given a terry-cloth-covered "mother."

(Courtesy of the Harlow Primate Laboratory, University of Wisconsin.)

FIGURE 2.11

This rhesus monkey raised in social isolation shows apathy, immobility, and an exaggerated fear of peers.

(Courtesy of the Harlow Primate Laboratory, University of Wisconsin.)

LaVigna, Zambito, & Thvedt, 1985; Menchetti, Rusch, & Lamson, 1981). In one of the most comprehensive studies of social skills, Hill and Bruininks (1984) followed 2,271 adults with mental retardation, many of whom were classified severely retarded. The study clearly demonstrated that relocation to a more normalized setting facilitated their functioning in adaptive behavior. This and other studies found that the vast majority of persons with severe mental retardation did not exhibit maladaptive behavior, were successfully integrated into the community, and did not represent a problem to the community in terms of delinquency or other undesirable behavior. These findings have been substantiated by a vast number of investigators (e.g., Conroy, 1977, 1982; Conroy, Efthimiou, & Lemanowicz, 1982; Eyman & Call, 1977; Nihira & Nihira, 1975).

Leisure Development

Historically, individuals with severe mental retardation were not taught leisure activities, although it has been documented that they have an abundance of free time. They spend most of it watching television passively, sitting idly, rambling aimlessly, or engaging in inappropriate behavior (Aveno, 1987; Dattilo, 1987; Wehman & McLaughlin, 1981). It has been widely recommended that they make better use of their leisure time. Wehman and McLaughlin suggest that age-appropriate leisure activities such as cooperative and interactive play could improve a host of skills, including communication, socialization, learning/memory, and motor skills. Wehman and his associates taught individuals with severe mental retardation to play dart games and pinball games that improved various skills through increased interactions with persons without mental retardation (Schlelen, Wehman, & Kiernan, 1982; Hill, Wehman, & Horst, 1982).

In determining which leisure activities should be taught to individuals with severe mental retardation, Wehman and McLaughlin suggest three basic principles. First, the activities should improve the person's other skills. In other words, there should be potential benefits for the individual from the leisure activity, and these benefits should be planned in the way a teacher makes a lesson plan. Second, the activities should capitalize on natural situations in the natural environment. That is, after the training period, there should be strong enough natural reinforcers to maintain and generalize the activity to other environments. Third, the activities should be age-appropriate—avocations that persons without mental retardation of the same chronological age would typically enjoy.

Games are not the only leisure activity recommended for persons with severe mental retardation. Feldman (1986), for instance, recommends pets. Sometimes called *pet therapy*, interaction with a pet can improve many of the same skills as a game and other skills as well. For example, persons with severe mental retardation can develop a sense of responsibility, self-worth, and com-

FIGURE 2.12

The range of leisure activities for persons with mental retardation is almost endless. The activity should be individualized, beneficial, and enjoyable.

(Courtesy of Cahokia School District 187, Illinois.)

passion from taking care of their pets. Other leisure activities are crafts, music, art, sports, shopping, going to museums, visiting friends, and religious activities (Grossman, 1983). In short, the leisure activities available to persons without mental retardation are, in most cases, available to those with severe mental retardation. The activities must be individualized (structured to the person's unique needs) and should be both beneficial to and enjoyed by the person.

Motor and Physical Development

Since individuals with severe mental retardation have a higher incidence of vision, hearing, and neurological problems, they naturally tend to have poorer motor and physical skills. These problems begin at or shortly after birth. It has been reported that infants and young children with severe mental retardation have pronounced problems in sucking, grasping, posture, range of motion, flexion, extension, and muscle tone. At 1 year of age they obtain scores from zero through three (on a ten-point scale) in such traits as heart rate, respiration, muscle tone, reflex responsiveness, and skin color (Apgar & James, 1962; Kennedy, Drage, & Schwartz, 1963). At age 4, they continue to exhibit low scores in those areas and show deficits in fine-motor, gross-motor, and eye-hand coordination (Drage, Berendes, & Fisher, 1969). As the children become older, these problems persist. Many children appear awkward and clumsy, walking with a stiff, robotlike gait; others are so motorically impaired that they cannot ambulate without a cane, a walker, or a wheelchair (see Levire, Carey, Crocker, & Gross, 1983).

Many individuals with severe retardation are developmentally delayed in the appearance and disappearance of the primitive reflexes, which are essential for normal development and condition the body for more strenuous and complicated movements (such as sitting and standing). As the body matures, the primitive reflexes disappear and are replaced by voluntary movement. In persons with severe mental retardation, these reflexes persist long after normal suppression occurs, making voluntary movement difficult, if not impossible (Kraemer, Cusick, & Bigge, 1982). Thus, such purposeful movements as visual tracking or grasping an object with the thumb and index finger are greatly delayed in comparison to persons without mental retardation. Since self-care tasks such as feeding and dressing are dependent on purposeful muscle movement, it is easy to see why individuals with severe retardation are significantly delayed in self-care.

Recently, motor development has received increased emphasis (Utley, 1982). While there are few published studies demonstrating the effectiveness of motor training, many professionals feel that systematic instruction in this area could reap dividends (Banerdt & Bricker, 1978; Moon & Bunker, 1987; Shane, Reynolds, & Geary, 1977). For example, Stein (1963) described an experiment in which students with mental retardation received ten weeks of adaptive physical education instead of their usual instruction. Compared to a control group, the experimental group achieved more academically and physically, suggesting that persons with severe mental retardation could greatly benefit from motor training.

Self-Care Development

The term **self-care development** is an evolving ambiguous concept essentially meaning achievement of any skill or behavior needed for an individual's full integration into the mainstream of school or society. While there is no consensus, self-care skills are generally accepted to include: (1) self-feeding, (2) self-dressing, (3) self-management, and (4) self-hygienics. In general, **self-feeding skills** are the tasks of independent eating and drinking, proper mealtime behavior, and at later stages food preparation, and cleanup after a meal. **Self-dressing skills** are those required to put on and take off clothing, including buttoning, zipping, and tying. At later stages, they should also include clothing selection, laundering clothing, and ultimately purchasing clothing. In

(Courtesy of Cahokia School District 187, Illinois.)

FIGURE 2.13

Persons with mental retardation can benefit significantly from motor activities such as bowling and baseball. Besides the motor skills benefits, the fact that the activities occur with and around persons without mental retardation offers an opportunity for social integration.

general, **self-management skills** refer to the elimination of inappropriate behaviors and the acquisition of community living skills, including community transportation skills, money management skills, household management skills, and etiquette skills. Finally, **self-hygienics skills** are the diverse components of toileting, grooming, and bathing. At the later stages, they should include oral and nasal hygiene, health care, first aid, and skin and nail care. Gender-specific tasks such as shaving for males and menstrual hygiene for females are also important.

The acquisition, maintenance, and generalization of self-care skills are especially important for individuals with severe mental retardation. In fact, probably nothing is more important for school and community integration (Adkins & Matson, 1980; Snell, 1987; Wehman & McLaughlin, 1981). Because of the importance of these skills, many researchers have found that teachers tend to provide training in self-care before initiating instruction in other areas, for instance, communication, socialization, leisure activities, and career and vocational education (Gruber, Reeser, & Reid, 1979; Snell, 1987; Whitman & Sciback, 1979).

Individuals with severe mental retardation often exhibit marked delays in acquiring even the simplest self-care skills. There are three possible explanations for this. First, parents may not have required the child to perform self-care tasks. Many parents mistakenly believe that it is easier to do the task themselves (e.g., buttoning the child's shirt) than to teach the child to do it. Second, the child may lack prerequisite motor skills. If a child cannot yet grasp, hold, or pull, it is difficult to teach him or her self-care tasks. Third, many children with severe mental retardation also have sensory and physical disabilities that hinder the acquisition process. For example, those who have little voluntary control over their hand movements have difficulty acquiring and integrating self-care skills.

Inappropriate Behaviors

Individuals with severe mental retardation frequently engage in inappropriate behaviors—behaviors that are highly repetitive, apparently nonpurposeful, and definitely undesirable. Inappropriate behaviors fall into four classes: (1) self-injurious behaviors, (2) stereotypic behaviors, (3) externally directed hazardous behaviors, and (4) nuisance behaviors. It has been estimated that approximately 70 percent of all institutionalized persons with severe mental retardation engage in some form of inappropriate behavior (Clements, Bost, DuBois, & Turpin, 1980; Spreat & Isett, 1981; Whitman & Sciback, 1979). It is widely reported that this is the most serious problem exhibited by the severely retarded (Guess & Rutherford, 1967; Kazdin, 1980; Wehman & McLaughlin, 1979). Inappropriate behaviors are a definite concern because they interfere with the instructional process, community integration, and the acquisition of desirable skills (Koegel, Firestone, Kramme, & Dunlap, 1974).

These behaviors are difficult to eliminate. For reasons not yet fully understood, they appear to have high reinforcing properties.

Self-injurious behaviors are actions that could "damage or disfigure a body part by one's own action" (Grossman, 1983, p. 194). The most common forms are head-banging, hair-pulling, eye-gouging, hitting, biting, and scratching. Elimination of self-injurious behaviors is imperative because they can lead to permanent physical damage (e.g., blindness or brain damage) (Kissel & Whitman, 1977).

Stereotypic behaviors are "complex, repetitive movements that appear to be nonfunctional" (Grossman, 1983, p. 198). Self-stimulatory behaviors are considered stereotypic. Common stereotypic behaviors include rocking, object-twirling, masturbation, rumination, random verbalizations, eye-rubbing, and finger-waving.

In general, **externally directed hazardous behaviors** are actions that are dangerous to other persons or their property. They are commonly the same as the self-injurious behaviors, but inflicted on others.

Nuisance behaviors are actions that make persons with severe mental retardation less acceptable to others. Although they are not dangerous, they should be reduced or eliminated. Typical nuisance behaviors include drooling, slobbering, expelling flatulence, inappropriate verbalizations, and throwing food.

The Case of Robert McGuire   EXAMPLE

Robert Andrew McGuire[4] was born in an agricultural community in a midwestern state following a gestation period of only 6 months and labor of 72 hours. At birth, he weighed slightly over three pounds and suffered from respiratory difficulties, that is, severe anoxia, cyanosis, and jaundice. He spent his first 4 months in the community hospital, and during that period he was first diagnosed as disabled. At 10 months, he was diagnosed as having spastic, quadriplegic cerebral palsy, and at 3 years, he experienced his first grand mal epileptic seizure. Because of these problems and a heart condition, Bobby spent his next 4 years shuttling between the hospital and the community preschool and school program.

Bobby's disability affected his family in general and his mother in particular. Shortly after Bobby was hospitalized for his first seizure, his father reportedly packed his bags and was never heard from again. Bobby grew up with his mother, a stepfather, and nine siblings, including direct siblings, step-siblings, and half-siblings. Mr. McGuire is employed in construction, and Mrs. McGuire worked outside the house in the past. Husband abandonment, periodic separation from her present husband, rearing nine children, and the frustration of obtaining necessary services for Bobby have given Mrs. McGuire many health problems. She has had surgery for ulcers and surgery after tearing her bladder when trying to lift Bobby from his wheelchair. She also has a heart problem and a nervous condition that she feels were brought on by trying to obtain appropriate services for Bobby.

Bobby began school in a class for the multiply disabled in an old, two-room country school building. The building is minimally accessible, with at least one step at every entrance. There is a nondisabled class in the other room of this building, but contact occurs only when both classes are outdoors, and this does not happen often, since the teachers have to push and pull the wheelchairs up and down the steps. Although Bobby's attitude toward school is positive, his education has not given him the skills he needs. For instance, he has been taught very few self-care, domestic, community, vocational, communication, or leisure skills. For over nine years, Mrs. McGuire has driven Bobby more than forty miles to a nursing home twice a week for occupational therapy and 125 miles three times a week for physical therapy. The McGuires have paid for both the transportation and Bobby's therapy.

The summer before what would have been his 8th grade, the school recommended that Bobby be placed in a hospital school about 300 miles away. The rationale was that he would receive better occupational, physical, and communication therapy than the local school system could provide. While this placement did result in improved therapeutic and educational services, Bobby never developed the functional skills needed for community integration. At age 19, he "graduated" from the hospital school. Today, Bobby lives at home with his parents and two younger brothers who are in high school. Recently, his mother, who just turned 60, asked, "What would happen to Bobby when we die?"

CONCLUSION

Severe mental retardation is a large component in the category of severe disabilities. Although the major deficiency of persons with severe mental retardation is lack of efficient cognitive processes, this disability affects other areas, causing problems in their efforts to become fully integrated into society. For instance, poor communication, self-care, physical, and social skills and the presence of inappropriate behaviors tend to isolate persons with severe mental retardation. But there also has not been a concerted effort to integrate them into either schools or society. Like Bobby, they are segregated into special classes and hospital schools. When they do graduate from school, they are often isolated from their communities.

The prospects should become brighter in the near future, now that research has indicated that individuals with severe mental retardation can learn and incorporate complex skills into their behavior repertoire. They can master sophisticated communication patterns, social interaction skills, domestic skills, general community skills, and leisure skills, as well as attaining a degree of self-sufficiency through employment. The trend toward community-based and family-based programming should gradually bring society toward the desired goal: full acceptance of individuals with severe mental retardation as *human beings* who simply think differently from the rest of us.

1. According to the most widely accepted definition, mental retardation re-   SUMMARY
fers to significantly subaverage general intellectual functioning existing concurrently with deficits in adaptive behavior and manifested during the developmental period.

2. There are three major aspects of the AAMR-Grossman definition: an IQ score of 75 or below on an individually administered intelligence test, impaired ability to meet expected standards of personal independence and social responsibility, and identification of the condition between birth and age 18. All three criteria must exist simultaneously.

3. Gold proposed a more optimistic definition that characterized a person with mental retardation "by the training process required for him or her to learn, and not by limitations in what he or she can learn."

4. Two systems are widely used in classifying persons with mental retardation: the AAMR-Grossman method and the educational method. The AAMR-Grossman system has four levels: mild, moderate, severe, and profound mental retardation. The educational classification has three levels: educable, trainable, and dependent (sometimes referred to as severe and profound or simply severe) mental retardation.

5. The prevalence of persons with mental retardation is approximately 3 percent of the school-age population and 2 percent of the preschool and postschool populations. The prevalence of severe retardation is approximately 0.4 percent of the general population.

6. Conditions leading to severe mental retardation include genetic and chromosomal disorders, nutritional and metabolic disorders, skull and brain disorders, and environmental disorders.

7. A dominant gene determines its specific trait (e.g., eye color) regardless of the other parent's gene. A recessive gene determines a trait only if it is matched by a recessive gene from the other parent.

8. Autosomal chromosomes are the first twenty-two matched pairs of chromosomes. While autosomal dominant genetic conditions can result in mental retardation, a more common cause of mental retardation is autosomal recessive genetic conditions.

9. The twenty-third pair, or sex chromosomes, can likewise create conditions that result in mental retardation. In general, this poses a greater risk for male than for female offspring.

10. Gene therapy may soon permit physicians to replace a defective gene with a normal gene in the body cells of a patient. This will reduce or eliminate the conditions created by the defective gene.

11. Some chromosomes have abnormal numbers or structures. A common abnormality is trisomy, more than two chromosomes in a pair. The most common form of Down syndrome, for instance, is caused by a trisomy of chromosome 21.

12. In nutritional and metabolic disorders, abnormal genes cause faulty formation of enzymes that are essential for metabolism. The enzymes accumulate in the cells, eventually reaching toxic levels that damage the young child's central nervous system, causing mental retardation and other neurological impairments. Nutritional and metabolic disorders are categorized by the type of faulty enzyme: carbohydrate disorders, amino acid disorders, lipid disorders, endocrine disorders, nucleotide disorders, and mineral disorders.

13. There are several types of craniofacial anomalies. The most common are microcephaly and hydrocephaly. Microcephaly means a smaller than typical head circumference. Hydrocephaly means increased cerebrospinal fluid within the skull, which ordinarily produces enlargement of the cranium.

14. Numerous environmental factors can result in mental retardation, including poisoning, Rh hemolytic disease, infections, malnutrition, and poverty/low-socioeconomic status.

15. Individuals with severe mental retardation have a number of communication disorders: small receptive and expressive vocabularies and disorders in articulation, semantics, and syntax. Some individuals have few or no speech skills and must communicate through manual sign language, communication boards, electronic devices, or yes-no gestures.

16. Many persons with severe retardation have social and emotional disorders that limit their integration into society. These disorders may be directly or indirectly related to their intellectual skills. Despite the prevalence of emotional disturbances, studies have demonstrated that persons with severe mental retardation can develop, maintain, and generalize sophisticated social skills.

17. Historically, persons with severe mental retardation were not taught leisure activities. A number of recent studies indicate conclusively that such persons can use their leisure time more productively in activities that develop desirable traits and skills.

18. Clearly, persons with mental retardation have a higher incidence of motor problems. Many with severe retardation are uncoordinated, awkward, and walk in a stiff robotlike gait. Others are so motorically impaired that they require canes, walkers, or wheelchairs to get from place to place.

19.   Self-care development refers to the behaviors required for full integration into the mainstream of school and society. Generally, these include self-feeding, self-dressing, self-management, and self-hygienics.

20.   Individuals with severe mental retardation frequently engage in inappropriate behaviors—highly repetitive, apparently nonpurposeful, and definitely undesirable behaviors—of four general classes: self-injurious behaviors, stereotypic behaviors, externally directed hazardous behaviors, and nuisance behaviors.

NOTES

[1]Throughout this chapter the term *severe mental retardation* is used to refer to severe and profound mental retardation in the educational classification. The term *profound mental retardation* will be used only for profound mental retardation in the AAMR classification.

[2]The scope of this book does not permit a detailed description of these syndromes or diseases. Interested readers are encouraged to read other works on these disorders. While the names given throughout this book are those primarily used, many of these syndromes and diseases also are known by other names, such as Sturge-Weber-Dimitri disease for Sturge-Weber syndrome or von Recklinghausen disease for neurofibromatosis.

[3]Precisely speaking, the *embryo* is the developing human in the first three months (trimester) of pregnancy; the *fetus* is the developing human from three months after conception to birth (the second and third trimesters). In this book, however, the word *fetus* is used to refer to the unborn child at any stage. *Embryo* is used only when the meaning is limited to the first trimester of pregnancy.

[4]All names used in the examples in this text are fictitious.

CHAPTER 3

Persons with Severe and Profound Behavior Disorders

(Courtesy of Tracy Hrbek.)

DEFINING BEHAVIOR DISORDERS

The demarcation of **behavior disorders**, like mental retardation, is clear and concise at the extremes of the continuum but confusing and inconsistent toward the middle. An individual who is continuously engaging in self-injurious behaviors and totally withdrawn into his or her own world would obviously be classified as behavior disordered; an immature child who displays inappropriate behavior may also be placed in that category. And, unlike categories such as sensory disabilities and mental retardation, which have quantitative linear criteria to assist in the identification process, emotion is nonrational, is nonlinear, and so far has eluded precise prose. A quiet child may be a withdrawn child, a shy child, a new child, a bilingual child, or an autistic child. An adolescent who cries in class may be mourning a death in the family, grieving over a chance remark by a classmate, suffering from a stomach ache, or responding to inner feelings of despair.

There is likewise little consensus about the name and definition of the category. Some opt for the term *emotional disturbances,* arguing that an underlying emotional problem is causing the inappropriate behavior, and the behavior will never truly become extinguished if the emotional problem is not treated. Others feel the term *behavior disorders* is more accurate, arguing that emotional problems may or may not be present, since some behaviors are learned responses; therefore, professionals must treat what can be seen, analyzed, and measured, namely the behaviors.

Nor is there one widely accepted definition. A recent perusal of journals and books revealed over thirty definitions that have some degree of acceptance in the field. To complicate this, some of the subcategories of behavior disorders, such as early infantile autism and childhood schizophrenia, have several widely accepted definitions.

Bower (1982) perceived persons with emotional disturbances as children and adolescents who exhibit one or more of the following five characteristics *to a marked extent* and *over a period of time:*

1. An inability to learn which cannot be explained by intellectual, sensory, or health factors . . .

2. An inability to build or maintain satisfactory impersonal relationships with peers and teachers . . .

3. Inappropriate behavior or feelings under normal conditions . . .

4. A general, pervasive mood of unhappiness or depression . . .

5. A tendency to develop physical symptoms, pains, or fears associated with personal or school problems [pp. 115–116].

Elaborating, Bower suggested that behavior disorders ranging from relatively normal to extremely aberrant behaviors formed a continuum, and that children with the disorders can be categorized along the continuum as follows:

(1) children who experience and demonstrate the normal problems of everyday living, growing, exploration, and reality testing . . . (2) children who develop a greater number and degree of symptoms of emotional problems as a result of normal crises or stressful experiences, such as death of father, birth of sibling, divorce of parents . . . (3) children in whom moderate symptoms of emotional maladjustment persist to some extent beyond normal expectations but who are

able to manage an adequate school adjustment . . . (4) children with fixed and recurring symptoms of emotional maladjustment who can with help profit by school attendance and maintain some positive relationships in the school setting . . . (5) children with fixed and recurring symptoms of emotional difficulties who are perhaps best educated in a residential school setting or temporarily in a home setting [p. 119].

While Bower's definition represents a significant attempt to quantify the category, it has some problems. Specifically, there is too much latitude in the interpretation of the terms *to a marked extent* and *over a period of time*. Just what is an *inability* to learn? Is it evinced by a six-month lag in achievement, by a one-year lag, by a two-year lag? Does it include an inability to learn appropriate social behaviors? Exactly what are *satisfactory* interpersonal relationships with peers? What behavior is *inappropriate,* and what are *normal* conditions? When is unhappiness *pervasive*? Many aspects of this definition require subjective judgments.

Nevertheless, Bower's definition has had a tremendous impact on public policy because it served as the model for the regulations governing implementation of Public Law 94–142. According to those regulations, children and adolescents with autism and schizophrenia are classified as seriously emotionally disturbed since they exhibit one or more of Bower's five characteristics to a marked degree over an extended period of time.[1]

CLASSIFICATIONS OF BEHAVIOR DISORDERS

In the past, category distinctions among behavioral or emotional problems have emerged from psychiatry, such as the third revision of the American Psychiatric Association's *Diagnostic and Statistical Manual of Mental Disorders (DSM–III)* (1980). This approach is useful for psychologists but holds little value for educators. Taking a different approach, Achenbach and Edelbrock used statistical techniques, computer analyses, and behavior ratings of children with and without behavioral and emotional problems to sort out clusters of stable and pervasive behavior patterns. They identified three general or broad-band syndromes in children with behavior disorders: internalizing syndrome, externalizing syndrome, and mixed syndrome (Achenbach, 1982a, 1982b, Achenbach & Edelbrock, 1978, 1981, 1983; Edelbrock & Achenbach, 1984).

Children and adolescents with **internalizing syndrome** exhibit behaviors that imply a retreat from the environment rather than a hostile response to it. They are frequently described as socially withdrawn, unresponsive, and immature. Typical behaviors include disordered speech and language patterns, distorted motor movements, disturbances in perception, and inappropriate responses to environmental events. Children and adolescents with **externaliz-**

ing syndrome generally exhibit behaviors at variance with the expectations of schools and other social institutions. They are aggressive, disruptive, defiant, disobedient, and irresponsible. As the label suggests, children and adolescents with **mixed syndrome** generally display behaviors symptomatic of both internalizing and externalizing syndromes, including immaturity, hyperactivity, anxiety, withdrawal, and a negative self-concept.

Persons with behavior disorders vary not only in category but also in degree, from the mild and transient problems displayed by perhaps 30 percent of all children sometime during their development (Kauffman, 1985) to very marked and chronic disorders that seriously impede every aspect of development. Children or adolescents who exhibit internalizing behaviors to a very marked and chronic degree are typically referred to as schizophrenic, autistic, or psychotic. Behaviors symptomatic of this population include impairment in developing personal relationships, preoccupation with inanimate objects, resistance to change in the environment, failure to acquire meaningful speech and language, and distorted motor and movement patterns. Their childhood years are characterized by intellectual retardation, lack of daily living skills, bizarre behaviors, and extreme social withdrawal.

PREVALENCE OF BEHAVIOR DISORDERS

The variables affecting prevalence of severe disability described in chapter 1 likewise play a role in behavior disorders. Studies on the prevalence of the overall category show great disparities, from around 2 percent (Froomkin, 1972), to 8 percent (Ullmann, 1952), to 10 percent (Bower, 1960), to 20 and 24 percent (Kelly, Bullock, & Dykes, 1977; Salvia, Schultz, & Chapin, 1974). Wood and Zabel (1978) offer an explanation: In these studies, an individual is found to have a behavior disorder at a specific time. Apparently, many individuals (especially children) manifest behavior problems at one time but not at any other. Therefore, a one-time screening may identify some as having behavior disorders who are actually exhibiting a temporary problem that does not warrant the label.

What, then, is the prevalence of persons with behavior disorders? According to many investigators, the rate is between 2 and 3 percent of the general population (Hewett & Taylor, 1980; Kauffman, 1980; Kelly, Bullock, & Dykes, 1977; Morse & Coopchik, 1979; Wood & Zabel, 1978). The prevalence of persons with severe behavior disorders[2] arouses some disagreement as well. Estimates range from 1 and 2 percent of the general population (Bower, 1982; Goldstein, Baker, & Jamison, 1980; Knoblock, 1983), to 0.04 and 0.05 percent of the general population (Calhoun, Acocella, & Goldstein, 1977; Paluszny, 1979; Ritvo & Freeman, 1977). While it is at best an educated estimate, approximately 0.4 percent of the general population appears to be

the prevalence rate. More males than females are identified as severely behavior disordered. Again estimates vary, but the most accurate ratio appears to
be four or five males to one female (Hington & Bryson, 1972; Morse, 1975;
Paluszny, 1979).

ETIOLOGY OF SEVERE BEHAVIOR DISORDERS

Why do some individuals behave so differently from the general population?
While many theories have been proposed, there is no convincing evidence yet
to explain the dramatically strange behavior of persons with severe behavior
disorders. The many explanations can be roughly categorized into three
groups: organic theory, environmental theory, and interaction theory.

Organic Theory

The **organic theory** is based on the belief that severe behavior disorders have
physical determinants that produce a cognitive disorder in the individual.
Supporters argue that such characteristics as resistance to change in the environment (often called *preservation of sameness*), failure to acquire meaningful
language and disturbances in perception are primarily congitive disorders that
result from an organic deficit. Studies of direct relatives of persons with severe
behavior disorders offer some support for this theory. For instance, the rate of
siblings becoming severely behavior disordered is approximately 2 percent
(Kauffman, 1985). Stronger evidence comes from studies of twins. In a review
of the research, Pollin (1972) found a concordance rate for monozygotic (identical) twins of approximately 50 percent. A concordance figure of less than 20
percent for dizygotic (fraternal) twins has been reported by other researchers
(Buss, 1966; Pollin, 1972; Ritvo & Brothers, 1982). Both figures are significantly higher than the expected rate of about 0.4 percent.

Researchers have accumulated a good deal of evidence suggesting that
persons with severe behavior disorders also suffer from neurological impairments. For example, DeMyer, Barton, DeMyer, Norton and Steele (1973)
reported that 73.4 percent of persons with severe behavior disorders have
signs of neurological dysfunction and 69 percent have grossly abnormal elec-
troencephalogram (EEG) patterns. Recent studies of cerebral-evoked voltages
(CEVs), the electrical measurement of neurological responses to specific stimuli, show that persons with severe behavior disorders have weaker auditory
and visual responses, reach their maximum response more quickly, and have
less consistent responses than do peers without disabilities. However, a cause-
and-effect relationship remains to be demonstrated. Various investigators
have proposed that the deficit is limited to audiovisual modalities, which would
explain why children with severe behavior disorders show a preference for

tactile-kinesthetic stimuli (Dunlap, Koegel, & Burke, 1981; Frankel, Simmons, Fichter, & Freeman, 1984; Hermalin & O'Connor, 1970; Koegel, Rincover, & Egel, 1982; Schopler & Reichler, 1971; Schreibman, Charlop, & Britten, 1983).

Lovaas and his associates, focusing on the question of cognitive disorders in the organic theory, analyzed disturbances in perception. In a laboratory study, children with severe behavior disorders, children with mental retardation, and children without disabilities were reinforced for responding to a complex stimulus involving the simultaneous presentation of auditory, visual, and tactile cues. After the cues were learned, they were presented separately. Children with severe behavior disorders responded primarily to one stimulus component; children with mental retardation responded to two; and children without disabilities responded to all three. Although no modality was preferred by the children with severe behavior disorders, apparently they had attended selectively to only one modality while learning the task (Lovaas, Koegel, & Schreibman, 1979; Lovaas, Schreibman, Koegel, & Rehm, 1971). Because much learning involves complex stimuli, this selective attention may be important in understanding why such children often have problems in social and environmental situations. The studies by Lovaas and his associates do not conclusively prove that organic factors cause severe behavior disorders, however.

There are three offshoots of the organic theory: the vitamin theory, the neuropsychopharmacology theory, and the orthomolecular theory. Essentially, they all suggest that some kind of biophysical deficiency causes the severe behavior disorders. Supporters of the organic theory suggest that if these biophysical deficiencies could be eliminated the individuals would no longer have the disability. The **vitamin theory** holds that the person has vitamin deficiencies that could be eliminated through large doses of the appropriate vitamins and minerals (Lelord et al., 1981; Rimland, Callaway, & Dreyfus, 1978). The **neuropsychopharmacology theory** hypothesizes that a chemical imbalance causes the severe behavior disorders, and antipsychotic drugs may be able to restore the proper balance (Schroeder & Schroeder, 1982). The **orthomolecular theory** points out that certain allergies give rise to symptoms similar to those of persons with severe behavior disorders (for instance, screaming, head-banging, and cessation of speech) and that these individuals should be treated as allergy patients are treated (Rimland & Meyer, 1967). While the arguments for these theories have won many supporters, at this point the recommended therapies have not proved successful. The American Academy of Pediatrics (1976) found no valid evidence that these approaches reduced the incidence of severe behavior disorders.

While it is appealing to think that persons with severe behavior disorders have an organic defect that causes them to fail socially and intellectually, research has not yet identified any such defect. Therefore, all current vitamin, drug, or allergy-based treatments are entirely experimental.

Environmental Theory

At the opposite end of the continuum is the **environmental theory**. Its supporters believe some environmental factor triggers severe behavior disorders. Diet, pollutants, illnesses, and rearing patterns have all been linked, in some way, to severe behavior problems (Knoblock, 1983). Most of the research has analyzed the relationship between the child and the parents. Proponents of this theory argue that the child's early experiences, particularly interactions between child and parents, form the cornerstone of all subsequent problems (Wing, 1985). Kanner (1943) wrote that parents of children with severe behavior disorders are intelligent and obsessive, detached and cold. In a later paper, he coined the term "emotional refrigerator" to describe the detached rearing patterns of these parents.

A major supporter of this theory, Bettelheim (1967) suggests that parents of children with severe behavior disorders never wanted their child and thus rejected the infant during critical periods of development in the first year of life. Slowly, the child withdraws from the real world into a world of his or her own making. Factors such as preservation of sameness and social isolation, Bettelheim indicates, are a means of coping with the rejecting environment. Other researchers interpret the data somewhat differently, although they agree with some of Bettelheim's points. They suggest that parents of children with severe behavior disorders do not reinforce socially appropriate or desirable behaviors, or at best reinforce them inconsistently, so that the children acquire bizarre behavior patterns (Goldstein, 1983; Strain, Odom, & McConnell, 1984).

Efforts to specify the kinds of rearing practices that may contribute to severe behavior disorders have prompted a number of research studies. Typical studies examine double-bind communication, in which a parent simultaneously gives the child mutually contradictory messages (e.g., both rejection and affection) while implicitly forcing the child to make a choice. Regardless of which alternative is selected, the child will experience pain. Researchers have noted that parents of children with severe behavior disorders frequently give their offspring double-bind messages (Bateson, Jackson, Haley, & Weakland, 1956; Crittenden & Bonvillian, 1984; Martin, 1980). One study compared the verbal communication patterns of mothers of children with severe behavior disorders to mothers of children without disabilities. The former conveyed less information, were less supportive, were less explicit, and were more ambiguous than the latter (Goldfarb, Yudkovitz, & Goldfarb, 1973).

Again, we must be cautious about drawing etiological conclusions from such evidence. Many very rejecting parents, for instance, rear children who show no signs of disability; and parents of children with severe behavior disorders rear siblings who are not at all disabled. Many studies found no evidence that parents of children with severe behavior disorders behave differently from parents of children without disabilities; in particular, they are neither too introverted nor obsessive (Byasee & Murrell, 1975; Sameroff &

Seifer, 1983; Sameroff, Seifer, & Zax, 1982; Schreibman & Mills, 1983). If the parents of disturbed children do exhibit different communication patterns, it is highly possible that the patterns result from simple weariness and pessimism after years of having their verbal instructions and questions ignored. To conclude that the parents' behavior caused the child's disorder is illogical; it is equally plausible that parental attitudes and behaviors became different because the child was so unusual. Sadly, this hypothesis has largely been overlooked in a rush to demonstrate parental culpability.

An entirely different environmental theory holds that severe behavior disorders result from an interplay between the child's drive to adapt to the environment and the demands of that environment. The child's attempts to organize the environment in a positive manner are frustrated by the environment itself, which is changing too quickly for the young child. Normal children manage to withstand this stress. They explore their environment and interact with it, becoming more confident and competent with each experience. However, the environmental stress gives rise to an intense motivational conflict in the child with severe behavior disorders. The instability of the environment makes the child apprehensive, this fear prevents the child from responding to others, and language fails to develop because the child is too afraid to engage in social interactions that lead to speech (Calhoun, Acocella, & Goldstein, 1977). As a result, the child exhibits a general failure to adapt to his or her environment, and adopts such traits as preservation of sameness, disturbances in language and perception, stereotypic and ritualistic movements, and social isolation in an attempt to manipulate and gain control over the environment.

Interaction Theory

Midway between the poles of the organic theory and the environmental theory is a hybrid of them, referred to as the **interaction theory** or the *diathesis-stress theory*. It asserts that an innate vulnerability (diathesis) to severe behavior disorders is much higher in some persons than others, and a stressful event may "set off" the severe behavior disorders in a vulnerable individual (Goldstein, Baker, & Jamison, 1980; Gottesman & Schields, 1972; Rosenthal, 1968). The trigger may be chronic stress in the form of a persistently disturbed family relationship or an acute temporary stress such as rejection by a loved one. According to Selye (1975), a reaction to stress may occur in two stages. The first, **alarm reaction**, is marked by excitation and resistance. If alarm reaction does not satisfactorily address the stressful situation, then **countershock** occurs. This stage is marked by adaptation and defense. Both of these responses can be seen in individuals with severe behavior disorders. Suomi's studies of rhesus monkeys offer support for the interaction theory. Suomi found a hereditary risk factor for emotional disturbances in the monkeys that was expressed only after a traumatic environmental experience (reported in Alper, 1986).

Zaslow and Breger (1969) offer an example of a diathesis-stress etiology of severe behavior disorders. These investigators assert that normal attachment develops through the pairing of stress reduction with sensorimotor stimulation from the parents. That is, the child develops an attachment for the parents through repeatedly having his or her stress relieved by parental holding, cuddling, patting, rocking, and playing. However, if a child is constitutionally active, noncuddly, or disease-prone and the parents tend to be distant and withdrawn, the child may never be held or patted long enough to dissipate his or her stress, and parent–child attachment may not develop. Because of the lack of attachment, child and parent become locked into an increasingly negative relationship, which prevents the child from developing cognitively or socially. Instead, the child becomes attached to objects, while cognitive activity is arrested. Thus, according to Zaslow and Breger, the child relies on such resistance activities as tantrums, stiffening, and gaze aversion to maintain his or her independence.

However, the interaction theory is not free of problems. Like the organic theory, it does not pinpoint the organic vulnerability or offer a way to identify which individuals are vulnerable. Like the environmental theory, it does not specify the types of stressful events that are likely to precipitate the breakdown. But, because the interaction theory easily accommodates and assimilates the research and arguments for both other theories, it is presently the most widely accepted perspective on the etiology of severe behavior disorders.

CATEGORIES OF SEVERE BEHAVIOR DISORDERS

Many professionals lump all children with severe behavior disorders into one category (**childhood psychosis**) based on the appearance of certain symptoms before the onset of puberty. Others contend that these disorders have two distinct categories: **early infantile autism** and **childhood schizophrenia** (sometimes referred to as *schizophreniform*).[3] Four decades ago, it was widely accepted that severe behavior disorders constituted a single category. Then, in 1943, Leo Kanner described eleven cases in which an inability to relate to others, an obsession with sameness, and impaired speech appeared very early in infancy. Kanner proposed that these children suffered from an inborn disorder that could be differentiated from other severe behavior disturbances of childhood. Since the primary symptom seemed to be inability to relate to anything beyond the self, Kanner initially described the disorder as *autistic disturbance of affective contact*. Later he coined the term *early infantile autism*, from the Greek *autos* meaning "self."

Since then, a number of attempts have been made to develop a classification scheme for autism and the other subcategories. Schemes proposed by the World Health Organization (Rutter, Lebovic, et al., 1969), the Group for the Advancement of Psychiatry (1966), and the National Society for Autistic

Children (Ritvo & Freeman, 1978) distinguish two subcategories, autism and childhood schizophrenia, on the following dimensions (Rimland, 1964; Rutter, 1968, 1978; Wing, 1972):

1. *Onset and course.* The child with autism is disordered from birth; the child with schizophrenia experiences a period of normal or nearly normal development, after which he or she regresses.

2. *Health and appearance.* Children with autism are not only in good physical health but also identified as "beautiful," whereas children with schizophrenia may or may not have health problems and are no more or less attractive than the general population.

3. *Physical responsiveness.* The child with autism exhibits stiff withdrawal. The child with schizophrenia may be physically responsive to social contact.

4. *Aloneness.* Children with autism are severely withdrawn. Children with schizophrenia sometimes respond to their social environment.

5. *Preservation of sameness.* Children with schizophrenia may not exhibit the same need to maintain the physical environment exactly that children with autism exhibit.

6. *Personal orientation.* Children with schizophrenia have a disoriented perception of their environment. Children with autism are unoriented—they generally give no indication of perceiving the environment, beyond the need to preserve sameness.

7. *Hallucinations.* While hallucinations are not common, they have been reported in children with schizophrenia but not in children with autism.

8. *Motor performance.* Children with schizophrenia may have some motor difficulties. Children with autism appear well coordinated and able to perform complex motor tasks.

9. *Language.* Children with autism use speech in noncommunicative ways. Children with schizophrenia can communicate, but they use speech to communicate bizarre thoughts.

10. *Intellectual abilities.* It is argued that children with autism have a higher intelligence level than children with schizophrenia. (However, the IQ scores of individuals with autism are usually in the 50s or lower; the scores of those with childhood schizophrenia are usually in the 60s and 70s or lower.)

11. *Savant syndrome performances.* Savant syndrome performances (inappropriately called idiot savant performances) are seen in a small proportion of children with autism but not in children with schizophrenia. These are displays of remarkable ability in isolated areas, for instance, playing a song on the piano after hearing it for the first time,

skillfully carving figures of animals, or indicating the day of a certain date in the future or in the past.

12. *Family background.* Parents of children with autism have higher intellectual ability and come from higher socioeconomic strata than parents of children with schizophrenia.

13. *Family history of mental disorders.* The incidence of mental illness in parents and grandparents is lower than average for children with autism but higher than average for children with schizophrenia.

14. *Sex ratio.* While the incidence of autism is three to eight times higher in males than in females, there is no sex differential in childhood schizophrenia.

Is there some justification for classifying children with autism separately from children with childhood schizophrenia? Many of these distinguishing features are based on little more than guesswork while others have failed to receive confirmation from subsequent research. For instance, there is no empirical support for the belief that children with autism have a higher intellectual potential than those with childhood schizophrenia. In fact, subsequent research has reported just the opposite (DeMyer, Hingtgen, & Jackson, 1981; Hingtgen & Churchill, 1971). There is no firm evidence that parents of children with autism have above average intelligence or come from higher socio-economic strata. Subsequent research has found little or no difference between children with autism and those with childhood schizophrenia on the following traits: health and appearance, physical responsiveness, personal orientation, motor performance, and sex ratio (Calhoun, Acocella, & Goldstein, 1977). Reports of savant syndrome performances, while appealing to the popular press, are open to question. For instance, Restak (1982) found that about an equal proportion of persons with mental retardation who display no autistic tendencies also exhibited savant behaviors.

Does this mean, then, there are no differences between children with autism and children with childhood schizophrenia? While there are no symptomatic differences, there may be intensity differences. For instance, it may be said that childhood schizophrenia is manifested in symptoms closer to normalcy, and thus less severe, than autism. Though children with schizophrenia may also spend hours contorting their bodies and engaging in repetitive and nonfunctional motor behaviors, they are much less likely to mutilate themselves than children with autism. Though their behavior is bizarre, it is less obsessive. But these differences may be more a factor of the earlier age of onset than of symptom distinctions between the two conditions. Autism and childhood schizophrenia may represent an artificial division of the same category, with schizophrenia depicting a milder form than autism, just as an IQ of 40 represents a milder form of severe mental retardation than an IQ of 20. However, Bauer (1983) in her review of the research stated, "the lack of differentiation between autism and childhood schizophrenia is not supported in the literature" (p. 229).

CHARACTERISTICS OF PERSONS WITH SEVERE BEHAVIOR DISORDERS

Clearly, persons with severe behavior disorders differ from those with mild and moderate behavior disorders along a number of significant dimensions. Severe behavior disorders bring a number of characteristics that limit the individual's ability to develop functional skills. The identified characteristics differ from study to study, but the most widely accepted list was proposed by Creak and his associates (1963). They found the following nine characteristics systemic and representative of severe behavior disorders:

1. Serious and sustained impairment in the development of personal relationships.
2. Unawareness of personal identity, manifested by personal disorientation, grotesque posturing, and self-mutilation.
3. Preoccupation with and personal attachment to inanimate objects or certain characteristics of objects without regard for their use or function.
4. Resistance to any change in the environment and compulsive rituals aimed at preserving "sameness" in the environment.
5. Abnormal perceptual experiences, which may lead to unpredictable and unexplainable responses to sensory stimuli.
6. Acute, excessive, and seemingly illogical anxiety or terror of common objects.
7. Arrest in acquiring or failure to acquire meaningful communication; speech marked by mutism, echolalia, neologisms, and other language disorders.
8. Distorted motor behavior, which may take the form of catatonia, contortions, hyperactivity, or—most commonly—endlessly repeated ritualistic mannerisms.
9. Significant delays in the acquisition of functional skills.

Rarely will an individual manifest all these symptoms, according to Creak and his associates, but individuals diagnosed with severe behavior disorders invariably exhibit the three central traits: serious impairment in social relationships, inability to use speech for communicative purposes, and bizarre motor movements.

Disturbances in social relationships, sometimes identified as the cardinal trait, may take many forms, from total withdrawal and refusal to interact with other persons to obsessive attachment to inanimate objects such as a small piece of garden hose, a metal clothes hanger, or an old plastic plate. In short, persons with severe behavior disorders fail to respond to their social environment or respond in an excessive and inappropriate manner.

The second most distinguishing trait is communication abnormalities. Many persons with severe behavior disorders are nonverbal; they may babble, whine, or cry. Those who use speech may exhibit peculiarities and almost always use it in a noncommunicative fashion or to communicate bizarre or incoherent ideas.

To the casual observer, the most striking trait is bizarre motor behavior, ranging from total lack of movement to self-induced vomiting, feces-smearing, and unrestrainable prolonged tantrums. Typical is a limited repertoire of movements repeated endlessly in stereotypic fashion for no apparent reason. Examples include twirling, toe-walking, rocking, and hand-flapping. If left alone, according to Lovaas, Litrownik, and Mann (1971), the child with severe behavior disorders will spend up to 90 percent of waking hours engaging in these behaviors. Even more striking are repetitive movements that result in self-multilation, such as face-hitting, head-banging, eye-gouging, and hand-biting. Persons with severe behavior disorders have been known to pull out their teeth, bite off the ends of their fingers, chew their shoulders to the bone, and pull off large layers of their skin.

Clearly, this distinct cluster of characteristics distinguishes severe behavior disorders from other disabling conditions. To understand persons with these disorders better and to distinguish them more clearly, we will examine some of the characteristics in greater detail.

Social Isolation

Social withdrawal and isolation are usually evident in the 1st or 2nd year of the child's life. Parents often recall that their child was an "ideal" baby who typically did not pester adults for attention and, in fact, seemed happier when left alone. These babies often are very hard to hold and cuddle, arching their backs and stiffening when picked up, whereas normal babies instinctively mold to the body of the adult holding them. As the infant grows into childhood, this recoiling from personal contact becomes even more marked. The child fails to acquire the social smile, avoids looking anyone in the face, and treats people as if they simply do not exist. The child does not listen if spoken to, does not come when called, and for all practical purposes seems to be completely absorbed in his or her own aimless activities. If the child is touched or grabbed in any way or asked to engage in an undesirable activity, he or she can become abusive and physically assault the "offending" person, without showing any remorse.

The lack of eye contact, to some researchers, is the source of disturbed interpersonal relationships. In a laboratory experiment, children with severe behavior disorders were compared to children without disabilities in gaze avoidance. Both groups of children were given ten minutes to explore an otherwise empty room containing five line drawings of faces mounted on stands. As figure 3.1 illustrates, the children without disabilities showed about equal interest in all faces, except less interest in the blank one. The children with severe behavior disorders looked the least at the happy face, somewhat

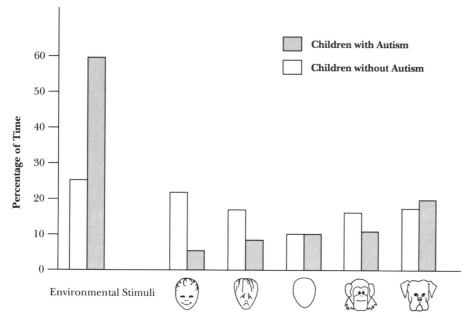

FIGURE 3.1

The Proportions of Time Spent by Children with Autism and Children without Autism Attending to Five Model Faces and to Environmental Stimuli

(Adapted from "The Behavioral Significance of Gaze Aversion with Particular Reference to the Syndrome of Infantile Autism," C. Hutt & C. Ounsted, 1966, *Behavioral Science, 11,* p. 349. Reprinted with permission from *Behavioral Science,* a publication of the General Systems Science Foundation.)

more at the animal faces, and by far the most at environmental stimuli such as light switches and baseboards (Hutt & Ounsted, 1966). The investigators concluded that children with severe behavior disorders avoid the gaze of other people to decrease their level of arousal. It is simply more comfortable for such children to look away than to look directly into someone's face. Whether this explanation proves correct, avoiding the gaze of another person is a distinct and disconcerting trait in persons with severe behavior disorders.

To illustrate social isolation in children with severe behavior disorders, Morgan (1981) cites a case study:

> When Timmy was about four or five months of age, I noticed that he didn't respond to us in the same way as our other children had done. He showed no reaction as I approached his crib. He didn't seem to care whether we were around or whether we picked him up. When I picked him up and held him, he was like a sack of flour at first. Later when I held him, he would hit his head over and over against my shoulder. He also would bang his head in his crib. At this point, we became concerned. As we look back now, Timmy was always unresponsive to

human contact, both in a physical and social sense. He always preferred being alone and doing his own thing—over and over [p. 13].

Communication Patterns

The social isolation of persons with severe behavior disorders is exponentially increased by their failure to use language for communicative purposes. From the beginning, most parents report, the child's language is delayed and deviant. In imitative social tasks, such as "waving bye-bye," they show little skill. Their use of small toys in imaginative play is greatly limited, if indeed it ever develops. Because both social imitation and imaginative play are essential for language development, the speech of these children falters badly. Unlike children with hearing impairments, who understand the principle of communication and who develop nonverbal skills for communicating, children with severe behavior disorders do not use gestures and mime to make their needs known. They may point to objects they need, but their ability to communicate is greatly restricted if the object is not present (Rosenhan & Seligman, 1984).

About half of all persons with severe behavior disorders are nonverbal. In the other half, speech is usually limited to **echolalia**: the child merely repeats, either immediately or at some later time, words or phrases heard earlier. These snatches of speech are echoed not in an apparent attempt to communicate but aimlessly, without concern for the meaning of the words. Echolalia is usually spoken in a high-pitched, parrotlike, squeaky monotone.

If children with severe behavior disorders do develop communicative speech, they make many of the same grammatical errors that normal children do. But the errors persist longer and some are unusual. Pronominal reversals are common (i.e., the child refers to himself or herself as "you," "he," "her," or his or her proper name rather than as "I"). Many misuse the suffix -*ing*. For instance, a 9-year-old girl was observed to say "Daddy piping" to describe an unrelated man smoking a pipe and "boy bubbling" to describe a boy blowing bubbles (Wing, 1976). These children often describe objects by their use rather than their name. For instance, a 12-year-old boy used "go-from-place-to-place" for automobile and "sweep-the-floor" for broom.

In communicative individuals, speech is marked by extreme literalness, repetition, and lack of spontaneity or originality. There are no colloquialisms. Conversation is stilted. Such persons can maintain a concrete question-and-answer interchange, but the subtleties of emotional tone are missing. They seem to know the formal rules of language, but they do not comprehend the idea of communication (Rosenhan & Seligman, 1984). Bender (1947) offers the following example of unusual speech patterns in a child with severe behavior disorders:

I say, hello, doctor, have you any new toys? Let me open your radiator with this screwdriver. I say let me open it. I say so what. Can I copy your animals? I am in a doctor's office. You and I are twins, aren't we? I am coloring this camel brown. I said I am coloring it brown. Have you a little scissors? Have you a big scissors? I say, have you a big scissors? Well, here's what I will use, what do you think? It is called a knife. How does my voice sound? What? What? Judy, what? Is that your name? I'm cutting out this camel. It is pretty enough to hang on the wall? Can you cut as pretty as this? My sister says camel talk. Isn't that funny? Camel talk. My voice sounds like up in the library. Doesn't it? In the hospital my voice sounds like up in the library. Can you say li-bra-ri-an? The library is where you get books [pp. 49–50].

This person has a rather high level of speech functioning, but his communication pattern is still extremely disjointed.

Insistence on Preserving Sameness

Persons with severe behavior disorders have an obsessive desire to maintain sameness in their environment. Toys must be placed in the same position on the same shelves. The arrangement of the furniture may never be changed. Clothes in the closet must hang in the same order. At breakfast, the egg must be eaten first, then the vitamin pill, then the toast, followed by milk and orange juice. In the bath, the face must be washed first, then the arms, and so on. Even a slight disturbance in this intricate pattern may elicit a tantrum.

The insistence on sameness may occur in other ways. Creak (1952) described a young boy who loved chocolate but would eat it only if it was cut into squares; round chocolate was summarily rejected. Creak described another boy who cried violently while getting ready for bed on the first night of summer camp. After a short time, the counselor surmised that the child wanted to wear his underwear beneath his pajamas. After he was dressed in the accustomed way, the child immediately quieted down.

Many children without disabilities react badly to changes in their environment, particularly sudden changes. But persons with severe behavior disorders show this trait to an exaggerated degree. Normal children at $2^1/2$ years of age commonly exhibit this concern for sameness, so it is possible that children with severe behavior disorders experienced developmental stall. Morgan (1981) provides the following example of preservation of sameness:

Robert has always been concerned with order and ritual. When he was only two, he would arrange blocks in lines for hours. If we altered this arrangement in even the slightest way, he would become upset. Or if we interrupted his activity, he might fall down, kick, and scream. Now he goes through certain rituals. He strikes the kitchen table and taps his fingers on it—at least twice a day. He will not go to bed at night until the telephone directory is on the table by his bed and turned to a certain page. Then he gets up several times to check the page before going to sleep [p. 20].

Stereotypic and Ritualistic Movements

Another distinguishing characteristic of persons with severe behavior disorders is their total absorption in stereotypic and ritualistic movements—complex, repetitive, apparently nonfunctional movements that recur frequently and with high intensity. They may be solitary activities or include manipulation of an object. Solitary movements typically include rocking, waving the fingers in front of the eyes, flapping the hands and arms, head-rolling, and staccato lunging and darting movements with sudden stops. Stereotypic movements with an object include spinning lids or plates, waving a piece of garden hose in front of the face, and flipping a clothes hanger between thumb and middle finger. Such activities have been known to continue for over eight hours and often take precedence over food. One study found that a group of children with severe behavior disorders who had not eaten for twenty-four hours would not respond to a signal that food was available when they were engaged in ritualistic movements. The children all knew what the signal meant and would respond to it immediately when they were not engaged in such movements (Lovaas, Litrownik, & Mann, 1971).

Persons with severe behavior disorders often have a deep emotional attachment to the objects they use in stereotypic activities. Many can distinguish their own object from others closely resembling it. For example, school personnel substituted an apparently identical clothes hanger for the one a young boy flipped. He had a tantrum until his original hanger was returned. The boy who waved a foot-long piece of garden hose in front of his face would hug the hose each night as he went to sleep. Morgan (1981) again cites the case of Robert to illustrate the preference for objects to people:

> Even when he was only one, he began to manipulate objects in a repetitive way. We gave him a set of blocks which he became very attached to. It was rather disturbing to us as parents to see that he cared more for the blocks than us. His first word, rather than "mama" or "dada" was "block" [p. 17].

Self-Injurious Behaviors

Like persons with severe mental retardation, persons with severe behavior disorders frequently engage in self-injurious behaviors. The most common forms are head-banging, hair-pulling, eye-gouging, hitting, biting, and scratching. These are typically not mild slaps or slight taps of their head against a wall but rather significant physical insults. A few examples may illustrate: A young man with severe behavior disorders who wore a professional football helmet cracked it by banging it against the floor a couple of times. When he was not wearing the helmet, he had split his head open and knocked himself out from the force of banging his head. A girl beat and bit herself so frequently and violently that a thick layer of calluses had formed across her forehead and the backs of her hands. Another young woman pulled out virtually every hair on her body. A young boy bit off the tips of all ten of his fingers to the first joint. A teenage boy pulled most of the skin off his forearms. Such self-injurious behavior can lead to permanent physical damage. But these behaviors need not occur; they can be eliminated through behavior modification techniques (Meyer & Evans, 1986).

Other Behavior Problems

Persons with severe behavior disorders frequently exhibit a number of other problem behaviors. Tantrums are quite common. They are not the tantrums typical of a 2- or 3-year-old child; rather they are more intense and more frequent. For example, the boy who flipped a clothes hanger once unleashed a tantrum that lasted well over three hours, in which he ran in a circle, hitting, kicking, and biting anyone who got in his way and kocking over and destroying any object he encountered. Injuries are common during such tantrums.

Another common problem is externally directed hazardous behavior, which is dangerous to other people and property. While hitting, biting, and scratching are the most common, such behaviors include head-butting, hair-pulling, eye-gouging, arm-twisting, bear-hugging, and kicking. For instance, the girl who had calluses on her forehead and the backs of her hands had injured three people to the point where they required hospitalization, one for a week.

Other behaviors that interfere with the social integration of persons with severe behavior disorders include lack of self-care skills (self-feeding, self-dressing, self-management, and self-hygienics), inability to learn, maintain, and generalize desirable behaviors, unexplainable and illogical responses to sensory stimuli, nuisance behaviors, bizarre gestures, odd patterns of motility, and unusual movements such as lunging, darting, and sudden stops.

The Case of William Robert Harrington   EXAMPLE

On the last day of December 1965, Billy Bob was born at a major hospital in a large, midwestern city. He was, in many ways, the perfect child—cute, warm, and cuddly, and he enjoyed the attention he got from his parents and older sisters. As the first male grandchild on both sides of the family, he was showered with gifts and attention, and he seemed to revel in it.

In most respects, Billy Bob's home life was typical. He was the second youngest of five children in what appeared to be a supportive and nurturing family. His father was assistant manager of a warehouse at an automobile manufacturing plant, and his mother worked as a clerk in a retail hardware store. Billy Bob's infancy was uneventful. His parents reported that he progressed through the developmental sequence like a normal child: he sat up at 6 months, he walked at 10 months, and he began talking at 11 months.

When Billy Bob was 14 months old, the Morrises, Mrs. Harrington's parents, separated, and Mrs. Morris and her two teenage sons moved in with the Harringtons. Initially, the Harringtons thought this would only require a reshuffling of the physical space within the home; they thought that they could continue with the same life-style they had enjoyed before. For example, the Harringtons attempted to treat both her parents equally, but this proved extremely difficult. Mr. Morris tried to pressure the Harringtons into forcing a reconciliation, and Mrs. Morris resented the Harringtons' socializing with Mr. Morris. To complicate matters, the teenage boys proved unruly and hardly controllable. At first, the Harringtons expected Mrs. Morris to curb her sons' unmanageable behavior. When she failed to do this, the Harringtons established rules that they expected the boys to follow. Unfortunately, not only did both Mr. and Mrs. Morris resent these rules, but also the boys refused to follow them. This brought a great deal of arguing, fighting, and bickering into the home.

The changed atmosphere was especially traumatic to Billy Bob. From that point on, he was not the same. His parents reported that he withdrew into a shell, he no longer smiled, and he didn't socialize. His behavior became unpredictable and explosive, marked by inappropriate and out-of-context associations. His speech skills—articulation, fluency, and desire to communicate—deteriorated to nonexistence. The Harringtons eventually took Billy Bob to a psychologist, who diagnosed him as a childhood psychotic functioning at the severely mentally retarded level.

Because of this diagnosis, when Billy Bob was 6 years old his suburban school district refused to accept him, but they did arrange to place him in a special day school. The day school referred Billy Bob to the regional diagnostic center for a complete educational evaluation. The evaluators found that he was functioning at the 2 years, 6 months level. They classified him as autistic and functioning at the severely mentally retarded level. In general, they found that his behavior was unpredictable and explosive and that he appeared to have lost contact with reality. Shortly after returning from the diagnostic center, Billy Bob was placed in a psychiatric hospital. The admission report did not list the precipitating event, but it stated that Billy Bob "needed a structured twenty-four-hour program on a seven-day-a-week basis." It also stated that he was having more frequent and more explosive outbursts of violent and aggressive behavior directed not only toward the staff but also toward his parents and siblings. (Billy Bob's explosive and aggressive behavior had twice injured his mother and once injured his oldest sister to the point where they required hospitalization.) The hospital placement was not successful, and in April 1973 Billy Bob was referred to a center that specialized in treating children with severe behavior disorders. It appears that this was intended to be a short-term placement, to conduct a complete educational evaluation on Billy Bob and to eliminate some of his explosive, aggressive behaviors.

In this evaluation, Billy Bob was diagnosed as autistic with acute brain damage that caused him to function at the severely mentally retarded level.

The psychologist indicated that the boy was in a private world of fantasy, was extremely hyperactive, laughed inappropriately, and used echolalic speech extensively. (Billy Bob essentially used only two echolalic statements; the first was, "Billy Bob's a bad boy" and the second was the theme song to the television show "The Flintstones.") Socially, the psychologist noted, Billy Bob could function neither in group situations nor with individuals. The majority of the psychologist's report dealt with the boy's aggressive behavior. He exhibited such self-injurious behaviors as violently hitting himself, biting his arms and index fingers, and ripping his clothes apart. Relative to externally directed hazardous behaviors, Billy Bob has been known to violently hit, kick, and pull the hair of others.

The speech pathologist indicated that Billy Bob had receptive language at about the 3-year-old level, but he exhibited no expressive speech skills. In self-care skills, he could dress and undress himself, put on his shoes, and button his clothes, but he could not tie his shoes; he could feed himself using knife, fork, or spoon, but his table manners were poor, marked by hurried and sloppy eating. In the dormitory, Billy Bob was described as stubborn, determined, and destructive. He often hit, kicked, or pulled the hair of other clients or the staff. Although he was physically healthy and free of physical defects, he appeared mildly clumsy and had balance problems. Finally, Billy Bob exhibited a large number of inappropriate behaviors. (In a series of five-minute intervals, Billy Bob exhibited an average of thirty-six inappropriate behaviors.)

In February 1974, the psychiatric hospital refused to accept Billy Bob back, and he was then formally placed in the training center. The curriculum was largely functional, and many attempts were made to integrate Billy Bob into the community (e.g., foster homes, group living homes), but he never stayed in an outside living arrangement for more than a month. As Billy Bob approaches his 21st birthday, the question of what will become of him takes on urgency. The license for the training center permits it to care for and train individuals only up to age 21. The Harringtons have not yet found an alternative placement for Billy Bob, either in a community-based living arrangement or in a hospital. They are now in their late 60s and feel they cannot physically take care of their son. Right now, no one knows for certain what will become of Billy Bob.

Conclusion

In his acceptance speech for the 1973 Nobel Prize, ethnologist Nikolaas Tinbergen (1974) expressed concern over the lack of agreement in the diagnosis and labeling of autistic children. "If the art of diagnosis has any objective basis," he affirmed, "there should be a positive correlation between first and second opinions" (p. 20). Citing a study by Rimland (1971) that demonstrated the absence of such a correlation in the diagnosis of 445 children with severe behavior disorders, Tinbergen observed: "What these doctors have been saying to parents is little more than 'You are quite right; there is something wrong with your child' " (p. 20).

Despite the lack of agreement in diagnosis, it cannot be denied that severe behavior disorders represent a problem of enormous magnitude to families, educational institutions, and society. There is an aura of mystery, a paradox, about a child who is potentially bright but is functioning at the severely mentally retarded level, a child who develops a personal attachment to an inanimate object but is unable to relate to parents and other people, a child who, for some unknown reason, unmercifully beats his or her head against the wall.

In recent years children with severe behavior disorders have caught the public eye. Articles in newspapers and popular magazines, television documentaries and dramas, and books by parents, such as Josh Greenfeld's *A Child Called Noah* (1972) and *A Place for Noah* (1978) and Barry Kaufman's *Son-rise* (1976), may ultimately bring a positive fallout for persons with severe behavior disorders. By spreading knowledge about the group, they dispel its mystery, and this should eventually aid the integration of persons with severe behavior disorders into school and society.

SUMMARY

1. In a widely accepted definition, Bower perceived persons with behavior disorders as children and adolescents who exhibit one or more of the following five characteristics to *a marked extent* and *over a period of time:* an inability to learn that cannot be explained by intellectual, sensory, or health factors; an inability to build or maintain satisfactory impersonal relationships; inappropriate behavior or feelings; a pervasive mood of unhappiness or depression; and a tendency to develop physical symptoms or fears associated with personal or school problems.

2. Achenbach and Edelbrock identified three broad-band syndromes—internalizing syndrome, externalizing syndrome, and mixed syndrome—and proposed a range of severity from mild to very marked for each syndrome.

3. Children and adolescents who exhibit internalizing behaviors to a very marked and chronic degree are typically referred to as having severe behavior disorders.

4. The prevalence of behavior disorders in the general population is approximately 2 to 3 percent. The prevalence of severe disorders is estimated to be 0.4 percent of the general population.

5. The ratio of males to females with severe behavior disorders is four or five to one.

6. Three major theories attempt to explain the etiology of severe behavior disorders: the organic theory, the environmental theory, and the interaction theory.

7. The organic theory holds that severe behavior disorders have physical determinants that produce cognitive and emotional disorders in the individual.

8. The environmental theory holds that some environmental factor (usually the parent–child relationship) causes the severe behavior disorders.

9. The interaction theory holds that some persons have a greater innate vulnerability to severe behavior disorders, and a stressful event or series of events then "sets off" the disorder.

10. Many professionals prefer a single classification (childhood psychosis) for severe behavior disorders while others contend that two subcategories (early infantile autism and childhood schizophrenia) are distinguishable.

11. Persons with severe behavior disorders usually manifest (1) social isolation, (2) serious impairments in communication patterns, (3) insistence on preserving sameness, (4) stereotypic and ritualistic movements, (5) self-injurious behaviors, (6) tantrum behaviors, and (7) externally directed hazardous behaviors.

12. Social withdrawal and isolation are usually evident in the 1st or 2nd year of the child's life and typically continue throughout life. In general, children with severe behavior disorders ignore other people and treat them as if they do not exist.

13. Typically language is not used for communicative purposes. Half of all persons with severe behavior disorders are nonverbal; in the other half, speech is usually limited to echolalia.

14. These children have an obsessive desire to maintain sameness in their environment.

15. They become totally absorbed in stereotypic and ritualistic movements, whether solitary (e.g., rocking or waving the fingers in front of the eyes) or with objects (e.g., spinning lids or plates or flipping a clothes hanger between thumb and middle finger).

16. Self-injurious behaviors include head-banging, hair-pulling, eye-gouging, hitting, biting, and scratching. They typically inflict great physical insults.

17. Other behavior problems include tantrums, externally directed hazardous behaviors, lack of self-care skills, an inability to maintain and generalize behaviors, and nuisance behaviors.

NOTES

[1]On January 16, 1981, the Department of Education recommended deletion of autism from the severely emotionally disturbed classification. Autism was made a subcategory under "other health impairments," on the premise that it may have biological causes. Autism is now defined under federal regulations as a condition manifested by severe

communication and other developmental disabilities. Nevertheless, Bower (1982) and many others argue that there is no significant research suggesting that autism is a product of other childhood diseases or a communication disorder. For the purposes of this chapter autism is considered a severe behavior disorder.

[2]Throughout this chapter the phrase *severe behavior disorders* is used for severe and profound behavior disorders, early infantile autism, childhood schizophrenia, childhood psychosis, pervasive developmental disorders, schizoid disorder of childhood or adolescence, schizophreniform, or autism. These other terms will be used only when the meaning is limited to that particular area or to clarify the meaning of a passage.

[3]*Schizophreniform* is the term recommended by the Group for the Advancement of Psychiatry to replace *childhood schizophrenia,* because the latter implies that the condition is an earlier version of adult schizophrenia. This may, in fact, be the case, since the two syndromes have several symptoms in common. However, they also have a number of important differences. For example, hallucinations and delusions are quite rare in children but not in adults with schizophrenia; and adults with schizophrenia generally seem indifferent to people, while children may be obsessively attached to their mothers.

CHAPTER 4

Persons with Severe
Physical Disabilities

(Courtesy of Jerry Howard, Positive Images.)

DEFINING PHYSICAL DISABILITIES

A small but diverse category of exceptional children is the physically disabled.
It includes a variety of conditions and levels of severity, from a relatively mild,
infrequent condition, such as asthma, that has a minimal impact on
functioning, to a long-standing physical and neurological impairment, such as
cerebral palsy, that severely limits mobility and functional integration. The
severity of some disabilities also varies with climatic conditions. For instance,

an individual with rheumatoid arthritis may be severely impaired during the cold, damp months in a northern climate but less disabled in a warm, dry climate. Some conditions have such divergent symptoms that for all practical purposes they represent two different syndromes. For instance, seizures may be so mild and infrequent that the child is not even aware he or she has a disability; or they may occur almost daily and be prolonged and debilitating. Both are classified as seizure disorders.

Because of its diversity, the physically disabled population is extremely difficult to define clearly and concisely. Definitions are often profiles of deficiencies in motor development. The best definition may be the one in Section 504 of the Rehabilitation Act of 1973, which covers any person who has a physical impairment that substantially limits his or her participation in one or more life activities (e.g., routine home, school, and community activities). By this delineation, a person who takes medication to control a musculoskeletal impairment (e.g., insulin to control juvenile diabetes mellitus) is not physically disabled. Nor would a person with an artificial arm be classified as physically disabled if he or she takes part in all home, school, and community activities. However, a person whose condition leaves the student unable to hold a pencil, walk from class to class, or care for his or her basic needs is considered physically disabled.

To fully understand persons with physical disabilities, this definition must also describe the components of the category, which can be classified as (1) neurological impairments, (2) spinal canal impairments, (3) musculoskeletal impairments, and (4) cardiopulmonary impairments. Each subcategory may be further divided; neurological impairments, for instance, include cerebral palsy and seizure disorders.

PREVALENCE OF PHYSICAL DISABILITIES

How many individuals are physically disabled? This question is difficult to answer. In addition to the reasons addressed in the preceding chapters, there are complications unique to this category. For instance, knowing the prevalence of a specific condition does not necessarily tell us the prevalence of physical disability from that condition. The Epilepsy Foundation of America (1982) reported that approximately 1 percent of the general population has seizure disorders. But medication completely controls seizures in half the cases and reduces the number of seizures in most others. Therefore, considerably less than half of that 1 percent are physically disabled.

Reports from school personnel on the number of children who require special education or related services because of a physical disability can be used to measure prevalence. These too can be inaccurate. For example, a physician may diagnose a muscle disorder before the problem begins to affect a child's school performance. Or a child may have a cardiac or blood impairment that affects his or her school, home, and community integration although it does not impair academic performance. In both of these situations, the severity of the child's symptoms may not justify placement in a special education program but would warrant classification as physically disabled. To complicate this, educational agencies vary in how they classify children. Most states and local school systems classify students with neurological impairments as physically disabled, but according to a U.S. Department of Education (1984) report, at least one state would classify such students as learning disabled and other states would classify them as multiply disabled.

At the federal level, there is no specific educational category for children with physical disabilities. Presently, two categories are used: orthopedic impairments and other health impairments. The U.S. Department of Education (1985a) indicates that 0.14 percent of the school population is classified as orthopedically impaired. Excluding children with early infantile autism and childhood schizophrenia, approximately 0.13 percent of the school population is classified as having other health impairments. This suggests that approximately 0.27 percent of the school population is classified as physically disabled. Because of state and local classification differences this probably is an underestimate.

Perhaps the most accurate prevalence estimate was made by Friedman and MacQueen (1971). In a study of approximately 45,000 children in a six-county area of Iowa, they found 195 persons with physical disabilities, or 0.44 percent of the school population. (The National Society for Crippled Children and Adults [1967] and the U.S. Department of Health, Education, and Welfare [1971] have found a higher prevalence for adults.) While there is still some disagreement, it appears that over half of those with physical disabilities, approximately 0.35 percent of the general population, may be classified as *severely* physically disabled.

Neurological Impairments

The neurological system is composed of the brain, the spinal cord, and the network of nerves that reaches out to all parts of the body. The spinal cord and nerves transmit messages between the brain and the rest of the body. Among its other functions, the brain sends instructions about movement to the muscles and other receptors while the muscles and joints send sensory feedback about speed, direction, and body position to the brain. A **neurological impairment** is an abnormal performance arising out of a dysfunction of the brain, spinal cord, and nerves, creating transmission of improper instructions, incorrect interpretation of feedback to the brain, or an uncontrolled burst of instructions from the brain.

Essentially, two types of physical disabilities result from a neurological impairment: cerebral palsy and seizure disorders.[1] With **cerebral palsy**, the brain either sends improper instructions or interprets feedback incorrectly. In either case the result is poorly coordinated or uncontrolled movements. With

seizure disorders, the brain sometimes emits an uncontrolled burst of neural transmissions, causing a seizure. Some children with seizure disorders have a momentary loss of attention; others fall to the floor with debilitating, prolonged, and uncontrolled movements; still others engage in what appear to be temper tantrums or purposeless activities. The common feature in almost all types of seizures is loss of consciousness. Fortunately, once diagnosed, seizure disorders usually can be controlled by medication and do not interfere with functional activities (Batshaw & Perret, 1986).

Cerebral Palsy

Cerebral palsy is a nonprogressive disorder of movement or posture caused by damage to the brain. A variety of motor defects appear at birth or in early childhood. The causes are diverse, ranging from inheritance and maternal infections to birth trauma and brain hemorrhages. Symptoms include muscle weakness or flaccidity, excessive involuntary motion, postural imbalance, and spasticity. Manifestations of the disorder differ according to the site and extent of the main lesion and may range from extremely mild motor incoordination to virtually complete impairment (Batshaw & Perret, 1986).

Classification of cerebral palsy occurs along two dimensions: a physiological classification of movement disorders and a topographical classification of limb involvements. The **physiological classification system** was developed by Minear in 1956 and adopted by the American Academy for Cerebral Palsy that year. It specifies six types of movement disorders: (1) spasticity, (2) rigidity, (3) athetosis, (4) ataxia, (5) tremor, and (6) mixed.

Spastic cerebral palsy is marked by tight limb muscles immobilized by muscular contractions. Movement is exaggerated to the extent that muscles continue to contract repetitively, giving a jerking appearance. As the individual becomes older, the spastic muscles become shorter, creating deformities of the limbs, pelvis, and spine (Bleck, 1975a). Spasticity accounts for about 60 percent of all cases of cerebral palsy (Best, 1978).

Although often identified as a separate class, **rigid cerebral palsy** appears to be a severe form of spasticity. It has been referred to as **lead pipe** or **cogwheel cerebral palsy**, in which there is a constant resistance to movement (lead pipe) or a resistance that lacks constancy (cogwheel).

Athetosis cerebral palsy is characterized by contorted, wormlike, purposeless movements of the limbs. The main features are rotation and twisting of the limbs, distorted positioning of the limbs, neck, or trunk, flailing of the limbs, and spontaneous jerking, usually of the fingers and toes. Approximately 20 percent of all cases of cerebral palsy are athetosis.

Ataxic cerebral palsy involves uncoordinated movement apparently caused by a lack of balance sensation or a poor concept of position in space. Persons with this disorder walk like sailors on a rolling ship at sea—feet apart, trunk weaving, with arms akimbo to maintain balance.

Tremor cerebral palsy, as the name suggests, is characterized by a shaking or tremor of the involved limbs.

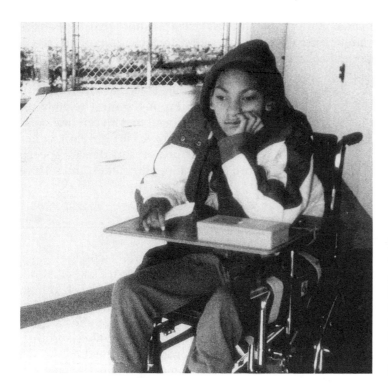

FIGURE 4.1

The term *cerebral palsy* covers a variety of motor defects that appear at birth or in early childhood. Some of the symptoms include muscle weakness or flaccidity, excessive involuntary motion, postural imbalance, and spasticity.

(Courtesy of Barbara Chatman.)

Mixed cerebral palsies are cases in which two or more movement disorders occur. Spasticity and athetosis are often found together; so are spasticity and tremor (Bleck, 1975b).

The **topographical classification system**, also proposed by Minear, is a description of the areas of the body where the motor problem occurs. This system has seven levels: (1) **monoplegia** is an involvement of one limb; (2) **hemiplegia** is the involvement of the upper and lower limb on the same side; (3) **paraplegia** is an impairment of the lower limbs only; (4) **triplegia** is an involvement of three limbs, usually one upper and two lower; (5) **quadriplegia** is a major involvement of all four limbs; this is occasionally called **tetraplegia** (Bleck, 1975b); (6) **diplegia** is a major involvement of the lower limbs and a minor involvement of the upper limbs; and (7) **double hemiplegia** is an impairment in which the upper limbs are more involved than the lower limbs. The physiological and topographical classification systems are used in combination in diagnosis, for instance, spastic hemiplegia cerebral palsy or athetosis quadriplegia cerebral palsy.

The frequency and extent of mental retardation in individuals with cerebral palsy has long been debated. Taking the results of intelligence tests at face value, some professionals have concluded that virtually every person with cerebral palsy is mentally retarded. Others have reported that 75 percent of all persons with cerebral palsy have IQs below 70 and about 25 percent have IQs in the borderline range. Still others have pointed out that individuals with cerebral palsy exhibit communication and physical limitations that impede the skills measured by intelligence tests. Furthermore, such children often have a more restricted experiential background, whereas the child without disabilities acquires many concepts through incidental activities such as visiting the zoo or shopping in a grocery store. Therefore, it is predictable that children with cerebral palsy would have depressed IQ scores. From the most reliable research, it appears that approximately 60 percent of persons with cerebral palsy have IQ scores in the mentally retarded range (Batshaw & Perret, 1986). Other problems typical of persons with cerebral palsy include sensory deficits, speech and language problems, perceptual disorders, learning difficulties, and seizure disorders.

EXAMPLE   **The Case of Mark Mitchelson**

Mark was born on a warm May day in 1962 to Donna and Patrick Mitchelson, a young working-class couple. These former high school sweethearts had high expectations for Mark, their first child. But numerous warning signs caused concern among the doctors. Mark was 6 weeks premature, he weighed slightly over four pounds, and he had numerous respiratory difficulties, producing severe anoxia, cyanosis, and jaundice. These problems seemed not to bother the Mitchelsons, and they brought Mark home cheerfully when he was 6 weeks old.

When Mark was about 18 months old, the Mitchelsons began to have serious concerns about him. He could not sit unassisted, he had no control over his movements, and he seemed to have seizures. Their pediatrician referred them to a large hospital associated with a major university, where Mark was diagnosed as having cerebral palsy, epilepsy, and mental retardation. Mark's disabilities and the birth of a daughter intensified problems the Mitchelsons were having. Shortly after the diagnosis, the parents separated and later divorced. Patrick moved to the West Coast and never saw Mark again.

When Mark was 30 months old, Donna checked him into a large psychiatric hospital. While the reason given for Mark's admission was his retarded functioning, the admission form also indicated he suffered from pneumonia and malnutrition. Donna and her infant daughter then left the area for one of the southern states. On Halloween Day in 1965, Patrick and Donna gave up parental rights to Mark, and he became a ward of the Division of Family Services. On leaving the hospital at age 3, Mark was placed in a private institution for persons with mental retardation. He was functioning at the level of a 7-month-old infant, which indicated severe mental retardation, and he had spastic quadriplegic cerebral palsy and mixed seizure disorders that were not completely controlled by medication. Sadly, most of the instructional activities at the institution were developmental; consequently, at age 5, Mark still exhibited many inappropriate behaviors and had not yet developed sophisticated communication, social interaction, ambulation, or self-care skills.

At age 6, Mark was placed in a public institution. Its goals for Mark were: (1) to develop spontaneous speech and language skills, (2) to improve his fine and gross motor skills, (3) to develop prevocational skills, (4) to develop social interaction skills, and (5) to develop academic skills. While some of these goals were appropriate, Mark made minimal progress in the nine years he was in this institution. Each year the goals were identical. Shortly after his 15th birthday, Mark was moved to another private institution.

At this point, he was evaluated again. He performed between the 2 years, 6 months level and the 3 years, 6 months level on all measurements. Records indicated that he could feebly copy a circle, slowly string three beads, and faultily sort buttons (he needed almost four minutes to string one bead). Again, the records indicated that Mark had not mastered the basic goals established by the previous institution. Three years later, Mark was moved to a different public institution.

The educational program at this institution was philosophically different from the previous institutions. The premise was to develop the skills an individual would need to be integrated successfully into the community. The school planned a hierarchy of functional skills intended to make Mark as self-sufficient as possible. At this point, Mark was edging toward his 19th birthday and had few functional skills. He had not been taught to feed himself or to dress himself totally. While Mark has made improvements in the last few years, he is still not to the point where he could be placed in a community group residence or vocational training program.

Granted, Mark may be properly classified as severely disabled; he has been labeled severely mentally retarded with spastic quadiplegic cerebral palsy and mixed seizure disorders. But a basic question must be asked: How much of his present condition can be attributed to his training and education (or lack of these), as opposed to organic disabilities? There is no easy answer. Nor is there an easy answer to the question: Where will Mark be a year from now, five years from now, ten years from now? Not in an institution, we hope!

Seizure Disorders

Seizure disorders are commonly defined as paroxysmal alterations of brain function that begin and end spontaneously and have a tendency to recur (Batshaw & Perret, 1986). The most common type is epilepsy. The causes of seizure disorders are quite diverse, ranging from brain anomalies, vascular malformations, and heredity to trauma, inflammation of the brain, and metabolic disorders. Estimates of prevalence are open to some debate. Selective Service statistics (Berg, 1975) indicate 0.5 percent of the general population while the Epilepsy Foundation of America (1982) proposes a prevalence of 1.0 percent. The correct figure is probably somewhere in between. Other notable prevalence factors are: (1) Seizure disorders are more common in infants,

FIGURE 4.2

During a seizure, children often become unconscious, lose voluntary control of their muscles, and fall to the floor. Many wear helmets to prevent additional injuries.

(Courtesy of Meri Houtchens-Kitchens.)

toddlers, and children under age 5 than in the rest of the population; roughly 2 percent are affected. (2) More males are affected than females, at roughly a 2:1 ratio. (3) Seizure disorders often occur with other disabling conditions, for instance, cerebral palsy and mental retardation.

While all seizures are different, they generally follow a common pattern. A seizure typically starts in an area of the cortex containing abnormal nerve cells. Initially, these cells depolarize due to an imbalance between the sodium outside the cell and the potassium inside the cell. The imbalance causes the cells to discharge. The discharge spreads, recruiting or involving normal neurons surrounding the abnormal cells much as a fire spreads through a forest. Soon, an entire area of the brain is discharging electrically. This excessive and periodic discharge constitutes a seizure. The discharge may lead to loss of consciousness, loss of voluntary movements, or abnormal sensory phenomena (Freeman & Lietman, 1973). The type and severity of the seizure are largely determined by the location where the discharges begin.

The most widely accepted classification system for seizure disorders, the International Classification of Epilepsy, was first proposed by Gastaut (1970) and subsequently adopted by the World Health Organization. It lists six types: (1) grand mal disorders, (2) focal seizure disorders, (3) petit mal triad disorders, (4) infantile seizure disorders, (5) autonomic seizure disorders, and (6) mixed seizure disorders. **Grand mal disorders** are very dramatic seizures. They are usually preceded by an **aura**, an unusual perception occurring moments before the seizure. After the aura, the individual loses consciousness, the arms are extended or flexed, the body becomes stiff, the legs are extended, and the person usually falls to the floor. As the muscles contract, air may be forced from the lungs through the vocal cords, resulting in a peculiar, eerie, sometimes frightening sound. There may be a loss of bowel and bladder control. Commonly the individual quivers and shakes, with the arms and legs jerking synchronously. After a few minutes, the jerking decreases in frequency and severity and stops. Following the seizure, the person may be confused, develop a headache, or fall into a deep sleep, for a few minutes or several hours.

The pattern of **focal seizure disorders** is milder and of shorter duration. Symptoms usually include a stiffening, jerking, or twitching of one or more parts of the body, such as a twitching at the corner of the mouth and in the thumb or fingers on the same side, or a stiffening and jerking of the arm and leg on the same side. Although the conscious state is altered during this seizure, the individual may not lose consciousness completely. Instead, he or she may be aware of the surroundings but unable to speak or respond normally to the environment. Occasionally, focal seizures are referred to as *march* or *Jackson* seizure disorders.

Petit mal triad disorders consist of three seizure patterns similar in symptoms and severity: (1) typical petit mal seizures, (2) myoclonic seizures, and (3) akinetic seizures. The **typical petit mal seizure** is a momentary suspension of all activity for about five to ten seconds. Besides losing consciousness, the person suddenly stares vacantly into space or slightly flutters his or her eyelids. The **myoclonic seizure** is a paroxysmal, brief contraction of part of a muscle or a group of muscles. There may be a brief, sudden neck flexion or extension, so that the head suddenly drops forward or backward; the arms may jerk upward; or the trunk may bend sharply. The **akinetic seizure** is characterized by a sudden loss of muscle tone, during which the individual usually falls to the floor but rises again shortly. This triad is sometimes called the *Lennox-Gastaut syndrome*.

Infantile seizure disorders typically occur in the first few years of life and appear to be associated with immature central nervous system development. They are marked by synchronous muscle contractions in which the infant flexes the arms, neck, and trunk forward and backward in a "jackknifing" motion. The seizures typically occur in a series, one after the other, for approximately thirty seconds and recur as often as every ten minutes.

Autonomic seizure disorders, or psychomotor seizures, are recurring, paroxysmal, abdominal cramps, often manifested by episodes of headaches, skin-flushing, pupillary dilation, and olfactory sensations. As part of the seizure, the individual may smell acrid or sweet odors, have a funny taste in his or her mouth, experience auditory hallucinations, or feel fearful or angry.

Mixed seizure disorders are two different types of seizures that occur concurrently. A person who suffers from both grand mal disorders and myoclonic seizures, for instance, is said to have mixed seizure disorders.

Seizure disorders are usually treated with anticonvulsant medication (e.g., barbiturates, hydantoins, oxazolidines, or succinimides). For about half the affected individuals, one drug is sufficient to control the seizures. For others, multiple medications, diet, and, less frequently, surgery are used. Seizure disorders are often part of a condition that includes other disabilities. In such cases, the prognosis is generally determined more by the degree of the other disabling conditions (e.g., cerebral palsy and mental retardation) than by the seizures.

EXAMPLE   **The Case of Kevin Garrett**

In 1973, a four-pound, six-ounce boy named Kevin Michael was born to Stephen and Alexandria Garrett. Stephen was employed as an aeronautical engineer, and Andria taught third grade in the suburb of a large, midwestern city. Kevin was born five years after his sister, Kathryn Lynn. Although Andria had a difficult and complicated pregnancy, the family was excited and optimistic at Kevin's birth. Almost immediately, Kevin developed several serious health problems and was labeled "medically fragile." He had a persistent high fever, which the doctors could not shake, he was jaundiced, and he could not breathe without a respirator. After a six-week stay, Kevin was discharged from the hospital. The pediatrician reassured the Garretts that in "six or seven months" everything would be "all right."

But everything was not all right. After a year, Kevin could not sit without assistance, he had little or no control of his arm, leg, and head movements, and he had muscle contractions in which his arms, neck, and trunk jerked forward and backward uncontrollably. Kevin's pediatrician suggested that these conditions were not serious and would probably go away in a very short time. Again and again Stephen and Andria returned to the pediatrician only to be told that they were too "impatient" and were "looking for problems that just weren't there." Less than six months after making that statement, the pediatrician recommended that Kevin be hospitalized to diagnose "the extent of his problems." The diagnosis indicated that Kevin had mental retardation, cerebral palsy, and seizure disorder. The pediatrician then recommended that Kevin be institutionalized so that Stephen and Andria could get on with their lives.

The parents refused to institutionalize Kevin, but they realized that he had to learn to control his arms, legs, and head. Andria's aunt, after reading a magazine article, recommended patterning. In this technique a different person controls each body part as the person with disabilities is put through a normal motor skill, such as walking. The article suggested that after a few months of training, Kevin would not only control his arms, legs, and head, but, in fact would become normal. After enlisting friends, neighbors, and high school students, the Garretts had Kevin "crawled" on his hands and knees six hours every day. He made minimal progress. The realization that Kevin would never become normal, the continuous argument over institutionalization, and the "railroad station" atmosphere of the home slowly eroded the Garretts' delicate marriage. Shortly after Kevin's 4th birthday, Stephen and Andria were granted a divorce.

Giving up on patterning, Andria had Kevin evaluated by a neurologist. She was concerned that his seizures were becoming more severe and frequent. After a lengthy examination, the neurologist prescribed phenytoin sodium, phenobarbital, and primidone. He also recommended that Kevin be enrolled in a private, church-run day program for young children with disabilities, housed in the basement of the church. "The program wasn't much help for Kevin," said Andria, "but it did wonders for me. After the divorce, I felt alone and isolated, but this program allowed me to meet other parents of handicapped children. It gave me the support and information I needed." It also gave Andria the freedom to return to teaching. "That," she said, "gave me a new lease on life." Her days had been completely taken up by Kevin and Kathryn Lynn, and that had "made me somewhat bitter. This gave me a chance to meet new people and to develop new friendships."

After two years, the special day school program closed. Since the public schools offered nothing for children with severe disabilities, Andria enrolled Kevin in a program directed by a private, nonprofit agency for children with mental retardation. It "was the worst possible excuse for an educational program," Andria noted. "Kevin had fifteen different teachers in two years, and, if any were qualified, they met [only] the minimum standards." There was no supervision and no programming. After two years, Kevin was not toilet trained, could not feed or dress himself, and could not get around without assistance. After pressing the local school district, Andria was offered an unstructured class placement for students with mental retardation 7 to 14 years old. Andria refused this placement.

Over the summer, she searched for programs and interviewed parents of children with disabilities. In August, before Kevin's 9th birthday, Andria moved to a neighboring district that had a special school for students with trainable mental retardation. Unfortunately this did not make a dramatic improvement in Kevin's education. He reportedly spent most of the day in "time out." He was still not toilet trained, nor was he receiving any self-care instruction.

At about the time his mother's dissatisfaction with the special school program was peaking, Kevin attended a summer day camp program for children with disabilities. The teacher was "excellent" according to Andria, and within two weeks, Kevin was completely toilet trained. Within six weeks, he could feed himself, dress himself, get around without assistance, and begin to communicate, awkwardly, through sign language. These experiences convinced Andria that her son could progress in a proper educational program. "It strengthened my commitment. . . . I knew that Kevin could learn." Andria contacted a local university, where Kevin was given a complete transdisciplinary evaluation. A proposed educational program was developed for him.

Armed with this report, Andria met with the local school administrators to discuss an individual educational program, or IEP. Six weeks later, the school district informed her that the proposed program was unacceptable, unrealistic, and impossible to provide. The school administrators refused to compromise, and Andria filed for a due process hearing. The hearing was lengthy and detailed, but it resulted in what Andria called "a decent decision." It clearly outlined the educational program that had to be provided for Kevin, specifying class size, daily schedule, materials, and supplemental services. In addition, the decision specified staff qualifications, home activities, and instructional strategies to ensure continuity in approach among all persons working with Kevin.

Andria spent the next three years trying to get the program implemented. Kevin's education during this time was "less than adequate. . . . I felt betrayed and deeply distressed," Andria confessed. She had thought the school personnel, as educators, would want the best program possible. "All they wanted was to get me out of their hair. But what really hurt me the most were the lies they were telling my superintendent." (It seems they misrepresented everything from her teaching ability to her personal life. Their lies nearly ruined her engagement to Theodore Jamison, a principal in the district where she taught.) She wrote letters, visited other programs, discussed the IEP with various professionals, and discussed different approaches with the administration, but Kevin's program largely remained unimplemented.

Finally, the school district offered to enroll Kevin in a special class for students with severe disabilities in a regular junior high school. Andria agreed almost immediately. With a heavy community participation component, the program emphasized six domains: general community, domestic, leisure-recreational, communication, social-personal, and vocational. While Kevin's contact with students without disabilities was limited and somewhat structured, he had daily contacts with peer tutors and peer buddies. Further, every student with disabilities was enrolled in a regular class and was encouraged to participate in classroom, social, and recreational activities. For instance, Kevin was involved in an after-school cooking class with students without disabilities.

Andria is minimally satisfied with the current program and is quite pleased with the teacher. She likes the fact that the program is individual and the teaching activities relate closely to the natural environment. Kevin's contact with students without disabilities has been extremely successful. "Kevin is much happier than ever before, he learns more, he is better behaved, and he really doesn't consider himself different from all those other kids," Andria noted with some pride.

There are two basic questions that must be asked about this case: Why did it take over a decade to get Kevin into an appropriate, integrated educational program? And will the previous lack of educational training ultimately hinder his community integration and acceptance?

Impairments from *in Utero* Exposure to Cocaine

Epidemiologic data indicate that **cocaine** abuse continues to escalate dramatically (Miller, 1987). From existing evidence it appears that over 5,000 Americans each day try cocaine for the first time, over 5 million are frequent and regular users, and over 30 million have used cocaine more than once (Grabowski, 1984). The National Institute on Drug Abuse (1987) reported for the first time in the fifteen years it has collected data that cocaine was the most frequent drug-related cause of an emergency hospital visit, surpassing ethanol and narcotics (Shannon, Lacouture, Rao, & Woolf, 1989).

Cocaine appears to be the number one illicit drug used by women of childbearing age. About 15 percent of all pregnant women test positive for cocaine use at some point during their pregnancy (Adams & Durell, 1984; Bingol, Fuchs, Diaz, Stone, & Gromisch, 1987; Pollin, 1985). Actual cocaine use by pregnant women probably approaches 25 percent, since the presence of cocaine metabolites in the serum and urine indicates exposure within the previous eight and forty-eight hours respectively, and women who do not wish to be detected simply avoid or postpone prenatal visits until the metabolites have disappeared (Shannon, Lacouture, Rao, & Woolf, 1989; Smith, 1988; Woods, Plessinger, & Clark, 1987). Emergency hospital admissions for cocaine abuse showed that the average female patient was 25 years old and that 67 percent had been using cocaine for five years or more (Woods, Plessinger, & Clark, 1987).

Cocaine is transmitted to the fetus through simple diffusion from an area of high concentration on the maternal side of the placenta to an area of low concentration on the fetal side. Since cocaine is lipophilic and has a relatively low molecular weight, it freely crosses the placenta. The vasoconstrictive properties of cocaine do somewhat reduce its transfer. When the placental vessels constrict, blood flow to the fetus is reduced and the amount of cocaine transferred is lessened, but the fetus is also deprived of essential gas and nutrient exchanges.

Infants may suffer greatly from exposure *in utero*. Cocaine is a powerful drug with an array of perils that have not yet been thoroughly explored. "It's a new problem, but a very real one," says Dr. Mackles, a neonatologist. "We are only now realizing how serious this could be" (Barol, 1986, p. 56). The severe and serious health problems that cocaine-affected babies suffer may be clustered into four categories: physical, emotional, cognitive, and motor.

Physical Problems

Cocaine causes peripheral vasoconstriction, fetal heart disorders, and hyperthermia or a raising of the body temperature above normal by three to five degrees centigrade. These factors and others in concert result in teratogenesis, increased and irregular heart rate, increased and dramatic fluctuations in blood pressure, decreased blood flow, lung damage, spontaneous bleeding in the brain, severe damage to the brain, stroke, paralysis, vision and hearing disorders, exencephaly and skeletal defects, limb defects, and growth delays (Bingol, Fuchs, Diaz, Stone, & Gromisch, 1987; Chasnoff, 1987; Chasnoff, Burns, Schnoll, & Burns, 1985; Chasnoff, Bussey, Savich, & Stack, 1986; Cregler & Mark, 1986; Flandermeyher, 1987; MacGregor et al., 1987; Mittleman, Mittleman, & Elser, 1984; Smith, 1988; Wallis, 1986).

Mothers who have used cocaine during pregnancy tend to have shorter infants with lower birth weights and smaller head circumferences than drug-free women have (Chasnoff, 1987; Smith, 1988; MacGregor et al., 1987). These infants are at increased risk for sudden infant death syndrome (SIDS). Their rate of SIDS is 15 percent, more than three times higher than heroin-exposed infants and more than thirty times higher than the general population. This suggests that cocaine-exposed infants have a high level of cerebral infarction (stroke), respiratory abnormalities, and sleep apnea (Chasnoff, 1987).

Psychological Problems

Psychological evaluations of cocaine-exposed infants reveal that they are unable to respond to the human voice and face, they have problems orienting themselves to space, they do not seem cognizant of the location of their hands and feet, they are unable to interact with others, they cannot express their emotions appropriately, and they respond poorly to comforting (Chasnoff, 1987; Telsey, Merrit, & Dixon, 1988; Wallis, 1986).

Cocaine-exposed infants are highly irritable and tremulous. They can be screaming and inconsolable one moment and then fall asleep the next. Since withdrawal from cocaine addiction produces a psychological rather than a physical response, cocaine babies cannot be weaned with a substitute drug the way heroin babies can. Withdrawal can take up to a month. Swaddling the babies in warm blankets gives them a sense of security and prevents them from thrashing around and hurting themselves. That done, the doctors wait and watch. Some physicians sedate the infants with valium, thorazine, or phenobarbital, although such sedation can lead to cognitive, physical, and emotional problems as well as possible addiction to those drugs (Chasnoff, 1987; Flandermeyher, 1987).

Cocaine babies do not respond well to attempts at comforting by caregivers. A woman who feels the anxieties of motherhood coupled with guilt and worry about her drug abuse during pregnancy has an extremely difficult time responding to and interacting with a baby who is withdrawn and irritable. Bonding is thus hindered, and this may be exacerbated by constant neglect, common to cocaine-addicted mothers. It should therefore be no surprise to find that child abuse is dramatically increased among infants born to women who use cocaine (Chasnoff, 1987; Telsey, Merrit, & Dixon, 1988).

Cognitive Problems

Since cocaine is a central nervous system stimulant, infants exposed *in utero* suffer from neurological and brain impairments. As early as 3 weeks after birth they exhibit jitteriness, hypertonicity, irritability and poor alertness. Electroencephalograms are typically abnormal with excessive bitemporal sharp waves. Cranial ultrasounds and visual evoked potentials show a pattern of acute cerebral infarctions that reflect serious brain damage (Chasnoff, 1987; Dixon & Bejar, 1988; Telsey, Merrit, & Dixon, 1988; Smith, 1988). Most cocaine-exposed infants are born prematurely with poorly formed and severely damaged brains (Barol, 1986; Dixon, Coen, & Crutchfield, 1987; Schneider & Chasnoff, 1987).

Cocaine-exposed toddlers are seriously delayed in indices that reflect average intellectual functioning. Their language, for instance, is delayed in onset and marked by numerous syntax and semantic problems. Articulation disorders in their speech are common. Their vocabulary is extremely limited, and their sentences reflect poor thought formation (Barol, 1986; Chasnoff, 1987). Cocaine-exposed toddlers engage in play behavior typical of much younger children. Rather than interacting with other children during play, they often engage in nonpurposeful, unoccupied behavior, solitary play, or watching other children play. They seldom, if ever, interact with other children (Chasnoff, 1987; Pittman, 1989).

Motor Problems

Infants born to mothers who have used cocaine during pregnancy show mild to severe motor disorders. As infants, they may be limp, lack muscle tone, be rigid, and fail to show a startle response. They have a poor tolerance for oral feeding and have disturbed patterns of sleep. Cocaine infants exhibit paralysis, multiple focal seizures, convulsive disorders, and tremors (Holland, 1982; Smith, 1988; Smith & Deitch, 1987). They appear to have difficulties doing simple motor movements and cannot perform complex motor tasks such as self-feeding or self-dressing (Wallis, 1986).

While it is easy to assume that cocaine is the villain causing these impairments, other variables confute a causative relationship. For instance, the low socioeconomic status of most cocaine-addicted mothers puts the fetus at risk for a number of problems. Lack of prenatal care, malnutrition, and tobacco use have all been associated with diminished fetal growth (Dixon, Coen, & Crutchfield, 1987; Oro & Dixon, 1987). About two-thirds of all cocaine abusers have a marked tendency to abuse alcohol, heroin, and other drugs that can have a detrimental effect on the fetus (MacGregor et al., 1987). Finally, street cocaine frequently contains undetermined adulterants in unknown quantities, which can potentially cause fetal defects (Smith & Deitch, 1987). It is equally clear, however, that the extent and severity of the disabilities found in cocaine-exposed infants cannot be fully explained by these other factors.

In a case study of a family called the Marshalls, Chasnoff (1987) illustrates the impact of cocaine on a neonate. Mrs. Marshall was a white, middle-class woman who used cocaine casually during the first 5 weeks of her pregnancy. During the pregnancy she did not use alcohol or heroin. During the 40th week of her pregnancy, however, she snorted five grams of cocaine over the course of three days. She noticed that her baby become extremely active during the first two days that she used the drug; on the third day she used one gram of cocaine, and the baby stopped moving. Three hours after she took the last dose of cocaine, her membranes ruptured and contractions began.

When Mrs. Marshall was admitted to the maternity ward, she was disoriented and her speech was slurred. Her heart rate was 120 beats per minute; that of the fetus was 180 to 200 beats per minute. Mrs. Marshall's baby, a boy, was delivered about fifteen hours after she had last used cocaine. He weighed eight pounds, one ounce. He was despondent, limp, and lacked muscle tone. He was given oxygen briefly and markedly improved. He was taken to the newborn nursery and appeared normal except for a heart rate that raced as high as 180 beats per minute.

When the Marshall baby was about 16 hours old, he stopped breathing and turned blue several times. He had several seizures on his right side and decreased muscle tone in his right arm, shoulder, and hip. His heart rate was intermittently high, and his blood pressure was also raised. Tomography of the baby's brain performed when he was 24 hours old revealed acute infarction (stroke) on the left side of his brain. He was given phenobarbital to control his seizures, and, although the seizures stopped, his right side was still mildly paralyzed. The baby's infarction may have been caused either by his high blood pressure before and after birth, by a subsequent cerebral hemorrhage, or by decreased blood flow to the brain at birth. It is impossible to know whether the stroke happened before or after he was born.

SPINAL CORD IMPAIRMENTS

The spinal cord and nerves transmit messages between the brain and the rest of the body. In a **spinal cord impairment**, the pathways from brain to muscles is interrupted. Messages are transmitted but not received. The result is paralysis and loss of sensation in muscles served by the spinal cord below the point of damage. Motor skill deficits may range from incoordination to paralysis of the entire body. Many individuals with spinal cord impairments suffer from respiratory, urinary, and skin infections, and can get from place to place only in a wheelchair. The most severely impaired are dependent on other people, trained animals, or sophisticated equipment to carry out various functional tasks.

To understand the effects of spinal cord impairments fully, we need to examine the function of the spinal cord. The spine is a flexible column of bones called *vertebrae,* encasing a cable (the spinal cord) with millions of nerve fibers. The vertebrae are numbered in three series from the neck down: seven **cervical vertebrae,** twelve **thoracic vertebrae,** and five **lumbar vertebrae.** Spinal nerves from these areas affect different parts of the body. Cervical vertebrae affect the upper body: C4 (the fourth cervical vertebra) affects the neck muscles, C5 the shoulders, and so forth. The nerves of the thoracic vertebrae affect the upper torso and trunk, and the nerves of the lumbar vertebrae affect the lower trunk and legs. The higher the impairment on the spinal cord, the more severe the deficits, as figure 4.3 shows; the lower the impairment on the spinal cord, the less severe the deficits.

Spina Bifida

Spina bifida is a generic term used to describe three congenital defects: spina bifida occulta, meningocele, and myelomeningocele. Spina bifida is one of the most prevalent congenital disorders in childhood, with a rate of approximately 0.4 percent of the newborn population (Bleck, 1975c). It results from faulty embryologic development of the central nervous system, in particular a failure of the lower end of the spinal cord to close. The nervous system originates from a thickening of cells on the back of the embryo. This plate then forms a groove as the cell layer thickens. The groove begins to close and form a tube by the 20th day of fetal life and should be completely closed by the 30th day. This tube is the basic feature from which the brain, brain stem, and spinal cord develop. The vertebrae are formed on either side of this tube and grow to encase it, protecting the delicate nervous tissue inside. For some unknown reason, in spina bifida the neural tube fails to develop completely and close on the 30th day of pregnancy.

Spina bifida varies in severity. **Spina bifida occulta,** the least severe of these disorders, is a failure of the back arches of the vertebrae to form. The skin may be intact and the spinal cord undamaged. The bone defect is covered with skin, and the back appears normal. In **meningocele** the covering bulges out in a sac filled with cerebrospinal fluid; there is no defect of the nerve fibers. The most serious and common form of spina bifida is **myelomeningocele,** in which the defective nerve fibers of the spinal cord and their covering protrude in a sac filled with fluid through an opening in the lower back. Figure 4.5 illustrates the differences between meningocele and myelomeningocele.

The disabilities associated with spina bifida are in most cases related to flaccid paralysis of the lower limbs and trunk. Probably the most embarrassing and one of the more life threatening disabilities is bladder and bowel paralysis, which can lead to kidney infection, loss of kidney function, and death. Other possible disabilities are hydrocephaly, club foot, dislocation of the hip, severe rocker-bottom flatfoot, and various abnormalities of the vertebrae, including

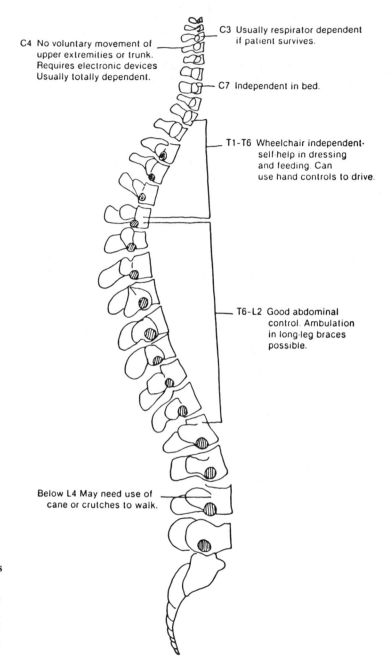

C3 Usually respirator dependent if patient survives.

C4 No voluntary movement of upper extremities or trunk. Requires electronic devices Usually totally dependent.

C7 Independent in bed.

T1-T6 Wheelchair independent-self-help in dressing and feeding. Can use hand controls to drive.

T6-L2 Good abdominal control. Ambulation in long-leg braces possible.

Below L4 May need use of cane or crutches to walk.

FIGURE 4.3

Effects of Injuries at Various Points of the Spinal Cord

(From *Educating the Chronically Ill Child* (p. 139) by S. Kleinberg, 1982, Rockville, MD: Aspen Publishers. Reprinted by permission of PRO-ED, Inc., Austin, TX.)

FIGURE 4.4

Students with physical disabilities can enjoy a positive social relationship with students without disabilities when they are integrated into the school program.

(Courtesy of Lynda Atherton.)

scoliosis (lateral curvature of the spine), kyphosis (humpback), and lordosis (swayback). Many individuals with spina bifida experience a loss of the sensations of pain, touch, and temperature; this may lead to burns and pressure ulcers.

The contemporary treatment for individuals with spina bifida often has three features. First, the myelomeningocele is closed early in infancy; while this does not necessarily ameliorate paralysis, it helps avoid life-threatening infection of the spinal cord. Second, about the same time, hydrocephaly is treated. Third, braces, physical therapy, and orthopedic surgical procedures are used to reduce or prevent any dislocation of the hip, foot deformities, and spinal deformities.

Spinal Muscular Atrophy

Spinal muscular atrophy is characterized by a progressive degeneration of the spinal cord and the cranial nerves of the brain stem. Symptoms range from a chronic, minimally disabling weakness to a rapid degeneration with complete incapacitation, total dependence, and early death. A variety of muscular disorders may result from this degenerative atrophy. For instance, hip muscle weakness in infants may cause delay or difficulty in sitting or walking and later

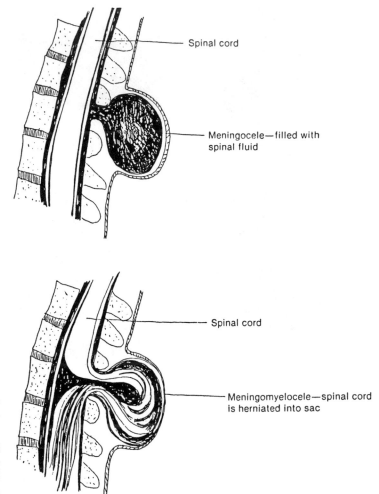

Spinal cord

Meningocele—filled with spinal fluid

Spinal cord

Meningomyelocele—spinal cord is herniated into sac

FIGURE 4.5

The Spinal Cord and Vertebrae Illustrating Meningocele and Myelomeningocele

(From *Educating the Chronically Ill Child* (p. 156) by S. Kleinberg, 1982, Rockville, MD: Aspen Publishers. Reprinted by permission of PRO-ED, Inc., Austin, TX.)

frequent falling and unsteadiness. Shoulder muscle weakness may cause fatigue in lifting objects, raising the arms, and even combing the hair. Back muscle weakness may cause back pain or spinal curvature problems similar to spina bifida. Involvement of the lower cranial nerves may cause difficulty in swallowing, difficulty in aspiration, poor cough reflex, and slurred speech. Diaphragmatic and chest muscle weakness may result in respiratory problems. Finally, muscular atrophy may cause weakness of the feet, ankles, hands, and wrists, producing a variety of fine motor problems.

Orthopedic problems are common in individuals with spinal muscular atrophy. Usually atrophy and loss of muscle strength are followed by tightening of the muscles and secondary joint contractures. The muscle shrinks when not used, loss of bone substance occurs, susceptibility to fracture increases, and

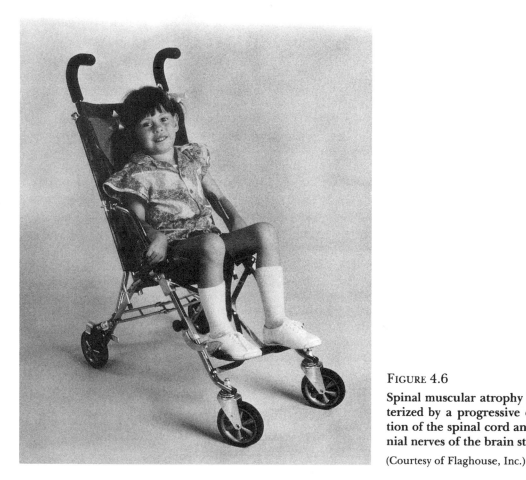

FIGURE 4.6

Spinal muscular atrophy is characterized by a progressive degeneration of the spinal cord and the cranial nerves of the brain stem.

(Courtesy of Flaghouse, Inc.)

sometimes growth is arrested. Heart disease, particularly irregular or slow heartbeat, has been reported.

Usually treatment is directed toward prevention of secondary joint and bone complications. Daily, progressive range-of-motion exercises of all joints and mild to moderate exercises should be performed daily. Lightweight braces for the knee, ankle, or spine may be necessary as the atrophy progresses, and surgical correction of spinal curvature may also be required (Koehler, 1975).

The Case of Rebecca Kimberly Sanders   EXAMPLE

Becky was born on May 24, 1978, to Perry and Lois Sanders in a large southern city, their third daughter. Shortly after her birth, the pediatrician informed the Sanderses that Becky had hydrocephaly, myelomeningocele, and paralysis from the upper torso down. The doctor recommended surgery to cover the hernia of the spinal cord and a ventriculoatrial shunt to drain the cerebrospinal fluid from the head. The Sanderses readily agreed to the surgery.

At Becky's 18-month pediatric checkup the doctor noted that she was making slow developmental progress. She had almost no motor skills in the upper limbs, and she was nonverbal, although she produced a lot of vocalizations. At 2 years, she could sit unassisted if placed in a sitting position, she could roll on her side using only her arms, and she had a vocabulary of five words. The doctor recommended braces for her lower limbs and physical therapy. The Sanderses obtained the braces and enrolled Becky in a physical therapy program. At 3 years, she was learning to feed herself, was beginning to use a wheelchair for mobility, and had increased her vocabulary to about twenty words.

Shortly after her 3rd birthday, Becky attended a preschool program sponsored by the local school district. Test results indicated that she was generally functioning at the 1 year, 8 months level. During her three years in this program, Becky made substantial progress. Her language, self-feeding, self-dressing, motor, and wheelchair skills improved, and she developed some socialization skills, as evidenced by her cooperative play. Physical therapy continued. Becky still needed to wear diapers at age 6.

A little before her 7th birthday, surgery was performed and she was fitted with a ureterostomy for urine and a colostomy for bowel collection. (An ostomy is a surgical opening through the abdomen into a hollow organ from which waste material can be eliminated when normal functioning of the bowel or bladder is lost.) At the beginning of the school year, Becky was administered a test battery. It indicated that she was making progress in almost every area: language, self-care, socialization, and motor skills.

What does the future hold for Becky? No one knows for sure. On the one hand, she could be totally dependent on her parents and society. But if she is provided with a functional program for the remainder of her school career, her prospects for living in the community, holding a remunerative job, and participating in society like anyone else could be very good. Only time will tell.

Musculoskeletal Impairments

The musculoskeletal system includes the muscles and their supporting framework, the skeleton. **Musculoskeletal impairments** may result in progressive muscle weakness, skeletal inflammation, stiff joints, or bone and muscle degeneration. Children with musculoskeletal conditions invariably have limitations in their motor skills. If the limitations are severe, the children may be unable to walk or sit independently or use their hands. Their dependence on others for basic needs can both frustrate and embarrass them. The impairment may also affect their appearance, increasing their social discomfort. Their hindered mobility may force them into a restricted life-style. They may have to attend distant schools, isolating them from friends and neighbors. Architectural barriers may hinder them from attending community and sporting events. As adults, they may be unemployed, forcing them into more dependence. They may not be able to find affordable, barrier-free living arrangements where they want to live. Thus, the motor impairments of these disorders impose limitations on the individual that are often intensified by community factors.

Arthrogryposis Multiplex Congenita

Arthrogryposis multiplex congenita is a disorder of either the muscles or the spinal cord cells controlling muscle contraction that results in stiff joints and weak muscles from birth. The child resembles a wooden marionette, which is why this disorder is sometimes referred to as the *Pinocchio syndrome*. Usually the shoulders are turned in, the forearms are turned palm down, the wrists are flexed and pushed inward, the fingers are curled in toward the palms, the hips are bent upward and outward, the knees are bent, the feet are turned in and down, the spine is curved laterally (scoliosis), the limbs are smaller and the joints larger than expected for the age, and the skin is dimpled over the joints. Associated conditions include heart disease, urinary tract and respiratory problems, abdominal hernias, and various facial problems (Bleck, 1975a). In general, affected individuals are deformed and stiff, with very limited joint motion. While many cannot walk, they can function quite well in wheelchairs.

Osteogenesis Imperfecta

Osteogenesis imperfecta literally means imperfect bone formation; the common term is *brittle bone disease*. The basic defect appears to be a reduced amount of calcium and phosphorus in the protein matrix of the bone, making the bones weak in structure and the connecting fibers immature. This results in greater elasticity of tissues such as the ligaments and skin. While brittleness of the bones is the basic symptom, there are other characteristics. The skull bones are soft, and, as the child grows, the forehead broadens and the temples bulge, so that the face becomes triangular. The limbs are small and often contorted due to repetitive fractures and healing. Outward bowing of the thigh bone and forward bowing of the leg bones are typical. X-rays show crooked bones that have thin outer shells and decreased whiteness or density. The chest is barrel-shaped, and the breast bone protrudes forward. The spine is rounded backward and often exhibits scoliosis. The teeth are easily broken, prone to cavities, and often discolored. The joints are easily mobile. The whites of the eyes have a blue discoloration. The skin is thin and appears transparent. Deafness due to bone defects of the inner ear is quite common (Bleck, 1975d).

Although treatment with magnesium oxide has received a lot of attention, the most widely used therapy is still surgery. The bone is cut into pieces, and a steel rod is inserted. Children who are mildly impaired may be partially ambulatory, but most children spend their lives in wheelchairs.

Juvenile Rheumatoid Arthritis

Rheumatoid arthritis, usually considered a disease of the middle-aged and elderly, may occur in children as young as 6 weeks. Estimates of the prevalence among children in the United States vary from 100,000 to 300,000. While the cause is unknown, many professionals believe that certain proteins, which usually destroy bacteria and viruses, in this instance attack the body's own healthy cells (Batshaw & Perret, 1986).

There are three types of juvenile rheumatoid arthritis: polyarticular, pauciarticular, and systemic. **Polyarticular** is the most common—over half of all arthitis in children. Symptoms include inflamed joints in the knees, ankles, wrists, fingers, elbows, and shoulders. Involvement of the hip and jaw are also common, causing difficulties in walking, talking, and eating. Because of great pain, the children usually sit as still as possible with their involved joints flexed, which is the most comfortable position.

Pauciarticular arthritis affects about 30 percent of arthritic children. In this form usually four or fewer joints are painful or swollen, and the iris and controlling muscle of the lens of the eye become inflamed. While the initial symptoms are mild, if left untreated they can quickly escalate to blindness.

The **systemic** type of juvenile rheumatoid arthritis is the least prevalent form. Symptoms are unusually high fevers once or twice a day, enlarged lymph nodes, enlarged spleen, and subsequent generalized illness and fatigue. Affected children look very ill when running temperatures of 105 or 106 degrees Fahrenheit, but a few hours later, when the temperature falls they appear healthy. After a few years, many develop pauciarticular arthritis (Miller, 1975).

Severe acute complications are quite common in juvenile rhematoid arthritis. The major problem in all three types is permanent joint changes. Any inflammation can cause some damage to a joint. The longer it goes untreated or uncontrolled, the greater the permanent crippling of the joint. Other severe complications actually result from therapy. Cortisone and related drugs are prescribed relatively often and their side effects can be dramatic. Some children stop growing, become obese, and develop a characteristic "moon face"; the bones become brittle, and resistance to severe infections decreases.

There is presently no cure for juvenile rheumatoid arthritis, only ways to control the inflammation and its secondary effects. Usually medication and rest for the joint or the body as a whole are prescribed. The medication for inflammation is aspirin, usually one and a half tablets per day for every ten pounds of weight. Surgery is used occasionally to remove diseased tissue from joints to reduce pain.

Muscular Dystrophy

Muscular dystrophy is a progressive diffuse weakness of all muscle groups, characterized by degeneration of muscle cells and their replacement by fat cells and fibrous tissue. While the cause is unknown, in almost every case boys are affected, which strongly suggests that it is a sex-linked recessive trait. Of the three types of muscular dystrophy, by far the most common form is **Duchenne type** (also referred to as *progressive muscular dystrophy* or *pseudohypertrophic muscular dystrophy*).

Typically, the child appears healthy at birth, but at age 3 the first symptoms appear. The child is awkward and clumsy and may walk on tiptoes, an early sign of lower leg and ankle muscle weakness. When getting up from the floor, the child may use arms and hands to "climb up" (hold onto) himself or herself. The disability progresses rapidly, soon involving the trunk muscles. At this stage the child may have poor posture, with a protruding abdomen and lordosis (swayback). Then the disability progresses more slowly to muscles in the arms, legs, and face. As muscles are increasingly infiltrated with fat and fibrous tissue, the body becomes increasingly deformed. Eventually the child loses the ability to walk, the use of upper and lower limbs, and in some cases, the ability to speak (Batshaw & Perret, 1986). In the early stages, children are often misdiagnosed, administered batteries of psychometric tests, and forced to attend family counseling. The family may then spend large amounts of time and money on needless activities (Bleck, 1975b).

In Duchenne muscular dystrophy the course is steadily downhill. Most children are in wheelchairs by age 10. The usual cause of death in the later teens is heart failure or overwhelming lung infection due to weakness of the breathing muscles. No effective treatment exists yet. Vitamins, special diets, amino acids, hormones, and even digitalis have been tried and failed. Physical therapy, braces, and surgery are used to prevent contractures and to extend the range of motion.

The Case of Ryan Daniel Haslam   EXAMPLE

The first few years of Ryan's life were extremely happy ones for his parents, Daniel and Elizabeth Haslam. Ryan appeared perfect, Dan and Beth both had good jobs, and they had just purchased a new house. They lived in the same town as both sets of Ryan's grandparents, who were excited about their grandson and eager to support the new parents. But sometime after Ryan turned 3, Dan and Beth noticed what they called "oddities." Instead of gaining physical skills, Ryan became clumsy, knocking over tables and lamps. Instead of running and walking on his feet, he used his tiptoes. While the Haslams were concerned, they thought Ryan was just passing through a stage.

The problems persisted, and when Ryan turned 4 Dan and Beth had their family doctor examine him. The doctor diagnosed Ryan as having "progressive cerebral dysfunction." That medical diagnosis "began an odyssey that lasted over four years," Dan noted, reaching for a looseleaf notebook overflowing with papers and forms. "During that time, we were referred to twenty-seven different professionals and spent close to a quarter of a million dollars." Finally, on the eve of Ryan's 10th birthday, a physician told them, "There is no easy way to say this, but we think your son has muscular dystrophy." Dan said he and Beth felt as though they had been cheated by the diagnostic runaround.

Then what Dan called the "tyranny of the disease" began to dominate their lives. Since someone had to be with Ryan, the parents and grandparents rearranged their schedules and jobs. Dan and Beth both had to turn down promotions. Business trips were cut short, business reports were left undone, and household duties began to pile up. Each morning and evening, Dan or Beth would position Ryan over sandbags and other equipment to stretch and exercise his muscles to prevent joint contractures. Each new fall or sign of muscular weakness was a matter of grave concern for the family.

The feeling of being cheated shadowed their lives. As Dan said, "it is hard to get excited about life when your only child is dying." Strains on the parents and grandparents were tremendous and seemed to come from all sides. Mortgage payments on the house were often overdue, and Ryan's medical bills ran into five figures. Dan and Beth often found themselves going in different ways, drifting apart. Their next door neighbors had a son just a few months younger than Ryan. Dan would stare out the window at this boy for hours at a time watching him play with his friends and wishing that Ryan could be out there with him. Dan admitted that his heart was breaking.

Ryan himself readily accepted his problems. Although his life-style was quite different from that of his friends and classmates and he had great pain from the disorder, he never complained or bemoaned his fate. Even when he realized that he could die, his concern was not for himself but for the effect his death would have on his parents and grandparents. As Ryan approached age 18, his physical condition became noticeably worse. He spent longer and longer periods in the hospital; he became progressively weaker. In March, he was hospitalized for a debilitating lung infection. On the first Sunday in May, still in the hospital, Ryan smiled at both his parents and died. The cause of death was heart failure.

Cardiopulmonary Impairments

The cardiopulmonary system includes the heart, lungs, and associated networks. The primary function of the lungs is to allow the blood to absorb oxygen and expel carbon dioxide. The heart pumps oxygen-rich blood to all the cells in the body, including the brain, where oxygen is needed for cell life. With **cardiopulmonary impairments**, an individual may have problems breathing, or the heart may not pump blood properly. Some children with these conditions cannot endure physical activities such as running, climbing stairs, walking from one part of the school to another, or even sitting in school all day. Their inability to take part in normal activities with classmates can create socialization problems. Since they have to limit all physical activities, they often have only limited contact with the general community, which further impairs their socialization. In addition, they are highly susceptible to illness.

Cystic Fibrosis

One of the most common hereditary diseases of childhood, **cystic fibrosis**, was not described until 1936. Just two years later it was recognized to affect many children when pathologist Dorothy Andersen reported a number of infants dead by 1 year of age from a lung disease in which there was involvement of the pancreas as well. She theorized that some disorder of the pancreas prevented absorption of vitamin A, which in turn caused lung changes. Andersen noted that the diseased pancreas had many cysts and much fibrous scarring, thus the name cystic fibrosis (Harvey, 1975).

It is estimated that one child in every 1,500 is born with this hereditary disorder and approximately one in twenty-five Caucasians carries the gene. It is the most common cause of death from a genetic disorder in the United States and the most common cause of chronic lung disease. It occurs much less frequently in black children and very rarely in Oriental children (Harvey, 1975). It is an autosomal recessive genetic disorder, so both parents must carry the gene for a child to inherit the disorder (see chapter 2 on recessive genetic inheritance).

The main source of complications is that the glands secrete unusually thick, gluey mucus. Normally mucus is thin and slippery; it helps keep air passages clear by carrying out dust particles and germs. In children with cystic fibrosis, the mucus does not move efficiently and the air passages are poorly cleared. A lung can be thought of as a tree, with the trachea being the main trunk and the bronchial tubes the branches. As cystic fibrosis progresses, mucus accumulates in many small peripheral branches and areas of the lungs become blocked.

Normally when a person inhales, the lungs become bigger and the bronchial tubes also dilate. When a person exhales, the lungs and bronchial tubes decrease in size. It is therefore easier for air to get into the lungs than out of them, since the diameter of the bronchial tubes is larger in inhalation than in exhalation. When mucus partially obstructs a bronchial tube, this difference in diameter between inhalation and exhalation becomes very important. The mucus can act as a "ball valve," trapping air in the periphery of the lung, so that those areas become overinflated. If enough mucus accumulates, a small bronchus may be obstructed so completely that air cannot pass either in or out of that portion of the lung. The trapped air will gradually be absorbed into the body and the blocked area of the lung will collapse. Children with cystic fibrosis also develop infections and illnesses caused by the inability to clear inhaled dust and germs. Another problem is damage to areas of the lung tissue (Harvey, 1975).

The treatment of children with cystic fibrosis takes several forms. They may be given an extract of the pancreas at mealtime. Since they have difficulty absorbing fat-soluble vitamins (i.e., vitamins A, D, E, and K) from foods, vitamin supplements are given. The prime treatment involves keeping the lungs as clear of mucus and as free of infection as possible so that an optimum airway is maintained. This is accomplished principally by postural drainage, in which the child is placed in various positions to drain different areas of the lungs while that portion of the chest is clapped vigorously and vibrated in an attempt to dislodge and move the mucus. (This can be a painful experience. In some instances, the mucus must be dislodged several times each day for up to an hour each time.)

Cystic fibrosis is progressive and relentless, but proper treatment can affect the rate of progression. If it is slowed enough, the child may grow to lead a relatively normal adult life with only minimal limitations. Early diagnosis and effective treatment are of paramount importance. The average age at death is now approximately 14 years with a definite upward trend. A large percentage of affected children will become adults, and many can expect to function well.

Cardiac Impairments

Cardiac impairments are a collection of disorders in which there is some structural defect of the heart, arteries, veins, or capillaries. Congenital heart impairments are about twenty times more common in childhood than acquired defects, with a prevalence of 0.06 percent of all live births. In reports describing the follow-up of untreated congenital heart impairments, the prevalence at 10 years of age is approximately 0.01 or 0.02 percent. Although some abnormal openings close by themselves, the attrition is largely the result of death from the more serious disorders. The largest number die within the first year of life, the majority within the first few months. This points to the need for early recognition, diagnosis, and therapy.

The fetal heart begins to take shape very early, toward the end of the 3rd week, when the fetus is 1.5 millimeters long. The heart begins as a tube, and, by a combination of differential growth, folding, and twisting, the major thoracic cardiovascular structures are formed by the end of the 7th week. The remaining development is largely growth. Consequently, any severe abnormality of the cardiovascular system probably occurs before the 8th fetal week (Batshaw & Perret, 1986; Baum, 1975). Although there is suggestive evidence that most congenital heart defects are caused by chromosomal disorders and infections, the etiology is unknown. Adventitious heart disease is acquired in essentially two ways, from rheumatic fever and hypertension.

Familial Hypercholesterolemia

Familial hypercholesterolemia is a hereditary defect in which a child has an extremely high level of blood cholesterol, which can cause a coronary. This disorder affects about one in 500 people in the United States in virtually all segments of the population. While the average baby has a cholesterol count of 60, those with familial hypercholesterolemia average about 800. In most children the disorder begins to show up at age 5, when unsightly, yellowish, lumpy areas loaded with cholesterol develop in the knees, elbows, heels, and areas between the fingers (Rosenfeld, 1981). Afflicted children fed nothing but fat-free foods still develop atherosclerosis and heart trouble. Rosenfeld cites three short examples to illustrate the nature of this disorder: "five-year-old Rachel, playing on a swing set in Toronto, suddenly collapses and dies of a heart attack. A young boy named Steven undergoes a triple bypass operation in Dallas to postpone the same fate. A baby is born in Japan with a cholesterol count of 1,000" (p. 46).

IMPAIRMENTS FROM AIDS INFECTION

Since first described in 1979, acquired immune deficiency syndrome (AIDS) has become a health problem of epidemic proportions (Dilley, Ochitill, Perl, & Volberding, 1985). The clinical characteristics are by now well known: the disease is probably mediated by an unidentified agent that reduces cellular immunity, leaving the individual susceptible to overwhelming opportunistic infections. There is presently no treatment for this immune deficiency, and the mortality rate of all diagnosed patients at any given time is 41 percent (Desforges, 1983; Dilley, Ochitill, Perl & Volberding, 1985; Frierson & Lippman, 1987; Olson, 1988).

While AIDS primarily occurs within at-risk subgroups (e.g., sexually active gay men, Haitians, and intravenous drug users), the disease has more recently expanded into other groups, namely neonates and children. AIDS can be transmitted to children in a multitude of ways: (1) from an infected mother to her fetus *in utero* by transplacental passage of the virus, (2) during labor and delivery through exposure to infected maternal blood and vaginal secretions, (3) through breastfeeding, (4) through blood transfusions, and (5) from drug abuse and sexual experimentation by the child (Abraham, 1988; Dilley, Ochitill, Perl, & Volberding, 1985; Olson, 1988; Osterholm & MacDonald, 1987; Hutchings, 1988). Not all children born to mothers with AIDS contract the disease; somewhere between 40 and 70 percent of such children born alive later develop AIDS, usually in their first 6 years of life (Abraham, 1988).

The Centers for Disease Control predict that by 1991 there will be over 3,000 neonates and children with AIDS. This estimate reflects only those reported to the CDC and does not include children infected with human immunodeficiency virus (HIV) and those who are in an earlier stage of the disease called AIDS-related complex (ARC). For every child who meets the definition for AIDS, there are three to seven who are HIV infected (Hutchings, 1988; Olson, 1988). While many children with HIV may never develop AIDS, they will have severe medical problems including mental retardation (Olson, 1988).

Although AIDS was first described in children in 1983, the growing numbers of children with AIDS have already seriously strained the medical, financial, social service, and foster care systems in many communities. Individuals with the least access to information and care face the greatest risk: low-income urban women and children (Fulton, Metress, & Price, 1987; Gurdin & Anderson, 1987; Hutchings, 1988; Monmaney, 1987). The natural history of the disease is different in children than adults. The effects of AIDS in children can be better understood if the symptoms are clustered into two categories: physical and psychosocial.

Typical physical symptoms of infants and children with AIDS include growth delays, chronic and recurrent diarrhea, persistent or recurrent fever, severe blood disorders, persistent and severe oral fungus infection, recurrent bacterial infections, encephalopathy, and lymphoid interstitial pneumonitis. These and other problems lead to involvement of the heart, liver, kidneys, and skin (Abraham, 1988; Hutchings, 1988; Koop, 1987). Facial features common in infants and children with AIDS include a small head with a boxlike forehead, a flattened nose bridge, and wide-set eyes with bluish whites (Seligmann, Katz, Hutchinson, & Huck, 1986). As HIV progresses and immune deficiency worsens, opportunistic infections occur. HIV infection in infants and children has various effects on the nervous system and virtually no child escapes some effect on development.

Psychosocial symptoms range from brain damage and mental retardation to social isolation and feelings of helplessness. Based on current projections, the National Coalition on Prevention of Mental Retardation suggests that HIV may become the largest infectious cause of mental retardation and brain damage in children within the next five years (Olson, 1988). Many children with AIDS report social isolation and open rejection by schoolmates and educational personnel, hospital staff members, and even family members (Fulton, Metress, & Price, 1987; Frierson & Lippman, 1987; Manning & Balson, 1987; Roe, 1987). A feeling of helplessness is exaggerated in children with AIDS. Some react by becoming behavior problems while others regress to complete dependence on caregivers and hospital personnel. In some cases, the feeling of helplessness is heightened by the child's inability to care for himself or herself (Frierson & Lippman, 1987).

The history of Toy Santiago's family illustrates the devastating effects HIV and AIDS have on the family. Toy had lost a drug-addicted daughter to AIDS and was now raising two grandchildren who were likewise infected. Stories about children with AIDS usually use pseudonyms. But this grandmother wanted to mask nothing; she wanted the children's real names used, and she wanted their lives described unsparingly. Even though she was warned that her family might suffer from the hostility that often confronts victims with AIDS, she boldly told her story to Terence Monmaney (1987), a staff writer for *Newsweek*. Toy Santiago's story asks desperately: What is happening to our children?

That Celeste is alive is a triumph of medicine, luck, and love. That she is exuberant is equally amazing, given the circumstances into which she was born. Her parents were heroin addicts who presumably became infected by using contaminated needles. Her father is terminally ill with AIDS; her mother died of it. She lives with her maternal grandmother, Toy Santiago, two older sisters, a younger brother, two cousins, and a young aunt in a five-room walk-up in a decaying section of the Bronx. Her 5-year-old brother, Eddie, is also infected with HIV.

AIDS has by no means robbed Celeste of poise or an appetite for ordinary pleasures. Her tastes run from cheeseburgers and boys to Masters of the Universe and Bon Jovi. When in a gregarious mood, Celeste shows off the scars and scrapes on her shins and knees; she looks like any kid tumbling into adolescence. A closer look, though, reveals that she and Eddie have the signs of an immune deficiency. Their hands are speckled with warts. His tongue and gums are covered with the white layer of yeast known as thrush, which is more hideous than dangerous. His doctors suggest that this gives him a "cotton mouth," which forces his teeth to form slowly and crookedly. A lung disorder sandpapers his voice and makes him wheeze and cough. Celeste suffers fewer discomforts. Her swollen salivary glands trouble her primarily because school-mates tease her about them.

The AIDS virus, according to medical researchers, first invaded New York's addict population around 1977, the year before Celeste's birth. It appears that Celeste was one of the first children in the nation born infected. Since then, pediatric cases have skyrocketed.

Every other week, Toy takes Celeste and Eddie to the Einstein College of Medicine where they receive the therapy that may be the key to their longevity. They have been coming to the clinic for three and a half years. The routine doesn't seem to depress Eddie as much as Celeste. He sits on the bed oblivious to the IV needle in the back of his hand delivering gamma globulin from a bottle hanging over his head like a question mark. Celeste and Eddie get their IVs hooked up at about the same time, but Eddie's smaller transfusion always empties first. "Beat ya," he taunts her. In the last half year Celeste has on occasion been uncharacteristically gloomy and withdrawn, pulling the sheet over her head and peering out with wide, moist eyes. Toy interprets this to mean that Celeste is beginning to fathom what it means to have AIDS.

Though Celeste and Eddie are both small for their age and lag a year or two in cognitive development, they have so far not shown signs of deep nervous system damage. The doctors at Einstein refuse to estimate how long they will survive but would not be surprised to see the children become teenagers. "They're bucking the odds," the attending physician says. "They're tough kids."

Children with HIV or AIDS would not be labeled severely disabled traditionally or under the definition proposed in chapter 1. These children can and should be educated in regular classrooms with children without disabilities. But this disease evokes intense concern in the general population because it is communicable, unpredictable, and uniformly fatal. It elicits great anxiety, almost hysteria, in educators and parents, who may try to exclude the child with AIDS forcibly from participating in school activities. Because children, parents, and educators must be taught how to respond appropriately to children with HIV and AIDS, these children should be classified as severely disabled until society openly and willingly accepts them and integrates them into the school and the community.

CONCLUSION

There is little doubt that physical disabilities have a tremendous impact on children and their families. As the examples of Mark, Kevin, Becky, and Ryan illustrate, children must not only adjust to and learn to live with their disabilities but also adjust to the "secondary" disabilities that society imposes on them. In many respects these are more disabling than the primary disability. Individuals with physical disabilities are often picked on, degraded, and belittled. They are isolated from society by architectural barriers, they may be isolated from friends by the difficulties of coping with their impairment, and they are often isolated in schools outside their neighborhood. As adults, they may not be able to find the type of job they want or any job. They may not be able to live where they wish because of the architectural barriers or financial considerations. If they have another handicapping condition, as Mark did, their problems are magnified and they are likely to be isolated at home or in an institution. But in the final analysis the individual with a physical disability, regardless of its severity, is just as deserving of a normal life-style as anyone else.

SUMMARY

1. Persons with physical disabilities comprise an extremely heterogeneous and diverse population, with many conditions and levels of severity.

2. Section 504 of the Rehabilitation Act of 1973 defines a physical disability as a physical impairment that substantially limits participation in one or more life activities.

3. The most widely used classification system divides physical disabilities into neurological impairments, spinal canal impairments, musculoskeletal impairments, and cardiopulmonary impairments.

4. The most accurate estimate of the prevalence of physical disabilities is approximately 0.44 percent of the school population. Approximately 0.25

percent of the school population is severely physically disabled. The prevalence rate is higher in the adult population.

5.   A neurological impairment is an abnormality from a dysfunction of the brain, spinal cord, and network of the nerves. The dysfunction may result in transmission of improper instructions to muscles, incorrect interpretation of feedback to the brain, or an uncontrolled burst of instructions from the brain.

6.   Cerebral palsy is a nonprogressive disorder of movement or posture caused by damage to the brain. Common symptoms include muscle weakness, excessive involuntary motion, postural imbalance, and spasticity.

7.   Cerebral palsy is classified according to physiological and topographical dimensions. The physiological classification consists of six movement disorders: spasticity, rigidity, athetosis, ataxia, tremor, and mixed. The topographical classification system has seven levels: monoplegia, hemiplegia, paraplegia, diplegia, triplegia, quadriplegia, and double hemiplegia.

8.   Seizure disorders are paroxysmal alterations of brain function that begin and end spontaneously and have a tendency to recur.

9.   Seizure disorders are classified into six types: grand mal, focal, petit mal triad, infantile, autonomic, and mixed.

10.   The exponential increase in cocaine use appears to be spreading to women of childbearing age. Cocaine is transmitted to the fetus through simple diffusion across the placenta. The child exposed to cocaine *in utero* may suffer problems in physical, emotional, cognitive, and motor development.

11.   The spinal cord and nerves transmit messages between the brain and the rest of the body. When the spinal cord is injured, the pathway is interrupted, so that messages are transmitted but never received.

12.   Spina bifida is a generic term for three congenital defects: spina bifida occulta, meningocele, and myelomeningocele. In spina bifida, the lower end of the spine fails to close during fetal development.

13.   Spinal muscular atrophy is a progressive degeneration of the spinal cord and the cranial nerves of the brain stem. Symptoms range from chronic, minimally disabling weakness to rapid degeneration, complete incapacitation, total dependence, and early death.

14.   The musculoskeletal system includes the muscles and their supporting framework, the skeleton. Musculoskeletal disorders invariably cause some limitations in motor skills; if the limitations are severe, individuals may be unable to walk, sit independently, or use their hands.

15.   Arthrogryposis multiplex congenita is a disorder of either the muscles or the spinal cord cells controlling muscle contraction. The result is stiff joints, weak muscles, and deformities of the joints from birth.

16. Osteogenesis imperfecta, or brittle bone disease, is a disorder of bone formation, leaving the bones weak in structure and the connecting fibers immature.

17. Juvenile rheumatoid arthritis is a disorder producing inflamed, stiff, and swollen joints in various areas, such as the knees, ankles, wrists, fingers, elbows, and shoulders.

18. Muscular dystrophy is a progressive generalized weakness of all muscle groups, characterized by a degeneration of muscle cells and their replacement by fat cells and fibrous tissue.

19. The cardiopulmonary system includes the heart, lungs, and associated networks. Its primary function is to absorb oxygen, expel carbon dioxide, and pump oxygen-rich blood to all the cells in the body.

20. In cystic fibrosis, the glands secrete thick, gluey mucus that does not clear out dust and germs and that eventually blocks the bronchial tubes of the lungs.

21. Cardiac impairments are structural defects of the heart, arteries, veins, and capillaries. They severely restrict an individual's physical activities.

22. Familial hypercholesterolemia is a hereditary defect in which a child has an extremely high level of blood cholesterol, which can cause a coronary.

23. Neonates and children infected with HIV and AIDS experience several physical and psychosocial symptoms, not the least of which is social isolation. The skyrocketing numbers of children with HIV and AIDS will seriously strain social services.

NOTE   [1] It is beyond the scope of this chapter to discuss every type of physical impairment. Rather, the intent is to illustrate the types of problems persons with physical disabilities experience, using disabilities that are relatively high in frequency and severity.

CHAPTER 5

Persons with Multiple Disabilities

(Courtesy of Bellerose Stock Boston, Inc.)

DEFINING MULTIPLE DISABILITIES

Thus far we have focused on single-category conditions. In this chapter, attention shifts to individuals with two or more disabling conditions simultaneously. Such persons constitute a diverse, heterogeneous population, not a distinct, unique population.

The definition of **multiple disabilities** proposed by the U.S. Office of Education is the same as that proposed for the severely disabled. Not only does it fail to mention or allude to multiple disabilities, but it also has many structural problems. Instead, this chapter will use the definition proposed in chapter 1:

> **Persons with severe disabilities or multiple disabilities have a very significant functional discrepancy in: (1) general developmental abilities, (2) caring and looking after themselves, (3) expressing thoughts, ideas, and feelings, (4) responding to environmental stimuli, and (5) interacting socially with chronological-age peers.**

PREVALENCE OF MULTIPLE DISABILITIES

Accurate estimates of the prevalence of multiple disabilities are hard to obtain for a number of reasons. First, should persons with multiple disabilities be classified in each category of disability that they have or in only one, and then which one? Second, some state educational agencies classify persons with physical disabilities as multiply disabled, while others classify persons with multiple disabilities as physically disabled (U.S. Department of Education, 1984). Third, different programs and service delivery systems use different definitions. Since prevalence varies from place to place, a national prevalence rate is difficult to obtain.

The most reliable prevalence estimates come from the medical, social, and educational agencies that provide services to persons with multiple disabilities. The U.S. Department of Education (1985a) reported 67,536 enrollments of children with multiple disabilities in the 1983–1984 school year. This does not include children with visual-hearing impairment.[1] Locket and Rudolph (1980) reported that there were 5,982 persons with visual-hearing impairment. Thus, approximately 74,000 persons or slightly over 0.07 percent of the school-age population would be classified as multiply disabled. The U.S. Department of Education (1985b) proposes a slightly higher prevalence for the multiply disabled, approximately 0.08 percent of the general population.

MULTIPLE DISABILITIES: AN OVERVIEW

An infinite number of combinations of disorders can lead to a multiple disability, but some combinations appear more often and are more difficult to cope with and so deserve special attention. The remainder of this chapter deals with the more frequent multiple disabilities centering around mental retardation, behavior disorders, and sensory impairments. It is widely believed that two

FIGURE 5.1

If there is an assault to one part of the neurological system, a corresponding assault to another part is likely.

(Courtesy of Cahokia School District 187, Illinois.)

disabling conditions have an additive relationship (one adds to the other). But in actuality they have an exponential relationship (the effects of one are multiplied by the effects of the other), so that the two are significantly greater in effect then either would be in isolation.

MULTIPLE DISABILITIES INVOLVING MENTAL RETARDATION

The neurological system is composed of the brain, the spinal cord, and the network of nerves reaching to all parts of the body. When there is an assault, genetic or environmental, to any part of the neurological system, there is likely to be a corresponding assault to another part of that system. This means that a person who is mentally retarded is likely to have another neurological impairment, such as cerebral palsy, epilepsy, or spina bifida. The individual's struggle to cope with cognitive limitations is then greatly compounded by the other neurological impairments.

Mental Retardation-Cerebral Palsy

There is a tendency to assume that all individuals with cerebral palsy are mentally retarded, but this definitely is not so. Approximately 60 percent of persons with cerebral palsy are mentally retarded (Batshaw & Perret, 1986). While a relationship exists between the two conditions, it is hard to justify a diagnosis of mental retardation in persons with cerebral palsy based on intelligence tests that are standardized on children with adequate speech, language, and motor abilities. Persons with cerebral palsy symptoms may be expected to have problems in both speech and psychomotor skills, two prime components in the assessment of intelligence. Therefore, the test scores of persons with cerebral palsy must be open to question.

The poor speech and uncontrolled spastic movements of persons with cerebral palsy cause many to correlate intelligence with the degree of physical impairment. Again, this is fallacious. A child with severe spasticity may be intellectually gifted, while one with only mild physical impairment may be severely mentally retarded.

Of course, a relatively large proportion of children do simultaneously exhibit mental retardation and cerebral palsy. This combination prolongs the instructional process and significantly increases the difficulty of finding appropriate instructional activities. Such children may not be able to express themselves either orally or by movements, making it almost impossible to assess their educational gains accurately. Because of their symptoms, it is also difficult for many to maintain and generalize recently acquired skills.

Mental Retardation-Other Physical Disabilities

Mental retardation occuring with other physical disabilities is relatively common. A high percentage of persons classified as mentally retarded have seizure disorders or spina bifida. As the case of Mark Mitchelson illustrated, many persons with mental retardation and cerebral palsy also have seizure disorders. In analyzing the presence of other disabilities with seizure disorders, Rodin, Shapiro, and Lennox (1976) found that 48 percent of persons with seizure disorders experienced some type of intellectual problem. Such persons have been reported to be more irritable, more fidgety, less sophisticated in social skills, and poorer in concentration skills than their chronological-age peers (Rutter, Graham, & Yule, 1970). These problems are probably not organic in origin but rather the result of society's response to persons with seizures.

Many persons with spina bifida also have hydrocephaly, which causes severe mental retardation. This combination has a profound impact on their performance, since they are likely to have mobility limitations, be socially isolated, have problems with bowel and bladder control, and have more infections and illnesses. Such problems by themselves can limit an individual's intellectual development, but coupled with the damage caused by the hydrocephaly they exert a profound impact on cognitive development.

FIGURE 5.2

Children with multiple disabilities can participate in the full range of family life.

(Courtesy of ABLENET® Inc.)

Mental Retardation-Severe Behavior Disorders

There is a relationship between mental retardation and behavior disorders. As a rule, the more severe the retardation, the greater the probability of emotional disturbance (Kirk & Gallagher, 1986). What is unknown is the exact frequency with which the two disabilities appear together. Estimates of persons with mental retardation who also have behavioral disorders range from 24 to 87 percent (Matson & Barrett, 1982; Senatore, Matson, & Kazdin, 1985). In a classical study on the Isle of Wight, a group of researchers estimated that emotional disturbances were four times more prevalent in people who were mentally retarded than those who were not (Rutter, Tizard, Yule, Graham, & Whitmore, 1974).

If the relationship is so prevalent, why has there been so little emphasis on behavior problems in persons with mental retardation? The primary reason is a phenomenon that Reiss, Levitan, and Szyszko (1982) called *diagnostic overshadowing.* The symptoms of mental retardation are so obvious and strong that the accompanying emotional difficulties tend to be ignored or put aside. In many cases, persons with severe behavior disorders exhibit the same behaviors to the same degree as persons with severe mental retardation, thus making a diagnostic separation difficult. What this often translates into for persons with both is that the needed psychotherapy and behavioral treatments tend not to be offered (Reiss, Levitan, & Szyszko, 1982).

Another problem is that certain stereotypic behaviors are often exhibited by persons with severe mental retardation, persons with severe behavior disorders, and persons with both. Berkson (1983) believes that persons with multiple disabilities receive positive feedback from the environment for engaging in these repetitive, stereotypic, or self-stimulatory behaviors. To decrease or prevent their occurrence, it is argued, the link between the behaviors and the rewards from the environment must be severed, and only functional, age-appropriate behaviors must be rewarded.

Mental Retardation-Visual Impairment

Mental retardation associated with a visual impairment may be caused by genetic disorders, infectious diseases, postnatal injuries, or a variety of other environmental or congenital events. Even with normal intelligence, the child with a visual impairment from birth will exhibit several developmental delays; with mental retardation, the delays are accentuated. For instance, muscle tone will be floppy and the development of fine and gross motor skills will be significantly delayed. The child may not sit unassisted until 14 or 15 months, will not crawl at all, and may not stand independently until 3 years (Adelson & Fraiberg, 1974). Since children learn to speak by imitating mouth movements, listening to sounds, and making cognitive associations between objects and sound symbols, the child with mental retardation-visual impairment may never develop speech and language skills or do so only by an extremely slow, painstaking process.

Children with mental retardation-visual impairments also tend to exhibit unusual behaviors. They engage in self-injurious behaviors such as head-banging, hair-pulling, eye-gouging, hitting, biting, scratching, and self-stimulatory behaviors such as rocking, rumination, eye-rubbing, and finger- or hand-waving more commonly than either the mentally retarded or the visually impaired population. Tantrums, externally directed hazardous behaviors, and social isolation are also common behavior patterns.

Mental Retardation-Hearing Impairment

Typically, persons with hearing impairments exhibit language and communication problems; persons with mental retardation display poor cognitive functioning and adaptive behavior problems. In combination, these disabilities create greater problems than either does in isolation. In a review of the research, Healey and Karp-Nortman (1975) reported that persons with both impairments have deficits in adaptive behavior, general intellectual functioning, and hearing (to no one's surprise) and that "the combination of these three factors requires services beyond those traditionally needed by persons with either mental retardation or hearing impairment" (p. 9).

The two most serious complications are limited communication skills and poor social interaction skills. Even when the individual is identified early and compensatory treatment is provided, he or she is not likely to develop a receptive vocabulary of more than fifty words and an expressive vocabulary of more than thirty words. This language impairment inhibits acquiring adaptive behavior skills and leads to a higher frustration level, tantrum behaviors, learning difficulties, and poor social interaction skills. The person with mental retardation-hearing impairment is very likely to be ostracized and shunned in attempts to interact with others. With socialization restricted, the person cannot learn the social nuances everyone else acquires through trial and error and slowly integrates into his or her social repertoire. The lack of social interaction skills then hinders any future attempts to interact. Over time, the person's social behaviors are perceived as increasingly abnormal. Besides communication and socialization problems, stereotypic behaviors, self-injurious behaviors, and externally directed hazardous behaviors are quite common in persons with mental retardation-hearing impairment.

MULTIPLE DISABILITIES INVOLVING SEVERE BEHAVIOR DISORDERS

Persons with disabilities are often mistreated, ignored, and punished for reasons that do not make sense to them, and they are often hindered in expressing their thoughts or ideas. These two factors easily explain why some exhibit behavior disorders. As a further complication, inappropriate behaviors may be unknowingly reinforced by people and events in their environment.

Severe Behavior Disorders-Physical Disabilities

The prevalence of severe behavior disorders occurring with a physical disability is uncertain, partly because of diagnostic overshadowing. In most cases, diagnosticians do not look beyond the surface features of physical disability when classifying an individual as physically disabled. Another factor, suggested by Lister (1970), is that a very large proportion of persons who are physically disabled become emotionally disturbed by having to adjust to their disability and society's discriminatory, degrading, and belittling treatment of them.

Though this argument makes sense, there is little substantiating research. One of the few studies that examined behavior disorders in persons with physical disabilities, conducted by Rodin, Shapiro, and Lennox (1976), found that 54 percent of persons with seizure disorders also had behavior disorders. Other research suggests that persons with physical disabilities may have a relatively high incidence of behavior disorders. Harvey and Greenway (1984) found that children with physical disabilities had "a lower sense of self-worth, greater anxiety, and a less integrated view of self" (p. 280) than children without physical disabilities, and the disabled children were often withdrawn, aggressive, and depressed. Feagans and McKinney (1981) found that persons who were withdrawn, depressed, anxious, and had a lower sense of self-worth had behavior disorders. A large proportion of persons with physical disabilities, therefore, appear to have behavior disorders. One of the primary characteristics of behavior disorders is aggression, a trait common in persons with physical disabilities. Thus, there is considerable suggestive evidence that persons with physical disabilities have behavior disorders.

Severe Behavior Disorders-Visual Impairment

Research on behavior disorders and visual impairment is only slightly more definitive than that on behavior disorders-physical disabilities. Tuttle (1984) indicated that persons with visual impairment tend to have low self-esteem, lack self-confidence, have social adjustment problems, and be passive and dependent. Tuttle concluded that many such persons have behavior disorders. Meighan (1971) gave the Tennessee Self-Concept Scale to 203 adolescents with visual impairments who were enrolled in state schools for the visually impaired. As a group, they "formed a very deviant and homogenous group whose scores on the basic dimensions on self-concept were all found to be in an extremely negative dimension" (p. 35). Head (1979) analyzed the self-concepts of persons with visual impairments who were enrolled in either a residential school or a public school program for the visually impaired. Corroborating Meighan's results, Head found few differences between the two groups of students, and he concluded that many persons with visual impairments are emotionally disturbed. Warren (1984) suggests that many visually impaired persons have behavior disorders because of being treated abnormally. At least 40 percent of individuals who are visually impaired engage in self-injurious behaviors, stereotypic behaviors, externally directed hazardous behaviors, nuisance behaviors, tantrums, or social isolation. While the research is not conclusive, it strongly suggests that a sizable proportion of persons with visual impairments have behavior disorders.

Severe Behavior Disorders-Hearing Impairment

An accurate estimate of the prevalence of behavior disorders-hearing impairment, like the other conditions, is difficult. Estimates vary with the criteria. Altshuler (1975), a psychiatrist specializing in the treatment of persons with behavior disorders-hearing impairments, reviewed the research and concluded that "the 8 percent estimate [of such persons] nationwide is a marked underrepresentation." He estimated that about three of every ten individuals who are hearing impaired have significant behavior disorders that warrant immediate attention and another two have less severe behavior disorders that would profit from treatment. Some hearing-impaired individuals have such severe behavior disorders that they are removed from schools because their teachers are unable to cope with their bizarre behavior. About these children, Ranier (1975) wrote:

It is my strong feeling on the basis of our two decades of experience in the psychiatric care of the deaf, as well as the reports of others, that there is a significant core of deaf children who cannot be educated or managed even in special education classes without a total therapeutic milieu under psychiatric direction. Temporary separation of the child from his environment and placement in a controlled therapeutic setting is essential to help the child develop better control, better socialization, and better identification [p. 19].

MULTIPLE SENSORY DISABILITIES

When either vision or hearing is impaired, special instruction emphasizes the unimpaired sense. The special education program for students who are visually impaired use verbal messages to compensate for the loss in vision. Students who are hearing impaired learn a communication system based on manual signing, finger spelling, or speech reading. When both channels are impaired, how can the individual communicate?

Visual Impairment-Hearing Impairment

When we think of persons with both visual and hearing impairments, we often think of Helen Keller. She has become a symbol of what can be done against great odds. With the help of Anne Sullivan, her teacher and constant companion, Keller achieved a level of academic competence and international achievement that is seldom matched. Her life and accomplishments can serve as a challenge for special educators, to develop more Helen Kellers from the 6,000 students with visual impairment-hearing impairment.[2]

The Bureau of Education for the Handicapped defines the category as follows:

Deaf-blind children are those who have auditory and visual handicaps, the combination of which causes such severe communication and educational problems that they cannot be properly accommodated in special education programs solely for the hearing handicapped and/or visually handicapped child [Bureau of Education for the Handicapped, 1975, p. 9].

The number of persons with visual and hearing impairments is compared with the number with hearing impairment alone in the decade 1977 to 1986 in table 5.1.

Sensory Impairment-Other Disabilities

Several diseases and conditions can affect both vision and hearing disabilities. As table 5.2 shows, maternal rubella, hereditary defects, and prematurity are the leading known etiologies of hearing impairments. Often these are accompanied by other disabilities, such as congenital heart disease, cerebral palsy, mental retardation, behavior disorders, and chronic health disorders

TABLE 5.1

Number of hearing-impaired students served by Public Laws 94–142 and 89–313, by primary handicapping condition, 1977–1978 to 1985–1986

Condition	School Year				
	1977–1978	1979–1980	1981–1982	1983–1984	1985–1986
Total	—	85,449	79,029	76,791	70,545
Deaf or hard of hearing	87,146	82,873	76,387	74,279	68,413
Deaf and blind	—	2,576	2,642	2,512	2,132

FROM: Office of Demographic Studies, Center for Assessment and Demographic Studies, Gallaudet University. Based on annual reports to Congress on implementation of the Education of the Handicapped Act by the Office of Special Education and Rehabilitation Services, U.S. Department of Education.

(Jensema, 1980). The prevalence of mental retardation among persons with visual impairment-hearing impairment appears rather high—approximately 70 percent, according to Fedum, Kiely, and Krugman (1969). And the overwhelming majority of these are in the severe and profound retardation ranges (Jensema, 1980; Stein, Palmer, & Weinberg, 1980). It appears that cerebral palsy and seizures are also common in persons with visual impairment-hearing impairment (Bobath & Bobath, 1972).

Classification of Visual Impairments

Contrary to popular misconception, a visual impairment (legal blindness) does not mean that the individual cannot see. Most persons with visual impairment have some residual vision and in fact can read normal print. Among several classification systems, a widely accepted one, developed by Colenbrander (1977) and adopted by the World Health Organization, has five levels: (1) **moderate visual impairment**—the individual needs special aids to perform most everyday tasks; (2) **severe visual impairment**—the individual can perform a visual task at a reduced level of speed, endurance, and precision with the use of special aids; (3) **profound visual impairment**—the individual has difficulty performing most detailed visual tasks; (4) **extreme visual impairment**—the individual cannot rely on vision and primarily relies on other senses; (5) **marked extreme visual impairment**—the individual is totally without sight and relies exclusively on other senses.

Classification of Hearing Impairments

People often think they can simulate a hearing impairment by placing their hands tightly over their ears. This is not so. A hearing impairment is both a reduction in loudness of sound and inability to hear certain frequencies. Those

TABLE 5.2

Percentage distribution of causes of hearing impairment among students, 1972–1973, 1982–1983, and 1985–1986

	School Year[a]		
Cause	*1972–1973*	*1982–1983*	*1985–1986*
Total, all causes	100.0	100.0	100.0
Cause unknown	48.6	39.5	43.0
Cause reported	51.4	60.5	57.0
Maternal rubella	17.6	16.3	8.0
Heredity	8.5	11.6	12.4
Meningitis	5.3	7.3	8.6
Otitis media	1.6	3.0	3.5
Other causes at birth			
Prematurity	5.2	4.0	4.4
Pregnancy complications	3.2	3.4	3.0
Trauma	2.3	2.4	2.4
Rh incompatibility	3.1	1.4	0.9
Other causes after birth			
High fever	2.3	3.1	3.1
Infection	1.5	2.7	2.8
Trauma	0.9	0.8	0.7
Measles	2.1	0.8	0.5
Mumps	0.6	0.2	0.1
Other causes	2.5	8.0	7.5

[a]Because some students reported more than one etiology, the sum of the cause-specific percentages exceeds the total for known causes.

FROM: Office of Demographic Studies, Center for Assessment and Demographic Studies, Gallaudet University. Based on annual surveys of hearing-impaired children and youth in the years listed.

frequencies are lost regardless of their amplification, and the individual therefore cannot reproduce them or even know that they exist.

A hearing aid is not necessarily the answer to a hearing impairment, since it merely is an amplification device whose primary function is to make sounds louder. It cannot select which sounds should be made louder and which should be make softer, so it amplifies background noises as well as the words the individual is trying to hear. (A rough analogy would be to listen to a tape-recorded lecture in a noisy classroom.) If the person has a sensorineural hearing disorder (as most persons with multiple disabilities do), an amplifying device is of little value because the damage is in the auditory nerve, which transmits sound impulses to the brain.

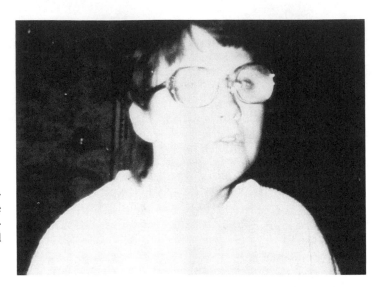

FIGURE 5.3

Vision is a continuous source of information; without it people have to rely on their other senses for information and for orientation and mobility.

(Courtesy of Tracy Hrbek.)

One of the most widely accepted classification systems for hearing impairments, proposed by Davis (1970), has five levels: (1) **mild hearing impairment**—the individual has difficulty with distant sounds; (2) **moderate hearing impairment**—the individual has trouble with conversational speech and class discussions, may need a hearing aid, and requires speech and language therapy; (3) **marked hearing impairment**—the individual requires hearing aids, auditory training, and intensive speech and language training; (4) **severe hearing impairment**—the individual can hear only very loud, nearby sounds and needs intensive special education, hearing aids, auditory training, and speech and language training; (5) **profound hearing impairment**—the individual may be aware of very loud sounds and vibrations and must rely on vision for processing information.

To roughly illustrate each level, here is what a person would hear in a line from the nursery rhyme, *Hey diddle diddle, The cat and the fiddle,* if spoken as ordinary conversational speech: (1) mild: Hey -i--le -i--le, The -at an- the fi--le; the volume would be a trifle diminished; (2) moderate: -ey -i--le -i--le, --e -at an- --e -i--le; the volume would be diminished more than if the individual had a severe cold; (3) marked: -ey -i--le -i--le, --e -a- an- --e -i--le; the volume would be faint but not as soft as a whisper; (4) severe: -e- -i---- -i----, --e -a- a-- --e -i----; the volume would be as faint as a whisper; (5) profound: the person would hear nothing and would not even be aware that someone was talking.

Education of Persons with Visual Impairment-Hearing Impairment

In the past children with visual impairment-hearing impairment were educated largely in residential schools if the parents could afford this highly specialized training. In 1968 the federal government passed legislation to establish eight model centers for the education of children with both visual and hearing impairments. Each center was responsible for a wide geographic area, to offer some degree of help to families of children with multiple disabilities wherever they lived in the United States. This program, which began in 1969, provides a wide variety of family counseling services, medical and educational services, and vocational training opportunities.

The program has been modified several times. In 1978, the federal government developed eight multistate centers. It was believed necessary to establish regional and state centers because of the low incidence of children with both visual and hearing impairments. In 1983, the federal government awarded state agencies the funds to develop their own programs for children and adolescents. The states are now responsible for the appropriate education, transition, and rehabilitation services for persons with visual impairment-hearing impairment "from education to employment" including "vocational, independent living, and other post-secondary services" (U.S. Department of Education, 1985a, pp. 2–3). These programs have brought comprehensive diagnostic facilities and trained personnel in contact with children and adolescents with both impairments and have encouraged educators to think seriously about how to cope with students who have this rare and difficult problem.

Stewart (1981) has proposed a five-level classification system for persons with both visual and hearing impairments that attempts to specify their programmatic needs. Stewart notes that an individual with moderate visual impairment and mild hearing impairment has very different instruction needs from a person with extreme visual impairment and profound hearing impairment. Other disabling conditions, such as mental retardation, functionally limit the performance level of an individual who has a sensory impairment. Stewart's classifications are:

1. **Mild sensory impairment.** These children should learn in a regular classroom. The teacher may from time-to-time need consultant services by a professional knowledgable about children and adolescents with visual and hearing impairments. These children can maintain normal academic achievement and compete with classmates without disabilities but may need speech and language training and ancillary services from an audiologist, a low-vision specialist, and an orientation and mobility trainer. Although the children may need occasional assistance, they should be totally integrated into society.

2. **Moderate sensory impairment.** These children should be educated in the regular school building and as much as possible in classrooms of peers without disabilities. The classroom teacher should be provided with adequate consultant services. Children who cannot be educated in the regular classroom should be placed in the most normalized educational program that can be provided, given intensive speech and language services, and provided with any ancillary services that can maximize their school performance. Even though they may need social services throughout life, they should be totally integrated into society.

3. **Severe sensory impairment.** These children require unique educational and instructional services. They may be able to acquire gestures and signs that lead to the development of effective communication. (While the optimum communication method is speech, the method selected must consider the unique skills and abilities of the individual. There is no "universal" communication method for a person at level 3.) Academic achievement may be as high as the sixth-grade level and include reading and writing skills. These individuals should be competitively employed and should live in an independent living arrangement.

4. **Profound sensory impairment.** These children need special methods of training to develop social, self-care, and daily living skills. They will probably have limited academic growth. Remunerative employment and independent living arrangements should not be excluded.

5. **Sensory impairment and immaturity.** Children who are too immature to profit from formal education need a program of stimulation training coupled with occupational and physical therapy. They should be trained in communication, self-care, socialization, daily living, orientation, and mobility. Older immature children should be taught to handle domestic chores. Community living and competitive, remunerative employment should not be ruled out for these individuals.

There are several unique aspects to Stewart's classifications. First, Stewart optimistically attempts to project a person's potential performance at all five levels, recommending education in regular classrooms to the maximum extent and suggesting that all persons may reside in the community and be employed in competitive, remunerative jobs. The underlying message is upbeat; it emphasizes the normal treatment of persons with multiple sensory disabilities. Second, this system encourages academic performance. Stewart suggests that children at level 1 and some at level 2 can compete academically with children without disabilities. Those at level 3 may reach sixth-grade level. Finally, Stewart strongly recommends that education and training programs be geared to the skills children need to become integrated into society, in particular, communication, social, self-care, daily living, domestic, employment, orientation, and mobility skills.

EXAMPLE   **The Case of Samuel Robert Hadden II**

Sammy was born on July 2, 1975, to David and Elaine Hadden, an automobile executive and a high school social studies teacher. The baby was named after his father's older brother, who had died in a boating accident while trying to save David and a younger brother. Shortly after the accident, David promised that his first child would be named in Sam's memory.

Elaine had contracted meningitis during the first trimester of pregnancy, but other than that the pregnancy was uneventful. Sammy was born at full term, and he weighed an even ten pounds. During labor and delivery the umbilical cord was wrapped around Sammy's neck. Shortly after his birth, he was diagnosed with mildly spastic quadriplegic cerebral palsy. At the time, neither the parents nor the doctors questioned whether Sammy had a sensory impairment. "In hindsight," David said, "we should have recognized that there was a problem. You know, he didn't ever seem to recognize us, he never reached for his rattle, or for his bottle, or for anything. And, loud noises never seemed to startle him. But he was our only child, and we both felt that these problems were common for cerebral palsy children."

When he was 12 months old, the Haddens expressed some of their concerns about their son to the pediatrician. The doctor prescribed leg braces and suggested that Sammy's behavior was symptomatic of children with mental retardation. To placate the parents, the pediatrician indicated that if the problems persisted, he would examine Sammy further. At his 18-month examination, Sammy was still nonverbal, not walking (although he could stand unassisted), and not reaching for objects. This time, the pediatrician recommended that Sammy's vision and hearing be tested. The tests showed that Sammy had profound visual impairment and marked hearing impairment. The ophthalmologist and the audiologist could each recommend programs in their specialty, but neither could recommend procedures the Haddens could use to interact with Sammy.

Shortly after Sammy turned 2, the Haddens visited a nearby regional center for persons with visual and hearing impairments. At this point, Sammy was for practical purposes noncommunicative, although he had some gestures and loud grunting sounds, which he used when he wanted to eat. He was learning to walk, but he often fell and bumped into furniture, causing injuries requiring medical services. While the professionals at the regional center did suggest methods and strategies the Haddens could use to work with their son, according to David, "all they wanted to do was to tell us that we were emotionally unstable and to consider enrolling him in their infant stimulation program."

This visit intensified the Haddens' feelings of frustration and failure. As Elaine stated, "We both felt that we would make very good parents, but with Sammy, we don't know whether we have helped him or harmed him." The parents felt totally helpless. For most of Sammy's first 20 months, he went to a day-care center, but shortly after he was diagnosed as visually impaired-hearing impaired, the center indicated it would no longer accept Sammy, implying that its insurance policy prohibited caring for a child with such a disability. The search for another day-care center proved fruitless, as did the search for a baby-sitter. Finally, Elaine applied for and was granted a leave of absence to care for Sammy.

The next few months were frustrating. Almost every spare moment was spent working with Sammy; every new method the Haddens heard about they tried. David even skipped work to be with Sammy and to provide some relief for Elaine. Yet Sammy was beginning to develop inappropriate behaviors, such as banging his head against the wall, rocking back and forth endlessly, and waving his fingers in front of his eyes. He even started hitting and kicking his parents.

In August after Sammy turned 3, the Haddens enrolled him in the state training school for the visually impaired, which had a program for students who also had hearing impairments. The objectives they developed were designed to improve his communication, self-care, and socialization skills. For the next six years, Sammy attended school at this residential facility. During that time he improved his self-care and socialization skills and stopped his inappropriate behaviors. Sadly though, his communication skills made only minimal improvement. He developed an expressive vocabulary of about eighty words and a receptive vocabulary of slightly over one hundred words.

At age 9, Sammy returned home to live. Even though he had spent at least one weekend a month and every vacation with his parents, the transition to home and a community school program was very difficult. The Haddens by then had two other children, Jon and Kimberly, so they couldn't devote themselves to Sammy as they used to. But now that Sammy is living with his family, they hope he will continue to improve, especially in his receptive and expressive skills, and that eventually he will be able to obtain a remunerative job and continue to live in the community.

In most respects, the Haddens are fortunate—Sammy is surprisingly well behaved and well adjusted. Klein (1977) describes a composite case study based on stories related by parents that is dramatically different and indicates the problems a person with visual impairment-hearing impairment may have. Klein calls her subject Johnny.

Although Johnny is 11 years old, his size suggests that he is only about 8. However, his parents know that he has the strength of someone twice his age and the stubbornness to use it to his advantage. When Johnny gets off the bus on Friday afternoon after a week in the residential facility, he lies on the sidewalk kicking, hitting, and screaming as his mother runs frantically to and from the house with various foods that might appease his anger and reduce the severity of the tantrum. Over the weekend Johnny takes charge of the television dial and permits no one else to select a program. While most of the world is asleep, Johnny's family lies awake listening to his ear-piercing screams. In the morning they find a ransacked kitchen, mutilated books, and a war-torn living room.

The tantrum routine continues the following morning as his mother attempts to find an acceptable outfit. Johnny expresses his preference very directly: He rips apart the clothes he does not want to wear, and then throws a tantrum. Trying to reason with Johnny is not very successful since the family cannot decode the manual form of communication he is being taught in school. Four separate letters from the school this week have notified his parents that Johnny needs a new hearing aid, an ophthamological examination to check his glaucoma, more scizure medication, and larger orthopedic shoes.

The cases of Johnny and Sammy both illustrate the problems the child with visual and hearing impairments and his or her family face.

CONCLUSION

The law of organization in Gestalt psychology suggests that the whole is greater than the sum of its parts. This is also true of multiple disabilities. Two disabilities have an exponential rather than an additive relationship. A person who is visually impaired may have difficulty developing communicative skills but is likely to become verbally proficient. An individual who is hearing impaired may likewise have some difficulty developing communicative skills but is likely to become proficient, if not in speech then in the use of manual signs. But a person who is both visually and hearing-impaired has greatly reduced prospects of becoming proficient in communication and many such persons never develop any communication skills.

Sailor and Haring (1977) found that many persons with multiple disabilities were functioning in the mentally retarded range. However, at least some could potentially function at higher levels. There is great danger that educators and other service providers will incorrectly assume that persons who are multiply disabled must also be mentally retarded. How many such children are assumed to be mentally retarded when they have much higher potential? The challenge that faces special educators is to develop more Helen Kellers from the thousands now classified as multiply disabled.

1. Like persons with severe disabilities, those with multiple disabilities have a very significant functional discrepancy in: (1) general developmental abilities; (2) caring and looking after themselves; (3) expressing thoughts, ideas, and feelings; (4) responding to environmental stimuli; and (5) interacting socially with chronological-age peers. **SUMMARY**

2. Estimates indicate that 74,000 school-age children are multiple disabled; the prevalence of multiple disabilities is approximately 0.08 percent of the general population.

3. There is an exponential relationship when two or more disabilities simultaneously occur in the same individual.

4. One of the most prevalent categories of multiple disabilities is cerebral palsy-mental retardation. Approximately 60 percent of persons with cerebral palsy are mentally retarded.

5. Between 24 and 84 percent of persons with mental retardation are also emotionally disturbed.

6. Children with mental retardation-visual impairment often have significantly delayed development in skills such as sitting, walking, speech, and language.

7. Children with mental retardation-hearing impairments are significantly delayed in communication, adaptive behavior, and intellectual functioning. Even using manual communication, such persons seldom develop a receptive vocabulary of more than fifty words and an expressive vocabulary of more than thirty. Stereotypic, self-injurious, and externally directed hazardous behaviors are common.

8. Since persons with disabilities are often mistreated, ignored, and punished for reasons they cannot understand or change and many are hindered in expressing their thoughts, ideas, and feelings, it is easy to see why many develop emotional problems.

9. Research suggests that a very large proportion of persons with physical disabilities also have behavior disorders. As a group, persons with physical disabilities are withdrawn, depressed, anxious, and aggressive and have a lower sense of self-worth.

10. A solid majority of persons with visual impairments are likewise emotionally disturbed. About 40 percent engage in self-injurious behaviors, stereotypic behaviors, externally directed hazardous behaviors, nuisance behaviors, tantrums, and social isolation.

11. Between 10 and 30 percent of persons with hearing impairments have serious behavior disorders.

12. The Bureau of Education for the Handicapped defines the visually impaired-hearing impaired as "those who have auditory and visual handicaps, the combination of which causes such severe communication and educational problems that they cannot be properly accommodated in special education programs solely for the hearing handicapped and/or visually handicapped child."

13. Persons with visual impairment-hearing impairment often have other disabling conditions, such as cerebral palsy, behavior disorders, and mental retardation (or functional retardation).

14. Colenbrander's classification system for visual impairments has five levels: (1) moderate, (2) severe, (3) profound, (4) extreme, and (5) marked extreme.

15. Davis's classification system for hearing impairments has five levels: (1) mild, (2) moderate, (3) marked, (4) severe, and (5) profound.

16. State educational agencies are presently responsible for educational, transitional, and rehabilitative services for persons with visual impairment-hearing impairment. These services must cover everything from "education to employment," including "vocational, independent living, and other post-secondary services."

17. Stewart proposed a five-level classification system describing the programmatic and functional needs of children with visual impairment-hearing impairment. This system recommends that such children be educated to the maximum extent possible in regular classes, reside in the community, and engage in competitive, remunerative employment.

[1]Throughout this book, the terms *visual impairment* and *hearing impairment* will be used   **NOTES** instead of the terms *blindness* and *deafness,* because the former are more normalizing and less stigmatizing, although they may be less definitive. When *blindness* is used, it refers to visual acuity of 20/200 in the better eye after correction and a central visual field of no greater than twenty degrees.
[2]Many professionals feel that persons with visual impairment-hearing impairment become functionally retarded and develop behavior disorders. These conditions are acquired and not organic. Because of sensory deprivation and lack of stimulation, such persons may function at a mentally retarded level. Likewise, because of frustration and anger at not being able to express their needs, they may use socially unacceptable behaviors as means of expression.

CHAPTER 6

Integration of Persons with Severe Disabilities

(Courtesy of U.S. Department of Education, Office of Civil Rights.)

Over tea, Lewis Carroll's Mad Hatter asks Alice a riddle: "Why is a raven like a writing desk?" Sensible Alice is stumped. Ravens and writing desks have little in common; the riddle is nonsense. But questions like the Hatter's are not always as nonsensical as they seem. In the mid-1960's, some social scientists began asking questions that then seemed as unexpected and as nonsensical as the Hatter's: Why shouldn't persons with severe disabilities live and be educated in a manner as close as possible to that of their peers without disabilities?

School Integration of Persons with Severe Disabilities

Before widespread acceptance of the principle of **normalization**, most children and adolescents with severe disabilities were excluded from public school programs in the belief that their disabilities made efforts to educate them a fruitless waste of valuable resources. Instead these children lived in institutions or were cared for by family members at home. Determined educational efforts were often made, with results ranging from modest to extraordinary (Hunt, 1967; Keller, 1955; Killilea, 1962). As successful educational efforts accumulated, parents and charitable groups began private schools. Their services were sketchy and incomplete at best, operating across ages and disability levels. The personnel frequently were high school graduates not trained in the techniques of educating students with severe disabilities. Facilities were located in church basements, private homes, closed business establishments, and abandoned schools. Despite the limitations of such schools, most parents felt fortunate to have some education for their children with severe disabilities (Donder & York, 1984; Guess & Horner, 1979). Occasionally programs were able to build their own private schools and hire certified teachers. Still they were separated from the public school system, housed in inadequate facilities, and equipped with insufficient and inappropriate supplies.

After many years of efforts by parents, advocates, and professionals, local educational agencies began to assume responsibility for educating children with severe disabilities. Largely owing to past practices, the majority of parents and special educators assumed it was not possible for children with severe disabilities to learn and thrive in the regular schools. It was widely and firmly believed that neither those children nor children without disabilities could benefit from a shared school program. Few considered the possibility that both groups of students might interact positively (Brown, Branston, et al., 1979). Besides, many professionals felt, "clustering" programs for students with severe disabilities provided desirable pedagogical features: staff proximity, a common curriculum, the collaborative expertise of support staff, and administrative convenience (Donder & York, 1984).

The Rationale for Integration

Despite notable improvements, the predominant educational model continues to be the cluster approach. Nevertheless, recent litigation, legislation, and work by parent and professional advocates have solidified and intensified the trend to integrate individuals with severe disabilities into the mainstream of society (Novak & Heal, 1980). The major thrust is for normalization, the delivery of services in environments and under circumstances that are as culturally normal as possible (Nirje, 1969; Wolfensberger, 1972). Recent interpretations stress programs for persons with severe disabilities that encompass the broad array of services and activities available to most residents of a community (Rusch & Schutz, 1986).

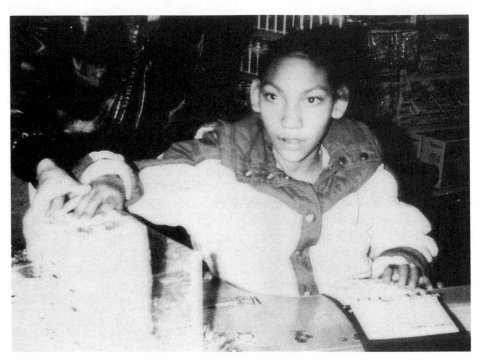

FIGURE 6.1

It is essential that students with severe disabilities have opportunities to learn functional skills to help them participate in community-based programs.

(Courtesy of Barbara Chatman.)

Community integration is a multifaceted process that involves much more than physically removing the children from segregated settings and placing them in community programs. For persons with severe disabilities to succeed in community settings, they must learn functional skills to participate as independently as possible in a variety of activities (Schutz, Vogelsberg, & Rusch, 1980). They and others in the community must acquire the skills and experience necessary for them to interact socially in integrated environments (Brown, Ford, et al., 1979).

This broadened concept of the range and type of services needed for community integration of persons with severe disabilities has far-reaching implications for the public schools. The major goal of education changes from a nebulous developmental curriculum to an approach that enables such students to live and function as effectively as possible in natural community environments. Minimally this includes the right to live in the community, to work in the community, to play in the community, and to socialize in the community. As Bank-Mikkelsen (1969), Nirje (1969), and Wolfensberger (1972) have suggested, this approach recognizes the essential humanness of individuals with disabilities and the fact that they have the same basic wants and needs as other people. Rather than emphasizing differences, the normalization principle focuses on commonalities. There is no need to create a separate world to which those with severe disabilities are relegated; instead, the "real" world that all people share must serve as the basis for determining educational goals and judging the success of education.

A commitment to normalization produces an unavoidable conflict with the practices of segregation. If persons with severe disabilities are to function adequately in myriad community settings, it is absolutely imperative for their educational environments to prepare them. In other words, schools must provide daily interactions between students with and without severe disabilities (Brown, Ford, et al., 1979, 1983). Students who do not grow up interacting with a wide variety of other students will be very different from those who do. The chances are increased that those differences will become deficits that restrict the lives of both adults with disabilities and those without (Brown, Ford, et al., 1983).

In this context, consistent opportunities for interaction must be provided and fostered (Bricker, 1978; Guralnick, 1976; Snyder, Apolloni, & Cooke, 1976). At the very least, school districts must disperse clusters of classes for students with severe disabilities throughout the district and place them next to classes of students without disabilities, to increase the probability that the two groups will interact socially. Some argue that even this does not go far enough, that students with severe disabilities should be educated in neighborhood schools in classes composed mainly of students without disabilities (Thomason & Arkell, 1980).

Benefits of Integration

It is widely believed that segregated schools are in the best interests of students with severe disabilities. It is commonly argued that integration will subject these students to ridicule and exploitation by students without disabilities. Yet many interactions between students with and without disabilities already occur in churches, stores, restaurants, and other community settings. Just as the public school experience should prepare students without disabilities to function meaningfully with students with severe disabilities, so it should prepare students with severe disabilities to function with students without disabilities. If a disabled student is educated in a chronologically age-appropriate regular school, increased opportunities to benefit from interactions with peers will occur naturally. These opportunities are not present or would have to be contrived in a segregated school setting.

If students with severe disabilities are to acquire the skills and behaviors needed in the real world, they must experience the various environments that are part of that world. They must learn to interact with people who live, work, and play in that world. Learning in school encompasses far more than acquiring the skills formally taught in class. Learning to interact with others, to

FIGURE 6.2

It has been clearly demonstrated that increased interactions between students with and without severe disabilities increase the nondisabled students' positive attitudes about peers with severe disabilities.

(Courtesy of Project ADEPT, South Bay Union School District, Imperial Beach, California.)

achieve optimal independence, and to make meaningful choices are critical skills that must be learned in integrated environments, because ultimately they are used in integrated settings. The public school experience should prepare all students for the realities of life after school. Increasingly students with severe disabilities will function in the wide variety of nonschool environments frequented by persons without disabilities. This can be difficult for the inexperienced. Stares, fears, negative comments, and interruptions in routine will be minimized if all students have opportunities to grow up and attend school with students with severe disabilities (Brown, Ford, et al., 1983). Giving students with severe disabilities more experiences with their peers magnifies their prospects of responding in age-appropriate ways. Awareness and acceptance of persons with severe disabilities by persons without disabilities must be taught in the formative school years (Donder & York, 1984).

Several studies have begun to substantiate the effectiveness and positive benefits of integrated settings to both persons with and persons without disabilities. In an early study, Ziegler and Hambleton (1976) analyzed two classes of students with severe disabilities who were transferred from a segregated facility to an integrated public school at which they could interact with other students. The transferred students were compared to a matched group of students still attending the segregated facility. Ziegler and Hambleton found that interactions between the students at the public school were predominantly positive, that there were fewer acts of aggression and other undesirable behaviors among the transferred students, and that a large number of public school students knew the transferred students by name. The researchers concluded that there is "little doubt that the placement of the special classes in a regular school was extremely effective in promoting interaction between the retarded and nonretarded students, thus providing a more normal environment for retarded children" (p. 460).

In four similar studies, Almond, Rodgers, and Krug (1979), McCarthy and Stodden (1979), McHale and Simeonsson (1980), and Poorman (1980) reported on the outcomes of having students without disabilities provide instruction to students with severe disabilities sometime during the school day. In both elementary and secondary schools, this instruction resulted in an attitude of acceptance and understanding of the students with severe disabilities by both their peers and the "regular" faculty. Most of the tutoring students reported that this was their first opportunity to interact with severely disabled students. In all of these studies, the nondisabled students' understanding of their peers with severe disabilities improved significantly. Thus, it appears that increased interactions between the two groups increase the nondisabled students' positive attitudes about their peers with severe disabilities. For instance, McCarthy and Stodden (1979) stated that "these accepting experiences and attitudes [would] carry over into the community and [should] facilitate post-school adjustment" (p. 163).

The School Integrative Approach

Integration of students with severe disabilities is a relatively recent strategy. The physical placement of students with severe disabilities into integrated settings is only the initial step. Systematic efforts must be made to maximize opportunities in which those students can become socially integrated into the school setting. In the **school integrative approach,** a hierarchy of opportunities has been generated to encourage the development of progressively sophisticated levels of integration (Schutz, Williams, Iverson, & Duncan, 1984), from the most restrictive to the most normalized: (1) physical integration, (2) systematic integration, (3) participatory integration, (4) reciprocal integration, and (5) associative integration.

Physical integration.   In **physical integration,** students with severe disabilities are placed, are taught, and interact in programs in close proximity to students without disabilities. Classrooms for the two groups may be next to each other, and the students may also be in physical proximity in noninstructional areas, such as the cafeteria, the school bus, or the gymnasium during sports events. Nevertheless, there is no actual contact between the two groups. This approach provides a minimum of social interaction, and consequently, it is very low on the hierarchy of integrative opportunities.

Systematic integration. In systematic integration, students without disabilities provide direct instruction or assistance to students with severe disabilities. Although the primary responsibilities of the student assistants are instructional, they also serve as models for imitation in social skills. However, interactions between the two types of students are limited, somewhat artificially, to instructional activities. All other activities take place with only physical integration. Systematic integration, in other words, is physical integration with planned instructional interactions.

Participatory integration. In participatory integration, students without disabilities provide direct instruction and assistance in service activities to students with severe disabilities. Service activities include escorting students to the cafeteria, pushing their wheelchairs, accompanying them on field trips, or helping them to put on their coats. Again the student assistants also serve as models for desirable social skills. But participatory integration is a contrived dependency situation.

Reciprocal integration. In reciprocal integration, students with and without disabilities interact socially in school. The major difference between this and the previous levels is in-school integration of such activities as eating lunch, attending assemblies, sitting on the school bus, participating in dances and school parties, and socializing in the halls. Students with severe disabilities attend regular classes primarily composed of students without disabilities. The basic theme is active interaction between the two types of students on a somewhat equal basis, so that a mutual exchange of benefits occurs.

Associative integration. In associative integration, students with and without disabilities interact socially before, during, and after school. Integration is so complete that students with severe disabilities are part of the school community and treated like all other students. For instance, a student with severe disabilities may be invited to a friend's home to listen to records after school, gossip about school activities, or sleep over.

The Peer Interactive Approach

A strategy frequently used to promote systematic and normalizing integration is the use of student assistants (e.g., Almond, Rodgers, & Krug, 1979; Fenerick & McDonnell, 1980; McCarthy & Stodden, 1979; Poorman, 1980). It is designed to increase interactions between students with severe disabilities and their nondisabled counterparts in a range of peer role relationships. There are four levels in the **peer interactive approach:** (1) peer tutors, (2) peer buddies, (3) special friends, and (4) reverse-role tutors.

Peer tutors. In **peer tutor** programs, students without disabilities volunteer or are recruited to assist professional staff as tutors, like classroom aides.

Essentially, teachers of students with severe disabilities give the peer tutors specific assignments, teach them to do the assignments, and supervise their performance. Peer tutors may teach specific skills, chart student performance, or attempt to modify certain behaviors (Voeltz, Johnson, & McQuarter, 1983). Tutor preparation generally focuses on changing the tutor's attitudes, providing information on students with severe disabilities, and instructing the tutor in teaching procedures, behavior modification, nonverbal communication, and data recording (Jenkins & Jenkins, 1985). To maintain a successful peer tutoring program, teachers must ensure that the experiences are pleasant and that tutors are reinforced for their efforts.

Peer buddies.   In **peer buddy** activities, students without disabilities volunteer to interact socially with students with severe disabilities outside a classroom or instructional situation. Peer buddies may be used in tasks such as escorting students with severe disabilities to the cafeteria, helping them get around the building, accompanying them on field trips, or helping them board the bus. The buddy system emphasizes a more normal social interaction than the peer tutor paradigm, in which the student without disabilities is always the helper and the student with severe disabilities always receives the instruction. The peer buddy system encourages a more realistic social interaction between chronological-age schoolmates whose abilities and skills are quite discrepant.

Special friends.   In the **special friends** approach, the emphasis is on friendship, leisure integration, and social interaction. The special friends approach emphasizes a horizontal interaction (i.e., the friends interact on an equal basis) whereas the peer tutor and peer buddy approaches are more of a vertical interaction (i.e., students without disabilities direct the activities for students with severe disabilities) (Voeltz, Johnson, & McQuarter, 1983). The special friends model is based on the assumption that students with and without disabilities can develop meaningful social relationships that endure beyond the school years and extend outside of school. It is thus essential that special friends be matched in factors that foster friendship, for instance, similarity of age, neighborhood, interests, and preferred activities. Both students need to have the social, play, and communication skills essential to their interactions. The nondisabled friend generally is not taught tutoring or management skills, although he or she may be taught the forms of behavioral responses the friend with severe disabilities will use. Many students who begin as peer tutors or peer buddies "graduate" to become special friends.

Reverse-role tutors.   In the **reverse-role tutor** approach, students with severe disabilities tutor students without disabilities in a skill such as sign language. In a sense, the students trade places, and the nondisabled students became somewhat dependent on the disabled tutors, if only for a short time. Typically, reverse-role tutors are taught how to demonstrate, monitor, and give feedback and how to provide training and supervision of the content area. In a review of a number of studies of reverse-role tutors, Osguthorpe, Top, Eiserman, Scruggs, and Shisler (1988) found that such tutors could quickly and efficiently acquire these complex instructional skills, made significant improvements in self-esteem and self-concept, and gained greater social acceptance. The positive interaction skills continued long after the reverse-role tutoring sessions were discontinued.

Cascade Model of School Integration

The **cascade model of school integration** synthesizes the two integrative approaches discussed above. Cascade systems have been widely employed in special education to analyze the least restrictive educational placement for students with disabilities. They are usually continuums from the most integrated to the most segregated school setting (Chaffin, 1975; Deno, 1970; Dunn, 1973; Reynolds, 1962). Deno, for instance, described her cascade model as "a system which facilitates tailoring of treatment to individual needs rather than a system for sorting out children so they will fit conditions designed according to group standards not necessarily suitable for the particular case" (p. 235).

As figure 6.3 illustrates, the cascade model attempts to delineate more fully the different school placements needed to meet the individual needs of students with severe disabilities. Depicted as an inverted pyramid, the model has three major characteristics. First, it projects an array of school placement options. Second, it illustrates that they extend downward from the most normalized, integrated settings to the most segregated. Third, it clearly indicates that the largest number of students with severe disabilities should be served in the most normalized school placements and very few, if any, should be served in segregated arrangements.

The goal should be to move students as far upward as quickly as possible. Students with severe disabilities should be constantly evaluated to determine if they can advance to a higher placement. While some students may require a certain level of services for a relatively long period of time, others may need that level for only a few months, and still others may skip it altogether. For instance, a student may move from Participatory Integrative Setting I to Reciprocal Integrative Setting II, skipping a level. The cascade model of school integration may also be used as a training instrument. Suppose Robert, a student with severe disabilities, is presently educated in a Reciprocal Integrative Setting II and there is a desire to "promote" him to Reciprocal Integrative Setting I. The teacher can determine from the model the skills Robert requires to progress to this higher level.

The characteristics of the nine levels of integration in the cascade model and a tenth segregated level are described below.

Associative Integrative Setting I. Associative Integrative Setting I is the most normalized of the nine levels. At this level, students with and without

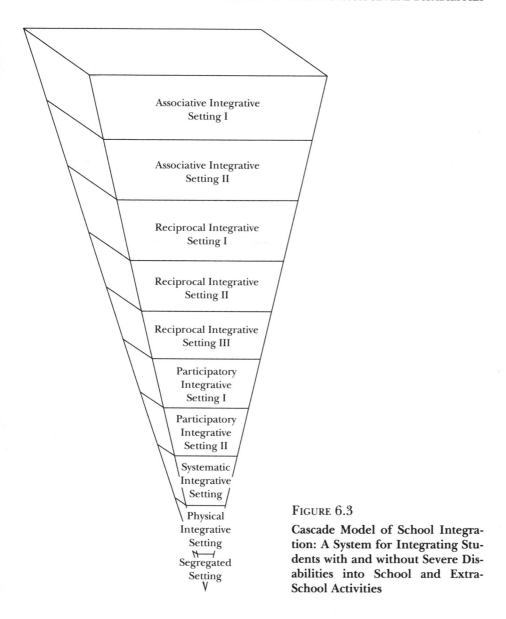

FIGURE 6.3

Cascade Model of School Integration: A System for Integrating Students with and without Severe Disabilities into School and Extra-School Activities

severe disabilities are totally integrated in every aspect of daily life, both inside and outside school. Students with severe disabilities are treated the way students without disabilities are treated. They may be invited to have a soda after school with a friend or to visit a friend's home to "hang out" or watch television. Interactions between students are not restricted or limited to a special friend; rather the student with severe disabilities forms friendships with other students naturally the way everyone else does.

Associative Integrative Setting II. In Associative Integrative Setting II, students with severe disabilities interact with other students largely through the special friend system. The student with severe disabilities participates in all inside and outside school activities, but largely with the assistance of a special friend or through activities arranged by a special friend.

Reciprocal Integrative Setting I. In Reciprocal Integrative Setting I, students with and without severe disabilities are integrated as active participants in the school environment. Disabled students actively participate in some regular classroom and school activities with a special friend. Integration is limited to in-school activities.

Reciprocal Integrative Setting II. In Reciprocal Integrative Setting II, students with and without severe disabilities are integrated as passive participants in the school environment. Students with severe disabilities participate passively, or at a less active level, in regular classes and school activities, either with or under the direction of a special friend.

Reciprocal Integrative Setting III. In Reciprocal Integrative Setting III, students with severe disabilities are passive participants with nondisabled students in the school environment outside regular classes, that is, in nonclassroom school activities, with and under the direction of a special friend. The students with severe disabilities are not in regular classes. Peer buddies and peer tutors may provide assistance to them at this level.

Participatory Integrative Setting I. Participatory Integrative Setting I attempts to integrate students with severe disabilities using peer buddies and peer tutors in special education classes for at least half the school day. While the major strategy is to use peer buddies and peer tutors, a student with severe disabilities may begin to form a relationship with a special friend. Students have only limited interactive contact outside of the special education classes.

Participatory Integrative Setting II. In Participatory Integrative Setting II, peer buddies and peer tutors are used in special education classes for less than half the school day. Nondisabled students provide direct instruction and assistance in service activities, but outside of the special education classes direct contact is almost nonexistent.

Systematic Integrative Setting. The Systematic Integrative Setting uses peer tutors in the education of students with severe disabilities. This is the only direct contact between the two types of students, and it is typically limited to instruction, assistance, or directing activities.

Physical Integrative Setting. In the Physical Integrative Setting, students with severe disabilities are in physical proximity to students without disabilities. Both groups are taught in programs that are next to each other, but there is no actual contact between the students.

Segregated Setting.   In the Segregated Setting, students with severe disabilities are not educated next to or in close proximity to students without disabilities. The special education classroom may be in the same building or a building away from the main campus. Students with severe disabilities do not come in contact with their nondisabled peers either before, during, or after school.

The Case of Benjamin Michael Gaines   EXAMPLE

Ben Gaines is a 12-year-old boy with severe mental retardation. He is presently enrolled in a special education program in a regular middle school located in a small, midwestern city. Ben's program focuses on domestic skills, community living skills, leisure skills, and vocational skills. A peer tutor assists Ben in the special education classroom, and Ben is enrolled in a regular English class, where he sits next to his special friend, who lives two houses away. According to his mother, Kathleen Gaines, this program is designed to develop the skills Ben will need when he graduates from school. But, until this past year, Ben has been segregated and restricted from interacting with peers without disabilities.

Ben was not identified as disabled either at or shortly after birth. Despite what Kathleen described as a "complicated delivery," doctors assured her and her husband, Stuart, that Ben would be a normal, healthy boy. Nevertheless, at age 1, Ben was not sitting without assistance and had not started to crawl, so the Gaineses expressed their concern to their pediatrician. After quickly examining Ben, he reported that he was likely a "late bloomer." Nevertheless, Ben's slow development continued. When he was 4, Kathleen and Stuart attempted to enroll him in a preschool program; the preschool staff refused to accept him because they felt that Ben was retarded. Kathleen returned to the pediatrician and insisted that Ben be reexamined. After a week of tests and evaluations of Ben, Kathleen and Stuart were told that he had severe mental retardation. When asked what they could do to help Ben, all this pediatrician suggested was, "Take him home and make him happy." As an afterthought, the doctor said, "You should consider placing him in an institution," and he referred Kathleen and Stuart to the local headquarters of the Association for Retarded Citizens. There Ben was enrolled in a half-day special preschool program and began to receive speech therapy and other educational services. He spent the afternoons in a neighborhood day-care center.

Ben attended the special preschool until age 6, when Kathleen and Stuart contacted the local school system to discuss Ben's placement in their district. The Gaineses requested that Ben attend a special education program in the neighborhood school and be enrolled in classes primarily attended by students without disabilities. The school psychologist agreed to this placement on a trial basis with the understanding that if it did not work out Ben would be placed in a segregated special school. The regular school, however, never gave Ben the trial placement. On the first day of school, the bus picked Ben up and took him directly to the special school. When Kathleen and Stuart protested, the psychologist denied the original agreement. School officials assured the parents that the special school was a trial placement until they could find a more suitable site, but they also maintained that "this is where Ben belongs." At the end of the school year, school officials determined that the segregated, isolated setting was the most appropriate one and that Ben was to remain there.

During Ben's second year at the special school, a friend suggested that Kathleen and Stuart talk to a professor at the state university. They wanted to know two things: what level could they expect Ben to reach, and how could they best educate Ben? After this visit, the Gaineses again approached school officials about an alternative school placement for Ben. Over Kathleen's and Stuart's continuous objections, Ben was kept in the special school for three more years. During this time, the parents felt that he gained very little. Furthermore, he began exhibiting severe behavior problems. At age 10, Ben was not dressing himself, he was beginning to self-feed, and it appeared to both Kathleen and Stuart that he was not learning appreciably. At this time, Kathleen arranged for an evaluation of Ben. It was determined that Ben was functioning at the level of a 2-year-old and that he had made only minimal progress since his last evaluation at age 4. To determine if Ben could learn, Kathleen quit her job to stay home and teach Ben shape discrimination and shape recognition. To her surprise, Ben quickly learned this task and other tasks the parents developed for him. Convinced that Ben was capable of doing more, Kathleen and Stuart demanded a change in placement for him.

The school district refused to move Ben. Undeterred, Kathleen and Stuart obtained assistance from a legal aid agency to bring the school district to a due process hearing. They won! The decision not only specified a structured educational program for Ben that included community living, domestic, leisure, and vocational skills, but also specified placement in an integrated setting. The school district could not provide such a program; however, officials agreed to a trial placement in a self-contained class for adolescents with mild mental retardation in one of the district's middle schools.

While Kathleen and Stuart acknowledge that Ben's behavior problems disappeared when he was in that class, nevertheless he was "babied" by the other students, and the educational program was inappropriate. The parents requested another placement.

District officials agreed to try to find placement for Ben within a regular school. In the meantime, however, over the parents' objections, the district returned Ben to the segregated school for the next eighteen months. As Stuart said, "It seems like we hit rock bottom; some of Ben's behavior problems returned, and Ben seemed to lose all hope." Again the parents filed for a due process hearing. Before the hearing, district officials met with the Gaineses and their lawyer to discuss their concerns. It was agreed that the parents and the superintendent would visit a program similar to the one they wanted in a neighboring district's middle school. The district also agreed to hire a consultant to develop a program for Ben.

Now Ben is enrolled in an integrated school program with students who are his chronological age. He is making tremendous strides and is readily accepted by both students and staff. But it has not been easy on the Gaineses. It took them years of requesting, fighting for, and demanding an appropriate education for Ben—a right to which they and their son are entitled.

COMMUNITY INTEGRATION OF PERSONS WITH SEVERE DISABILITIES

Foremost among the rights long denied to persons with severe disabilities has been the opportunity for habilitation in the least restrictive residential environment. Large residential public institutions, once regarded as a humane setting where individuals could learn competence and independence, fall far short of these optimistic goals. Consequently, many professionals have proposed a shift away from their restrictive, isolated services toward integrated, community residential services that are more normalizing, are more humane, and result in the acquisition of more skills.

Community integration, according to Close, O'Connor, and Peterson (1981), is the cornerstone of true normalization. Normalization, as defined by Nirje (1980), is providing to persons with severe disabilities the "patterns of life and conditions of everyday living which are as close as possible to the regular circumstances and ways of life" (p. 33). Application of this principle to residential services requires that persons being trained for independent functioning receive that training in the environment they will be expected to adapt to in the future (Wolfensberger, Nirje, Olshansky, Perske, & Roos, 1972). To develop, learn, and live as fully as possible, persons with severe disabilities require access to services that meet their individual needs within the community in which they will reside.

Services need to augment rather than deter the disabled person's interactions with his or her community. Many professionals feel that community-based services should reflect the full range of options typically enjoyed by those without disabilities. At a minimum these include the right to live in a normal, community-based apartment or home, to hold a job, and to be fully integrated into the community.

Categories of Community Normalization

The foundation of community placement is normalization. According to Wolfensberger (1972), normalization and true community integration go far beyond physical placement in a community residence. In true community normalization, persons with severe disabilities interact with the general community in normal patterns, for instance, shopping at neighborhood stores,

FIGURE 6.4

Persons with severe disabilities should be permitted to participate in day-to-day activities typically found in their community.

(Courtesy of Barbara Chatman.)

traveling on public transportation, visiting with neighbors, and participating in cultural and recreational activities. They develop social relationships, for instance, expressing affection toward, interest in, a positive regard for, and friendship for others. A community residence should promote a totally normal life-style.

Community integration can vary from life in a group home in a residential neighborhood to complete independence and social integration. Nirje (1980) proposed six categories of community residential integration: (1) physical integration, (2) functional integration, (3) social integration, (4) personal integration, (5) societal integration, and (6) organizational integration.

Physical integration.   **Physical integration** refers to the structural integration of persons with severe disabilities. It can include living in a house that is typical of a residential neighborhood with appropriate landscaping and home furnishings, the availability of privacy, a personalized sleeping area, and a supportive atmosphere. Residents take responsibility for many of the duties around the house: food preparation, housecleaning, and dish washing. Physical integration also means remunerative employment in an industrial or business location.

Functional integration.   **Functional integration** is an extension of physical integration in which persons with severe disabilities engage in the day-to-day activities typically found in their community, for instance, using restaurants, swimming pools, rest rooms, parks, shopping malls, miniature golf courses, arcade galleries, and public transportation.

Social integration.   **Social integration** refers to the natural development of social relationships with nondisabled persons in the neighborhood, workplace, and community at large. Since the attitudes other people have about persons with severe disabilities vitally affect successful social integration, the public image of disabled persons largely determines the rate of social integration. A disabled person's development of traits such as manners, respect, and acceptance of criticism are also essential to social integration.

Personal integration.   In **personal integration** persons with severe disabilities experience changing, developing, and differing needs for personal relationships with "valued" persons. This integration mode incorporates the opportunities to have meaningful relationships with siblings, parents, relatives, friends, and a spouse. Persons with severe disabilities have the right to the same range and intensity of personal relationships as others do, including the right to move out of their parents' home and into a house in the community, the right to develop friendships, the right to date and develop relationships with the same and opposite sex, and the right to marry.

Societal integration.   In **societal integration**, persons with severe disabilities are responsible for their own opportunities for growth, maturity, and self-fulfillment. As much as possible, program and planning decisions belong to the person whose life is affected. Persons with severe disabilities must assist in determining their conditions of life, options, and future. In many ways, the right of self-determination is more important for persons with severe disabilities than for others because of their differential treatment, their denial of rights, and their segregation from society.

Organizational integration.   **Organizational integration** refers to the structures that support the integration of persons with severe disabilities. Integration is achieved by using public generic services, the services typically available to persons without disabilities (e.g., mass transit, movie theaters, hospitals, and shopping centers). If necessary services are not available or simply do not exist in the generic sector, the development of special services should be patterned after and aligned with generic services.

FIGURE 6.5

An important aspect of integration and normalization is the opportunity to develop meaningful relationships with others of the same and the opposite sex.

(Courtesy of Cahokia School District 187, Illinois.)

Cascade Model of Community Integration

Community residential placement is broad and varied, not homogeneous. Community residential arrangements differ from community to community and from residential site to residential site. Community integration is not a single option, but rather a sequence of options geared to the needs of different individuals (Cone, Bourland, & Wood-Shuman, 1986; Schalock & Jensen, 1986). The very concept of the least restrictive placement as applied to community living strongly implies a range of options. This range allows the residential needs of persons with severe disabilities to be met in the most appropriate manner.

The **cascade model of community integration** tailors community residential arrangements to the individual needs of persons with disabilities. As figure 6.6 illustrates, the cascade model is an inverted pyramid. It portrays four major concepts. First, it projects an array of community placement options. Second, it shows them extending downward from the most integrated, normalized arrangements to the most segregated ones. Third, it clearly points out that the largest number of persons with severe disabilities should be served in the most normalized arrangements and that very few, if any, should be served in segre-

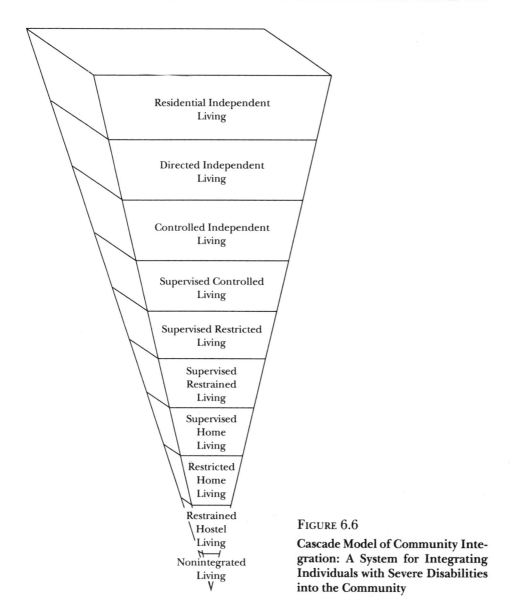

FIGURE 6.6

Cascade Model of Community Integration: A System for Integrating Individuals with Severe Disabilities into the Community

gated arrangements. Fourth, it incorporates Nirje's six levels of community normalization.

Like the cascade model of school integration, this cascade model is designed to move individuals as far upward as quickly as possible. An adult in this system is constantly evaluated to determine if he or she can graduate to a higher level. While some persons require one level of services for a relatively long period of time, others may need it only for a few months, and still others may be able to skip it altogether. This model too may be used as a training instrument. For instance, if an individual is presently residing in Supervised Controlled Living, trainers could determine the skills he or she would need to progress to Controlled Independent Living.

Five basic variables determine the levels in the cascade model: (1) the type of community integration, (2) the amount of supervision, (3) the type of dwelling, (4) the selection of roommates or residents, and (5) the number of residents in the dwelling. These variables, in turn, may have subcomponents. The amount of supervision, for instance, may be (1) no supervision, (2) intermittent supervision, (3) infrequent, regular supervision, (4) frequent, regular supervision, or (5) constant, continuous supervision. The subcomponents may be clustered in a variety of ways to provide a continuum of placement options.

The characteristics of the nine integrative levels and a tenth nonintegrative level in the cascade model of residential options are discussed below.

Residential Independent Living. Residential Independent Living is the most integrated option. At this level, adults with severe disabilities live in a house or an apartment of their choice in the community without supervision and support beyond that normally obtained from public generic services. An individual at this level may select his or her roommate.

Directed Independent Living. In Directed Independent Living, adults with severe disabilities live in a house or an apartment of their choice in the community with intermittent (when needed) supervision. They may select their roommates and will not receive external support beyond that normally obtained from public generic services.

Controlled Independent Living. In Controlled Independent Living, adults with severe disabilities live in an apartment in a complex with a small number of apartments (less than 15 percent) also inhabited by persons with disabilities. The person with severe disabilities may select his or her roommate and receives intermittent supervision.

Supervised Controlled Living. In Supervised Controlled Living, adults with severe disabilities live in an apartment complex with a small number of apartments (again less than 15 percent) inhabited by other persons with disabilities. The resident receives infrequent, regular supervision and may select his or her roommate.

Supervised Restricted Living. In Supervised Restricted Living, adults with severe disabilities live in an apartment complex where about half the apartments are inhabited by persons with disabilities. The resident receives infrequent, regular supervision and may select his or her roommate.

Supervised Restrained Living.   In Supervised Restrained Living, adults with severe disabilities live in an apartment in a complex fully inhabited by persons with disabilities. Supervision is frequent and regular; the resident may select his or her roommate.

Supervised Home Living.   In Supervised Home Living, adults with severe disabilities live in a group home where all the other residents are disabled. There are eight or fewer residents, and supervision is regular and frequent. Roommates are selected by the staff with some input from the resident.

Restricted Home Living.   In Restricted Home Living, adults with severe disabilities live in a group home where all the other residents are disabled. There are eight or fewer residents under constant supervision. Roommates are selected by the staff with some input from the resident.

Restrained Hostel Living.   In Restrained Hostel Living, adults with severe disabilities live in a hostel that meets one of the following conditions: (1) it has more than eight residents but fewer than twelve, or (2) it is located in a nonresidential section of the community. All the residents are disabled and under constant supervision. Roommates are selected by the staff.

Nonintegrated Living.   Individuals at this final level reside in a segregated environment exclusively for persons with disabilities. They are under constant and continuous supervision, and roommates are randomly assigned. The facility is located in a nonresidential area and has more than ten residents. Residents have little or no contact with persons outside the facility.

Services for Families

One type of community living arrangement was intentionally not addressed by this continuum: living with parents, relatives, friends, foster parents, or adoptive parents. These living situations are difficult to categorize because they are comprised of many variables that lack consistency. Some parents, for instance, encourage the integration of their child into the community while others actively discourage integrative opportunities. While it is true that adults with severe disabilities have the right to live away from their parents, services should be made available to those who live with their parents or relatives. The National Information Center for Handicapped Children and Youth (1986) recommends the following services: (1) respite care, (2) case management, (3) habilitation services, (4) homemaker services, (5) nursing care, and (6) parent training.

Respite care.   Respite care provides relief to the primary caregivers from the constant physical and emotional demands of caring for a person with severe disabilities. Relatives may need a reliable caregiver when they are coping with a divorce, illness, or the death of a family member. They may also need relief from time to time just to go shopping, have a night out, visit friends, or take a vacation. Respite care provides someone the family can trust to look after the person with severe disabilities properly (Cohen & Warren, 1985; Salisbury & Griggs, 1983; Warren & Dickman, 1981).

Case management.   The person who provides **case management** helps the relatives and the disabled adult to identify needs, coordinate the delivery of services, maintain records, and monitor services to ensure that they are in fact meeting the identified needs. In a sense, the case manager serves as an advocate for the adult with severe disabilities, and, if necessary, obtains services even if the primary caregivers are opposed to providing those services.

Habilitation services.   **Habilitation services** are designed to train the adult with severe disabilities in the skills he or she needs to become fully integrated into society. The habilitation trainer not only provides such training but also attempts to generalize those skills into the community at large.

Homemaker services.   Trained persons who provide **homemaker services** instruct adults with severe disabilities in routine domestic duties such as meal preparation, cleaning, and laundry. The trainer also teaches the primary caregivers how to give instruction and reinforcement to the adult with severe disabilities.

Nursing care.   **Nursing care** providers primarily offer health care to persons with severe disabilities, but they may also teach self-care skills, teach health and hygienic practices, and care for special medical needs. Nursing instruction is given to both the adult with severe disabilities and the primary caregiver.

Parent training.   **Parent training** programs use a variety of methods to help the primary caregiver teach socially acceptable skills to the adult with severe disabilities. Instructional techniques range from behavior modification to vocational instruction, and subjects range from community mobility skills to domestic living skills.

EXAMPLE   **The Case of Kenneth Justin Wooliver**

Ken was born February 18, 1963, to Debbie and Paul Wooliver. He was a beautiful baby—with olive skin, dark brown eyes, and a tuft of black hair. According to Paul, the nurses proclaimed him the cutest baby they had ever seen. Ken smiled often, he ate eagerly, and he enjoyed being held; in every way, he appeared to be perfect. But as Ken approached his 1st birthday it became clear that he was experiencing some difficulties in development. He still had problems sitting unassisted, he had yet to crawl, and his eye-hand coordination was almost nonexistent. When Paul and Debbie took Ken to the pediatrician for his 12-month physical, all the doctor would tell them was that Ken was progressing a little slowly, but that everything would be fine.

At 30 months, Ken was still progressing slowly and was significantly delayed in almost every developmental area. He had yet to say a word, he could barely walk, he was just beginning to feed himself with finger foods, and he had recently learned to reach for and grasp objects. At that physical, the doctor said that Ken was mildly mentally retarded and recommended that the Woolivers enroll him in a preschool program directed by the local Association of Retarded Citizens.

During his three years in this program, Ken progressed significantly, and compared to his classmates in kindergarten he was only slightly delayed. But in April of that year Ken experienced a grand mal seizure in school that lasted for well over an hour. During the seizure, Ken struck his head on the side of a table, opening a cut from above his eye to well into his hairline. He was taken to the hospital.

At the hospital, Paul and Debbie were told that Ken probably had suffered some brain damage and would show slight regression. There was brain damage, but the regression was anything but slight. Ken lost all self-care skills, he could no longer communicate, he could barely walk, and he slept for only one or two hours at a time. He could no longer attend school and required continuous supervision. As a result, Paul and Debbie were forced to spend every moment with Ken. They made repeated attempts to find a daily caregiver and obtain respite care but to no avail. Paul's parents agreed to watch Ken until a more permanent solution could be found, so that Paul and Debbie could return to work. About a month later, when Paul returned home after picking up Ken, he found a six-word note taped to the front door: "I can't take it anymore. Debbie." Paul was left to care for Ken continuously. Some nights, he slept for less than two hours. When not sleeping or working, Paul spent every moment with Ken. He did not have a moment to himself. About fourteen months after Debbie left, Paul was hospitalized for what his doctor called "nervous exhaustion." Out of desperation, Paul's parents began to look for a residential placement for Ken. Nevertheless, almost a year passed before they found an acceptable place.

Ken was placed in a small, residential, out-of-state facility that specialized in individualized treatment. After only three months, Paul was informed that the facility could not handle Ken's severe behavior problems; he had to be removed. A second placement was then found. In this facility, Ken was beaten and abused so severely that he had to be hospitalized. At that point one of his eyes was swollen almost shut, three teeth were missing, a finger was broken, and he had lost almost forty pounds. A third placement was found. During a weekend visit to Ken at this institution, Paul noticed while trying to feed Ken that his son was drooling and unable to chew his food. Paul discovered that Ken was being given large doses of psychotropic drugs. Again Paul actively sought an acceptable placement for Ken. He visited approximately forty places before he found one. In this facility, Ken regained many of the skills he had lost and made improvements in other areas, but the agency was licensed to care for people only until age 18. As a result, in 1981, Ken was forced to leave.

In June Ken returned to live with Paul. While Paul had not yet remarried, he was engaged to Carmen, who was very accepting of Ken. While Ken was able to live at home, Paul realized that home living might not be in Ken's best long-term interests. So in May 1982, Paul decided to form a not-for-profit corporation designed to establish a group home. Paul's work had just begun. With Carmen's help, he wrote countless letters, made numerous telephone calls, attended multitudinous meetings, and traveled to the state capital untold times. Slowly, with the help of other parents and professionals, the corporation was formed. It then negotiated with the state for the funding of a small group home for Ken and five other young men. After receiving the go-ahead from the state, Paul made the down payment on a house in a neighboring subdivision.

After the purchase of the house, Paul worked fourteen to sixteen hours a day, skipping meals and sleep, using all his vacation time, to bring the house up to code standards. He carried heavy fire doors, gutted and rebuilt rooms, installed a sprinkler system, and completely remodeled the basement. At the same time, as the corporation's treasurer, he continued to keep the organization's finances straight. Paul persevered through an endless number of frustrations and obstacles. Finally, on September 12, Ken moved into the group home.

It has not always been easy for Ken in the group home, but he has continued to improve during his time there. With his roommate, Ken takes care of his room. He does his own laundry, he prepares one meal a week, and he cleans the kitchen, the living room, and a bathroom twice a week. He is employed in two part-time jobs and works about thirty hours a week at minimum wage. On those days, Ken packs his own lunch. On Wednesday night, Ken walks to his father's house and has dinner with Paul and Carmen. He spends part of every weekend with them. About once a month he goes to a movie, and a couple of times a season he attends a baseball game. Paul noted, "Our relationship has really matured since he moved into the group home. It's . . . it's more like a father-and-son relationship." With a smile on his face, leaning back in his chair, and clasping his hands behind his head, Paul recently observed, "Who would have ever thought that Ken would be where he is now? I am so proud of him. I am just so proud of him!"

CONCLUSION

Historically, most children and adolescents with severe disabilities have been excluded from public education and general community services on the assumption that efforts to integrate them would be a fruitless waste of scarce resources. After years of work by parents, advocates, and professionals, the concepts of integration and normalization have taken hold and flourished. Today, integration and normalization in schools and the community are seen as the most appropriate policies on moral, philosophical, and legal grounds. Persons with severe disabilities have the right to function as effectively as possible in natural community environments: to live, be educated, work, play, and socialize in the community. They have the fundamental civil right to function in situations as similar as possible to those enjoyed by people without disabilities.

Integration and normalization also offer financial benefits. Community services are more cost effective than services in isolation. Templeman, Gage, and Fredericks (1982), for instance, noticed a 57-percent savings for persons with severe disabilities who were trained to live in the community over those who lived in a segregated environment. Similar savings accrue to educational services provided in the community over those in an isolated program.

Social integration in the public school and the community is an exciting and challenging frontier in service delivery. The torch has passed from restrictive service delivery models to integrative, normalized models. The challenge for the next decade is to serve persons with severe disabilities in the least restrictive, most integrated settings, and to promote appropriate social interactions with persons without disabilities.

SUMMARY

1. Until recently, it was widely believed that neither students with severe disabilities nor students without disabilities would benefit from a shared school program.

2. The principle of normalization emphasizes the commonalities between persons with and without disabilities, holding that persons with severe disabilities should be educated and treated as much as possible like persons without disabilities.

3. Many professionals have proposed that students with severe disabilities be educated in age-appropriate public schools and that interactions with other students be promoted. Some educators argue that students with severe disabilities should be educated in their neighborhood schools in classes composed mainly of students without disabilities.

4. Research studies have clearly and repeatedly demonstrated that students with and without disabilities benefit from school integration.

5. Integration entails much more than physical placement of students into integrated settings. To encourage progressively sophisticated levels of interaction, the school integrative approach has generated a hierarchy of procedures: (1) physical integration, (2) systematic integration, (3) participatory integration, (4) reciprocal integration, and (5) associative integration.

6. In physical integration, persons with severe disabilities are in close proximity but not in actual contact with nondisabled persons.

7. In systematic integration, students without disabilities provide direct instruction and assistance to students with severe disabilities.

8. In participatory integration, students without disabilities provide assistance in service activities to students with severe disabilities.

9. In reciprocal integration, students with and without disabilities have in-school social interactions.

10. In associative integration students with and without disabilities interact socially inside and outside the school.

11. The peer interactive approach has four levels: (1) peer tutors, (2) peer buddies, (3) special friends, and (4) reverse-role tutors.

12. Peer tutors are nondisabled student volunteers who act as classroom aides to students with severe disabilities.

13. Peer buddies are nondisabled student volunteers who interact socially with students with severe disabilities in noninstructional situations.

14. Special friends are nondisabled student volunteers who are friends to students with severe disabilities, interacting on an equal basis.

15. Reverse-role tutors are students with severe disabilities who tutor nondisabled students in a content area such as sign language. Reverse-role tutors were found to make significant improvements in self-esteem and self-concept and impressive gains in acceptance by and interaction with nondisabled persons.

16. The peer interactive approach and the school integrative approach are merged in the cascade model of school integration, an inverted pyramid with nine levels of integration (plus a level of segregation) designed to promote the most normalized school placement for students with severe disabilities. The levels are: (1) Associative Integrative Setting I, (2) Associative Integrative Setting II, (3) Reciprocal Integrative Setting I, (4) Reciprocal Integrative Setting II, (5) Reciprocal Integrative Setting III, (6) Participatory Integrative Setting I, (7) Participatory Integrative Setting II, (8) Systematic Integrative Setting, (9) Physical Integrative Setting, and (10) Segregated Setting.

17. Many professionals feel that community-based services should reflect all the options typically enjoyed by persons without disabilities. Minimally, these include the right to live in a normalized, community-based apartment or home, to be employed, and to participate in community activities.

18. Nirje proposed six categories of community residential integration: (1) physical integration, (2) functional integration, (3) social integration, (4) personal integration, (5) societal integration, and (6) organizational integration.

19. The cascade model of community integration consists of nine integrated levels plus a segregated level: (1) Residential Independent Living, (2) Directed

Independent Living, (3) Controlled Independent Living, (4) Supervised Controlled Living, (5) Supervised Restricted Living, (6) Supervised Restrained Living, (7) Supervised Home Living, (8) Restricted Home Living, (9) Restrained Hostel Living, and (10) Nonintegrated Living.

20. Five major variables determine the level of integration in the cascade model: (1) the type of community integration, (2) the amount of supervision, (3) the type of dwelling, (4) the selection of roommates or residents, and (5) the number of residents in the dwelling. The variables, in turn, have subcomponents.

21. A number of services should be extended to adults with severe disabilities who live with parents, relatives, or friends: (1) respite care, (2) case management, (3) habilitation services, (4) homemaker services, (5) nursing care, and (6) parent training.

CHAPTER 7

Communication Problems in Persons with Severe Disabilities

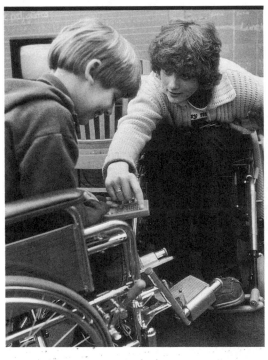

(Courtesy of Evan Johnson, Jeroboam, Inc.)

COMMUNICATION, LANGUAGE, AND SPEECH: AN OVERVIEW

In the modern world, the ability to communicate is a basic skill. Anything that interferes with communication can create serious problems. Before we discuss the communication problems that plague persons with severe disabilities, it is important to distinguish three terms: communication, language, and speech.

Communication is the process of imparting feelings, ideas, and perceptions (Barney & Landis, 1988; Moerk, 1977). It encompasses both formal and relatively informal methods (e.g., a twinkling of the eyes, a smile, or a nervous laugh). Whether formal or informal, communication involves three factors: (1) a sender; (2) the information message; and (3) a receiver (Irwin, 1982). Communication can be **intentional**, for example, when Jack smiles at Martha, or **fortuitous**, for example, when a gambler smiles inadvertently as he is dealt a good poker hand.

Language may enter the communication process when the sender has a message that cannot be transmitted informally. Language is the process of sending a message through a formal symbol system (Cole & Cole, 1981). If Jack wants to ask Martha for a date, a smile will not communicate that. He must formulate a message according to the conventions of a particular language: specific words and a specific word pattern so that Martha will understand that he is asking her out.

If on Wednesday night, Jack dials Martha's telephone number and verbally transmits his message to her, it is called **speech**. Speech is the oral transmission of language (Musselwhite & St. Louis, 1982). Martha hears the sounds Jack is making and decodes them according to a cognitive pattern; she puts meaning to the sounds Jack has produced. If there is no interference in the encoding and decoding processes, the message is transmitted to the receiver. In this case, Martha understands that Jack is asking her to go to the school dance with him on Saturday night.

Prelinguistic Behaviors

The foundations of language are established in early interactions between infants and their social and physical environment. Within months, young children begin to respond to parent communications and passively experience the rules that govern language. To illustrate, many researchers (Bateson, 1975; Collis & Schaffer, 1975) have found that parents engage in a bidirectional exchange of responses with their infants. Vocal exchanges with infants as young as 3 months show a turn-taking quality like adult conversation. Even at the stage when the infant cannot imitate or intentionally control an interaction, parents are incidentally teaching the rules that govern language.

Gradually, specific nonlinguistic behaviors of the child come to be treated as language events by the parents. As the infant's motor abilities develop and become more controlled, he or she can alter the environment. By 6 months of age, a child may use a simple technique such as banging a rattle to produce the apparently desired result, a noise. A child may request an object by reaching for or attempting to grasp it, and may express displeasure by pushing it away. Normally developing children use a variety of these **prelinguistic behaviors** when their expressive abilities are limited to nonverbal gestures. Eventually, these gestures evolve into expressive language behaviors, according to many researchers (Bullis, Rowland, Schweigert, & Stremel-Campbell, 1986).

FIGURE 7.1

This young person with cerebral palsy uses a light sensor to activate a keyboard and communicate to her "listener."

(Courtesy of Prentke Romich Company.)

The research suggests that other prelinguistic motor behaviors are critical to the development of conventional language. For instance, Sugarman (1978) asserts that several sensorimotor behaviors may underlie the development of communication and language. She found that infants between 9 and 13 months develop what is called **means-end behavior**, using a person to obtain an object or an object to get a person's attention. A child at this stage may shake or even throw a rattle not to produce noise but rather to get the parent's attention. According to Sugarman and others, the first signs of expressive language appear when a child firmly establishes means-end behaviors. Parents tend to interpret their child's communicative behaviors richly, sometimes deriving a complex sentence from a gesture or vocalization that would be meaningless to a stranger.

Certain social and cognitive skills are also apparently related to the development of language skills. Bruner (1975) suggests that the rule-governed play routines between parents and child or among children set the stage for acquiring the rules that govern language and communication skills. Although the child's early linguistic utterances are limited in function, they effectively regulate the environment even at the **proto-word** or one-word stage (Dore, 1975;

Halliday, 1975). Other studies (Bruner, Roy, & Ratner, 1978; Pea, 1980; Stevenson & Lamb, 1981; Tronick, 1981) have identified a number of social factors, including frequency of interaction, variety of social experiences, responsiveness of the primary caregiver, and structuring of social activities, as possible contributors to the development of both receptive and expressive language.

To illustrate, Bates, Benigni, Bretherton, Camaioni, and Volterra (1979) conducted a longitudinal study of the relationship between various social-cognitive play behaviors and language development in infants between 9 and 13 months. They found that imitation, tool use, symbolic play, and combinational play were all good predicators of both gestural communication and language. Uzgiris (1981), discussing the possible relationship of play experiences and imitation to language, suggests that they may be another means of communication for the child. Play and language are both symbolic processes through which young children assimilate experiences. Play can also serve a nonverbal function, reflecting the child's nonlinguistic symbolic skills (Bullis, Rowland, Schweigert, & Stremel-Campbell, 1986).

Persons with severe disabilities commonly have communication and language impairments. From the research just cited, it appears that their impairments first appear at the prelinguistic level and that deficits in motor, social, cognitive, and play development hinder their acquisition of prelinguistic skills, which, in turn, affects their acquisition of communication skills. Thus, children with severe disabilities may not develop many of the skills on which language is based, or may develop them at dramatically later ages than the typical child. Persons with severe disabilities are linguistically delayed from shortly after birth onward.

Extralinguistic Behaviors

Some behaviors may compete or interfere with learning to communicate. These are referred to as **extralinguistic behaviors**. An almost endless number of extralinguistic factors may impede the language process in persons with severe disabilities. Perhaps the most common was first described in a classic study by Zeaman and House (1963). These researchers noticed that persons with severe mental retardation were unable to attend to the stimuli available to them. Their attention deficits made them easily distractable.

Other extralinguistic behaviors include self-stimulatory, stereotypic, and ritualistic behaviors, such as head-banging, rumination, object-twirling, rocking, eye-rubbing, and flapping the hands and arms. Many individuals with severe disabilities are anxious and apprehensive around other people; they become withdrawn and generally do not relate to others. When they are forced to associate with people, they may become quite aggressive and engage in externally directed hazardous behaviors such as head-banging, eye-gouging, hair-pulling, hitting, kicking, biting, and scratching. Many utter random vocalizations that are completely unintelligible and apparently have no meaning. Others are echolalic, parroting anything said to them. Visual and hearing impairments further limit an individual's speech and language skills. A person with visual impairment, for example, cannot imitate the manner in which speech sounds are made. A hearing impairment obviously makes it extremely difficult to reproduce sounds.

It appears from the research that many persons with severe disabilities both do not develop the prelinguistic skills prerequisite to language and do develop extralinguistic behaviors that inhibit their acquisition of an adequate language system.

LANGUAGE PROGRAMMING AND INTERVENTION FOR PERSONS WITH SEVERE DISABILITIES

Although the importance of early intervention for persons with severe disabilities has long been recognized, the usual practice has been to wait until there is evidence of a significant delay in the development of communication skills. Recent discussions of the relationship of early cognitive development to language acquisition have resulted in early intervention programs designed to produce specific cognitive behaviors and linguistic structures. Many researchers have suggested that an early program may actually be preventive as well as corrective, because it develops the child's deficient prelinguistic behaviors while minimizing extralinguistic behaviors (Alberto, Garrett, Briggs, & Umberger, 1983; Reichle & Karlan, 1985). Early intervention may also facilitate the learning of later communication skills that are important in social and vocation situations (Barney & Landis, 1988; Stillman, Alymer, & Vandivort, 1983).

Goals of Language Programming

The terminal goal of a language training program is not necessarily to teach the child with severe disabilities the adult system of communication. Many factors may restrict the level of language acquisition the child can achieve. The major goal should be to provide a system of communication that is functional for that child in the particular environment and takes into account the child's unique future needs. The focus is to develop an appropriate and socially useful system (Keogh & Reichle, 1985; Owens, 1988). With such a system the child will discover how to manipulate the environment, which should motivate greater learning and use of language in the future (Kaiser, Alpert, & Warren, 1987; Luftig, 1984; Owens, 1988). Thus language usage reinforces itself.

Luftig (1984) has noted that persons vary in their use of **pragmatics** or the way information is relayed to others through language. A vocabulary that is functional for one child may have little or no relevance for another. Each child's expressive needs are determined by the child's relationships with other people and with objects in everyday living. The pragmatics of a person with severe disabilities who lives in a group home, for instance, are very different

FIGURE 7.2

A training program should provide a system of communication that is effective and functional for the individual in his or her environment.

(Courtesy of Prentke Romich Company.)

from those needed by that same individual living at home or living in an institution. As a number of researchers have noted, the goal for any language training program should be to eliminate, or at least to reduce, the gap between the child's current pragmatic skills and the language requirements of the child's present and likely future environment (Chapman, 1981; Barney & Landis, 1988; Owens, 1988; Peterson, 1987).

Once the goals of a language training program are set, the design of the program can begin. The design sets a series of intermediate goals, which are progressive approximations of the desired terminal behavior. The intermediate goals and the terminal behavior must be geared to the individual's skills, traits, and disabilities as well as present and future pragmatic needs. The selection and sequencing of the intermediate goals should be based on the most efficient and effective way in which persons with severe disabilities can acquire communication. From the first step, the person should benefit from the program in terms of improved communication and improved social and emotional interaction.

Approaches to Language Intervention

The differences in language training approaches boil down to two basic questions: what to teach and how to teach it. There is considerable variation in content and sequence, but somewhat less in instructional procedures. Most language programs for persons with severe disabilities use behavior modification techniques in teaching language skills and generalizing those skills to new environments (Bricker & Bricker, 1970; Reichle, Rogers, & Barrett, 1984). Of the many approaches, only two, the developmental and the functional, will be presented; most others are based on and are variants of those.

Developmental approach.   The **developmental approach** to language intervention uses the sequence in which persons without disabilities learn and master language as its basis. The child with severe disabilities is taught skills in the sequence suggested by the data on the language acquisition of toddlers and children. For instance, if toddlers without disabilities acquire means-end behavior immediately prior to gestural communication, and if a child with severe disabilities has just mastered means-end behavior, then he or she would actively be taught gestural communication. Since language behaviors are often based on cognitive skills, the developmental approach assumes that cognitive development and language development go hand-in-hand (Chapman & Miller, 1980; Owens, 1988).

Recently, several developmental language training programs have appeared that are designed to integrate cognition with language training. They assume that certain cognitive strategies are necessary prerequisites to the development of language. Many researchers (e.g., Clark, 1984; Chapman & Miller, 1980; Owens, 1988; Shane, 1980; Shane & Bashir, 1980) advocate teaching an augmentative system (e.g., use of a communication board and manual signs) through a developmental approach. For instance, Chapman and Miller state that acquisition of language, whether spoken or nonspoken, is predicated on the development of a certain level of cognitive performance.

Several criticisms have been leveled against the developmental approach to language intervention, however. Some researches feel there are insufficient developmental data on which to base language intervention strategies. Others note that psycholinguists' descriptions of what the child is learning when acquiring language have undergone so many changes over such a short period of time that it is difficult to discover a consistent theoretical base for planning intervention strategies. Still other researchers find insufficient evidence of a causal link between cognitive development and the acquisition of communication skills. Even if the manner in which children without disabilities acquire language can be determined conclusively, there is no reason to assume that this is the most effective method to teach children with severe disabilities. Many professionals have questioned applying the developmental approach to pragmatic and functional use of language. For example, the expressive needs of a 10-year-old boy with severe disabilities is dramatically different from those of a toddler without disabilities; is it logical, then, to use the toddler's expressive skills as a language model for the boy?

Functional approach.   The **functional approach** to language intervention focuses on the forms and skills most useful to the individual in controlling, modifying, and interacting with the environment. This approach asserts that, since persons with severe disabilities cannot acquire language in the normal manner, they should not be instructed in the normal developmental sequence. Kaiser, Alpert, and Warren (1987) and Leonard (1981), for instance, argue that the very fact that language is delayed may indicate that older disabled persons use different processes to acquire language than young children.

In the functional approach, the interventionist determines the pragmatic communication skills a person needs at the time to facilitate integration into society. Once he or she has acquired those, the interventionist determines the set of skills the person will need for the next level of integration. For instance, if a person with severe disabilities has acquired the communication skills for integration into school, the interventionist would determine the skills the person will need for integration into the community and would teach the person those skills. Whereas the developmental approach teaches language skills in isolation, the functional approach teaches them in the environment in which they are used. That is, if a girl is expected to shop at Nel's Corner Grocery Store when she graduates from school, her instruction in communication skills will take place at Nel's. The communication skills taught must be tailored to the individual's present and future needs.

The functional approach, too, has critics and opponents. One criticism is directed at the items taught to persons with severe disabilities. Many researchers contend that the words or signs are often selected without any theoretical basis or thought to their practical application. Billingsley (1984) noted that the selected language items were often nonfunctional and nongeneralizable. This makes them of little value and, many investigators maintain, they could even be counterproductive to the integration of persons with severe disabilities (e.g., Bates, Benigni, Bretherton, Camaioni, & Volterra, 1979; Gopnik & Meltzoff, 1984; Rice, 1984; Wiig & Semel, 1984). The second criticism is directed at the approach. While it is universally agreed that an integrated environment is best, many contend that programs cannot justify taking one or two students into the environment while an aide stays in the classroom with the other students.

Selection and Development of Expressive Language

The ability to communicate is basic to human development. It is through communicative interaction that people relate and exchange thoughts, ideas, feelings, needs, and experiences. For many persons with severe disabilities, effective communication is not possible through traditional channels. Often, they can produce only undifferentiated guttural sounds and gross gestures. To become truly integrated into school and society, they must have an effective means of expressing their thoughts, feelings, and ideas.

Now that programs have been enacted to provide an integrated education for persons with severe disabilities, these children must have an effective means of expression. If oral means are not possible, nonverbal methods must be used. Various methods may augment the children's communication abilities and make them more effective. It is important that these methods be considered augmentative channels, not substitute channels, of communication. They are not meant to replace verbal communication but rather to add to it, much as gesturing conveys added information for a verbal child. Some people fear that introducing augmentative channels can decrease or discourage speech development. However, many studies have demonstrated that nonvocal communication techniques do not decrease functional vocalization or speech development (Barney & Landis, 1988; Clark, 1984; McNaughton & Kates, 1980; Harris-Vanderheiden, Brown, MacKenzie, Reiner, & Scheibel, 1975; Vicker, 1974). In fact, it can be argued that augmentative systems improve oral communication.

Augmentative Expressive Systems

A variety of **augmentative expressive systems** are available, and selecting the appropriate ones for a child is not an easy task. Augmentative systems range from concrete, pictorial systems to orthographic systems that require the ability to spell and read. Selection of an appropriate system is critical and should be done with care. The choice should not be cast in stone, never to be altered. The system used may change as the individual develops and acquires skills. Thus, selection is a continual process, examining where the person is at the time and the most normal communicative style possible for that person.

Manual communication.   **Manual communication** is the traditional language used by the hearing impaired, although recently it has also been applied to nonverbal persons with severe disabilities. Since it is a nongenerative system, the individual has to learn each sign as an independent, unique symbol. Signs are made by (1) hand and arm configurations, (2) placement of the hands and arms in relation to the body and face, and (3) movements of the hands and arms. Approximately a half dozen manual communication systems are presently used in the United States; the most common one is **American Sign Language** (after Spanish and Italian, the third most common non-English language in the United States). Each system has not only different symbols for each word but also a different syntax, semantics, and grammar. Thus, it is difficult, if not impossible, for a person conversant in American Sign Language to communicate with someone using another manual system without a translator.

Manual communication systems can be used by persons with severe disabilities for expressive purposes. But, while people with hearing impairments use manual communication the way other people use speech, those with severe disabilities use signs in a **holophrastic** manner to represent whole sentences. To illustrate, when a boy with severe disabilities makes the sign for cookie, he is probably asking, "May I have a cookie, please?" If he makes the sign for drink, he may be saying, "I am thirsty. May I have a glass of water?"

Presently, manual communication is the predominant form of nonspeech communication for persons with severe disabilities (Fristoe & Lloyd, 1978).

Nevertheless, many researchers (Clark, 1984; Sailor & Guess, 1983) suggest that logographic systems will soon equal and surpass manual signs. As Sailor and Guess indicate, logographic symbols with spelled translations below them promote easier integration of persons with severe disabilities into the community, because the symbols can be understood by the general public. Manual communication requires an interpreter, since most of the general public cannot understand manual signs. Therefore, many professionals now recommend logographic systems for persons with severe disabilities.

Picture systems.   One symbol system uses pictures. **Picture systems** use illustrations, line drawings, or photographs to represent thoughts, ideas, things, or feelings. Typically, an individual using a picture vocabulary system points to pictures to communicate thoughts to another person. Children often communicate through pictures on a holophrastic level. For instance, if a girl points to a picture of food, she is probably saying, "I want something to eat"; if she points to a picture of a bathroom, she may be saying, "I need to use the bathroom." The message receiver almost always has to use contextual clues to interpret the child's message. Confusion and misinterpreted messages are common. Because of that, and because pictures lack versatility and functionality, many researchers argue against the use of such systems by persons with severe disabilities, contending that holophrastic picture systems can inhibit integration.

Rebus systems.   **Rebuses** are largely iconic pictorial symbols that represent words. They are easy to encode and decode. Widely used for well over a century, rebuses have only recently been applied to persons with severe disabilities. The system most widely used by such persons is the **Standard Rebus Glossary** (Clark, Davies, & Woodcock, 1974). Largely a nongenerative system, it contains 818 rebuses plus over 1,200 combinations of rebuses or rebuses with letters. Rebus symbols in general may be classified into three types: (1) pictographic, (2) relational, and (3) abstract. Figure 7.3 presents examples of the three types and a passage written completely with rebus symbols and combinations. Because rebuses were intended to correspond to English words, the system incorporates English syntax and permits the construction of highly complex sentences.

There are strengths and weaknesses in using the rebus system for persons with severe disabilities. Because it is a nongenerative system, individuals have to learn each symbol independently. But because the symbols are largely concrete pictographs, they are easier to learn and apply than other symbols. Many researchers (Clark, 1981, 1984; Clark, Moores, & Woodcock, 1976; Harris-Vanderheiden, Brown, MacKenzie, Reiner, & Scheibel, 1975; Wolf & McAloniue, 1977) report success in teaching, applying, and generalizing the rebus symbols with severely disabled persons. According to those studies, such persons found the rebus symbols easier to learn and apply than other symbol systems, including manual signs and Blissymbols.

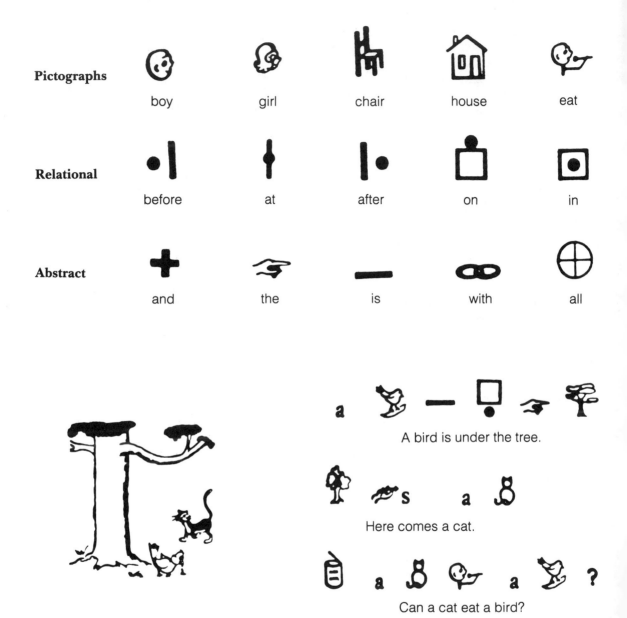

Pictographs

boy   girl   chair   house   eat

Relational

before   at   after   on   in

Abstract

and   the   is   with   all

A bird is under the tree.

Here comes a cat.

Can a cat eat a bird?

FIGURE 7.3

Examples of Pictographic, Relational, and Abstract Rebus Symbols and a Passage Written with Rebus Symbols

(The rebuses and illustration are reprinted with permission of American Guidance Service, Publishers' Building, Circle Pines, MN 55014, from *Introducing Reading—Book Two* [Peabody Rebus Reading Program] by Richard W. Woodcock. Copyright 1967. All rights reserved.)

Blissymbolics.   Blissymbols are unique, generative symbols. In the rebus system, each symbol corresponds to a word; each Blissymbol, however, corresponds to a concept. Since Blissymbols are conceptual, they can be interpreted without reference to sounds or words. The Blissymbolic system consists of approximately 100 meaning-based symbols, which can be combined to generate thousands of symbols (Bliss, 1965). Their successful use by persons with physical disabilities has been well documented (Clark, 1984; McDonald, 1980; Silverman, McNaughton, & Kates, 1978). Nevertheless, they have received limited use by persons with severe disabilities.

In general, there are four types of Blissymbols: (1) pictographic, (2) ideographic, (3) relational, and (4) abstract. Examples of the types and a passage written with Blissymbols are shown in figure 7.4. The first four ideographic symbols in figure 7.4 have a similar component, the heart, indicating that they deal with some sort of emotion. The heart symbol represents the concept of emotion throughout the system. A word describing the basic meaning of the symbol is always printed directly beneath the Blissymbol. Thus, this system can be used with total strangers who have not learned it. But, unlike the rebus system, Blissymbolics does not follow the morphological or syntactical rules of English, although it can handle tense changes, plurals, and so on.

Blissymbolics has strengths and weaknesses, of course. Since it is a generative system, only approximately one hundred symbols must be learned to master the entire language. Perhaps because of this, people who master Blissymbols make the transition to language more easily than those who learn other systems. Blissymbols are less pictographic than rebuses, so they may take longer to learn. To use them, a person has to apply the rules of a generative system. As McNaughton and Kates (1980) have pointed out, Blissymbolics "can more appropriately be employed when the user is capable of understanding its logic and meaning-based symbols rather than responding by rote to meaningless visual configurations" (p. 319).

While the success of Blissymbols for persons with physical disabilities cannot be denied, it appears that persons with severe disabilities acquire and use rebus symbols more easily. Nevertheless, they can learn and use Blissymbols (Clark, 1981, 1984; Hurlbut, Iwata, & Green, 1982; Song, 1979). The major obstacle for them appears to be learning the rules used to generate new symbols. Therefore, each collection of symbols that forms a word has to be learned independently; over time this can become counterproductive. Consequently, it appears that the best system for persons with severe disabilities may be the rebus system.

Augmentative Aids and Techniques

In essence, communication has three elements: a symbol component, a structural component, and a physical component. The **symbol component** consists of symbols used to represent ideas, thoughts, and feelings. For persons with severe disabilities, these may be manual signs, rebus symbols, Blissymbols, or

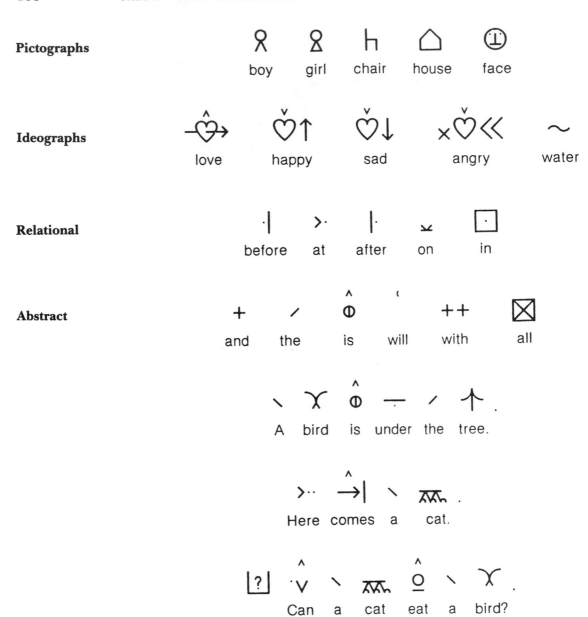

Figure 7.4

Examples of Pictographic, Ideographic, Relational, and Abstract Blissymbols and a Passage Written with Blissymbols

(The Blissymbols used herein are derived from the symbols described in the work *Semantography*, original copyright© C. K. Bliss 1949. Blissymbolics Communication International exclusive licensee, 1982.)

FIGURE 7.5

Selecting and adapting the appropriate augmentative aids and techniques must take into account a number of variables, from the type of disability to the person's social environment.

(Courtesy of Prentke Romich Company.)

traditional orthography. The **structural component** is the manner in which the symbols are combined or arranged so that they are meaningful to the receiver—the semantics and syntax of the symbol system. The **physical component** is the means of transmitting the symbols to a receiver. The first two components have been discussed above. The remainder of this chapter will analyze the physical component. In persons without disabilities, it is muscles and organs (e.g., teeth, mouth, lips, larynx) that transmit sound patterns. In persons with severe disabilities, it may be a communication board, a communication notebook, or a computerized communication device.

Selecting the appropriate **augmentative techniques** for a particular child is not easy. Augmentative aids range from simple "yes" and "no" cards taped to the arms of a wheelchair to highly sophisticated iconic communication systems. Just as there is great diversity in the form and degree of disabilities, so there is great diversity in the types, sophistication, benefits, and usability of aids. The benefit of a particular aid depends on a great many variables: (1) the type and degree of disability, (2) the person's cognitive abilities, (3) the social environment, (4) the physical environment, (5) the person's level of receptive language, (6) the communication functions to be fulfilled, and (7) the person's present and future communication needs. There is no ideal or most appropriate aid for any disability. Neither are cost, sophistication, and number of features necessarily indicators of a better aid. In many cases, a simpler, less sophisticated choice may be more appropriate than a complicated, more advanced aid.

Communication boards. In general, **communication boards** (conversation boards) are series of pictures or symbols through which people can relay their thoughts, ideas, and feelings. The size, shape, and location of the information on the board depend on the needs and skills of the user and must be individualized. It is often recommended that the user be tested on a preliminary communication board to ascertain that information is conveyed quickly and easily before a "permanent" board is created. In fact, no board is truly permanent. Since it reflects the individual's current vocabulary, needs, and skills, the communication board must continually evolve with the sophistication of the user.

While the common format is a large board divided into segments with a symbol in each segment, there are several variations. One is a series of small cards connected by a ring. When not in use, they can be kept in a pocket or purse. Another variation is a series of sheets in an ordinary three-ring binder with as many as nine symbols per sheet. A third variation is an expanding plastic photo holder with a symbol in each section. While these alternatives are just as effective as traditional conversation boards, they look more normal. All portable communication boards can be designed so that different sheets can be inserted depending on the kind of information desired at a particular time. For instance, a sheet of rebus symbols depicting play activities could be inserted just before a child goes to the playground or a sheet depicting different leisure activities could be inserted during the individual's free time at home. Bigge (1982) recommends a large tick-tack-toe pattern as a good format. Regardless of the format, when a person is just learning to use a communication board, it is usually best to start with four symbols the person presently needs, for instance, thirst, bathroom, yes, and no.

The means of indicating the symbol vary. While most individuals with severe disabilities can point with a finger or hand, those who cannot point may use other means, such as a head mounted wand or a direct focus headlight, to identify a symbol.

Electronic communication aids. Due to the recent expansion of the electronic microchip and computer industries, exciting electronic communication devices are continually becoming available. Most are designed to be activated in several ways, depending on characteristics of the user. Borden and Vanderheiden (1988), Brandenburg and Vanderheiden (1987a, 1987b, 1987c), and Blackstone (1987) illustrate and describe a variety of augmentative communication devices developed for persons with severe disabilities. Many electronic devices are designed in a matrix with a light above or behind each cell. Pictures

FIGURE 7.6

Augmentative aids can range from highly sophisticated iconic communicative systems, such as these electronic communication boards, to simple hand-written cards.

(Courtesy of Prentke Romich Company.)

FIGURE 7.7

Persons who have problems controlling their motion may use pressure-sensitive pads to direct the pattern of light in the matrices or to control the scanning process.

(Courtesy of Prentke Romich Company.)

or symbols are displayed in each square of the matrix. While the content in some is permanent, most matrices are designed so that the content can be changed with the needs of the user. Some matrices contain only a few squares while others have as many as one hundred.

Some electronic devices are activated by direct selection. The user touches the matrix cell, and the information is recorded or the word is phonetically pronounced. For users who have problems controlling their movements, joysticks, headsticks, mouth sticks, and pressure sensitive pads may be used to direct the pattern of light in the matrices or to control the scanning process. Interfaces and governors may assist in activation of the desired cells. It is important to select the most efficient and normalizing output features for a particular person.

FACTORS IN APPROACH SELECTION

While the ideal communication method for persons with severe disabilities is speech, it must be recognized that many such persons may never learn to speak. They need augmentative communication methods and aids that permit them to express their thoughts, ideas, and concerns accurately and effectively. Selecting an appropriate method and aid is of prime importance; therefore, careful monitoring and evaluation must be conducted before, during, and after selection.

Factors to Evaluate Before Selection

The following are some of the factors that should be carefully evaluated before selection of an augmentative method and aid:

1. The individual's current communication ability and amount of functional communication.
2. The individual's current and future communication needs.
3. The individual's motivation to communicate and prior attempts at communication.
4. The individual's prognosis for developing effective speech.
5. The individual's physical and social environment and their influence on his or her communication development.
6. The individual's primary message receivers or communicative audience and their motivation to communicate with him or her.
7. The individual's current and future educational, vocational, and community integration goals.
8. The most normalized communication mode that is possible for the individual.
9. The individual's communicative style and whether it is appropriate for his or her level of receptive and expressive communication.
10. How the proposed communication mode enhances or fosters the individual's attempts to communicate.
11. The flexibility of the communication mode in adapting to the individual's changing communication needs.

12. The adaptability of the communication mode to current therapy and educational procedures.
13. The amount and type of professional and parental help available.

Factors to Evaluate During Selection

The following are some of the factors that should be carefully monitored during selection of an augmentative method and aid:

1. The individual's present visual and hearing skills.
2. The individual's ability to associate, store, and retrieve the meaning of pictures and symbols.
3. The individual's present level of physical skill.
4. The individual's speed of response.

Factors to Evaluate After Selection

The following are some of the factors that should be carefully monitored after selecting an augmentative method and aid:

1. How effectively and appropriately the individual communicates using the aid.
2. How effectively and appropriately the individual communicates through the symbols selected.
3. How the individual's present communication skills will meet his or her changing communicative, educational, vocational, and environmental needs.

The Case of Louis Franklin Steiner   EXAMPLE

Louis was born in the middle of June on his mother's 33rd birthday and his parents' eleventh wedding anniversary. He was the third child and only son of Franklin and Louise Steiner. At the time of his birth, his sister Elizabeth had just completed kindergarten and his sister Jennifer was slightly over 3. Though the Steiners were delighted with Louis, they had some concerns. Louise had contracted a urinary tract infection in the first trimester of pregnancy that had been treated with an unknown medication. And, although labor and delivery were apparently uneventful, Louis was born with a fractured clavicle. His birth weight was six pounds, fourteen ounces, and he was born full term.

According to his parents, Louis's development was always slow. He did not sit until 14 months of age, and he did not walk until 4 years. At 6, Louis's receptive language skills were limited to a few simple commands, and his expressive skills consisted of three unintelligible sounds. His hearing and vision were described by his doctor as "grossly adequate" although the physician noted that Louis held objects close to his eyes and sat close to the television set. According to his parents, Louis's behavior was characterized by tantrums, social isolation, stereotypic movements, and self-injurious behaviors. His teachers indicated that he exhibited the same behaviors at school and was quite disruptive. The school system diagnosed Louis as severely mentally retarded with secondary diagnoses of autism and seizure disorder. Twice a day he received phenytoin sodium for the seizure disorder. At age 8, there was no change in his language production, ability to play, and ability to respond to environmental events. The doctor estimated Louis's overall development at "well below the 2-year level."

His school performance during his 9th year did not improve. The language training he received was largely directed by the speech and language therapist. Although he still made only three unintelligible sounds, his speech and language program centered around articulation training. During that year the severity and frequency of his externally directed hazardous behaviors increased.

The next school year, a new teacher, Mr. Rankin, decided to teach the rebus system to Louis. He began by introducing four symbols: yes, no, thirst, and hunger. This program was warmly accepted and reinforced both at home and by other school personnel. It took almost six months before Louis could reliably use all four symbols for communicative purposes. Mr. Rankin also expected Louis to vocalize as he pointed to the symbols on a small communication board. Slowly the teacher added to the vocabulary, and by the end of the year Louis had an expressive vocabulary of fifteen rebus symbols. As his expressive skills developed, a number of other positive changes took place. His tantrums, self-injurious behaviors, externally directed hazardous behaviors, and stereotypic behaviors decreased, and there were marked improvements in his self-care, social, and motor skills. At the end of the year, Louise, in tears, thanked the teacher. "For the first time, Louis can talk to us, and we can talk to him! I just can't tell you how happy we are."

The following year, Louis increased his expressive vocabulary to thirty-eight rebus symbols. He continued to vocalize as he pointed to the symbols, and three of his sounds were distinct and clear enough to be understood by his parents and Mr. Rankin without the rebuses. His undesirable traits continued to decrease in severity while many of his desirable traits increased in sophistication. Over the subsequent years, Louis mastered more and more rebus symbols while improving his oral communication. The format of his augmentative aid changed from a large lap board to a set of flip cards, which he keeps in his back trouser pocket. His progress enabled him to participate in a vocational training program and an independent living program. At present, Louis lives at home with his parents and a younger sister and works at three part-time jobs. He gets around on his own using the community mass transportation system. About once a week, Louis goes to the movies with his girlfriend, and afterwards they often go out for a pizza or ice cream. Louis has made tremendous strides from the days of his three unintelligible sounds. At that time, who would have expected him to be where he is today? His improvements are largely the result of one teacher introducing Louis to four rebuses one September day when he was 10 years old.

Conclusion

The ability to express thoughts, ideas, and feelings clearly and concisely is not a luxury in today's society, it is a necessity. For people to be actively and totally integrated into a community, they must be able to communicate. The closer their communication method is to the normal mode, the greater the prospects for integration. The ideal mode of communication is speech; any other method restricts integration. But for many people with severe disabilities speech is not a realistic option. If they can produce only unintelligible sounds, it is unlikely they will speak in the immediate future. Alternative augmentative methods must be provided for persons with severe disabilities to communicate with other people.

Teaching a person with severe disabilities communication skills may accomplish more than the ability to utilize symbols and lexicons. Research has indicated that, with communication, many undesirable behaviors decrease in frequency and severity and desirable behaviors increase in frequency and acceptability (Eason, White, & Newson, 1982; Donnellan, Mirenda, Mesaros, & Fassbender, 1984; Horner & Budd, 1983). Tantrums, social isolation, stereotypic movements, self-injurious behaviors, and externally directed hazardous behaviors may be dramatically decreased by learning communicative skills, as they were in Louis's case. Acquisition of desirable traits such as self-care skills, socialization skills, vocational skills, and integrative skills may be accelerated. When people can communicate, even if it is through an aid, they may become more sophisticated in skills such as socialization than they could by being taught that particular skill alone.

SUMMARY

1. Communication is the process of imparting feelings, ideas, and perceptions. Language is the process of sending a message through a formal symbol system. Speech is the oral transmission of language.

2. Persons with severe disabilities have deficits in prelinguistic skills, which delay their acquisition of communication skills.

3. Persons with severe disabilities often exhibit extralinguistic behaviors (e.g., attention deficits, distractability, self-stimulatory and stereotypic behaviors, and echolalia), which impede the process of communication.

4. The focus of a communication training program for persons with severe disabilities is to develop effective and functional communication for that person in his or her present and future environment.

5. The developmental approach to language intervention uses the sequence in which children without disabilities learn language as the instructional basis of intervention.

6. Criticisms of the developmental approach are: (1) the developmental data on which to base language strategies are insufficient and (2) the communication instruction lacks functionality.

7. The functional approach to language intervention focuses on the skills deemed most useful to the individual for controlling, modifying, and interacting with his or her environment.

8. In the functional approach, the interventionist determines the communication skills a person will need at the time in the particular environment to facilitate integration.

9. The two major criticisms of the functional approach are: (1) the words selected are often nonfunctional and nongeneralizable, and (2) few programs can justify having the teacher take one or two students into an integrated environment while the aide stays in the classroom with the other students.

10. Augmentative methods of communication are designed to supplement verbal communication and in many cases actually improve oral communication.

11. Manual communication is a nongenerative augmentative system that produces a word or concept through hand and arm movements. Persons with severe disabilities tend to use manual communication in a holophrastic manner. Although this is presently their predominant form of nonspeech communication, it will soon be replaced by logographic, pictorial systems, many professionals contend.

12. Picture symbol systems use illustrations, line drawings, or photographs to represent ideas, thoughts, and feelings holophrastically.

13. Rebuses are nongenerative, iconic, pictorial symbols that directly represent words. Because of their pictorial nature, they are easier for persons with severe disabilities to learn and apply than other symbol systems.

14. Blissymbols are a generative symbol system in which each symbol corresponds to a concept. Persons with severe disabilities often have difficulty learning the rules that govern the generation of symbols into concepts, so

they have to learn each group of symbols independently. Nevertheless, successful use of Blissymbols by persons with physical disabilities has been well documented.

15. Augmentative aids range from simple "yes" and "no" cards taped to the arms of a wheelchair to highly sophisticated complex, iconic communication systems.

16. Communication boards are series of pictures or symbols people can use to relay thoughts, ideas, and feelings.

17. New electronic communication devices are now available. Most use a matrix format.

18. The augmentative method and aid must be matched to the person with severe disabilities. Careful monitoring and evaluation must be conducted before, during, and after selecting an approach, to ensure that it is appropriate.

CHAPTER 8

Social and Personal Skills in Persons with Severe Disabilities

(Courtesy of Eugene Strattman and Judith Mantz.)

Lack of culturally acceptable social responses is a significant behavioral deficiency that distinguishes persons with severe disabilities from persons without disabilities. Follow-up studies have consistently revealed that these social skill deficits significantly interfere with school integration, community adjustment, and vocational success. The studies have repeatedly demonstrated that, prior to training, well over 90 percent of all persons with severe disabilities have a significant social skill problem, ranging from lack of social awareness to openly aggressive behaviors toward others and from stereotypic and other nondirective behaviors to an absence of grooming and hygiene skills. Certain common characteristics apparently intensify the social skill deficits. Short attention span, low frustration tolerance, limited language skills, and poor cognitive abilities contribute to a person's inability to acquire and use social skills.

In large part acceptable **social-personal behavior** is determined by its context. To behave appropriately under a variety of conditions, a person must perceive the critical nuances of specific situations with different people in various settings. It is entirely appropriate, for instance, to act one way with close friends and another way with strangers. The behavior standards appropriate for a baseball game are very different from those for a symphony concert. Teaching socially valid behaviors for a specific situation and setting does not guarantee socially valid behavior in another circumstance (Wehman, Renzaglia, & Bates, 1985). According to Kazdin (1980), the major criteria for evaluating behavior change are how well the individual performs relative to others and how competent he or she is perceived to be by others. Consequently, it is important not only to teach persons with severe disabilities to perform in a "normative" manner, but also to teach **social-personal skills** that meet relevant and acceptable standards.

PARAMETERS OF SOCIAL COMPETENCE

Unlike other skills typically required of persons with severe disabilities, social-personal skills are determined by their social context. The person with severe disabilities must perceive the critical aspects of specific situations and alter his or her response accordingly. Such social perception is extremely important in social situations with different people in different settings. In contrast, making a bed remains relatively consistent from one setting to the next.

Variations may be illustrated by the relatively commonplace conventions about the distance that separates two people while conversing. The distance Sally maintains from a gas station attendant when they are talking about adding oil to her car is quite different from the distance Sally maintains from a fellow student when discussing a class, which is different from the distance between Sally and her sister when they are sharing secrets in her bedroom, which is different from the distance between Sally and her boyfriend while standing in the movie lobby on a Saturday night date. The appropriate distance varies according to the salient dimensions of the situation, in this case, Sally's relationship with the other person and the amount of privacy they have. Over time, Sally has assimilated these varying distances, and today she takes them for granted, responding without conscious thought.

However, an individual from a different culture, Yuri, has assimilated very different appropriate distances in his native culture from those in our culture. Consequently, Yuri may stand at an "inappropriate" distance while conversing with John. If so, he will likely receive negative reactions from John. If he stands at an appropriate distance, he will likely receive positive reactions. Over time, Yuri will assimilate these distances, integrating them into his repertoire.

Yuri's example is not necessarily applicable to Byron, a person with severe disabilities. Byron is likely to have only limited contact with persons without disabilities. The gradual process that permitted Yuri to assimilate the appropriate distances is not available to Byron. To optimize his integration possibilities, Yuri had to perform three operations simultaneously: analyze the salient dimensions of each setting; analyze his behavior in that setting; and analyze the response he received. Trial and error then forces Yuri to make sophisticated decisions quickly. Because of his inability to attend to all the salient dimensions of the setting, Byron probably requires more repetitions than Yuri to assimilate this standard, but in all likelihood Byron will have fewer repetitions. Byron probably will attend to nonsalient dimensions when forming a hypothesis, he will continue to receive negative reactions from others, and eventually he may isolate himself from others.

While the importance of social-personal skill development is well substantiated, few agree on the exact components and parameters of social and personal skills. This lack of consensus has precluded accurate measurement and evaluation of instructional procedures. Sadly, these conditions have suppressed curriculum and instructional technology development. Where specific social and personal skills have been defined, much of the research has centered on relatively discrete behaviors and has failed to tie them into a broader concept. For instance, studies of social skill development have examined training in the use of video games (Dattilo & Mirenda, 1987; Sedlak, Doyle, & Schloss, 1982), social integration during break time (Breen, Haring, Pitts-Conway, & Gaylord-Ross, 1985), and social control (Peck, 1985).

For the purposes of this discussion, social and personal skills may be defined as those behaviors that maximize social interactions with others and are perceived as socially appropriate by peers and significant others (Wehman, Renzaglia, & Bates, 1985). According to this definition, social-personal behaviors include those that facilitate direct and indirect social integration. They include behaviors used for contact with other people (e.g., greeting responses), behaviors that facilitate contact (e.g., grooming skills), and behaviors that usually occur in a social context (e.g., leisure activities). In this concept, the terms *social* and *personal* are adjectives that characterize interactions between people. Any time people interact, they are manifesting social and personal skills. Social-personal behaviors typically encompass four areas: (1) grooming, hygiene, and personal appearance, (2) social interaction and involvement, (3) self-development, and (4) sexual awareness. Each area has subcomponents.

Grooming, Hygiene, and Personal Appearance

Proper grooming and hygiene and an acceptable physical appearance are essential for persons with severe disabilities. Competence in achieving these is directly linked to social integration, normalization, and acceptance. In general,

FIGURE 8.1

When students with severe disabilities are integrated into the public schools, they can see age-appropriate behavior and develop social relationships with peers without disabilities.

(Courtesy of Lynda Atherton.)

grooming, hygiene, and personal appearance skills involve looking after and caring for oneself, one's dress, and one's appearance. In the early stages, grooming and hygiene skills include bathing, brushing teeth, and combing hair; personal appearance skills include putting on and taking off clothing, including buttoning, zipping, and tying. In later stages, grooming and hygiene skills extend to nasal hygiene, health care, first aid, and skin and nail care; personal appearance skills include the ability to select, launder, and, ultimately, purchase one's clothing. Instruction in clothing selection, makeup, shaving, use of cosmetics, and menstrual hygiene is, of course, sex-specific.

While other social-personal skills directly create integrative activities, grooming, hygiene, and personal appearance skills take a more facilitative or passive role in integration, and lack of these skills can greatly hinder a person's prospects of integration. A person with severe disabilities who has an offensive odor or an unkempt appearance is likely to be ostracized regardless of his or her competence in interacting with other people. Grooming, hygiene, and personal appearance skills must be mastered by the person with severe disabilities before he or she can actively be integrated into society.

Social Interaction and Social Involvement

Social interaction and involvement skills range from manners to greeting skills and from the elimination of stereotypic behavior to acceptance of criticism. They should not be considered a separate curricular area but rather woven into other instructional domains and taught in the community to the maximum extent possible. Many researchers perceive three components of social interaction and involvement: (1) self-related behaviors, (2) self-management behaviors, and (3) integrative behaviors. Each of these also has component skills. For instance, **self-related behaviors** include (1) accepting consequences, (2) accepting criticism, (3) developing manners, (4) developing politeness, (5) accepting authority, (6) responding to demands and requests, (7) developing responsible behaviors, (8) displaying self-control, and (9) coping with conflict. **Self-management skills** typically include (1) elimination of self-injurious behaviors, (2) elimination of stereotypic behaviors, (3) elimination of externally directed hazardous behaviors, and (4) elimination of nuisance behaviors. The components of **integrative skills** are (1) engaging in eye contact, (2) greeting others, (3) helping others, (4) making conversation, (5) participating in leisure activities, (6) developing a positive attitude toward others, and (7) respecting others' property.

Social interaction and social involvement behaviors should be selected according to Wolf's (1978) delineation of **social validity**. Social validity, according to Wolf, is an analysis of the frequency and duration of specific social-personal responses in certain contexts. It quantifies the behaviors that are socially normal, acceptable, and typically exhibited by persons without disabilities at a particular chronological age. Social validity is usually established by significant others, who determine whether the behaviors of a person with severe disabilities accord with the behaviors of persons without disabilities. Significant others include peers without disabilities who live in the same community and parents or guardians. The goals that evolve from this analysis reflect skills that enable a person to function as normally as possible. Teaching a person with severe disabilities to behave according to social norms dramatically increases the chances of that person functioning successfully in community life.

An extension of Wolf's social validity hypothesis that has recently attracted attention is the concept of **stranger training**. This approach teaches persons with severe disabilities acceptable, responsible, and cautious interaction patterns with unfamiliar persons, using strangers as trainers. Through years of schooling and other programming activities, persons with severe disabilities develop a reliance on and trust in other people that they extend unquestioningly to unfamiliar persons. In most cases this is not a problem. But, as their community integration increases, they are more likely to encounter potentially dangerous, harmful, or unscrupulous strangers. Therefore, they must be taught how to interact with a stranger or an unfamiliar trainer. Later, this behavior must be generalized to the community with other stranger trainers.

Self-Development

Self-development skills are those necessary for personal achievement and satisfactory relationships with other people. Self-development has two subcomponents: (1) self-esteem and self-understanding, and (2) development of a better relationship with others. **Self-esteem and self-understanding** also have two components: (1) nurturing one's abilities, interests, needs, and wants, and (2) learning how to interact constructively, appropriately, and responsibly. Both elements are concerned with acquiring self-awareness (e.g., identifying one's interests, abilities, emotions, and needs) and acquiring self-confidence (e.g., feelings of worth, importance, and competence). **Development of a bet-**

FIGURE 8.2

The skills needed to establish and maintain friendships can best be learned and practiced in school with nondisabled students.

(Courtesy of Lynda Atherton.)

ter relationship with others explores the skills needed to establish and maintain successful interpersonal relationships (e.g., forming and maintaining friendships and understanding the impact of one's behaviors on others). While at first glance, the two components of self-development may appear discrete, they are highly interdependent. An improvement in self-confidence results in the development of more friendships with persons without disabilities and this in turn results in an improvement in self-confidence.

Seven self-development skills, each with subcomponents, have emerged from these two generic components (Kokaska & Brolin, 1985):

1. Achieving self-awareness
    a. Attaining a sense of body
    b. Identifying interests and abilities
    c. Identifying emotions
    d. Identifying needs
2. Acquiring self-confidence
    a. Expressing feelings of worth
    b. Telling how others see one
    c. Accepting praise
    d. Accepting criticism
    e. Developing faith in oneself

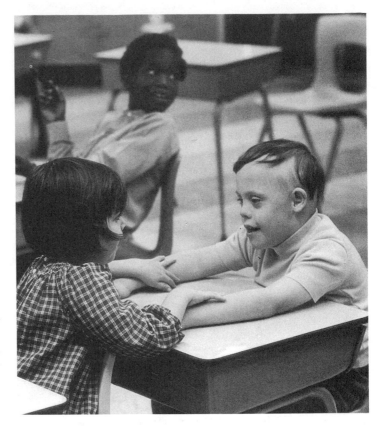

FIGURE 8.3

When students with severe disabilities are integrated into the regular classroom, they can learn appropriate behaviors by modeling and being around children without disabilities.

(Courtesy of Bruce Roberts, Rapho/ Photo Researchers, Inc.)

3. Developing socially responsible behavior

   a. Knowing character traits needed for acceptance
   b. Knowing proper behavior in public places
   c. Developing respect for the rights of others
   d. Recognizing and following instructions
   e. Knowing one's role

4. Maintaining adequate interpersonal skills

   a. Knowing how to listen and respond
   b. Knowing how to make and maintain friendships
   c. Establishing appropriate sexual relationships
   d. Knowing how to establish close relationships

5. Achieving independence

   a. Understanding the impact of one's behavior on others
   b. Understanding self-organization
   c. Developing goal-seeking behavior
   d. Striving toward self-actualization

FIGURE 8.4

The opportunity to develop friendships and intimacy with persons of the same and the opposite sex is an important aspect of social development.

(Courtesy of Cahokia School District 187, Illinois.)

6. Developing problem-solving skills
   a. Differentiating bipolar concepts
   b. Understanding the need for goals
   c. Looking at alternatives
   d. Anticipating consequences
   e. Knowing where to find good advice

7. Communicating adequately with others
   a. Recognizing emergency situations
   b. Understanding the subtleties of communication
   c. Communicating adequately to be understood

Sexual Awareness

Sexual awareness skills require ongoing education. It includes traditional sex education, such as knowledge about human reproduction and fertility, plus factors historically considered to be outside the realm of sex education, such as awareness of self and intimate behaviors with persons of the same and opposite sex. Traditionally, sex education has been neglected for persons with severe disabilities or, if taught, has been restricted to pubescent changes and identification of major body parts. But, if people with severe disabilities are truly going to be integrated and normalized, they must have the same training provided to persons without disabilities. Sexual awareness training covers six items: (1) male puberty, (2) female puberty, (3) social relations with the same and the opposite sex, (4) human reproduction, (5) fertility regulation, and (6) marriage. Each category may be subdivided. For instance, social relations with the same and the opposite sex may include friendships, intimacy, and dating customs. Sexual awareness must be taught in context with the other social-personal behaviors.

ALTERNATIVE APPROACHES TO SOCIAL-PERSONAL DEVELOPMENT

Teaching a person with severe disabilities to behave according to established social norms and values greatly increases the chances that he or she will be successfully integrated into community life. But simply teaching the whole spectrum of social-personal skills discussed above may not guarantee integration and normalization. In fact, some argue that teaching all the prerequisite social-personal skills may waste valuable instructional time because certain skills may never be used. Moreover, it is unlikely that a person with severe disabilities can be taught to respond effectively to all the nuances of every interaction. Many professionals suggest, instead, teaching only high priority competencies for use in the community. Skills that have a low probability of being used in the community should not be taught, since they would not foster integration.

Self-Regulatory Model

An alternative to full-spectrum social-personal instruction is the **self-regulatory model.** According to this paradigm, ability to function in social-personal situations depends on three factors: (1) thinking critically, (2) determining relevant information, and (3) acting independently (Williams, Brown, & Certo, 1975). Since persons with severe disabilities have an **external locus of control**, they often depend on authority figures to tell them how and when to perform certain skills. However, in numerous situations, social-personal performance is crucial but authorities are not present. Then persons with severe disabilities are particularly deficient and quite vulnerable. One way to compensate for this is to teach not only specific skills but also how to perform those skills appropriately across environmental configurations without specific cues from persons in authority. The learner must engage in a series of responses, evaluate the appropriateness of such responses, and, if necessary, alter his or her behavior without being cued by a person in authority.

In recent years, researchers have attempted to teach persons with severe disabilities self-regulatory skills. These skills enable the person to respond effectively to all the nuances of each social-personal situation without being cued by an authority figure or being taught the correct response to that specific situation. Self-regulation consists of five interrelated skills, each based on the previous one but more sophisticated and complex: (1) self-monitoring, (2) self-standard setting, (3) self-evaluation, (4) self-reward, and (5) self-delaying of gratification. It was found that persons who can self-delay gratification can effectively respond to varied social-personal environmental configurations without specific cues from a person in authority (Brimer, 1985).

Nietupski and Williams (1974) conceived self-regulation as consisting of at least four interrelated steps: (1) detecting or defining the task, (2) arriving at alternative ways to complete the task, (3) implementing an alternative, and (4) assessing the outcome of the alternative. According to Nietupski and Williams, an individual who can complete all four steps is likely to respond effectively to varied social-personal settings without receiving external cues.

An extension of the self-regulatory concept was proposed by Liberty (1984) and White (1983), although not conceived as a method for acquiring social-personal skills. These researchers argue that persons with severe disabilities develop a dependence on positive artificial antecedent events—events that are set up to stimulate a desirable response from them. They learn to respond only to these artificial events, and they do not learn to respond to the varied events that occur in the natural environment. Over the long-term, Liberty argues, this greatly hinders their maintenance and generalization of social-personal skills. The investigators recommend, in contrast, that antecedent events vary along a continuum from positive to irrelevant to negative, and, of greater importance, that antecedent stimuli be provided by events occurring naturally in the environment rather than by artificial methods.

Behavioral-Analytic Model

A somewhat different approach is the **behavioral-analytic model**. Proposed by Goldfried and D'Zurilla (1969), this model too is more cost effective than teaching the full spectrum of social-personal skills. Instead, Goldfried and D'Zurilla suggest that teachers identify and prioritize situations and skills that will help a person to function in a normal manner with others. The skills are then taught in order of priority. The procedural sequence of the behavioral-analytic model has three steps: (1) situational analysis, (2) response enumeration, and (3) response evaluation.

Situational analysis.   In the initial step, a large sample of social-personal situations is identified, from generic situations that a large number of persons would likely experience to specific situations experienced infrequently by anyone other than a person with severe disabilities. For instance, almost everyone engages in social greetings (e.g., "Hello, Ernie. How are you?") and social requests (e.g., "Bertha, would you like a cup of coffee?"). But persons with severe disabilities encounter unique criticisms that others are not likely to

FIGURE 8.5

To gain social acceptance, people with or without disabilities have to exhibit behaviors similar to those of everyone else.

(Courtesy of United Features Syndicate, Inc.)

experience at all or in the same manner (e.g., "Edward, stop hitting the table with your spoon!").

The methods typically used for **situational analysis** are observations and interviews. The observation phase may include self-observation by the person with severe disabilities and direct observation by someone else. Self-observation may be reported through personal interviews or simplified self-recordings in which the person describes the social-personal situations he or she experiences. To obtain a complete picture, direct behavioral observations should be conducted in every setting the individual now uses or is likely to use in the immediate future (e.g., school, work, home, and community). Interviews with others who have direct contact with the person with severe disabilities help to provide a comprehensive listing of the social-personal skills he or she will need to function and become integrated.

Response enumeration.   Once problematic or frequently encountered social-personal situations are identified, Goldfried and D'Zurilla recommend **response enumeration**, listing potential responses to these situations. Selected situations are presented to a group of individuals, who are asked how they would respond, or else people are watched responding to simulated situations. From this sampling process, a range of possible responses is identified for each social-personal situation.

Response evaluation.   Goldfried and D'Zurilla recommend using a rating scale to rank the responses, from the most effective to the least effective, in the **response evaluation** step. The response selected as most effective in a specific social-personal situation is then, if possible, used as the training objective for persons with severe disabilities.

FIGURE 8.6

Teaching a person with severe disabilities to behave according to social norms increases the probability that he or she will be accepted by others in society.

(Courtesy of Tracy Hrbek.)

Normative Analysis Model

Several other methods are philosophically similar to the behavioral-analytic model. Although less systematic, the **normative analysis model** also attempts to determine the social-personal skills required in a particular setting, using analysis of (1) the frequency and duration of specific responses to specific situations, (2) the appropriate time and place to engage in specific behaviors, and (3) the chronological age at which specific behaviors are appropriate. The goals that evolve from this analysis should reflect skills that are appropriate in terms of frequency, duration, time, place, and chronological age, enabling a person to function as normally as possible in that particular setting at that particular time (Williams, Hamre-Nietupski, Pumpian, McDaniel-Marx, & Wheeler, 1978).

Ecological Model

The **ecological model** likewise attempts first to identify normal and acceptable behavioral standards for persons with severe disabilities in a variety of environments (i.e., domestic, leisure, general community, vocational, and school). Then, through in-depth interviews with significant others and observations of the person's performance in these settings, a discrepancy analysis identifies inappropriate behaviors he or she presently exhibits in those environments (Brimer, 1985; Brown, Branston, Hamre-Nietupski, Pumpian, et al., 1979). From the discrepancy analysis, skills that would maximize integration and normalization are selected for instruction in the natural environment where they are needed. The individual then develops the specific social-personal skills required to maximize integration in each environment.

SOCIAL-PERSONAL SKILL DEVELOPMENT STRATEGIES

Regardless of the approach used, certain strategies can assist persons with severe disabilities in the acquisition, maintenance, and generalization of social-personal skills. These strategies are equally appropriate to traditional and alternative approaches and fall into three categories: (1) the environmental approach, (2) the consequence approach, and (3) the response approach.

Environmental Approach

The **environmental approach** holds that planned activities in the natural environment have a beneficial and powerful influence on the development of social-personal skills in persons with severe disabilities. These persons benefit from exposure to more socially competent models in integrated environments, and exposure enhances the development and expression of desirable skills. To illustrate this positive influence, Peterson and Haralick (1977) systematically arranged free-play activities between youngsters with severe disabilities and youngsters without disabilities. The children with severe disabilities engaged in more sophisticated play behavior than when they were associating only with peers with severe disabilities. These results argue against strict homogeneity of groups on the basis of functional level and suggest that integrated, normalized opportunities be provided to persons with severe disabilities.

Obviously, different social-personal behaviors are required in different settings. If persons with severe disabilities are to develop full social-personal repertoires, they must experience the unique situational demands of a wide variety of settings. Restricting them to only certain settings substantially reduces their chance to learn more effective behavior. Parents, teachers, and other service providers must share responsibility for expanding the opportunities of persons with severe disabilities to explore and experience their home communities fully.

Acceptable and desirable social-personal behavior may require manipulation of materials. In far too many cases, persons with severe disabilities use materials intended for much younger children. When an adult with severe disabilities uses materials intended for preschoolers without disabilities, he or she is often viewed as socially immature and incapable of adult behavior. Consider, for instance, the divergent impressions generated by observing a 20-year-old adult using crayons on a coloring book or using a pen to fill out a crossword puzzle from the *New York Times*. Although the materials are structurally similar, the crossword puzzle is without question more appropriate for an individual who is 20. Clearly, persons with severe disabilities must be given

FIGURE 8.7

The environmental approach holds that persons with severe disabilities benefit from exposure to more socially competent models in integrated environments.

(Courtesy of Lynda Atherton.)

access to age-appropriate materials, particularly when these items are found in places that encourage greater integration and greater spontaneity in social behavior (Wehman, 1979). Playing with a pinball machine at home would probably not result in a behavior change, but playing in an arcade alongside adolescents without disabilities increases the prospects of social integration. Increasing the proximity of and exposure to such materials can promote more productive and acceptable social-personal behavior in persons with severe disabilities.

Consequence Approach

Although careful arrangement of environmental conditions may facilitate the acquisition of desirable social-personal skills, persons with severe disabilities frequently require more direct intervention. The **consequence approach** uses direct intervention following social-personal behaviors. In particular, the occurrence and frequency of desirable behaviors depend on reinforcing consequences. Preferably, reinforcing consequences naturally result from appropriate social-personal behaviors. For instance, when a student with severe disabilities makes eye contact with a schoolmate, the schoolmate reinforces the contact by engaging in friendly conversation. This increases the likelihood that the student will make eye contact in similar situations in the future.

When natural events are not reinforcing enough, additional consequences may be arranged. Both externally administered reinforcers and self-administered reinforcers are used. **Externally administered reinforcers** are events

FIGURE 8.8

Students with severe disabilities can acquire appropriate social-personal skills by engaging in desirable leisure activities.

(Courtesy of Amy Shiverdeck.)

delivered by others contingent on the occurrence of targeted social-personal behaviors. **Self-administered reinforcers** can also strengthen socially appropriate behavior, although this strategy is not widely utilized for persons with severe disabilities. The individual gives himself or herself a reward for performing targeted social-personal objectives. For instance, a boy who attends a school dance could reinforce himself by buying a soda at the end of the evening. Reinforcing consequences potentially play a significant role in instructional programs for persons with severe disabilities. Every effort should be made to use natural consequences and self-administered reinforcers to maintain social-personal behaviors for long periods of time.

Response Approach

The **response approach** to developing social-personal behaviors focuses on making persons with severe disabilities aware of how to respond, what to do, and when to exhibit the behavior. It has four stages: (1) modeling, (2) rehearsal, (3) feedback, and (4) practice in the natural environment. **Modeling** is a process in which a person is shown through live models, audio or video tapes, or simulations how to do the targeted social-personal skills. Repeated exposure to a situation does not alter a person's behavior, but modeling combined with verbal instruction is a powerful technique for developing social-personal skills (Wehman, Renzaglia, & Bates, 1985). Factors that contribute to the success of modeling include the vividness of the model, the use of high-status and competent peers as models, the pairing of reinforcement and modeling, and the highlighting of relevant cues in the modeled situation. As a general rule, persons with severe disabilities should be coached to observe the model, and the situation should be as realistic as possible. It may prove advantageous to use peer tutors, peer buddies, or special friends as models for social-personal behavior.

Behavior **rehearsal**, or role playing, involves practicing positive social-personal behaviors acquired from modeling. Because persons with severe disabilities learn best by doing, behavior rehearsal is a critical ingredient in social-personal development. For maximum effectiveness, rehearsal must occur in the natural environment.

After the person with severe disabilities has rehearsed the social-personal skill, **feedback** should be given on the adequacy of his or her performance. Feedback typically includes reinforcing consequences.

After rehearsal and feedback, the person with severe disabilities must **practice** the skill **in the natural environment** to maintain and generalize it to a number of different situations. It is important to vary the relevant cues for the behavior in the natural environment.

Conclusion

Appropriate social-personal behavior is an intricate component in virtually every aspect of a person's life. For persons with severe disabilities, inadequate social-personal skills make integration into the natural environment much more difficult. Lack of culturally acceptable social responses often distinguishes persons with severe disabilities from persons without disabilities. There is no doubt that social skill deficits significantly interfere with integration and normalization.

It does not have to be that way! Persons with severe disabilities can develop acceptable and normal social-personal skills. They can become integrated into society. This goal requires consistent and dedicated efforts by parents, teachers, and other service providers. It requires teaching skills the person will use in the natural environment. And it requires the maintenance and generalization of those social-personal skills.

1. Unlike the skills typically taught to persons with severe disabilities, acceptable social-personal skills are determined by the social context in which they occur.   **Summary**

2. Social-personal skills are those behaviors that maximize direct social interactions with others and are perceived as socially appropriate by peers and significant others.

3.   Social-personal behaviors facilitate direct and indirect contact with other people. These behaviors encompass four areas: (1) grooming, hygiene, and personal appearance, (2) social interaction and social involvement, (3) self-development, and (4) sexual awareness.

4.   Grooming, hygiene, and personal appearance skills are critical skills directly linked to social integration, normalization, and acceptance. They are the skills involved in looking after and caring for oneself, one's dress, and one's appearance.

5.   Social interaction and social involvement skills range from manners to greeting skills and from the elimination of stereotypic behavior to accepting criticism. There are three groups of these skills: (1) self-related behaviors, (2) self-management behaviors, and (3) integrative behaviors.

6.   Social validity may be used as a basis for selecting the social interaction and social involvement behaviors to teach. Social validity identifies social-personal skills that are normal, acceptable, and valuable.

7.   Stranger training instructs students about how to behave when they encounter potentially dangerous, harmful, or unscrupulous strangers.

8.   Self-development skills are those necessary for personal achievement and satisfactory relationships with other people. There are seven components: (1) achieving self-awareness, (2) acquiring self-confidence, (3) developing socially responsible behavior, (4) maintaining adequate interpersonal skills, (5) achieving independence, (6) developing problem-solving skills, and (7) communicating adequately with others.

9.   Sexual awareness includes the tasks and knowledge of traditional sex education plus factors historically considered outside the realm of sex education. Sexual awareness has six components: (1) male puberty, (2) female puberty, (3) social relations with the same and the opposite sex, (4) human reproduction, (5) fertility regulation, and (6) marriage.

10.   Many professionals argue that the traditional method of developing social-personal skills is not always effective and cost efficient. Several alternative methods have been proposed.

11.   The self-regulatory model requires that persons with severe disabilities engage in a series of social-personal responses, evaluate the appropriateness of their responses, and if necessary alter their behavior without being cued by a person in authority.

12.   Self-regulation requires five competencies: (1) self-monitoring, (2) self-standard setting, (3) self-evaluation, (4) self-reward, and (5) self-delaying of gratification. Persons who can self-delay gratification can respond effectively to varied environmental situations without specific cues from others. To self-regulate, a person with severe disabilities must be able to (1) detect and define the task, (2) arrive at alternative ways to complete it, (3) implement an alternative, and (4) assess the outcome.

13. The behavioral-analytic model prioritizes the skills that would help a person with severe disabilities to function in a normal and acceptable manner with other persons. The procedural sequence of this model has three stages: (1) situational analysis, (2) response enumeration, and (3) response evaluation.

14. In the situational analysis stage, a large sample of generic and specific social situations is identified and prioritized. In the response enumeration stage, all potential responses to the prioritized situations are identified. The response evaluation stage determines the most appropriate response to each situation. This response is then taught to the person with severe disabilities.

15. The normative analysis model determines the frequency, duration, and appropriateness of specific social-personal behaviors in a particular setting to enable persons with severe disabilities to function as normally as possible in that setting at that time.

16. The ecological model identifies acceptable social-personal behavior standards for persons with severe disabilities in a variety of environments (i.e., domestic, leisure, general community, vocational, and school), from interviews with significant others.

17. Three strategies have been utilized to facilitate social-personal skill development in persons with severe disabilities: the environmental approach, the consequence approach, and the response approach.

18. The environmental approach holds that planned activities in the natural environment have a beneficial and powerful influence on the acquisition of social-personal skills by persons with severe disabilities. Exposure to more socially competent models facilitates the development of more appropriate and normal skills.

19. The consequence approach holds that the occurrence and frequency of desirable social-personal behaviors depend on reinforcing consequences. Preferably, reinforcing consequences result naturally from performing appropriate behaviors. When natural events are not reinforcing enough, additional consequences may be arranged. Both externally administered reinforcers and self-administered reinforcers are used.

20. The response approach to developing social-personal behaviors has four steps: (1) modeling, (2) rehearsal, (3) feedback, and (4) practice in the natural environment. Modeling uses live models, audio or video tapes, and simulations to show how to perform a targeted social-personal skill. Behavior rehearsal involves practicing the skills taught by modeling. After rehearsal in the natural environment, feedback is provided on the adequacy of the performance. Practice of the skill maintains it and generalizes it to different environments in the community.

CHAPTER 9

Transfer, Generalization, and Maintenance Problems in Persons with Severe Disabilities

(Courtesy of Lynda Atherton.)

TRANSFER, GENERALIZATION, AND MAINTENANCE: AN OVERVIEW

After weeks of instruction, Earl Roy had learned all the steps in an age-appropriate, leisure skill: playing an electronic pinball machine independently. Earl Roy could drop a quarter into the coin slot, keep each ball in play for at least fifteen seconds, and flip each ball at least once. After Earl Roy was proficient in this skill at school, Ms. Lutz, his teacher, took him to the Land of Oz, a video arcade in the local shipping mall. At the Land of Oz, Earl Roy was not able to put a quarter into the slot or play the pinball machine.

Ms. Stafford wanted to teach her high school students with severe disabilities how to board and ride a public bus. In her classroom she arranged eight chairs in a double row and put one chair at the head of the row with a small cup next to it. In this simulation, one student was to "board the bus," drop a token into the small cup, and take a vacant seat. The aide would "drive" to the "next bus stop," and another student would "board the bus." After each student became proficient in this task, Mrs. Stafford took four students to a bus stop in the community. To her surprise, the students had a great deal of difficulty boarding the bus; they could not drop the tokens into the slot; they had trouble selecting a seat; and one of the students fell on his way to a seat.

Why were the students in these two examples unable to perform the skills in a new environment? Although this question has long puzzled teachers, recently it has attracted the attention of researchers. A number of investigators have identified transfer, generalization, and maintenance as the heart of the problem. Although often used as synonyms, these intertwined terms have subtle differences in meaning. Essentially, the most encompassing term is transfer. A component of transfer is generalization, and maintenance is a component of generalization.

Transfer is the process of causing a learned task to be applied to a similar subsequent task by *varying either the stimulus or the response conditions* (Crowder, 1976). In the typical transfer task, the teacher tries to have students actively apply a previous learning experience to a new but similar situation. To illustrate, Nash, a 9-year-old boy with severe disabilities, exhibited a number of self-injurious behaviors such as head-banging, self-hitting, and self-biting. Using a treatment program, Ms. Newsom, Nash's teacher, eliminated these behaviors in the classroom. She then extended the treatment program to other environments in the school: gymnasium, cafeteria, hallways, and outside play areas. In these environments other persons (i.e., cafeteria workers, the principal, other teachers, students) were enlisted to deliver reinforcers to Nash.

In this example, Ms. Newsom systematically varied the stimulus conditions by extending the treatment program to other locations. She also systematically varied the response conditions by requiring other persons to provide reinforcement.

Generalization entails causing a learned behavior to be applied in a new situation *by varying the stimulus conditions.* It is based on a connection between a behavior and discernible, relevant features of a particular training condition. Appropriate, desirable behavior then occurs in a nontraining situation due to that situation's similarity to the training conditions (Stokes & Osnes, 1988). In subsequent situations with the discernible, relevant features of the training conditions, those features will elicit a similar response (Albin & Horner, 1988). The greater the similarity in features, the greater the prospects of generalization (Houston, 1976). Consider, for example, teaching Leigh to use an unfamiliar fast food restaurant after he had learned to use McDonald's. A number of discernible, relevant features are common to all fast food restaurants (e.g., food is ordered by the patron at a counter, food is placed on the tray by the salesperson, food is carried to the table by the patron, food wrappers and containers are discarded in the waste receptacle by the patron). These features form a stimulus class that includes any restaurant with the features and excludes any restaurant without them. To begin, the trainer teaches Leigh to recognize the discernible, relevant features of all fast food restaurants. Next, Leigh is taught a precise responding pattern that he could use successfully in any fast food restaurant. Finally, he is taught enough about the stimulus class so that he would not walk into a sit-down restaurant or a cafeteria and place an order with the person at the cash register.

Maintenance is causing performance of a learned behavior to continue beyond the training period by varying the conditions of practice (Drabman, Hammer, & Rosenbaum, 1979; Mank & Horner, 1987). It is the stable and sustained performance of a learned targeted behavior. A behavior is maintained when it is performed over time and across the range of stimulus situations the learner encounters in day-to-day activities (e.g., new people, weather changes, different environments) (Horner, Bellamy, & Colvin, 1984; Horner & Billingsley, 1988). To illustrate the difference between maintenance and generalization, suppose that Mr. Robinson has taught Randy to walk across the street in the crosswalk in front of the school. At this point, Mr. Robinson is not concerned with teaching Randy to cross other streets. Therefore, training was specific to that particular crosswalk. When Randy continues to use that crosswalk during rainy and snowy days, when he is alone or other children are crossing, when traffic is heavy or light, Mr. Robinson can conclude that Randy is maintaining this skill. But, if he wanted to generalize that skill, Mr. Robinson would teach Randy to recognize the discernible and relevant features of all crosswalks, have Randy apply this skill to other similar streets with crosswalks, and eventually have him apply it across the instructional universe to "all streets in town with crosswalks."

The basic transfer and generalization task involves two stages. The individual first masters a task. Then he or she attempts to apply that task to a somewhat similar situation. In other words, the individual learns to respond to a specific set of conditions; thereafter, a similar set of conditions will elicit a similar pattern of responses. The greater the similarity between the two conditions, the greater the tendency to elicit the originally learned behavior. In the earlier example, after Earl Roy failed to transfer his skills from the training site to the Land of Oz, Ms. Lutz isolated the discernible and relevant features in the Land of Oz and duplicated those features in the training site. On his second visit to the Land of Oz, Earl Roy was able to drop the quarter into the slot, keep each ball in play for fifteen seconds, and flip each ball at least once. Why was Earl Roy unsuccessful on his first visit to the Land of Oz but successful on his return visit? The answer obviously hinges on his recognition of the similarity in features between the training site and the Land of Oz.

It is abundantly clear that the principles of transfer, generalization, and maintenance have been successfully applied to persons with severe disabilities. Now there is greater interest in identifying the conditions that contribute to transfer, generalization, and maintenance and the variables that affect the **generalization gradient**. Among the most important variables are: (1) extended training, (2) partial reinforcement, (3) motivation, (4) experience, and (5) discrimination.

The Effect of Extended Training

What is the effect on generalization of increasing reinforced responses to the training condition? For instance, Theo has been taught to eat at Steve's Diner. Is he more likely to generalize his eating skills to a different diner if there is an increase in reinforcement for eating at Steve's Diner? There is often an initial increase in generalization. When Theo first received reinforcement, he did not recognize a number of highly distinctive features of Steve's Diner. Hence, he did not distinguish clearly between Steve's Diner and Greg's Cafe. But, as Theo's training and reinforcement continue, Steve's Diner becomes more distinctive to him, and he becomes much less likely to identify the features common to all diners. Generalization then decreases. Thus, there is an inverse relationship between generalization and reinforced responding to the training situation. Beyond **training to criterion**, as reinforced responding increases, generalization decreases, according to research data from a variety of situations (Houston, 1976; Salzberg & Villani, 1983; Stokes & Osnes, 1986, 1988).

This has important implications for teachers. It strongly suggests that training beyond task mastery may hinder generalization to other settings dramatically. Many researchers suggest that, once task mastery is acquired, generalization must be actively taught (Guevremont, Osnes, & Stokes, 1988; Hill, Wehman, & Horst, 1982; Pancsofar & Bates, 1985).

The Effect of Partial Reinforcement

What is the effect on generalization when a person's behavior is partially or inconsistently reinforced? Suppose when Matthew tries to use a stereo record player, he is sometimes rewarded (music) and sometimes not (silence). Is he more or less likely to generalize his behavior to other similar situations? Research data suggest that generalization is more extensive following **partial reinforcement** (Houston, 1976; Koegel & Koegel, 1988; Rhode, Morgan, & Young, 1983; Schreibman, Kohlenberg, & Britten, 1986). Matthew is likely to generalize his record playing skills to other situations more quickly if he is partially reinforced than if he is continuously reinforced. Thus, it is more appropriate for the teacher of students with severe disabilities to use intermittent reinforcement, at least after the skill is acquired, to foster task generalization.

The Effect of Motivation

Will a response acquired under conditions of high motivation result in more or less generalization than a response acquired with low motivation? Daniel has a great desire to listen to a cassette tape player at home, but he has almost no desire to put his dirty clothes in the hamper at home. If these two tasks were taught to Daniel in a training environment (e.g., school), what are the prospects that each would be generalized to the home? A high level of motivation tends to foster generalization, and low motivation tends to hinder it. Thus, Daniel is more likely to generalize his cassette tape playing than putting his dirty clothes in the hamper. The experimental results appear to be consistent that increased desire increases transfer and generalization (Goldstein & Wickstrom, 1986; Kirkland & Caughlin-Carver, 1982; Koegel & Mentis, 1985).

The Effect of Experience

What is the effect of prior experience on an individual's prospects of generalization? Once a day Greg buys a soda from the vending machine at his neighborhood grocery store. Because it is very old, it is quite different from any other soda vending machine in the community. While Greg is extremely proficient with this machine, he has no experience with any other soda machine. Will Greg generalize more or less than a person who has been exposed to many different types of vending machines all along? There are essentially two general positions concerning this issue. Some professionals argue that the inexperienced Greg will respond equally to all vending machines. The generalization gradient will be flat. They argue that the stimulus dimension (e.g., a dimension of vending machines varying in similarity to one another) does not "exist" for Greg until he has had experience with it. Until Greg has had a chance to distinguish among or compare soda vending machines, all vending machines will be equivalent to him. He will perceive all machines, including the one in his neighborhood, as the same and will respond to them identically. Other professionals argue that Greg will be less likely to respond to other soda vending machines even though he has never had the opportunity to experience various points along the stimulus dimension. They contend that the gradient generated by the inexperienced Greg would be extremely steep, not flat.

Some evidence supports the first position. In a classical experiment, Peterson (1963) raised ducks in yellow light (589 nanometers, or nm, in wavelength). They did not have the opportunity to distinguish one wavelength from another. A control group was raised in normal light. Both groups were then trained to peck a key illuminated by 589 nm of light. Next, generalization was tested by illuminating the key with eight different wavelengths, ranging from 490 nm to 650 nm. The ducks raised in yellow light generalized perfectly, or failed to discriminate among the various test stimuli. The controls, on the other hand, sharply limited their responses to stimuli that were similar to the training conditions. These findings, replicated by a number of other researchers, support the argument that experience with only one dimension of a stimulus is important in producing generalization.

Other data indicate that steep rather than flat gradients may be obtained in the absence of prior exposure to many points along the stimulus dimension (Borkowski & Varnhagen, 1984; Storey, Bates, & Hanson, 1984). These investigators have found steep gradients under certain rather specific conditions when an individual has experienced only a single stimulus condition. The conclusion that can be drawn from the conflicting data is that prior experience with many stimulus conditions may not be absolutely essential for generalization but it helps. The inexperienced Greg may be less likely to obtain sodas from other vending machines, but he is more likely to try other machines if he has prior experience with a variety of vending machines. Thus, to maximize generalization, teachers should expose students with severe disabilities to as many dimensions as possible of the condition to be generalized.

The Effect of Discrimination

Generalization and discrimination may well be opposite sides of the same coin. Besides being complementary processes, they have an inverse relationship, so that an increase in one is matched by a decrease in the other. A decrease in generalization is a decrease in the tendency to give the same response in similar conditions. An increase in discrimination is the same thing—the tendency to restrict responses to one condition chosen from a set of similar conditions. Discrimination is a breakdown in the tendency to generalize.

The following example may illustrate. Doug learned how to turn on the radio in the training site. He was taught to discriminate the radio from other items in the training site and to discriminate the operating features on the radio. After the training, Doug correctly turned on the radio in his room, using both discrimination and generalization. He first discriminated the radio from the other items in his room, then discriminated the operating features of the radio, and finally generalized the skills he had learned in the training site. In this example, as in most cases, discrimination is required in order to generalize a task. The example shows the complementary relationship between the two processes. But suppose that Doug "overdiscriminates" the radio in the training site. He may not recognize an object as a radio then unless it is identical to the radio in the training site and unless the setting has many of the same stimuli as the training site. As Doug receives more reinforcement for use of the training radio, he will almost naturally develop additional discrimination and thus become less likely to generalize this skill to the operation of other radios, even if they are physically and functionally very similar. This generalization-discrimination continuum strongly reinforces an earlier point: for generalization to occur, it must be actively taught to individuals with severe disabilities.

IMPORTANCE OF GENERALIZATION FOR PERSONS WITH SEVERE DISABILITIES

For practical and ethical reasons, teachers of students with severe disabilities have recently increased their use of generalization. Abundant documentation clearly indicates that such persons can generalize a previously learned skill to a new or different situation. Generalization has been used for skills from street crossing to operating soap dispensers and from leisure activity training to social interaction training. A brief example may illustrate its importance. Ms. Cole has taught Ginger all the steps necessary to obtain a soda from a vending machine. After analyzing all the soda machines in the community, Ms. Cole identified five types. Rather than teaching Ginger to operate each vending machine independently, she wants Ginger to identify the common features of all the vending machines so that she can operate them based on her knowledge of operating one type.

This example illustrates how generalization can save valuable instructional time. If Ginger can generalize her skill to other types of vending machines, Ms. Cole can use her time to teach Ginger other skills. Furthermore, Ginger's ability to generalize to other soda vending machines may develop her proficiency in an area in which she did not receive any instruction, for instance, operating a candy vending machine or perhaps even a video arcade game. Generalization also has important ramifications for future integration. As new technologies develop, today's objects and equipment change. Soda vending machines today differ from those of a decade ago, and those of the twenty-first century will be dramatically different. If an individual with severe disabilities is going to adapt to a changing society, he or she must be able to generalize.

The growing emphasis on teaching functional, community-referenced skills to persons with severe disabilities has heightened the need for instructional techniques for generalization. Paradoxically, some functional skills, such as crossing a street, are potentially dangerous until an individual has mastered

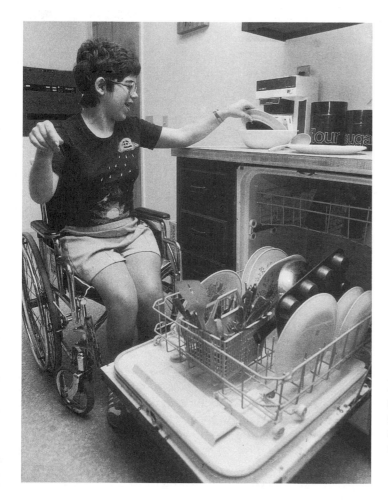

FIGURE 9.1

Generalization extends acquired skills to other conditions and situations, saving valuable instructional time for new learning.

(Courtesy of Bohdan Hrynewych, Southern Light.)

them. How can this important functional skill be safely taught to a person with severe disabilities? Fortunately, the answer is through generalization. In a study by Matson (1980), students were taught street crossing skills on a life-size, mock intersection. After the simulated training, the skill was applied to an actual intersection, and later generalized to other nontrained intersections (Horner, Jones, & Williams, 1985; Martchetti, McCartney, Drain, Hooper, & Dix, 1983).

Thus far, the discussion of generalization has been limited to its application across nontrained situations. But skill maintenance is a component of stimulus generalization. Sometimes called *generalization over time* or *class one generalization,* skill maintenance is application of a skill to conditions essentially the same as the training condition. The maintenance program is a continuation of the formal treatment program after the skill is learned to criterion. The intent of maintenance is to ensure that the learned behavior is stable and

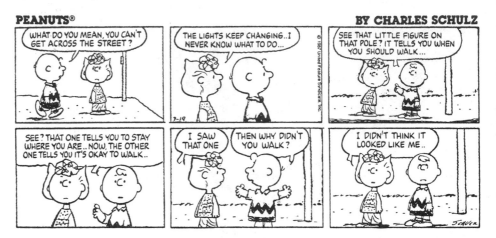

FIGURE 9.2

Crossing an intersection is a complex skill that requires the person to exercise a high degree of safety and caution.

(Courtesy of United Feature Syndicate, Inc.)

sustained, not to apply it to nontrained conditions. Suppose that Alex is being taught to obtain and eat his lunch appropriately in the high school cafeteria. Mr. Tankersley, his teacher, has taught Alex to go through the cafeteria line, select a tray, place a napkin, knife, fork, and spoon on the tray, place a plate of lunch, a dessert, and a container of milk on the tray, select and sit in a vacant chair, and eat his lunch with good manners at the table. Alex has mastered this skill to criterion. If Mr. Tankersley now wants to sustain and solidify Alex's school cafeteria behavior, he will use a maintenance program. At present he has no desire to extend this skill to a community cafeteria or restaurant (i.e., to generalize it to a new setting).

An important and often overlooked factor to assess before the treatment-then-maintenance sequence is whether the maintenance procedures alone can produce the desired behavior or whether additional treatment or reinforcement is required. Goetz, Gee, and Sailor (1985) taught Chuck, a 12-year-old with severe disabilities, to make toast using a two-phase sequence. In phase one, Chuck selected the appropriate sequenced card from an array of three cards. In phase two, Chuck made toast according to the sequence specified in the cards. Although Chuck learned and performed the task to criterion, the researchers noticed that he could not maintain the skill after training. Once Chuck was retaught the skill, he was quickly able to perform the task to criterion. Thus, it appears that the only way Chuck could "maintain" the toast-making skill was to perform it continuously, or as Drabman, Hammer, and Rosenbaum (1979) put it, in skill maintenance, there must be "contingencies for as long as the behavior change is desired" (p. 209).

FIGURE 9.3

Since persons with severe disabilities require intensive interventions to effect small amounts of behavior change, generalization offers an economical method for them to develop proficiency in a number of functional skills.

(Courtesy of W. Densies Ward.)

COMPONENTS OF GENERALIZATION

Although a wealth of research has documented the effectiveness of generalization with different populations and in different settings, only recently has there been a serious attempt to apply generalization to persons with severe disabilities. Since they require intensive interventions to effect small amounts of behavior change, generalization offers an economical method for them to develop proficiency in a number of functional skills (Albin & Horner, 1988; Horner, Eberhard, & Sheehan, 1986; Pancsofar & Bates, 1985; Snell & Browder, 1986). In a classical study on generalization, Drabman, Hammer, and Rosenbaum (1979) specified four major categories of generalization: (1) generalization across time, (2) generalization across settings, (3) generalization across behaviors, and (4) generalization across subjects.

Generalization across Time

Generalization across time, or maintenance, is a continuation of the behavior change after the program contingencies have been withdrawn. The purpose is to maintain the behavior once the skill has been learned to criterion and the formal treatment program has been discontinued. Usually, the maintenance procedure has three stages. In stage one, the trainer obtains a baseline level of the behavior. In stage two, the training program is conducted. In stage three, the program returns to the baseline conditions. Behavior maintenance is measured by comparing the original baseline to the second baseline when treatment is withdrawn. An example is a study conducted by Breen, Haring, Pitts-Conway, and Gaylord-Ross (1985), analyzing the social interaction between workers with severe disabilities and fellow employees without disabilities on the job site during break. In stage one, the baseline phase, none of the employees with severe disabilities exhibited any social interaction skills. In the treatment phase (stage two), all four employees with severe disabilities exceeded or reached the training criterion of socially interacting 83 percent of the time during break. In phase three, the return to baseline stage, the interaction percentage dropped to 27 percent. The difference between stages one and three illustrates the maintenance achieved by the program.

Generalization across Settings

Generalization across settings is continuation of a behavior change in another environment from the one in which treatment occurred. The criterion for determining whether the new environment is the same or different is the presence or absence of the salient discriminative stimuli present in the treatment environment. This criterion occasionally requires an arbitrary judgment of what constitutes "salient discriminative stimuli." Of course, a change from a student's home to the school or from the school to the general community is readily considered a change in environments. However, not all changes are so obvious. Suppose a different trainer is brought into the treatment environment. Would that constitute a change in settings? According to Drabman, Hammer, and Rosenbaum (1979), a different trainer would constitute a change in the "salient discriminative stimuli," and thus a different setting, even though treatment took place in the same physical environment. Since generalization across settings (e.g., from school to community) is of prime importance in the education of persons with severe disabilities, every attempt should be made to maximize it.

Generalization across Behaviors

Generalization across behaviors is application of a change to a behavior other than the one specifically targeted for change. The criterion used for judging whether a behavior is the same or different is whether the generalized behavior can be defined independently of the treatment behavior. If a targeted behavior, for instance, was inappropriate behaviors, then changes in any behavior contained in the operational definition of inappropriate behaviors (e.g., self-injurious behaviors, stereotypic behaviors) would not be classified as generalization. In contrast, if the targeted behavior was specifically self-injurious behaviors, then changes in other forms of inappropriate behaviors (e.g., stereotypic behaviors) would be classified as generalization. Suppose, Leo, a 15-year-old with severe disabilities, was socially reinforced for playing with an electronic pinball machine. Playing with the machine was the targeted behavior; it was the behavior the trainer wanted to increase. While playing with the electronic pinball machine, Leo's social skills (e.g., interacting with others, talking to others, exhibiting proper behavior at the arcade) likewise increased. In this example, the increased social skills constitute the generalized behavior.

Generalization across Subjects

Generalization across subjects is a behavior change in a nontargeted person which is similar to the behavior change in the targeted person. Three criteria must be fulfilled in this form of generalization. First, no contingencies may be applied to the nontargeted subject; second, the generalized behavior in the nontargeted subject has to occur after the initiation of treatment in the targeted subject; and third, the behavior change has to be similar to the treatment program provided to the targeted subject. Suppose Walter accompanies Leo to the video arcade. Walter has never seen an electronic pinball machine, let alone play with one. Ms. Carson, their teacher, is attempting to generalize Leo's pinball machine playing from the treatment setting to the arcade. She brought Walter along to generalize some of his social skills. After watching Leo play for a few moments, Walter decides, on his own, to play with the pinball machine. The pinball playing behavior has been generalized across subjects.

GENERALIZATION STRATEGIES

The four types of generalization do not describe how generalization may be used by persons with severe disabilities. Stokes and Baer (1977), in a study destined to become a classic, conducted an extensive review of applied behavior analysis research and described nine strategies that have been used to facilitate generalization. White (1983), expanding on their work, observed twelve generalization approaches in research studies assessing generalization. Arranged in hierarchical order, their combined strategies are: (1) train and hope, (2) train in natural settings, (3) train to sequential modification, (4) train to natural maintaining contingencies, (5) train sufficient exemplars, (6) train loosely, (7) train to indiscriminable contingencies, (8) train common stimuli, (9) train multiple case, (10) train general case, (11) train to mediate generalization, and (12) train to generalization.

Train and hope

Train and hope, as the name suggests, is a strategy used after treatment and behavior change has occurred; generalization across time, settings, behaviors, or subjects is hoped for and passively planned but not actively pursued. The trainer hopes that generalization will occur but does not explicitly implement

it. This method is by far the most common, accounting for almost half the cases of applied generalization (Liberty, 1984). Most train and hope cases involve maintenance, and according to Stokes and Baer approximately 90 percent of all train and hope studies report successful maintenance or generalization. Yet it should not be concluded that the train and hope paradigm is a highly successful generalization strategy. Two factors may account for the high reported success. First, some researchers may simply not report their generalization data if measurement indicates that generalization did not occur. Second, if generalization clearly did not occur and was deemed important, the trainer may have provided additional programming to ensure generalization. The rate of successful train and hope generalization may be significantly lower than reported.

Train in Natural Settings

Train in natural settings is a behavior change procedure carried out in the environment followed by a hope phase, identical to that in train and hope. The only difference from train and hope is that the training occurs in the natural environment rather than a training site such as a classroom (Stokes & Baer, 1977). The method of generalization is passive rather than active. While the success of this strategy was not reported, it is probably slightly more effective than train and hope.

Train to Sequential Modification

Train to sequential modification is a two-step strategy. In step one, behavior change is effected, and generalization across time, settings, behaviors, or subjects is planned but not pursued. The sufficiency of generalization is then assessed. If generalization is absent or deficient, step two, additional training and generalization, is initiated. Usually the second attempt at generalization incorporates more components than the first. In a sense, this strategy is an extension of the train and hope method: it consists of a first train and hope sequence, an assessment, and a second train and hope sequence (Liberty, 1984). Ms. Williams has taught Kevin to wash his hands to criterion. In the generalization assessment phase, she found that Kevin was unable to wash his hands outside of the treatment environment. Ms. Williams then provided additional training. After the second training phase, Kevin was able to wash his hands outside the treatment environment.

Train to Natural Maintaining Contingencies

Train to natural maintaining contingencies is a generalization strategy in which the behavior change is maintained in the new environment by natural reinforcers in that environment (Stokes & Osnes, 1988). Ms. Wapner taught Robert to play foosball to criterion in the training environment. She took Robert and Tim, his special friend, to Aladdin's Lamp, a local pinball arcade. At Aladdin's Lamp, Robert not only beat Tim in foosball but also beat Vallery, Tim's girlfriend. When Robert, Tim, and Vallery left Aladdin's Lamp, Robert was so excited that he asked Tim and Vallery if they wanted to go back to Aladdin's Lamp the next day after school. In the treatment phase, Ms. Wapner had reinforced Robert for appropriate foosball playing. Even though her reinforcement was removed in the generalization phase, Robert's foosball playing skills are likely to remain because of the natural reinforcing contingencies present (e.g., the pleasant feeling Robert gets when playing foosball). Because reinforcers are already present in the natural environment, this behavior is likely to be sharpened, refined, and generalized to different conditions and situations.

Unfortunately, for some skills there are no natural reinforcing contingencies. Self-care skills such as tooth-brushing do not have easily discernible natural reinforcers. Contrived or redesigned "natural" reinforcers may be developed at times. For instance, Horner, Jones, and Williams (1985) taught three persons with severe disabilities to cross up to twenty street intersections by selecting intersections the learners naturally used to get where they wanted to go (i.e., to school or work).

Train Sufficient Exemplars

Train sufficient exemplars is a strategy through which generalization may be maximized if the environment contains a number of discernible and relevant exemplars that were present in the training (Stokes & Osnes, 1988). (Albin and

Horner [1988] described **exemplars** as teaching examples present during the training; they are used to teach both how to perform the targeted skill and the set of conditions in which to perform it.) What is a sufficient number of exemplars? If teaching one exemplar of a skill results in mastery of that exemplar only with no generalization, the obvious route is to introduce another exemplar, and then another, and then another, until generalization occurs (Albin & Horner, 1988). An example is a study conducted by Stokes, Baer, and Jackson (1974) on the generalization of children's greeting responses not established through training. Varying the features of the setting by introducing another trainer, Stokes, Baer, and Jackson found that generalization was achieved. This raises an important question about the structure of the exemplars needed to maximize generalization. Apparently, diversity of exemplars is the rule to follow for maximum generalization. Diversity should be sufficient to reflect the dimensions of the desired generalization. However, diversity can also be an enemy: too much diversity and not enough similarity of exemplars may reduce generalization gains. A sufficient combination of similar and diverse exemplars clearly maximizes generalization efforts.

Train Loosely

Train loosely is a strategy of reducing the discernible and relevant features of the training by deliberately incorporating diversity. The diversity of the training conditions should result in greater similarity between the treatment setting and the generalization setting, which should then facilitate generalization (Stokes & Osnes, 1988). As mentioned earlier, generalization and discrimination may be inversely related, thus the less discrimination is taught to the learner, the greater the prospects for generalization. In this procedure, times, settings, behaviors, and subjects are intentionally varied from treatment period to treatment period. While this strategy has produced the greatest amount of generalization (White, 1983) in persons without disabilities, it may not be an effective generalization method for persons with severe disabilities (Wehman, Renzaglia, & Bates, 1985).

Train to Indiscriminable Contingencies

Train to indiscriminable contingencies is a strategy in which the learner cannot readily and reliably differentiate the features of the treatment setting from the features of the generalization setting. Predictability of consequences enables a person to discriminate occasions and behaviors that will be followed by positive consequences from those that will not. Most training situations want the learner to stay under the control of the training procedures. But in this generalization strategy, consequences are made progressively less discriminable until the learner cannot tell which occasions and behaviors will be reinforced and which will not (Dunlap & Plienis, 1988; Stokes & Osnes, 1988).

Since it is impossible to discriminate reinforcement conditions from nonreinforcement conditions, this strategy should result in greater maintenance and

FIGURE 9.5

An environment may contain a number of discernible and relevant exemplars that can enhance generalization.

(Courtesy of the Illinois School for the Visually Handicapped.)

generalization. The strength of the strategy may be illustrated by an experiment conducted by Schwarz and Hawkins (1970), in which the behavior of a sixth-grade student was videotaped during classes. After each school day, the student was shown the tape of only the math class and awarded reinforcers according to how often certain behaviors were evident on that tape. Although reinforcers were awarded only on the basis of the math class, desirable improvements were observed in the other classes as well. The success of generalization in this study may well be attributable to the partly indiscriminable nature of the reinforcement contingency. While delayed reinforcement may result in greater generalization with some populations, it has thus far proved inefficient in persons with severe disabilities.

Train Common Stimuli

Train common stimuli is a generalization strategy in which the training program contains the same stimuli typically encountered in the natural environment. If stimuli are common in both the training and the generalization settings, and if those stimuli play a key role in the training procedures, their presence should facilitate generalization of the behaviors across settings (Fowler, 1988; Stokes & Osnes, 1988). To program for generalization, various aspects of the natural environment must be systematically introduced into the training environment to maximize generalization.

One way to control for the salient features in both the training and generalized settings is through social stimuli. Peers, parents, siblings, and teachers are examples of social stimuli associated with certain behaviors (e.g., polite conversation, instruction, directions). They are likely to function as discriminative stimuli if they have frequently and actively been present or have participated in training procedures in which certain behaviors were reinforced. Generalization is programmed by systematically introducing the social stimuli into relevant nontraining environments. Peers are particularly logical social stimuli because they often are naturally present in diverse environments.

Train Multiple Case

Train multiple case is a generalization strategy in which a person is trained to use items typical of a subcategory or set, and then is asked to generalize to subcategory items that were not part of the training set. In this procedure, set membership is narrowly conceptualized; the set members must be structurally and functionally similar (Carr & Kologinsky, 1983; Horner & Billingsley, 1988; White, 1985). To illustrate, Anthony's teacher, Ms. Adkins, wants to teach him to use the soap dispensers in Pasadena. She determines that three types of soap dispensers are used in Pasadena. In the first type, soap is obtained by pushing up the spout directly beneath the dispenser. In the second type, soap is obtained by pushing in a knob above the spout; the spout moves with the knob, so Anthony has to move his hands with the spout. In the third type, soap is obtained by pulling a lever toward the front of the dispenser behind the spout. Ms. Adkins trains Anthony on each type of soap dispenser independent of the other two. While individual dispensers vary in size, shape, and color, Ms. Adkins teaches Anthony to use two or three dispensers of the first type. After Anthony generalizes that type of dispenser into Pasadena, he is taught a set of the second type of dispensers. After he generalizes that type into the other settings, he is taught a set of the third type, and he generalizes that type into Pasadena. The basic intent of this generalization strategy is to teach the person the commonalities of a subcategory that can be extrapolated to all members of that subcategory.

Train General Case

Train general case is a generalization strategy in which a person is trained to use a particular category of items and is then asked to generalize the skill to category members that were not part of the training process. This strategy conceptualizes category membership more broadly. In train multiple case, each subcategory of soap dispensers was taught independently. In train general case they would all be taught as one generic category (Albin & Horner, 1988; Horner & Billingsley, 1988). To illustrate, Betsy was trained to use three fast-food restaurants determined to be typical of those in Shelbyville (e.g., McDonald's, Taco Bell, Captain D's). After treatment, Betsy was taken to another fast-food restaurant in Shelbyville, Burger King, with the expectation that she would generalize and apply the skills learned in the training to the untrained restaurant. At Burger King Betsy was expected to purchase the meal she wanted, carry it to an unoccupied table, sit down, eat the meal, and discard the papers and cartons in a trash receptacle. The basic intent of this procedure is for the person to generalize behaviors based on category commonalities.

Train to Mediate Generalization

Train to mediate generalization is a two-step strategy. The first step is establishing a trained response that is likely to be used with other conditions and situations. This response is referred to as a **mediator**. In the second step, the mediator is used as a sufficient commonality between treatment and generalization (Guevremont, Osnes, & Stokes, 1988; Koegel & Koegel, 1988; Stokes & Osnes, 1988). The most commonly used mediator is language. To illustrate, Ms. Rogers has taught Jason to order a cheeseburger, french fries, and a strawberry milk shake from a fast-food restaurant, Burger Heaven. After he has eaten, Ms. Rogers asks him to describe his behavior from the time he entered Burger Heaven to the time he left. If he accurately describes the process, he is rewarded. Reinforcement is not contingent on Jason's behavior in Burger Heaven but rather on the mediator, the verbal report of his behavior. The language mediator serves as a salient common stimulus in both treatment and generalization phases.

Train to Generalization

Train to generalization is a strategy in which the learner generalizes from one untrained generalized situation to another untrained situation. The person is generalizing a skill recently acquired through generalization. For instance, Sherry was taught to grocery shop at Allen's Shop-and-Save Market. The treatment phase consisted of teaching Sherry to shop only at this particular market. A few days later, Sherry passed Fenton's Grocery Store, an unfamiliar facility. Thinking of something she needed, she went into Fenton's and purchased the item. In effect, Sherry generalized grocery purchasing skills from Allen's to Fenton's. Connected to Fenton's was a large department store, Springfield Bargain Center, which was structurally very similar to Fenton's. The color scheme, lighting, carts, checkout counters, and music were all the same. On impulse, Sherry went into the unfamiliar department store. Seeing some items she needed, Sherry purchased them. In effect, she generalized to the Springfield Bargain Center from Fenton's Grocery Store, from an untrained condition to another untrained condition.

While "generalized generalization" typically does not occur in persons with severe disabilities, it is possible to facilitate this strategy. If transfer does not occur after a behavior is taught, the trainer can tell the learner about the

FIGURE 9.6

Besides being an effective method for developing community, recreational, and social skills, generalization is an effective method for developing such domestic skills as cooking and preparing meals.

(Courtesy of the Illinois School for the Visually Impaired.)

possibility of generalization and specifically ask him or her to apply the recently acquired skill to an unfamiliar situation. This technique is often referred to as **train to instructional generalization.** For train to generalization to be effective, it must be systematically taught to persons with severe disabilities.

CONCLUSION

Transfer, generalization, and maintenance, like their experimental psychology cousin, behavior modification, send a simple but refreshingly positive message: behaviors can be changed, solidified, and applied to new situations. Transfer and generalization are particularly important to teachers of persons with severe disabilities because they save valuable instructional time, extend skills into other environments, ensure task proficiency and task maintenance, assist the learners to adapt to a dynamic society, and facilitate instruction in functional skills.

If transfer and generalization are such useful and valuable skills, why are they not more widely utilized? Billingsley (1984) indicated that less than 10 percent of the objectives on individualized education plans for students with severe disabilities specified generalization of the objectives. Reasons cited for the omission ranged from teacher disinterest in generalization to fear of promising too much to parents. White (1983) proposed three possible reasons for omission of generalization and generalized outcomes: (1) students with severe disabilities do not recognize opportunities to generalize a skill or a behavior, (2) they do not obtain desired reinforcers for a skill outside the training environment since the available natural reinforcers are insufficient; and (3) they find that other skills or strategies are simply more effective in obtaining desired consequences. Whatever the reasons, it is imperative that teachers of persons with severe disabilities become increasingly concerned about generalizing skills beyond the treatment environment. As Billingsley (1984) stated, "The expectation of a generalized outcome, therefore, is not too much. It is, instead, a priority" (p. 191).

What can be done to increase generalized outcomes? Besides the components, strategies, and factors already discussed, three factors merit reiteration. First, to the maximum extent possible, training environments should be in the natural community. In particular, trainers should use natural contingencies to reinforce desirable behaviors. Second, trainers should loosen control over the stimuli and the responses in the treatment setting. Teachers should concurrently train different examples while varying cues, social reinforcers, exemplars, and discernible and relevant stimuli. Third, trainers should use stimuli and exemplars that are typically found in the natural settings, specifically peer tutors, peer buddies, and special friends, to facilitate transfer and generalization.

1. Three terms for the continued performance of a learned behavior are SUMMARY transfer, generalization, and maintenance. Generalization is a component of transfer, and maintenance is a component of generalization.

2. Transfer is the process of causing a learned behavior to be applied to a subsequent task by varying either the stimulus conditions or the response conditions. Generalization entails causing a learned behavior to be applied in a new situation by varying the stimulus conditions. Maintenance is causing performance of a learned behavior to continue beyond the training period by varying the conditions of practice.

3. Five major variables affect generalization: (1) extended training, (2) partial reinforcement, (3) motivation, (4) experience, and (5) discrimination.

4. Increased competence occurs with additional training; but, as competence increases, the prospects of generalization decrease. Extended training and generalization have an inverse relationship.

5. Task generalization is more extensive and more efficient under partial reinforcement than consistent reinforcement.

6. Increased motivation appears to increase task generalization, and decreased motivation appears to decrease generalization.

7. Increased experience maximizes generalization.

8. Discrimination and generalization have a complementary and inverse relationship. A person needs discrimination skills to identify the discernible and relevant features common to the training and the generalization situations. However, as discrimination increases, generalization decreases.

9. For persons with severe disabilities, generalization serves a number of useful purposes: (1) it expands skills to other settings and conditions, (2) it saves valuable instructional time, (3) it produces task proficiency, (4) it assists in adapting to an increasingly complexed society, (5) it facilitates instruction in functional skills, and (6) it maintains skills.

10. Drabman, Hammer, and Rosenbaum categorized four major types of generalization: (1) across time, (2) across settings, (3) across behaviors, and (4) across subjects.

11. Generalization across time, or maintenance, is designed to continue the behavior change once the skill is learned to criterion.

12. Generalization across settings is a change of behavior in a setting other than the one in which training occurred. A change in setting is determined by the presence or absence of discernible and relevant stimuli.

13. Generalization across behaviors involves a change in a behavior not specifically targeted for change. The generalized behavior must be definable independently of the training behavior.

14. Generalization across subjects is a behavior change in a nontargeted person similar to the behavior change in the targeted person.

15. After an extensive review of the research, Stokes and Baer described nine generalization strategies, which White later extended to twelve: (1) train and hope, (2) train in natural settings, (3) train to sequential modification, (4) train to natural maintaining contingencies, (5) train sufficient exemplars, (6) train loosely, (7) train to indiscriminable contingencies, (8) train common stimuli, (9) train multiple case, (10) train general case, (11) train to mediate generalization, and (12) train to generalization.

16. In the train and hope strategy, after a skill is learned to criterion, generalization is hoped for but not actively pursued.

17. In the train in natural settings strategy, after a skill is learned to criterion in the natural environment, generalization is hoped for but not actively pursued.

18. Train to sequential modification is a two-step strategy. In step one, a targeted skill is learned to criterion and generalization is planned but not pursued. If generalization does not occur, in step two additional training is provided and generalization is again initiated.

19. In the train to natural maintaining contingencies strategy, generalization to the natural environment is maintained by natural reinforcers in that environment.

20. In the train sufficient exemplars strategy, generalization to untrained conditions may be maximized by a sufficient number of exemplars that were also present in the training conditions.

21. In the train loosely strategy, the discernible and relevant aspects of the training procedure are reduced, creating greater similarity between the training and the generalization settings to enhance the generalization process.

22. In the train to indiscriminable contingencies strategy, the learner cannot reliably identify the discernible and relevant generalization features which will result in reinforcement.

23. In the train common stimuli strategy, the training program contains the same discernible and relevant features typically encountered in the natural environment.

24. In the train multiple case strategy, the learner is trained to use items typical of a subcategorical set and then asked to generalize to subcategory members that were not part of the trained set.

25. In the train general case strategy, the learner is trained to use a general category of items and then asked to generalize to category members that were not part of the training process.

26. Train to mediate generalization is a two-step strategy. The first step is establishing a trained response, or mediator, that can be used in other situations. In the second step, the mediator is used as a sufficient commonality between training setting and generalization setting.

27. In the train to generalization strategy, the learner generalizes from one generalized untrained condition to another untrained condition.

CHAPTER 10

Vocational and Employment Concerns of Persons with Severe Disabilities

(Courtesy of American Guidance Service.)

CURRENT VOCATIONAL SERVICE APPROACHES

Historically, job training courses have either totally ignored persons with severe disabilities or have relegated them to nonvocational and prevocational roles (U.S. Department of Labor, 1977). As a result, such persons have had little work opportunity. Instead they have received prevocational readiness instruction that might someday lead to employment opportunities (Bellamy,

Sheehan, Horner, & Boles, 1980). Since it was widely believed that they could not benefit from vocational services, they were also denied sheltered employment opportunities. The rare sheltered employment offered turned out to be little more than long-term protective care devoid of vocational training.

More recently, though, families and professionals have developed work training programs for persons with severe disabilities, designed to prepare them to enter more advanced employment (Katz, 1968). Structured around sheltered workshops, these programs offered a continuum of services through which persons with severe disabilities were expected to move as they developed more sophisticated prevocational skills, work habits, and other traits necessary for employment. With the trend toward deinstitutionalization and normalization, it is not surprising that work training programs have become a focal point for many educators. If adults with severe disabilities are to succeed in community living and truly become integrated into society, it is increasingly important that they engage in meaningful employment. Sheltered work settings are one option for meaningful employment.

Sheltered Work Settings

Efforts to provide vocational services for persons with severe disabilities were limited, until recently, to **sheltered workshops**. Initially established as training facilities, sheltered workshops have evolved into long-term employment sites that, until recently, served only workers with mild disabilities (Hansen, 1980). In the past decade, however, increased emphasis has been placed on providing vocational services for adolescents and adults with severe disabilities. This trend resulted in enactment of the Rehabilitation Act of 1973, which mandated services for persons with severe disabilities as a priority, regardless of their potential for competitive employment. Since then, sheltered workshops have grown rapidly in size and number (Greenleigh Associates, 1975; Whitehead, 1979). Nevertheless, they still serve a majority of persons with mild, not severe, disabilities (Parmenter, 1980). While 280,000 adults with severe disabilities are now served in sheltered workshops, according to Whitehead (1979), over thirty times that number are served inappropriately or not at all. Sheltered work facilities may be categorized into four types of programs: (1) work activities, (2) work adjustment, (3) extended employment, and (4) transitional employment.

Work activities.   **Work activity programs** are long-term training procedures designed for persons considered unable to qualify for work adjustment, extended employment, or transitional employment. These centers usually provide exposure and training in domestic and daily living skills, social skills, leisure and recreation skills, and prevocational skills. In general, persons placed in such programs are considered unemployable and unable to contribute to the economy as productive employees (Rusch & Schutz, 1986). Work activity programs are required to pay workers a certain percentage of the hourly minimum wage for the amount of work completed on a project. Even this minimal pay can be avoided by placing persons with severe disabilities in nonvocationally oriented programs. A 1983–1984 survey by Bellamy and Buckley (1985) reported that approximately one in three persons in sheltered facilities was in a nonvocationally oriented program. Needless to say, the earnings of the vast majority of persons in work activity programs are inconsequential.

Work adjustment.   **Work adjustment programs** provide long-term placement for persons who have numerous behavior and skill deficits but are considered capable of acquiring the skills necessary for sheltered or transitional work. In addition to vocational and behavioral training, persons with severe disabilities usually receive academic, speech, and occupational instruction. Work adjustment clients are usually not paid much for the work they perform. The only stipulation is that they must be paid according to their productivity. The average wage for persons with severe disabilities in these programs was 39 cents per hour, and few worked a full week. They averaged twenty-one hours of work per week, with the average weekly salary being $10 or less (Elder, Conley, & Noble, 1986).

Extended employment.   **Extended employment programs** offer long-term sheltered work with little or no chance of progressing beyond the workshop setting in the immediate future. Persons in this setting are considered unable to compete in the job market and instead are placed in minimally paying jobs in the sheltered facility. They are usually persons who work steadily but slowly. They require very little staff time and few ancillary services (Wehman, Renzaglia, & Bates, 1985). Extended employment sheltered workshops typically fall into two broad categories: self-employed and contractual-employed. **Self-employed workshops** produce a service or commodity that is sold directly to the public—from refinishing and repairing furniture to manufacturing commodities and from salvaging materials to growing plants, fruits, and vegetables. **Contractual-employed workshops** have contracts to manufacture or assemble a product or perform a service for a local business or industry—from putting bolts, nuts, and washers into polyethylene bags to laundering items for a hospital or other business. The success of any workshop, whether self-employed or contractual-employed, depends on having enough work to subsidize its employees. Sadly, this is often not available, and employees may then spend most days playing cards, watching television, or doing meaningless tasks.

In his introduction to a comprehensive study of sheltered workshops conducted by the U.S. Department of Labor, former Secretary of Labor Ray Marshall described the basic purposes of sheltered workshops as preparing the worker with disabilities for "employment in the competitive labor market, and providing long-term sheltered employment and supportive services" for such workers (U.S. Department of Labor, 1977, p. 10). With some notable exceptions, sheltered workshops have dismal records of meeting these goals (Bellamy, Rhodes, & Albin, 1986; U.S. Department of Labor, 1977).

Transitional employment. **Transitional employment programs** offer short-term or temporary placement in a sheltered facility. Persons may be referred to this setting for extended evaluation, work adjustment, training in a specific vocational skill, or refinement of skills necessary for employment (Flexer & Martin, 1978). Their long-term expectation is competitive, remunerative employment in an integrated setting. On the surface, this placement makes heuristic sense; it should develop and refine the necessary skills. Due to the highly contrived nature of the setting, though, it prepares people inadequately for employment conditions outside a sheltered facility. Since individuals in this setting are expected to have a high level of vocational skills, it is infrequently used for adults and adolescents with severe disabilities.

The progression from work activities to work adjustment, to extended employment, and finally to transitional employment represents a continuum of sheltered employment services through which the adult or adolescent is projected to advance and eventually "graduate" to competitive, integrated employment. On the surface, it is an attractive approach, to progress from low employment skills to higher ones much as a child advances from one grade to the next until graduation from school (Bellamy, Rhodes, & Albin, 1986). However, the underlying logic and especially the results contradict the viability of this approach for persons with severe disabilities.

Movement to higher employment skills, the underlying concept of this continuum in services, remains only an illusion for most participants with severe disabilities. Studies consistently indicate that fewer than 5 percent of participants advance each year (Bellamy, Rhodes, & Albin, 1986). The failure of the current system is also evident in the wages participants earn. At least forty thousand adults are specifically disallowed from working by state regulations and earn no salary (Bellamy, Horner, Sheehan, & Boles, 1981). Another sixty thousand with severe disabilities participate in work activities centers, where the average wage is $288 per year, or less than $1 per working day (U.S. Department of Labor, 1979). A more recent study of programs in Minnesota found that 49 percent of adult clients of activity centers had no earnings at all during 1980; the average yearly earnings for the remaining 51 percent was only $155 (Minnesota Developmental Disabilities Program, 1982). Clearly, current services do not offer participants the financial benefits associated with employment. The results point to a life that is financially impoverished and segregated from the mainstream, with little hope of advancing to greater employment opportunities.

Implicit in the design of prevocational and nonvocational programs is the belief that skills and behaviors acquired in those environments can transfer to employment settings (Brolin, 1976). Such an assumption is increasingly viewed as untenable for persons with severe disabilities, although it may well be defensible for those with other disabling conditions (Brown, Nietupski, & Hamre-Nietupski, 1976). Recent data support the interpretation that persons with severe disabilities must receive training in the settings and circumstances of their ultimate performance (Boles, Bellamy, Horner, & Mank, 1984; Look, Dahl, & Gale, 1977; Kagan, 1978; Rusch & Mithaug, 1980; Wehman & Hill, 1982). The absence of co-workers without disabilities, the lack of pressure for work performance, and the continuous presence of supervisors or instructors all represent radical departures from most employment settings. Even if persons with severe disabilities did acquire prevocational skills in these programs, it is unlikely that they would directly translate the skills to employment opportunities.

Another problem underlying the continuum of sheltered employment services is lack of funding constancy as an individual moves to higher levels of vocational training. Conflicting funding contingencies and regulations arise because funding for vocational programs comes from many state and federal agencies. Movement from one program level to another usually means one agency is no longer paying for services and another agency is. Service providers often have powerful disincentives for movement. Medicaid offers a clear example: in its Home and Community Waiver program, states can shift the costs of community services to Medicaid, which pays a relatively high federal share of program costs. However, only work activity and work adjustment programs qualify, not vocational and prevocational programs, creating a disincentive for states to move individuals out of the lowest levels of the continuum (Bellamy, Rhodes, & Albin, 1986).

The problems of this continuum of vocational services are exacerbated by the growing number of unserved adults with severe disabilities. Children with severe disabilities who entered public school programs rather than institutions after the passage of Public Law 94–142 are now adolescents, creating a national expansion in secondary school classrooms. Data from Oregon show the dramatically increased numbers of "school leavers" now facing the adult service system. Five years ago fewer than fifteen students in Oregon reached the mandatory school-leaving age of 22 and entered adult services; now, more than one hundred students are projected to graduate each year for at least the next ten years (Bellamy, Rhodes, & Albin, 1986; Brodsky, 1983). Of the students who graduated from 1976 to 1981 and required some day program at graduation, 23 percent were still waiting for a program up to five years later. Only 20 percent of the graduates had received any vocational rehabilitation services, and most of these were services to persons with a single disability or vocational evaluations (Brodsky, 1983). The press of unserved graduates of public school programs may overwhelm the current ineffective service system before alternatives that create real employment benefits can be installed.

COMPETITIVE INTEGRATED EMPLOYMENT

Competitive integrated employment is a job that pays a salary at or close to minimum wage in a work group predominantly composed of persons without disabilities. Historically, most adults with severe disabilities have not been

FIGURE 10.1

Remunerative, competitive employment in an integrated community setting offers a viable, attractive, and normalizing alternative to sheltered employment.

(Courtesy of Cahokia School District 187, Illinois.)

employed competitively, and only in recent years have attempts been made to obtain meaningful gainful employment for them (Rusch & Mithaug, 1980; Wehman, 1981). Competitive employment in a community setting offers a viable, attractive, and normalizing alternative to sheltered employment in terms of salary, integration, advancement, independence, and self-concept.

Benefits of Competitive Employment

The first and obvious point in favor of competitive employment is the opportunity for better wages and benefits. A person with severe disabilities placed in an integrated job will earn a salary that easily beats the 75 cents a day typically earned by sheltered workshop counterparts. This higher salary, coupled with normalization, can provide more community and recreational activities than would otherwise be possible. In turn, these experiences develop greater socialization and interpersonal skills. Thus, a competitive salary plays a crucial role in the normalization of a person with severe disabilities.

Another important benefit is the integration opportunities offered by competitive employment. Opportunities to serve consumers without disabilities, to work with nondisabled co-workers, and to meet people without disabilities in everyday encounters enhance the worker's prospects of forming friend-ships and acquiring appropriate social interactive skills through observation and practice. In the restrictive environment of a sheltered workshop, employ-ees cannot observe and practice socially acceptable skills. Coworkers without disabilities in a competitive environment also model adjusting to changing demands of the workplace. In contrast, the continual insulation from real work obstacles in a sheltered workshop is a false panacea in the habilitation of adults with severe disabilities.

Competitive integrated employment addresses the same service delivery problems as sheltered workshops. Both approaches acknowledge that there are important discrepancies between the skills of adults with severe disabilities and the demands of the workplace and that the time- and resource-limited services of vocational training agencies probably cannot overcome these dis-crepancies. In the sheltered workshop, the discrepancy is treated as a problem of readiness; the person needs to develop skills and eliminate problems to permit his or her employment at some future time. Competitive, integrated employment treats the discrepancy as a need to teach job-specific skills.

This simple difference in interpretation has profound programmatic con-sequences. Since readiness is emphasized, sheltered employment services focus on training to prepare the person for later employment. The competitive interpretation focuses on a paid work opportunity and support services. Both approaches have as their ultimate objective a decent life in the community, which includes productive work, independence, and social integration. The readiness approach of sheltered employment addresses this by attempting to "fix" the individual—providing therapy, training, and related services in the hope of an integrated, productive future. The competitive integrated employ-ment approach provides immediate opportunities for work and community participation while offering whatever level of support the individual needs to participate in these opportunities. The main ingredient of competitive inte-grated employment for persons with severe disabilities is the support they receive throughout the employment.

The Process of Supported Employment

The Developmental Disabilities Act of 1984 defines **supported employment** as remunerative, competitive employment in an integrated community environ-ment that meets three requirements: (1) the person is unlikely to earn a salary at or above minimum wage because of the severity of his or her disability, (2) the work site employs primarily persons without disabilities, and (3) the person is likely to need ongoing support such as supervision, training, and transporta-tion to sustain paid employment. This definition is especially designed for persons with severe disabilities who need support to work and whose work may not meet the productivity requirements for payment at or near the minimum wage. Since supported employment requires no minimum entry ability, it offers a unique and innovative method of employment for persons with severe disabilities.

FIGURE 10.2

Supported employment is designed for persons with severe disabilities who need support at work and whose productivity may not meet the requirements for payment at or near the minimum wage.

(Courtesy of Cahokia School District 187, Illinois.)

Practically speaking, supported employment is designed for adults who typically receive services in day habilitation or sheltered workshops. The number requiring ongoing support in any community will reflect, in part, the quality of local educational training and employment opportunities. The better the educational training and the job market, the smaller the group who require ongoing support (Wehman, Renzaglia, & Bates, 1985). This does not mean, of course, that all persons with severe disabilities should be placed in work roles. Persons of retirement age, those of independent means, those who are medically fragile, and others may choose not to be candidates for supported employment, regardless of their disabling condition.

Today, many factors argue for large-scale implementation of supported employment. Three factors are critical to the success of this approach in serving persons with severe disabilities. First, employment trainers must search out every employment opportunity in the labor market. To limit work efforts to settings that have "training value" or high social status would unquestionably leave many more persons with severe disabilities in sheltered work programs because of lack of competitive employment. Second, employers need incentives to participate in supported employment programs. The Targeted Jobs Tax Credit is a step in that direction; more incentives need to be enacted to sway a fearful employer to try a disabled worker. Third, attitudinal barriers that hinder the employment process need to be erased. The President's Committee on Employment of the Handicapped (1981) lists three "idea barriers" hindering supported employment: a negative reaction to employees with mental retardation, nonacceptance by fellow workers without disabilities, and the belief that persons with mental retardation are more prone to job-related injuries. Treating these three factors as separate problems may well result in fewer supported employment opportunities as well as inferior services for persons with severe disabilities.

The crucial feature of supported employment is support. The employee presumably would lose the job without this support; that is why he or she is not a candidate for less expensive and less intrusive programs of preparation for competitive employment (Bergeron, Perschbacher-Melia, & Kiernan, 1986). The support required may involve counseling, transportation assistance, design of equipment, and constant or episodic intervention. Work site support requires more than the collection of follow-up data. It is intervention oriented, designed to improve the work behavior of the employee with severe disabilities or the related performance of co-workers and supervisors. Is this periodic intervention too costly to justify its use? Compare the alternative, serving these individuals in a sheltered workshop at more than $40 a month or serving them for the rest of their lives in an adult activity center at even greater cost (Bellamy, Rhodes, & Albin, 1986; Wehman, Kregel, Barcus, & Schalock, 1986).

Supported employment is designed to give persons with severe disabilities the same benefits and opportunities others obtain from employment. Of course, this represents a major shift from current service objectives, which use skill development or service procedures as indices of employment quality. Most adults ask three questions to evaluate whether their current job is satisfactory or whether a new job represents a desirable change. First, what income will this job provide? This index seeks information about both the salary and the life-style that salary would provide. Second, how attractive is the work? This index seeks information about the challenge and status of the job. Third, what benefits are associated with this job? This index seeks information about such employment benefits as job mobility, advancement, security, and insurance. Naturally the values attached to income, quality of work, and benefits differ for individuals, but most people, including those with severe disabilities, weigh these factors informally to evaluate their employment. These three indices, not measures of developmental growth, are the yardstick with which program quality and success may be measured (Kiernan & Stark, 1986; Shestakofsky, Van Gelder, & Kiernan, 1986).

Supported employment does not negate all existing services for persons with severe disabilities. Many service innovations of the past decade fit comfortably with this employment initiative. What the concept introduces is a basis for comparing different kinds of employment services in terms of consumer benefits and outcomes. While many existing services may meet the letter of the definition of supported employment, their value must be compared to alternatives that may be more integrated, more remunerative, and better able to accommodate persons with various levels of disability.

FIGURE 10.3

Supported employment should give persons with severe disabilities the same benefits and opportunities others in society receive from employment.

(Courtesy of Cahokia School District 187, Illinois.)

FOUR SUPPORTED EMPLOYMENT ALTERNATIVES

Placing persons with severe disabilities into supported employment can be very difficult. It requires perseverance and a carefully planned sequence of events, starting with a general assessment of the community and ending with follow-up support and assistance. Differences in service needs, public resources, and labor markets combine to form a kaleidoscopic array of program strategies. Each has advantages and drawbacks in terms of generating real employment, producing integrative outcomes, and overcoming barriers. The employment alternatives can be classified into four models: benchwork supported employment, mobile crew supported employment, enclave supported employment, and supported jobs employment.

The Benchwork Supported Employment Model

The most restrictive of the four models, the **benchwork supported employment model,** was originally designed to provide employment in contracted assembly work, typically in electronics. A small number of highly qualified staff provide intensive training and supervision on employment tasks and related services to approximately fifteen employees with severe disabilities. The work site is usually a leased commercial space either in the heart of the community or in a section of a factory.

The benchwork model shares many features and constraints with traditional sheltered employment. Work is performed in the program's own work space, reducing opportunities for social integration. Continuous employment depends entirely on the program's ability to secure an adequate supply of contract work. But, unlike sheltered employment, the benchwork model has several features specially designed to overcome the barriers to integration inherent in a separate work site. Integration is addressed in both program design and individual services. Work sites are close to stores, restaurants, and other community resources, providing an opportunity for integration before and after work, during breaks, and at lunch. An individualized catalog of these opportunities serves as a curriculum for nonvocational training. Possibilities for integration at work may also be available when commercially successful programs hire workers without disabilities (Wehman, Moon, Everson, Wood, & Barcus, 1988).

Recent data indicate that benchwork wages are twice to four times the national average in work activity centers, with the lowest salary at benchwork sites being $110 a month (Boles, Bellamy, Horner, & Mank, 1984). In addition to wages, employees receive training to participate in community activities surrounding the workplace. They are encouraged to do activities such as using public transit to travel to and from work, going to lunch in restaurants, and buying toothpaste during lunch breaks, the way other working adults do during the work day. Data on benchwork companies indicate that workers average more than seven integrated community activities per week (Mank, Rhodes, & Bellamy, 1986).

The Mobile Crew Supported Employment Model

In a sense, the **mobile crew supported employment model** is the benchwork model in a van instead of a building. A crew of five persons with disabilities spends the workday performing contracted groundskeeping and janitorial work in community settings. A crew manager is responsible for direct service and management functions to ensure that each worker learns and performs tasks to consumer specifications, that all jobs scheduled for the day are completed, and that each worker has access to meaningful community integration.

Data from companies using mobile crew supported employment demonstrate equal success in metropolitan areas, rural settings, and locales plagued by economic difficulties and high unemployment. Wages for the mobile crew range from $130 to $185 per employee per month, which exceeds that earned by employees in the benchwork system (Mank, Rhodes, & Bellamy, 1986). The data also clearly demonstrate that employees with severe disabilities have a broad range of social contacts with citizens without disabilities. Because employees move about the community in the performance of their jobs, they experience constant physical and social integration. They are also taught to

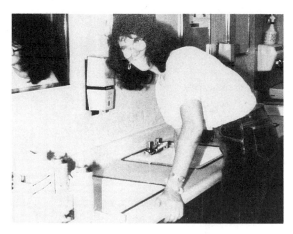

FIGURE 10.4

In the mobile crew supported employment model, a person with severe disabilities performs contracted groundskeeping and janitorial work in several community settings.

(Courtesy of Cahokia School District 187, Illinois.)

use such community services as stores, restaurants, banks, and medical facilities (Mank, Rhodes, & Bellamy, 1986).

The Enclave Supported Employment Model

In the broadest application of the **enclave supported employment model** employees with severe disabilities are trained and supervised by a model worker without disabilities employed in the same industry or business. Since they work alongside the model worker and other employees, this approach is more integrated than the mobile crew and benchwork models. The employees with disabilities are required to meet the same production schedules, quality standards, and performance levels as the other employees. Typically, six to eight employees with severe disabilities are employed in each enclave site; this affords the enclave supervisor the opportunity to provide and enhance integration activities in both the job site and the community (Wehman, Moon, Everson, Wood, & Barcus, 1988).

The company provides a model worker in the assembly area who has production responsibilities and assists the supervisor with ongoing supervision and training of the employees with severe disabilities. The model worker and the supervisor both ensure that enclave employees learn to use the company cafeteria and both support day-to-day integration. Payment is commensurate with that for other company employees doing the same type and amount of work. Access to work is guaranteed in the same manner as for other employees in the company.

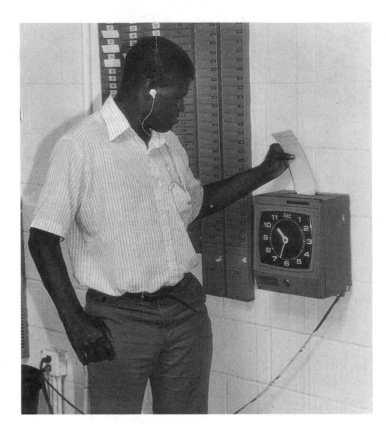

FIGURE 10.5

In the enclave supported employment model, employees with severe
disabilities are trained and supervised by a model worker employed
in that industry or business.

(Courtesy of Partlow State School, Tuscaloosa, Alabama.)

Preliminary data on the success of this strategy are highly positive. In one
work site, as employees with severe disabilities reached 65 percent of the
productivity standard set by the company, they received an average monthly
salary of $639 plus fringe benefits (medical insurance, vacations, and holiday
pay) (Rhodes & Valennta, 1985). Enclave companies have expressed great
satisfaction with this approach. On almost every measure, this model is an
excellent alternative to the present methods of employing persons with severe
disabilities, according to Mank, Rhodes, and Bellamy (1986).

The Supported Jobs Employment Model

The most integrated model, the **supported jobs employment model**, identifies
competitive employment sites in the community, places persons with severe
disabilities at those sites, and provides ongoing support at the work site until
the person masters the demands of the job. Although this model can apply to
a variety of jobs, it has principally been used in service businesses, such as
restaurants, offices, and stores. Employees in this model are integrated in both
their jobs and their communities. They perform their job duties in the same
areas as other employees doing similar work. Breaks and lunches occur with
other employees, ensuring physical and social integration.

FIGURE 10.6

In the supported jobs employment model, persons with severe disabilities are placed in competitive employment sites in the community. They receive ongoing support at the work site until they master the demands of the job.

(Courtesy of Cahokia School District 187, Illinois.)

To place a person with severe disabilities in a supported jobs employment setting requires a sequence of steps illustrated in figure 10.7 and discussed below.

Community assessment and job search.   The initial step in implementing the program is to conduct a careful analysis of all possible employment opportunities in the community. This entails working with community employment agencies, civic organizations, and local employers. These community contacts are crucial to integrative placement efforts. The range of jobs identified as viable will influence the jobs that will comprise the initial training program. Thus, the key step for both placement and training is identification of every possible employment site within the community. Work environments must also be evaluated for their physical and social interactive characteristics.

Communication with employer.   The second step is employer communication, talking with the supervisor or employer about a prospective employee's skills, traits, and capabilities. The trainer should discuss available tax credits, insurance, and any other information the employer may need to know. Once an employer agrees to use his or her business as a training site, a work schedule can be reviewed and transportation needs worked out. During the training period, the person with severe disabilities will continuously be evaluated and taught other skills necessary for employment.

Job assessment.   Next, persons with severe disabilities are assessed on the job demands of the site and the skills the job requires. In rare cases, standardized

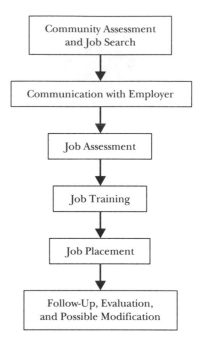

FIGURE 10.7

The placement of persons with severe disabilities in a supported jobs employment site, typically follows the sequence of steps illustrated in this figure.

(Courtesy of Parklow State School, Tuscaloosa, Alabama.)

assessment instruments are used; in most instances, job assessment is done by direct observation of the job site and generation of site-specific behavioral objectives, since each job has different demands. A person's job performance is then compared to the behavioral objectives. From the assessment data, realistic performance objectives are established. Objectives for each prospective employee are formulated in the areas deemed critical to placement. Relevance is the keystone of each objective.

Job training.   Job training, too, is highly job-specific. It should be conducted in an integrated community employment site. Training must develop not only the skills needed to perform the job, but also skills such as getting along with co-workers, accepting criticism, and following safety precautions. The first step, in most job training programs, is to compare the prospective employee's present job skills to the specific behavioral objectives generated for that job site, to determine any discrepancy between the two. This is followed by job training in the community setting. During training, data are consistently gathered to evaluate the prospective employee's job mastery. Training continues until he or she has met the criterion, which, in most cases, is 100 percent independent performance for ten consecutive days.

Job placement.   Once the prospective employee has mastered the job requirements and met the criteria at that site, he or she may be given a remunerative position doing that job. The trainer is gradually phased out of the job site, and the employer pays the recent trainee a salary at or near minimum wage.

Follow-up, evaluation, and possible modification.   The final step in this model is follow-up, evaluation, and possible modification of the job placement. Follow-up must be carefully planned to be effective and cost-efficient. Telephone communication and mailed supervisor evaluation forms with periodic site visits are sufficient follow-up services for employees who are well stabilized, but others may require frequent site visits and possible interventions. During conversations with employers, the trainer must be sensitive to possible cues that there are problems needing direct contact. It is imperative that the trainer maintain contact with the employee after job placement. The trainer may eliminate difficulties before they become traumatic or may help obtain an alternative job for an employee with severe disabilities who becomes dissatisfied with the job.

TWO EXAMPLES OF THE SUPPORTED JOBS EMPLOYMENT MODEL

Supported employment is first and foremost employment. It exists when a person's activities create goods and services that have economic value and result in payment from an employer or customer. Within this concept, supported jobs employment may be part-time or full-time. The remainder of this chapter offers an example of each.

Part-Time Employment

The supported jobs employment model was originally conceived as a full-time work approach but almost immediately changed to a part-time program due to the lack of full-time options for persons with severe disabilities.[1] There was a scarcity of full-time jobs, but there were numerous part-time jobs suitable for persons with severe disabilities. The program developers reasoned that a person with severe disabilities employed in two to four part-time jobs would have roughly full-time employment.

Part-time employment has a number of advantages for persons with severe disabilities. Top on the list is its availability. While few such persons are employed full-time (Mithaug, Horiuchi, & Fanning, 1985; Wehman, Kregel, & Zoller, 1984), through part-time employment, many work over thirty hours a week even during periods of high unemployment and negative economic growth. Second, part-time employment is a cushion against business failures. A closed business spells unemployment for a full-time worker, but a part-time colleague may still have two or three other jobs. Third, part-time supported employment increases an employee's opportunities for interacting with persons without disabilities. Fourth, part-time employment makes job mobility less risky. If a worker does not like a particular part-time job, leaving is not as traumatic as it would be if that were his or her only source of income.

But part-time employment also has some significant disadvantages. Part-time workers do not accrue the benefits usually available to full-time employees (e.g., paid vacations, medical insurance, retirement programs). They also may not accrue the pay raises full-time employees typically earn. These are serious losses. Further, transportation between jobs may present greater problems than transportation to and from one full-time job.

An example of a part-time employment opportunity for persons with severe disabilities is the pilot program for high school students in Oregon (Fredericks et al., 1986). Employment training sites for persons with severe disabilities were obtained through a process that closely resembled the sequence in figure 10.7. After identifying an integrated job in the community, the vocational coordinator arranged to meet with the prospective supervisor or employer and explained the parameters of the program. A nonpaid position was sought initially. Since employers had no responsibility for wages or for training, most readily accepted the students on a trial basis. With the assistance of the employer, a staff member identified the duties and requirements of the job. Baseline data were obtained by assessing the prospective worker's pretraining job performance level. The typical job training used a **total task teaching method**. In this method the entire job sequence is taught to the student as a unified task instead of dividing it into component parts and teaching each component separately. In complex tasks, the components were broken down and taught separately to the student with severe disabilities. For instance, the job of dishwasher requires loading and unloading dishes, removing food from dishes before they are washed, operating the washer, and stacking dishes after they are dried. Each of these duties is a component, and each component is taught using the total task teaching method.

During the initial stages, a trainer stayed with the student during the entire job training period. As the student progressed in job skills, volunteers were substituted for trainers. The use of volunteers allowed more students to be served. The goal of all training was independent performance by the student. When the student reached criterion, the trainer or volunteer gradually withdrew from the job site to demonstrate that the student could perform the job independently. However, the trainer was always available to the employer to remedy any problems or to assist in any further training. In addition to job-specific training, the student was instructed on a variety of associated work skills deemed important. Table 10.1 lists those skills.

When the student demonstrated job proficiency, the subject of wages was raised with the employer. Even then, pay was sought only for students within two years of graduation. If the employer indicated that a salary was not possible, the student was moved to another job site. If the employer agreed to hire the student, arrangements were completed. To ensure that the student maintained a high level of job performance, the trainer assured the employer that he or she was available to remedy any problem or to assist in further training. Follow-up contacts were made by telephone or in person and varied from twice a week to once every other week. These periodic evaluations were conducted even if the student was considered to be independent on the job. Often inappropriate behaviors reemerged or the speed of work decreased. Some employers changed the nature of the job and felt that the trainers were better able to retrain the employee than they were.

This supported jobs training program was school-based, but Fredericks and his associates note that the community has made a commitment to supported employment. A nonprofit corporation has been established to continue monitoring students who have graduated. Referrals are also made to the nonprofit corporation from sheltered workshops and work activity centers. Continuation of the part-time employment program into adulthood seems probable.

Full-Time Employment

Philosophically and conceptually, the full-time employment model is similar to the part-time model developed by Teaching Research.[2] This model, which is structurally similar to figure 10.7, was designed to facilitate the entry of persons with severe disabilities into integrated, competitive employment settings. It is argued that many individuals attend adult activity centers or sheltered workshops that exclude them from rehabilitative services because of limited or no employment potential. The intent of this model is to develop and implement procedures for training persons with severe disabilities and to place them in remunerative employment in the community.

The initial step is a careful analysis of job opportunities in the community. Potential employees are then assessed for general work and social skills. Data are collected on the job proficiency of each trainee, using standardized instruments and direct observation of performance on different tasks. Production rates are also assessed on industrial tasks. The proficiency and production assessments determine the jobs for which the individual is best suited.

After the trainee demonstrates some job proficiencies, a staff member contacts a potential employer and describes the program, the trainee's skills, and the employer's responsibilities. If the employer agrees to accept the trainee as an employee, the project staff analyzes the specific work environment to identify potential problems. Objectives for the trainee are then formulated in areas deemed critical to job placement. The trainee is reassessed and placed in a simulated pre-employment unit until he or she has mastered the objectives. Besides job-specific skills, the simulated training covers such generic work skills as grooming, communication, functional social behavior, and job break behavior. Once the trainee has met the objectives in the simulated pre-employment unit, he or she begins the transition to integrated community employment. At this point, the employee receives a salary and the usual benefits of full-time employment. After the employee meets the objectives in the employment setting, the project staff members are gradually phased out.

TABLE 10.1 Associated Work Skills Deemed Important in Developing Independent Workers

Work-Related Behavior	Transportation and Mobility	Self-Care and Grooming	Social Communication	Other Behaviors
Checks own work	Takes appropriate transportation to and from work	Dresses appropriately for work without assistance	Communicates basic needs, such as thirst, hunger, sickness and toileting needs	Displays willing, positive attitude
Corrects mistakes	Locates work station	Washes before coming to work without assistance	Does not engage in self-stimulatory or self-abusive behavior, aggressive or destructive behavior, or self-indulgent behavior	Is even tempered
Works alone without disruptions for specified periods without contact from supervisor	Locates rest room	Washes after using rest room without assistance	Engages in relevant, appropriate conversations	Displays cooperative behaviors
Works continuously at a job station for specified amount of time	Locates break and lunch area	Washes before eating without assistance	Responds calmly to emotional outbursts of others	Is trustworthy and dependable
Uses appropriate safety gear	Locates locker or coat area	Washes after eating without assistance	Talks about personal problems at appropriate times	Seeks additional work when completes assigned tasks
Responds appropriately during fire drill	Moves about work environment independently	Shaves regularly without assistance	Refrains from exhibiting inappropriate emotions at work	Exhibits flexibility
Follows safety precedures		Keeps hair combed without assistance	Refrains from bringing inappropriate items to work	Accepts criticism and suggestions for behavior change without becoming angry and in acceptable manner
Wears safe work clothing		Keeps nails clean without assistance	Refrains from tampering with or stealing other people's property	Displays pride in self and work
Cleans work area		Keeps teeth clean without assistance	Responds appropriately to changes in supervisors	Controls emotions and refrains from tantrums
Identifies and avoids dangerous areas		Uses deodorant without assistance	Interacts with co-workers at appropriate times	Displays loyalty to employer
Responds appropriately to emergency situations		Bathes regularly without assistance	Responds appropriately to social greetings such as "hello" or "good morning"	
Participates in work environment for specified periods of time		Cares for menstrual needs without assistance	Initiates greetings appropriately	
Works in group situation without being distracted		Cares for toileting needs without assistance		
Works faster when asked to do so		Eats lunch and takes breaks at appropriate times		
Completes work by specified time when told to do so		Brings lunch and snack independently		

Comes to work designated number of times per week

Arrives at work on time

Recognizes appropriate time to take breaks and lunch

Returns promptly from lunch, break, rest room

Uses time clock or clock appropriately

Does not leave work station without permission

Follows directions without questioning them

Has sufficient physical endurance for tasks

Operates vending machines without assistance

Uses napkin independently

Displays appropriate table manners

Exhibits acceptable and appropriate physical appearance

Ignores inappropriate behaviors and comments from co-workers

Refrains from inappropriate sexual behavior at work

Laughs, jokes, and teases at appropriate times

Responds appropriately to strangers

Approaches supervisor appropriately when he or she (a) needs more work, (b) makes a mistake that he or she cannot correct, (c) does not understand task, (d) has finished task, (e) recognizes that tools are defective, (f) notices that disruption has occurred, or (g) becomes sick

Complies with supervisor's requests in specified period of time

Responds appropriately to correctional feedback from supervisor

Responds appropriately to changes in routine

Follows instructions

Largely compiled from *Associated Work Skills: A Manual*, by I. Egan, B. Fredericks, J. Peters, K. Hendrickson, J. Toews, and J. Buckley, 1984, Monmouth, OR: Teaching Research Publications.

They assure the employer that they will be available to assist in remediation or further training. Periodic follow-up evaluations of the employee are conducted even if he or she is adequately functioning on the job.

Conclusion

The cornerstone to both deinstitutionalization and normalization is remunerative, integrated employment in the community. Through this route persons with and without severe disabilities achieve independence and community integration. There are two approaches to employment. The flow-through sheltered employment model envisions workers progressing from one service level to the next and eventually "graduating" to integrated competitive employment. In practice, however, individuals with severe disabilities rarely move to higher service levels and achieve the wage and integration benefits of employment in this model. The supported employment model offers a promising alternative. To achieve meaningful normalization for persons with severe disabilities, this model focuses on competitive integrated employment in the community at a salary at or near minimum wage. Supported employment has several programs to ensure flexibility in employment opportunities. If adults with severe disabilities are to succeed in community living and become integrated into society, they, like every other adult, must be able to engage in meaningful employment.

SUMMARY

1. Historically, work training programs have either ignored persons with severe disabilities or relegated them to nonvocational or prevocational roles.

2. The Rehabilitative Act of 1973 mandated priority services to persons with severe disabilities, increasing the number of such persons presently served in employment sites. Still, thirty times that number are served either inappropriately or not at all.

3. Sheltered work facilities have four types of programs: (1) work activities, (2) work adjustment, (3) extended employment, and (4) transitional employment.

4. Work activity programs offer long-term training designed for persons who are viewed as unemployable and nonproductive.

5. Work adjustment programs offer long-term training for persons who have numerous behavior and skill deficits but are considered potentially capable of sheltered employment in the future.

6. Extended employment programs offer long-term sheltered employment with little or no chance of progressing to community settings in the immediate future. Sheltered workshops may be self-employed or contractual-employed.

7. Transitional employment programs offer short-term sheltered placement to provide training or refinement of skills necessary for competitive, remunerative employment in an integrated job site.

8. The continuum of sheltered employment services suggests that participants will progress from work activities to work adjustment, extended employment, and transitional employment, but this progression is only an illusion for most persons with severe disabilities.

9. Persons with severe disabilities have to receive training at employment sites and under circumstances where performance is ultimately required.

10. A critical problem in sheltered employment services is lack of funding constancy as a person moves to higher levels of vocational training.

11. Competitive integrated employment is a job that pays or comes close to minimum wage in a work group predominantly composed of persons without disabilities.

12. Remunerative competitive employment in an integrated community setting offers a viable alternative to sheltered employment in terms of salary, integration, job advancement, independence, and self-concept.

13. Supported employment is competitive employment at or above minimum wage for a person with disabilities at a work site that employs primarily workers without disabilities and in which the person receives ongoing support because of the severity of his or her disabilities.

14. Supported employment is based on the assumption that an employee with severe disabilities would lose the job without access to ongoing support. There are four generic models: benchwork supported employment, mobile crew supported employment, enclave supported employment, and supported jobs employment.

15. In the benchwork supported employment model, employees with severe disabilities perform contracted assembly work at a centrally located facility or area in a factory. While the work site is not integrated, employees are trained and expected to participate in integrated community activities. Wages range from twice to four times the national average for persons in work activity centers.

16. In the mobile crew supported employment model, four to six persons with disabilities perform contracted groundskeeping and janitorial work in several community settings, traveling by van from site to site. Wages exceed those in the benchwork model.

17. In the enclave supported employment model, four to seven employees with severe disabilities are trained and supervised by a model worker without disabilities in the business. They have to meet the same production schedules, quality standards, and performance levels as other employees. The employees with severe disabilities are taught integration skills both in and out of the work site.

18.   In the supported jobs employment model, persons with severe disabilities are placed in competitive employment sites in the community and given ongoing support at the work site until they master the demands of the job. This model has six steps: (1) community assessment and job search, (2) communication with the employer, (3) job assessment, (4) job training, (5) job placement, and (6) follow-up, evaluation, and possible modification.

NOTES   [1]This program was developed by the Teaching Research Division of the Oregon State System of Higher Education. The information for this section was largely based on the article "Part Time Work for High School Students," by Fredericks, Covey, Hendrickson, Deane, Gallagher, and Schwindt (1985).

[2]The full-time employment model described in this section was Project Employability, which was developed through a grant from the Virginia State Department of Rehabilitative Services to the School of Education of Virginia Commonwealth University. The information for this section was largely taken from the books *Competitive Employment: New Horizons for Severely Disabled Individuals* by Wehman (1981) and *Vocational Training and Placement for Severely Disabled Individuals,* edited by Wehman & Hill (1979a, 1979b).

CHAPTER 11

The Families of Persons with Severe Disabilities

(Courtesy of Paul S. Conklin.)

EFFECTS OF A CHILD WITH SEVERE DISABILITIES ON THE FAMILY UNIT

A pregnancy ushers in a new stage of family life. The family begins to think about including another member in its circle of love and care, initially planning and furnishing the space the new infant will occupy and later perhaps

239

shifting friendships, social activities, and economic arrangements to "make room" for the child. Similarly, emotional relationships in the family unit undergo subtle but significant changes. Siblings, husband, and wife experience important social, leisure, economic, and domestic changes that can affect family structure and its relation to the outside world as it incorporates a new member. If the new child has severe disabilities, the impact on the family is intensified. Although it is difficult to generalize because of the heterogeneity of family members and "personality" of the family unit, it is widely accepted that the family of a child with severe disabilities experiences added stress. The amount, severity, and type of stress is directly related to the type and level of disability. If the child's appearance arouses comments, stares, and rejection, this may increase the stress felt by the family (Glidden, 1986; Wikler, 1986). The extra time and effort required for child care and supervision by parents and siblings increases the stress (Turnbull, 1981). The frequent rejection of a child's efforts to interact and socialize with others places an added load on everyone in the family. Because of the child's reduced peer contact, the parents have to spend more of their time entertaining and supervising the child (Shoultz & Kalyanpur, 1987).

The families of children with severe disabilities exhibit a number of **secondary characteristics** that add stress (Beckman-Bell, 1981). Worry about the child's day-to-day survival, guilt and anger about his or her future, the need for special therapies, and reduction in their leisure endeavors, social activities, and even sleep increase the family's stress exponentially. Extra expenses are often incurred for education, medical intervention, equipment, and therapies. At the same time, the family's income may be greatly reduced, as one working parent is forced to stay home to care for the child. Severe behavior problems compound this stress (Agosta, Bradley, Rugg, Spence, & Covert, 1985; Korn, Chess, & Fernandez, 1980). Self-abusive, self-destructive, and externally directed hazardous behaviors often produce additional problems and occasionally hospitalization of the primary caregiver.

The demands on parents are increased if the child has a wide range of skill deficiencies. Feeding problems, sleep disturbances, dressing problems, recurring seizures, chronic **enuresis** and **encopresis**, self-stimulation, and self-abusive behaviors are not uncommon. They usually occur with many other "secondary" problems (Snell & Beckman-Brindley, 1984). Further, many parents report anxieties simply from the realization that their child is severely disabled. Many fight against recognizing their child's disability (Fotheringham, Skelton, & Hoddinott, 1971). One parent stated: "Our oldest boy is no more than an idiot. We accept that fact. But until that day four years ago when both of us faced it, we had no family life, we were on the brink of divorce, and Joyce teetered dangerously on the terrifying edge of insanity" (Kvaraceus & Hayes, 1969, p. 97).

Stress alone cannot account for the pressures and burdens a family experiences, but it is often coupled with guilt, pressures from family, friends, and professionals, and the pressures inherent in living in a complex, technological

FIGURE 11.1

Besides heaping guilt and stress on the parents of children with severe disabilities, society also expects them to be superparents.

(Courtesy of Tracy Hrbek.)

society. Greer (1975), a special educator with a daughter with disabilities, indicates that, "if parents are unfortunate enough to have a handicapped child, society then hypocritically says they must be *superparents*. They must supply enormous additional amounts of care, love, and attention to their child. They must do this additionally, on a 24 hour a day, 365 day a year basis; otherwise they are *superbad*" (p. 519). Later, Greer suggests, "in the back of parents' minds, then, is a vague awareness that society is looking over their shoulders and judging if they are carrying out their prescribed duties, giving much love, attention, and devotion, not missing any treatment appointments, providing the best available care, etc. This is a 'goldfish bowl' type of existence which eventually takes its toll in energy, strength, and courage" (p. 519).

The presence of a child with severe disabilities influences a variety of family functions, often unfavorably. Fotheringham, Skelton, and Hoddinott (1971, 1972), indicated that families without disabled children generally demonstrated better functioning than families of children with severe disabilities in (1) health and health practices, (2) care and training of children, (3) relationships between family members, (4) individual behavior and adjustment, and (5) overall family functioning. There were no reported differences between the two groups in (1) home and household practices, (2) economic practices, and (3) social activities. Farber (1968) noted that having a child with severe disabilities in the home has adverse effects on (1) guilt and depression, (2) marital integration, (3) job promotion, (4) family roles, and (5) siblings' occupational expectations. Further, Byassee and Murrell (1975) noticed that there were significantly fewer mother-father agreements in families of children with severe disabilities than in those of children without disabilities. These investigators found that, after a child with severe disabilities was born, the parents communicated less and had fewer common interests than before.

Stages of Family Adjustment

The addition of a child with severe disabilities forces a complex readjustment pattern on the entire family: siblings, father, and mother (Bristol & Gallagher, 1986; Kaiser & Fox, 1986; Simeonsson & Bailey, 1986). The readjustment is an extremely arduous and protracted process, moving through loosely arranged stages toward adjustment and acceptance. The concept of stages has a history extending almost four decades in special education. One of the first continua was a three-step process centered around the concepts of pity and concern (Boyd, 1950). Later, Hay (1951) delineated a six-stage continuum that began with bewilderment and concluded with acceptance.

Since Hay's model, many continua have been proposed. A number resemble the five stages proposed by Kubler-Ross (1969) in her classical research on death and dying. This similarity is more than a coincidence, because, in addition to handling stress and developing acceptance of their child with severe disabilities, the parents must grieve for the death of their "idealized" child: the child about whom they dreamt, who was perfect in almost every way. They must pass through Kubler-Ross's stages of shock and denial, anger, bargaining, depression, and acceptance, plus stages that are unique to the parents of a child with severe disabilities.

The ten stages typical for parents of children with severe disabilities are:

1. **Unawareness.**   The family is totally unaware that the child has a disabling condition. Family members react to the infant as they would to any new baby. If the infant is diagnosed as disabled from birth, this stage is omitted.

2. **Uneasiness.**   As time passes, the child does not behave the way the parents expect. In this stage, the parents are generally uncomfortable about the child's lack of progress and search for an explanation. They compare the child to other babies and ask the opinions of friends, relatives, and professionals.

3. **Conscious recognition.**   The parents grope for the meaning of their child's condition. Nevertheless, they strongly cling to the belief that he or she is nondisabled and attempt to define the lack of performance in acceptable terms, for instance, "Claire doesn't crawl because of her stubborn nature" or "Donny just isn't interested in talking yet."

4. **Casual recognition.**   The nature of the child's problem and its consequences are explained to the parents. They may begin to understand some of the ramifications for them, but they may not fully recognize that the child is disabled and may still cling to the belief that there is nothing wrong.

5. **Denial.**   The parents deny that their child is severely disabled and find "growth" in their child to discount the professional diagnosis and

classification. From time to time, they return to the professionals, expecting them to find new evidence or to admit to some mistake. In this stage parents may visit a number of professional agencies, shopping for a more acceptable diagnosis. Denial is a very real attempt by the parents to avoid pain, sorrow, and suffering.

6. **Anger.**   The parents become angry about their child's severe disability and ask, "Why did it happen to me?" as the impact becomes more evident. In this stage, each parent may blame the other for the child's disability. Since inordinate demands are made on the parents' time, patience, and physical endurance, they often feel trapped and tied down. Gradually, these feelings of resentment extend to the spouse, the child, and the disability.

7. **Pity and self-pity.**   The parents feel sorry for or pity themselves for the death of their idealized child and their unfulfilled dreams for that child. While they can feel sympathy for the child with severe disabilities, sadly they cannot extend that sympathy to each other.

8. **Bargaining.**   The parents pray to their deity, offering to reform or to exchange something for making their child nondisabled. For instance, a parent may promise, "I'll go to church every Sunday if you will only make my son normal" or "I will become a better person if you will only help my daughter to be like everyone else."

9. **Depression.**   The parents understand that their child is severely disabled and that he or she will probably be that way permanently. They generally feel incapable of caring for their child and fulfilling all the responsibilities associated with his or her disabilities.

10. **Acceptance and accommodation.**   The parents accept the child just as he or she is and begin to plan a constructive course of action for the child. They not only make plans for the child's future but also become actively involved in the child's present education and training.

These reactions are not a sign of maladjustment on the family's part; rather they are normal responses to a traumatic, complicated event. In a process as complex as adjusting to and accepting a child with severe disabilities, descriptions of stages are necessarily simplified and somewhat symbolic. They represent an attempt to explain the process. In most multiple-stage processes, a person advances to a certain level, performs some function, and then progresses to the next, higher stage. In contrast, a parent may linger in one stage of this process or move back and forth between two stages several times. Parents may skip one or more stages or respond to situations as if they were in two or more stages simultaneously. After advancing to stage 9, a parent may regress to stage 5 because of a traumatic event. It should also be noted that the two parents do not progress through the stages in unison. A father may be in stage 5 while the mother is in stage 8. Each parent may be operating from

FIGURE 11.2

Parents of children with severe disabilities try to provide them with the normal range of experiences.

(Courtesy of Lynda Atherton.)

a different perspective, and this can obviously interfere with their communication, complicate their adjustment to the child, and impair their relationship with each other. There is strong but not conclusive evidence that siblings without disabilities progress through these stages as well (Simeonsson & Bailey, 1986). Therefore, each parent and sibling might be in a different stage, which could hinder, if not terminate, communication and impair the adjustment of the child with severe disabilities. These stages, then, should be viewed as guideposts to help others comprehend the parents' reactions.

EXAMPLE   **The Ticehurst Family**

Throughout that overcast December day, Caroline felt funny, even though she could never quite explain it. She had pains off and on, and, although the doctor told her not to worry, she felt she might have to go to the hospital sooner than expected. Her husband, Walter, teased: "You think you're the only woman in the world who ever had a baby?" The Ticehursts already had one child, Kevin, strong, healthy, and nearly 4 years old. So Caroline knew what a normal pregnancy felt like. "This one just didn't feel the same," she said. That night, as they were watching Johnny Carson, Caroline felt a hot rush of blood. Walter called the doctor, then called his sister-in-law to come stay with Kevin, and bundled his wife into the car for the short drive to the local hospital. When the doctor arrived, nearly two hours later, he performed a Caesarean. The baby boy was delivered 2 months premature, after a pregnancy of 32 weeks.[1] Although his color and respiration were good, he weighed only four pounds, three ounces; the doctor indicated that he needed careful watching. When Walter asked if the infant should be transferred to the better-equipped university hospital, the doctor asserted that the baby would be better off staying where he was. So Walter visited with his wife and then went home to relieve his sister-in-law.

Three hours later, the baby began to breathe irregularly. A chest X-ray showed severe respiratory distress syndrome (RDS), a hyaline membrane disease in which the film that helps prevent lung collapse is either missing or inadequate. Walter, summoned by telephone back to the hospital, could see that the baby was blue. The staff arranged for transferring him to the university hospital. During the trip, the baby had periods of interrupted breathing and was given artificial respiration. On arrival at the university hospital, he was placed on an respirator. Then a lung collapsed. The medical report summarized his condition as "extremely poor."

Late the next day, the baby was baptized Trevor Theodore Ticehurst; the head of the medical staff stood in as his godfather. For the first 3 weeks of his life, Trevor was on the respirator. Since he was losing substantial weight, the doctors started feeding him nutrients through a catheter in a vein above his heart. By the time he was 4 weeks old, Trevor was having seizures on his right side and around his mouth. His head size was increasing rapidly because of hydrocephaly. The usual shunt procedure, a tube inserted from head to stomach to drain the fluid, was not possible because a spinal tap showed Trevor had an infection, which the doctors thought might be associated with ventricular bleeding. Trevor also had hyperbilirubinemia, a type of jaundice in which the premature system cannot break down certain wastes; the condition can cause a toxic brain reaction leading to mental retardation, cerebral palsy, and hearing loss. When asked what else could happen to Trevor, his doctor replied, "He could also be blind." At 4 1/2 months, when his spinal fluid finally ran clear, he got a shunt to release fluid from the brain. At just over 5 months, he was finally discharged from the hospital, listed in "fair" condition; his prognosis was "guarded."

When Trevor was brought home, he was still underdeveloped and had not acquired the basic sucking and swallowing reflexes, so he gagged and vomited when fed. Caroline had to teach Trev to swallow by holding his nose, placing food far back on his tongue, and clamping his mouth shut. Each feeding took hours. He was slightly over 2 before he could swallow automatically. He could not control his head movements, and sitting was out of the question.

By the time Trev was 3, the family was bankrupt, living in a basement, surviving on welfare and food stamps. In the 1st year of life, Trevor had been back in the hospital half a dozen times. When Caroline took him in for a checkup, a month after a hernia operation, the doctor confirmed that Trevor was blind. Walter's insurance ran out; his firm did not carry any major medical coverage. Caroline had to have her gallbladder removed; Walter's high blood pressure and asthma flared up; and he lost his job at a Wall Street brokerage firm when he became unable to keep up with the pressure.

The Ticehursts took Trevor to a hospital that ran a preschool day-care program, but the director said that Trevor was too young, too sick, and besides the program "needed the space for children who could be helped." They applied for Social Security disability for Trevor. He qualified for $180 a month. Walter took on two jobs, but the bills kept mounting until they were overwhelming. In 1982, Trevor's Medicaid allowance of $500 a year for outpatient treatment was cut to $100 when the administration reduced spending on domestic social programs. But illnesses that would be routine for other children usually meant a trip to the emergency room for Trevor. He averaged five trips a year at an average cost of $400 each.

The Ticehursts' bills exceeded $40,000. Walter's hands shook as he sat at his kitchen table riffling through a folder bulging with letters and bills. He was intense, agitated. His blood pressure was dangerously high. He seemed older than 39, with deep pouches under his eyes and a gaunt, haggard look, as he declared, "I wrote to the president. I said, 'Do you realize it would cost taxpayers $30,000 to $40,000 a year if we would put Trev in an institution, and yet, by keeping him home, by keeping him home . . . ' " His voice died as if he had forgotten what he was saying.

Caroline broke in, "We are not going to put him in an institution." She added more vehemently, "We're not going to put him someplace where he sits in a chair all day and rots! We'll keep him home as long as we can!"

"It's what he's going to be like that worries me," Walter acknowledged. "He's cute now, but what happens when he's 35 years old and still needs diapering? When he's too big for Carry to lift and put in the bathtub?" He closed his folder, then opened it again, spreading out replies to the hundreds of letters he has mailed since Trevor's birth: letters to the president, to politicians, and to journalists. Many people wrote back to express their regrets, best wishes, and sympathy. "I don't want sympathy!" Walter said. "We are way past sympathy. And I don't want handouts. I want justice! I want some attention to this problem." He wanted to show the irrationality of a system that requires a family in distress to relinquish their assets, go broke, and remain at poverty level in order to qualify even for limited aid. He also questions the rationale by which a government that stresses its role in preserving life not only cuts a family adrift but also penalizes it. If Walter earns more than $1,200 a month, Trev's $325 a month will be jeopardized.

At a press conference in the spring of 1985 at Fordham University, Surgeon General C. Everett Koop was asked about the financial problems of families with disabled children. "Life is not fair," he reminded the press. "You and I cannot make it fair." He said too many quality-of-life decisions were made on behalf of the family, rather than the infant with disabilities, "because it might affect whether the sister can take ballet lessons." But he agreed that some families might have "the problem of expense," and indicated a study was under way to explore how "the medical bills are paid for and by whom, and what the impact is on society. I can't give you the answer, but it is possible— and don't say that I said it's probable—but it is possible that out of that [study], if the size of the problem is amenable to correction, and it seems it's something that Congress would want to do, that could lead to a kind of catastrophic insurance. But I don't know." Meantime, he expressed confidence that "the great majority are covered by Medicaid or by private insurance" (Barthel, 1985, p. 157).

Effects on Siblings

Because the family unit is an evolving and dynamic system, any analysis of a subsystem such as the adjustment of siblings[2] to a brother or sister with severe disabilities must take into account the complexity of the overall system. Among many paradigms advanced to characterize this complexity, the **triaxial model** proposed by Tseng and McDermott (1979) considers the longitudinal and structural nature of the family in terms of subgroups. To delineate the effects a child with severe disabilities has on siblings, the triaxial model suggests that two dimensions be examined: the parent-nondisabled child subsystem and the sibling-child with severe disabilities subsystem.

Parent-Nondisabled Child Subsystem

Research has identified a number of positive and negative effects on the parent-nondisabled child subsystem. Positive effects generally include the sibling's acceptance of the brother or sister with severe disabilities, because of the parental attitudes (Tseng & McDermott, 1979). Breslau, Weitzman, and Messenger (1981) found that siblings had similar total scores on a psychological inventory to the scores of a reference group. Along similar lines, Mates (1982) found that siblings were not significantly different from the normative values on measures of home and school adjustment, school achievement, and self-concept. Siblings were also reported to have more empathy and understanding than the general population.

On the negative side, numerous investigators have reported that siblings spend significantly less time with their parents than a matched set of peers do (McHale, Simeonsson, & Sloan, 1983; Taylor, 1980). Siblings generally have feelings of being left out and excluded (Blackard & Barsh, 1982; Taylor, 1980); they feel that more is expected of them (Blackard & Barsh, 1982; Harder & Bowditch, 1982); and they typically resent the added responsibilities (Chinitz, 1981). On formal inventories of psychological functioning, siblings were also found to have significantly higher scores on subscales reflecting inappropriate behaviors, such as fighting and delinquency, than a matched set of peers (Breslau, 1982; Breslau, Weitzman, & Messenger, 1981).

Sibling-Child with Severe Disabilities Subsystem

Investigators who have analyzed the relationship between a sibling and a brother or sister with severe disabilities have generally found both positive and negative effects. Among positive effects, Taylor (1980) indicated that many siblings assisted in the care of the brother or sister by administering treatments and medications. The vast majority of siblings have, at some time, been teachers and trainers of their brother or sister, and many of them used behavior change procedures effectively (Simeonsson & Bailey, 1986).

Among negative effects, Taylor (1980) reported that siblings typically had feelings of inferiority and guilt and entertained death wishes for their brother or sister. Other researchers have reported that siblings are more irritable, are socially withdrawn, and have poorer self-concepts than the general population (Ferrari, 1982; Harvey & Greenway, 1984; Lavigne & Ryan, 1978). Many siblings expressed diffused anger at the brother or sister over damage to personal belongings and the restriction of family activities (Chinitz, 1981).

As these two dimensions illustrate, sibling relationships do not conform to a consistent pattern. Clearly, variability in the type and quality of the investigations contributes to the difficulty of interpreting the findings. Despite these limitations, some tentative conclusions can be drawn. Several variables have been identified as important and pertinent in the adjustment and socialization pattern of the sibling: the age of the sibling, the gender of the sibling, and the type and severity of the disabling condition (Powell & Ogle, 1985).

Age of the sibling.   Age has consistently been identified as an important variable in the adjustment and socialization pattern of siblings. In a classical study, Farber (1960) described the effects of changing age on both the sibling and the child with severe disabilities. While the sibling develops social adjustment patterns appropriate to his or her sex and changing age, the child with severe disabilities progressively becomes the youngest child. While the

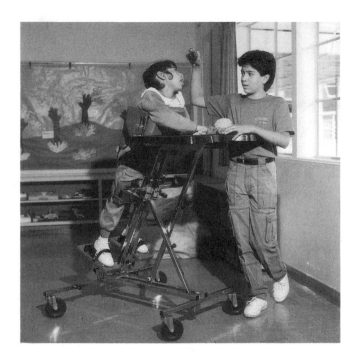

FIGURE 11.3

Siblings of children with severe disabilities are often used as trainers and employ a number of behavior change procedures effectively.

(Courtesy of Project ADEPT, South Bay Union School District, Imperial Beach, California.)

children are young, they interact on a somewhat equal basis, but as siblings become older, they become more protective and directive. The relative ages of the children play a subtle role in the sibling's self-perception. Siblings younger than or close in age to the brother or sister with severe disabilities had a poorer overall adjustment and less sophisticated socialization skills than a matched set of peers (Brody & Stoneman, 1983; Chinitz, 1981; Lavigne & Ryan, 1978; Simeonsson & Bailey, 1986; Taylor, 1980).

Gender of the sibling.   Although Farber (1960) concluded that gender was an important variable, subsequent researchers have argued that it may be less important. A number of studies found significant differences in the responsibilities delegated to male and female siblings (Brody & Stoneman, 1983; Lavigne & Ryan, 1978; Simeonsson & Bailey, 1986; Simeonsson & McHale, 1981; Taylor, 1980). They indicated that female siblings were often assigned caring and nurturing responsibility while male siblings were not. This responsibility, many have noted, was harmful to the female siblings' overall adjustment and socialization patterns.

Grossman (1972), in contrast, suggests that socioeconomic levels may directly influence the responsibilities assigned to male and female siblings. Female siblings from lower socioeconomic levels were expected, from the time they were quite young, to assume a major share of responsibility for nurturing

FIGURE 11.4

Social activities such as playing catch with a sibling with severe disabilities can improve the relationship between the children.

(Courtesy of Carol Evans.)

their brother or sister with severe disabilities; those from upper socioeconomic levels had few nurturing responsibilities. The upper socioeconomic male siblings had roughly the same level and range of nurturing responsibilities as female siblings. But males from lower socioeconomic levels were not even as involved as males from upper socioeconomic families; they were not expected to assist in either nurturing or caring for their brother or sister. Of all the siblings, Grossman acknowledged, these males were the least affected.

Breslau, Weitzman, and Messenger (1981), however, suggest that neither age nor gender may be analyzed separately. They found that male siblings who were younger than the child with severe disabilities had higher impairment scores than younger female siblings, while female siblings older than the child with severe disabilities had higher impairment scores than older males. In a subsequent study, Breslau (1982) indicated that a third variable, age spacing, may influence adjustment and socialization patterns. In particular, younger male siblings close in age to the child with disabilities had higher impairment scores than females. Given these findings, two conclusions seem reasonable. First, older female siblings, especially in lower socioeconomic families, are delegated responsibility for caring for the child with disabilities, which hinders their overall adjustment and socialization. Second, as Simeonsson and Bailey (1986) noted, male siblings, especially those younger than or close in age to the brother or sister, may have difficulty resolving the discrepancy between themselves and the child with severe disabilities, and thus are likely to have problems in overall adjustment and socialization.

Type and severity of the disabling condition. Simeonsson and Bailey (1986), after reviewing approximately twenty studies, concluded that neither the type nor the severity of the disabling condition influenced the sibling's overall adjustment. Specific disabilities do not appear to influence whether the sibling's reactions will be positive or negative. Responses across disabilities strongly suggest that individual differences in the traits, temperament, and functional behaviors of the disabled child influence the sibling's reactions and transcend the particulars of the disability. This interpretation accounts for the different reaction patterns of siblings to the same disabling condition.

Grossman (1972) suggests that children with more severe or multiple disabilities may require more time for care and nurturing than mildly disabled children and thus may have a greater impact on the overall adjustment and socialization of siblings, especially older female siblings. While this position makes sense heuristically, it is not yet supported by either research or anecdotal studies.

The Case of Thaddeus and Emily Morrisson   EXAMPLE

Emily stacked two pillows on the carpet, pounded them with her fist, and then sat down crossing one leg over the other. Taking a deep breath, she observed: "You know, sibling love is never easy and it is certainly not automatic, but when one sibling is forced into a care-giver role and the other into a care-receiver role, well, you know, it's like asking for trouble." After a long pause, as if studying her previous statement, Emily poignantly described how her parents had delegated to her the major responsibility for looking after Thaddeus, her brother with severe retardation, even though at age 6 she was not even sufficiently mature to care for herself. Punctuating her description with tears, Emily noted, "The responsibility I felt for Thad was tremendous, and at times frightening." Once while Emily was babysitting, Thad wandered off down the street, although he had been asleep when she checked him a few minutes earlier. She looked all over the neighborhood, and couldn't find him. "My mother hysterically told me that 'if anything happened to Thad, if anything at all, I would be totally to blame!' I felt terrible and confused and guilty. I was only 7."

Like a shadow, Thaddeus would accompany her wherever she went. "His differentness rubbed off on me in the eyes of my playmates. He was a drag for me and my playmates. He was difficult to communicate with, he often stank, and was wild and stubborn." Whenever someone belittled, degraded, or made fun of Thaddeus, Emily was expected to "gather him up and leave. I lost many playmates by always having to side with Thad, even if it was his fault." In school, she acknowledged, she never had a close friend with whom she could confide intimate thoughts and secrets, and she was never invited to spend the night with a friend or invited to a slumber party. "I felt neglected by my family and shunned by my peers. I was a very lonely girl." This isolation extended into high school. Although very attractive, Emily sadly admitted she was never invited on a date, not even to the prom.

Her role of constant baby-sitter posed a number of additional social problems for her. For instance, when the Morrissons enrolled their children in recreational activities, they always put Emily in the class for Thaddeus's age group. "I especially remember the swimming lessons. The teacher was uncomfortable around my retarded brother, and vented his discomfort in an antagonistic attitude toward me. Thad would merrily splash about, oblivious to the teacher's instructions and ignoring my explanations and demonstrations. Then [the teacher] would yell at me, 'Can't you do anything with that brother of yours?' " And, of course, on the way out, after class, Emily dreaded the embarrassment of meeting her friends going to the class that followed the "baby class."

The parents compounded many of the problems between Emily and Thaddeus. Thaddeus's minor accomplishments "always met with animated enthusiasm from our parents." In contrast, it seemed "our parents' response to my accomplishments was closer to the pat-on-the-back level. I was expected to perform well in every circumstance; and if I didn't, then all hell would break loose. I was expected to make straight A's even though my evenings consisted of looking after Thad." Emily did not begrudge Thaddeus the attention he got for his accomplishments—she often praised him enthusiastically herself. But she felt that she deserved enthusiasm for her accomplishments, too. "I didn't want to have to beg for praise; I didn't want to be taken for granted; I only wanted to be noticed!" Symptomatic of the lack of parental attention was the fact that only her grandparents attended her high school graduation; her parents "had to go" to a meeting at Thaddeus's school that night.

Other relatives could be just as bad, sometimes worse. With every visit, a relative would implore, "Emily, you have to be nice to Thad, because he can't help the way he is." But "try to explain to an 8-year-old girl whose brother had just destroyed all her toys that she should ignore it because he just 'can't help it.' Or try to explain to a 10-year-old girl why her brother would receive a gift with every visit from a relative and she didn't because 'God was good to you, but He wasn't good to your brother.' " These same relatives would rave about how "cute" Thaddeus was and "reproached me for not being more tolerant of him."

Pulling herself up slowly from the pillows, Emily said, "You know, the sad thing is that we should have been good friends." After a pause, she murmured, "Yes, we could have been good friends."

FAMILY INTERVENTIONS FOR CHILDREN WITH SEVERE DISABILITIES

A number of characteristics make it somewhat more difficult for families of children with severe disabilities to foster behavioral change in the child than it is for families of nondisabled children. Yet families of children with severe disabilities have long been recognized as a valuable resource in meeting the educational needs of their children. There are many valid reasons for encouraging parents and siblings to teach the child with severe disabilities: (1) parents can be powerful reinforcing agents, (2) parents generally spend more time with and know their child better than professionals do, (3) skills taught at school can be maintained and generalized to the community through family efforts, (4) parents receive gratification from contributing to the development of their child, and (5) parents can assist in the community integration and socialization of their child (Bronicki & Turnbull, 1987; Shoultz & Kalyanpur, 1987). Participating in their child's instructional program affords many parents an effective antidote for feelings of frustration and helplessness. For these reasons, many professionals view parents as primary interventionists whose actions can have wide-ranging and lifelong effects.

Therefore, many professionals automatically assume that **parent training** is necessary and valuable. This assumption needs to be critically examined. Winton and Turnbull (1981) interviewed mothers of children with severe disabilities about their perspectives on parent involvement. The majority indicated that their most preferred involvement was maintaining contact with their child's teacher, and only 13 percent chose parent training opportunities as most preferred. One mother (who incidentally was an elementary school teacher) commented: "Living with a child like this is just about an impossibility. It's just the constant supervision of a child like this that really gets to you after a while. It's frightening enough without having to teach them too" (Turnbull, 1983, p. 36). This should not be interpreted as lack of interest in helping their child develop skills at home; rather, parents were justifiably not interested in being their child's primary teacher.

Another consideration is the effect parent intervention may have on the child. While many parent training programs have resulted in substantial skill development for children with severe disabilities, they may also have unanticipated negative effects on the parent-child relationship. To illustrate, Diamond (1981) comments:

> Something happens in a parent when relating to his disabled child; he forgets that they're a kid first. I used to think about that a lot when I was a kid. I would be off in a euphoric state, drawing or coloring or cutting out paper dolls, and as often as not the activity would be turned into an occupational therapy session. "You're not holding your scissors right," "Sit up straight so your curvature doesn't get worse." That era was ended when I finally let loose a long and exhaustive tirade. "I'm just a kid! You can't therapize me all the time!" [p. 30].

Probably the most common skill taught by parents to their child with severe disabilities is elimination of inappropriate behavior (e.g., aggressive, noncompliant, self-injurious, and self-stimulatory behaviors). In most studies, variation in parental attention was the primary method of treatment for reducing inappropriate behaviors. It was generally an efficient programming technique. Snell and Beckman-Brindley (1984) reported that, in all but one of nine studies, there was a reduction of noncompliant and other inappropriate behaviors. Parent intervention has also been used successfully in dealing with feeding problems, unusual fears, mobility deficits, self-care problems, and communication disorders. Parents have used such techniques as behavior modification, appropriate instructions, physical guidance, prompting and fading of prompts, and modeling (Parke, 1986; Greenspan & Budd, 1986; Snell & Beckman-Brindley, 1984).

Three approaches have repeatedly been applied in parent intervention programs. One is the **home training program**, in which intervention skills are taught to parents in their home. Typically, a trainer works directly with the parents and the child and observes the parents interacting with and teaching the child. An example is the Portage Project (Shearer & Shearer, 1972), in which each family is assigned a **home teacher**, who is responsible for instructing the parents in the skills and principles they need to work effectively with their child. The home teacher usually visits one day per week and plans an individualized curriculum for the child in language, self-help, cognition, motor, and socialization skills.

Although the majority of home training programs have been conducted with parents of preschool children, this model is equally appropriate for parents of older children with severe disabilities. For instance, Fowler, Johnson, Whitman, and Zukotynski (1978) reported on a successful program to teach behavior management skills to the mother of a 24-year-old woman with severe disabilities. Results documented the success of the program in changing the mother's behavior, which in turn produced positive changes in the daughter's behavior. Similar results have been obtained with adolescents and adults with severe disabilities (Ashman, 1982; Nordquist & Wahler, 1973; Smith, 1985; Smith & Belcher, 1985; Whitman, Hurley, Johnson, & Christian, 1978; Zifferblatt, Burton, Horner, & White, 1977).

A second parent intervention approach is the **group training program**. Group training can be conducted in a variety of ways. In general, parents are asked to attend training sessions at their child's school, during which they are informed of the instructional activities provided to their child and how they can assist in the child's program. Clearly, the emphasis of training sessions varies with the needs of the parents and the students. In some instances, trainers help parents refine their teaching skills; in others, trainers may illustrate the best method to maintain and generalize new skills.

An example of group training for parent intervention is the Kansas Neurological Institute program (Baker, 1978). The core of the program was ten modules, which were taught to parents in weekly evening sessions. Five modules covered behavior management principles and techniques and five covered self-care skills, positioning, adaptive equipment, and legal rights. An individual session was also held with each set of parents. Parents were informed of their child's present instructional activities and encouraged to apply their new knowledge to assist in the program as much as their time, skills, and desires allowed. Pretest and posttest data indicated that parents made significant gains in knowledge and improvements in interactions with their child. In a group training program, parents and educators meet, discuss, and operationalize the instructional program so that efforts at school and home are directed toward the same objectives and reinforce each other.

The third parent intervention approach uses parents as classroom helpers. Participation in the classroom gives parents the chance to observe their child and other children with severe disabilities in an educational setting and to imitate the strategies used by the teacher. It also gives the teacher some valuable assistance. An example of a **classroom helper program** is the Regional Intervention Program in Nashville, Tennessee (Wiegerink & Parrish, 1976). Parents were expected to spend approximately six hours per week at the school working with their child. In the first phase, they worked with their child in individual sessions or on special behavioral problems, under the supervision of the teacher. Parents were expected to learn skills that would enable them to work successfully with their child at home—essential behavior modification skills and other instructional techniques.

Parent participation in the classroom requires careful and systematic planning. Parents need backup support to feel confident in this new role. Individual parents' expectations may differ, depending on their schedules, time commitment, previous teaching skills, and interest in participation. When parents first start to work in the classroom, professionals should arrange frequent conferences to answer questions and provide feedback on their performance. Parents should also be encouraged to evaluate themselves. Since many working parents are unable to participate in the classroom program, alternative methods need to be developed to increase their competence in working with their children.

Conclusion

Historically, parent-teacher interactions have not been as positive or productive as they should. The passage of the Education for All Handicapped Children Act of 1975, Public Law 94-142, and more recently the Education of the Handicapped Amendments of 1986, Public Law 99-457, established new ground rules for interactions between professionals and parents. These acts require shared decision making and responsibility in ensuring that students with severe disabilities receive an education appropriate to their present and future needs. An integral aspect of successful parent-teacher interactions is mutual respect and open communication. Preparing persons with severe disabilities for complete integration into the community is a complex process; it truly requires the best efforts of both parents and professionals working as partners to accomplish mutually defined goals systematically.

Professionals must remember that families of children with severe disabilities are pressured by burdens that are difficult for a nonparent to fathom. They are often frustrated by a slow, confusing, and rigid system in which authorities and professionals have given them little assistance and much humiliation. Their feelings of guilt are reinforced by society's prejudices. And, like the Ticehursts, they often bear financial burdens that are aggravated by bureaucratic inconsistencies. From this background of experiences, parents of children with severe disabilities enter the school system. It is mandatory that teachers listen to them, actively help them, and incorporate them into their child's educational program.

SUMMARY

1. The family of a child with severe disabilities experiences added stress from a variety of sources: (1) the child's limited peer involvement, (2) worry about the child's day-to-day survival, (3) guilt and anger about the child's future, (4) need for special services and therapies, (5) reduction in the family' leisure endeavors and social activities, (6) reduced income and extra expenses, (7) prolonged hospitalization, and (8) the child's self-abusive, self-destructive, and externally directed hazardous behaviors.

2. Society adds pressure by suggesting that parents must be superparents. If they cannot fulfill these responsibilities, they are viewed as superbad.

3. The presence of a child with severe disabilities can impair family functioning in such areas as (1) health and health practices, (2) care for and training of the children, (3) relationships between family members, (4) individual behavior and adjustment, (5) overall family functioning, (6) marital integration, (7) job promotion, (8) family roles, and (9) sibling occupational expectations.

4. The family unit must undergo a complex readjustment, which engulfs parents and siblings.

5. The family goes through a series of ten loosely arranged stages leading toward adjustment and acceptance: (1) unawareness, (2) uneasiness, (3) conscious recognition, (4) casual recognition, (5) denial, (6) anger, (7) pity and self-pity, (8) bargaining, (9) depression, and (10) acceptance and accommodation.

6. These stages are not signs of maladjustment but rather normal reactions to a traumatic, complicated event.

7. The parent-nondisabled child relationship experiences both positive and negative effects. Positive effects generally include the sibling's acceptance of his or her brother or sister. Negative effects center around having less time, feelings of being excluded, and having more responsibilities.

8. The relationship between a sibling and a child with severe disabilities

undergoes both positive and negative effects. Positive effects generally center around siblings being used as trainers. Negative effects generally include siblings' feelings of inferiority, guilt, and irritability; social withdrawal; and negative self-perceptions.

9.   Three important variables in siblings' adjustment and socialization are: (1) age of the sibling, (2) gender of the sibling, and (3) type and severity of the disability.

10.   Two conclusions about the age and gender of siblings seem reasonable. First, sisters, especially those in lower socioeconomic families, are often delegated much of the responsibility for nurturing the child with severe disabilities, and this hinders their overall adjustment and socialization. Second, brothers, especially those younger than or close in age to the child with severe disabilities are likely to have problems in overall adjustment and socialization.

11.   While numerous studies have indicated that neither the type nor the severity of the disability affects the sibling's overall adjustment, a severe or multiple disability may require more time for care and nurturing and thus hinder the overall adjustment and socialization of siblings, especially older females.

12.   Families of children with severe disabilities have long been recognized as a valuable resource in meeting the child's educational and therapeutic needs.

13.   The most common skill parents teach their child is elimination of inappropriate behaviors.

14.   Three parent intervention programs have been used to assist families in developing their child's skills: (1) the home training program, (2) the group training program, and (3) the classroom helper program.

15.   In the home training program, a trainer teaches parents at home how to teach and interact with their child with severe disabilities.

16.   In the group training program, parents meet with other parents and the teacher at the child's school for training, so that the efforts of home and school are directed toward the same objective and reinforce each other.

17.   In the classroom helper program, participating parents can observe their child and other children in an educational setting and imitate the teaching strategies used by the teacher.

---

[1]The World Health Organization has defined a premature child as one born before the   NOTES
37th week of pregnancy (the normal term is 40 weeks) and weighing less than five and one-half pounds. Babies born too small, too soon have always accounted for the great majority of infant deaths because they are undeveloped in various ways. The sucking and swallowing reflexes, for instance, are not developed until rather late in pregnancy.

[2]For practicality and to prevent confusion, the word *sibling* is used to refer to the nondisabled brother or sister of a child with severe disabilities.

CHAPTER 12

Preschool Programs for Children with Severe Disabilities

(Courtesy of United Cerebral Palsy Associations, Inc.)

Early intervention for young at-risk infants and children has long been recognized as a vital cornerstone of lifelong education and training. This realization, championed by parent and advocacy groups, led to passage of the Handicapped Children's Early Education Assistance Act (1968) and the Education for All Handicapped Children's Act (1975). Although these acts fell well short

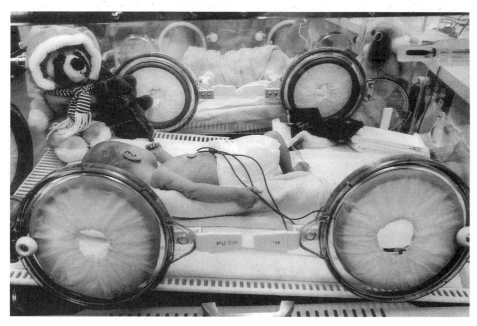

FIGURE 12.1

To serve the increasing number of at-risk infants appropriately, varied professionals must guide, assist, and work closely with the parents.

(Courtesy of St. Paul-Ramsey Medical Center, St. Paul, Minnesota.)

of providing education for young children with severe disabilities, they did create increased awareness of its importance. Preschool programs have been gaining momentum since the mid-1970s, but sadly educational programs for children 5 and under have not become widespread.

A recent law holds promise of serving these at-risk children and their families adequately. The Education of the Handicapped Amendments of 1986, Public Law 99-457, mandate that young children with severe disabilities between the ages of 3 and 5 be served adequately by 1991. Somewhat later, infants and toddlers under age 3 are to receive appropriate intervention services. This law encourages new and unique approaches for educating this previously underserved population. Teachers are to become consultants to parents, watching how they interact with their children and explaining more therapeutic ways to carry, feed, change, play, and talk to the infants. The law further encourages service delivery approaches in which all team members help families optimize the development of their children. These approaches to child and infant programming focus on the important role parents play in their child's early learning experiences. The law also prods professionals to reexamine existing approaches to ensure optimum development for all infants and children.

To serve infants and children appropriately under the guidelines of Public Law 99–457, instructional strategies and services must maximize each child's development. At the very least this requires that strategies and curricula encourage varied professionals to guide, assist, and work closely with parents. Parents would be seen not only as sources of valuable information but also as intervention agents and members of the service delivery team. Early intervention strategies must consider two factors: the kinds of services to be provided and the manner in which services are to be delivered.

CURRICULUM APPROACHES

Since the mid-1970s imposing empirical evidence has been presented in support of early stimulation for infants and children with severe disabilities. Investigators have conclusively illustrated that preschool programs can accelerate the development of an infant or child (Brofenbrenner, 1974; Karnes & Teska, 1980). A decade of experience with preschool intervention programs has produced unequivocal confirmation of the value of systematic service to infants and children with severe disabilities. From these programs, two widely used basic curriculum approaches have emerged: the developmental model and the functional model.

Developmental Curriculum Model

Programs for infants and children with severe disabilities have historically followed a **developmental curriculum model**, assuming that the normal sequence of development provides a logical structure for educational goals. Proponents argue that infants and children with severe disabilities follow the same developmental progression as children without disabilities. The acquisition of each skill serves a dual role: It is an advance through a developmental stage and an attainment of readiness for the next, more sophisticated skill (Anastasiow, 1978).

In the developmental model, objectives are generated from broad, generic categories of similar behaviors typically referred to as **content domains**. Communication, cognition, self-care, social-personal, and motor skills are the content domains in most preschool programs. Each content domain is divided into a detailed list of behaviors, sequenced according to their normal acquisition. This list is the core of the developmental approach, serving as both an assessment and a curriculum guide. For example, Ralph's present skills are compared to a developmental profile that lists the behaviors in each content domain sequentially. This is the assessment phase of the developmental approach. The first few assessment items that Ralph lacks in each content domain become targeted as objectives for Ralph's educational program. Since assessment and curriculum are closely intertwined in the developmental approach, this paradigm is sometimes characterized as an **assessment-linked curriculum** (Gentry & Adams, 1978).

Even proponents of the developmental approach acknowledge that it may not constitute a complete preschool curriculum for toddlers and children with severe disabilities. For instance, many such children exhibit undesirable and maladaptive behaviors. Since developmental programs are principally concerned with the acquisition of developmentally normal behaviors, they do not deal with elimination of inappropriate behaviors (Bricker, Bricker, Iacino, & Dennison, 1976). A second drawback was noted by Allen (1978). He argues that a developmental sequence should be used cautiously for young children with severe disabilities, since they usually arrive at developmental milestones through atypical routes. Repeated observations indicate, for example, that a child with severe disabilities may master a relatively sophisticated skill (e.g., walking up stairs) before being able to perform a lower level skill (e.g., throwing a ball). A third criticism concerns the acquisition of **critical skills**. Many skills (e.g., imitation) are critical for learning more advanced skills but are not developmental in nature (Hayden, McGinnes, & Dmitriev, 1976). These skills, typically called **tool skills**, should, nevertheless, be included in the preschool curriculum for young children with severe disabilities.

Developmental curricula may be traditional or follow a variation. One of the more noteworthy variations was proposed by Connor, Williamson, and Siepp (1978). Its theme is that developmental skills should be taught with other skills through integrated activities. Because skills do not develop in isolation, they should be paired with other skills regardless of their content domains.

Probably the most popular variation of the developmental model is an approach that was proposed by Piaget and applied to children with disabilities by Inhelder (1968), Stephens (1971, 1977), and Woodward (1963, 1979). The major emphasis of the **Piagetian curriculum** centers on structuring **antecedent events** in the environment. The goal is to produce conflict in the child, creating what is termed **disequilibrium**. The discomfort of being in disequilibrium encourages the child to try to restore **equilibrium**. Through this process of equilibrium-disequilibrium-equilibrium, a child progresses from a lower substage to the next more sophisticated substage within a developmental stage and ultimately to the next developmental stage. An example of this principle may be observed in the teaching of **object permanence**, the concept that objects still exist even though they may be out of sight. Suppose, for instance, that Matthew's ball rolls behind the curtain. This is a source of discomfort, or disequilibrium, that motivates Matthew to seek the ball by interacting with the environment and thus reestablish equilibrium.

Functional Curriculum Model

The **functional curriculum model** assumes that toddlers and young children with severe disabilities differ to such an extent from those without disabilities that the normal sequence of development is not necessarily the best approach

FIGURE 12.2

The ultimate criteria for the selection of goals in the functional curriculum are their relevance and usefulness to the infant or child in the particular environment.

(Courtesy of Houghton Mifflin Company.)

for meeting their needs (Sailor & Guess, 1983). Proponents of this model argue that instructional objectives chosen from a developmental perspective may have little or no relevance to the child and may not be useful or purposeful.

An example may illustrate. Hopping on one foot five successive times and stacking one block on top of another to form a three-block tower are two objectives in the developmental curriculum. These are unacceptable goals in a functional curriculum, which requires that goals be functional—that is, of practical use to the child now or in the immediate future. As chapter 1 stated, a functional task is one that must be performed for a person if he or she cannot perform it independently. Hopping on one foot five successive times and building a three-block tower are not practical, useful skills. In contrast, grasping a spoon is an objective in the functional curriculum, since it has relevant application to self-feeding. A functional curriculum may draw from developmental data, but the selection of objectives is based on relevance and usefulness to an infant or child in relation to the environment.

A functional curriculum may be traditional or one of two important variations. The first emphasizes the **criteria of the next educational environment**. This concept is an outgrowth of the **criterion of ultimate functioning**, which focuses on the skills needed by an adult with severe disabilities to perform productively and independently in the community (Brown, Nietupski, & Hamre-Nietupski, 1976). This criterion is difficult to apply to infants and children because objectives formulated from it would be irrelevant and essentially nonfunctional at such an early stage, so it was extended downward as the criteria of the next educational environment. Applied to toddlers and young children with severe disabilities, the next educational environment is the public school kindergarten. Vincent and her associates (1980) recommend that future environmental settings, not just the next one, be taken into consideration when setting objectives for toddlers and young children with severe disabilities.

The criteria of the next environment have implications for both the content and the instructional method of the curriculum. Research suggests that preacademic skills are minimum components in most regular kindergarten classes, but social-personal skills and self-care skills are more critical components for success or failure in the next environment, and the preschool curriculum should develop those skills. Vincent and her colleagues also recommend a gradual modification of the special education environment to approximate the kindergarten classroom.

A second functional variation is the **individualized curriculum sequencing model**. An individualized curriculum is developed for each infant or child, which systematically plans for response generalization while emphasizing environmentally functional skills. A **service delivery team** selects and prioritizes objectives unique to each child. A training program is then designed for each objective, following a typical **task analysis procedure** while identifying activities and events that offer opportunities for the behavior to be trained in a functional manner. From this training program, individual curriculum sequences are developed. The sequences combine skills across content areas in a logical manner so that one behavior naturally leads to the next in the sequence.

The distinction between the developmental curriculum and the functional curriculum is somewhat artificial in practical applications. A functional curriculum may draw from developmental data in selecting appropriate objectives, especially when teaching a new content domain or subject. The teaching of **skill clusters** draws heavily from developmental logic in identifying behaviors that should be taught together, based on the expected age of emergence. The organization of instructional units into clusters of related skills fits very nicely into the multiple normal environments of the functional approach. Skills that can easily be sequenced together in a cluster are often those most useful and meaningful to the student. Sailor and Guess (1983) suggest that a developmental approach is typically used with toddlers and young children with severe disabilities, while a functional approach is typically used with adolescents and young adults.

TREATMENT APPROACHES

Undoubtedly, the service delivery best suited for infants and children with severe disabilities is the **transdisciplinary team model**. Conceptualized by Hutchinson, this approach has been described as "a deliberate pooling and

FIGURE 12.3

Since children with severe disabilities differ from each other in behavioral, sensory, and cognitive deficiencies, professionals must coordinate their educational efforts.

(Courtesy of Ortho-Kinetics.)

exchange of information, knowledge and skills, crossing and recrossing traditional boundaries, by various team members" (Haynes et al., 1976, p. 2). Since children with severe disabilities differ from each other in behavioral, sensory, and cognitive deficiencies, the transdisciplinary model is the appropriate delivery approach to coordinate and integrate the services provided to them (Giangreco, 1986). It can provide a cross-pollination of professional expertise and parental knowledge in a manner that bears directly on the needs of the infant or child.

It may clarify the transdisciplinary approach to contrast it briefly to other educational service delivery systems. Presently, three other cross-disciplinary approaches are used in educational programs for infants and children: the unidisciplinary model, the multidisciplinary model, and the interdisciplinary model. In the **unidisciplinary model**, each professional works independently of the other specialists, developing programs based on the philosophy of his or her discipline without regard to the approaches of the other disciplines. The **multidisciplinary model** is based on many of the same premises. Each professional provides services in isolation from other specialists, and little or no communication occurs among professionals. However, the various professionals recognize that other disciplines make important contributions to the habilitation of the infants and children they are treating. In the **interdisciplinary**

model, the various professionals work with each other in jointly planned programs. The emphasis is on interaction among team members, who help and rely upon each other to provide well-coordinated services for the infant or child. Still, each professional develops separate goals and objectives specific to his or her discipline (Gallina, 1987; Peterson, 1987).

In contrast, the goals and objectives in the transdisciplinary model are jointly developed and prioritized by the team, including the parents. After the team identifies the child's strengths, weaknesses, and deficits in various natural environments (e.g., school, home), direct instruction is provided in those settings by the most appropriate specialists. For instance, the physical therapist may teach Janet to climb up and down the steps of the Metro bus to overcome her poor "equilibrium reactions," and the speech pathologist may document Janet's communication demands on the Metro bus and in Burton's Grocery.

The transdisciplinary approach effectively integrates program goals and objectives from various disciplines and professionals. Integration begins in the assessment process and extends through programming. Each team member is responsible for sharing information and skills so that multiple interventions with the child can occur simultaneously. Lyon and Lyon (1980) have identified three characteristics vital to the transdisciplinary approach. The first is a **joint team effort**. This implies that a group of professionals is jointly responsible for both program planning and program delivery. The second is a **staff development approach**. This emphasizes the need for the parents and team members to train one another, drawing upon their particular expertise, information, and experiences. As Lyon and Lyon state, the transdisciplinary approach requires that "members of an educational team need to realize and accept that other individual professionals bring uniquely different experience, information, and skills with them into the group" (p. 253). The third, and undoubtedly the core, characteristic is the **role release** concept. In this transcending mechanism, various specialists teach others (including the parents) to implement the training procedures traditionally relegated to their profession. Role release does not mean that professional responsibilities are abdicated. Hutchinson (1974) clearly stated that professional accountability was not relinquished in the transdisciplinary approach. Quite the contrary! Team members must remain accountable for what they teach others and for how well others acquire the skills. Role release from one team member to another can take several forms, with varying degrees of technical expertise.

A key ingredient in the transdisciplinary approach is the **program facilitator**, a member of the transdisciplinary team who is responsible for coordinating and integrating delivery of services from team members. This role, in most cases, is assumed by the classroom teacher, who typically has the most contact with the child. The program facilitator gathers information from the disciplines, synthesizes this information, and incorporates it into an effective, functional, integrated intervention strategy with the assistance and guidance of the other team members. The program facilitator does not formulate and develop the child's goals and objectives; the team jointly develops and prioritizes each child's unique goals and objectives. Regardless of who assumes the role of program facilitator, role release among all professionals is a fundamental and essential precept in the transdisciplinary approach.

SERVICE DELIVERY MODELS

The transdisciplinary approach dovetails neatly with the service delivery models typically used for infants and children with severe disabilities. Although there is much overlapping and many variations, basically there are six preschool delivery models: (1) home-based service delivery, (2) home-based followed by center-based service delivery, (3) home-based and center-based service delivery, (4) center-based service delivery, (5) integrated center-based service delivery, and (6) consultative service delivery. This list presents them in a hierarchy from the most restrictive to the most integrative physical placement. An apparently restrictive placement, however, can offer a high level of integration. Project Telstar, for instance, is a home-based service delivery program that systematically places children without disabilities in the home of a child with severe disabilities.

Home-Based Service Delivery Model

The central purpose of the **home-based service delivery** model is to serve infants and children with severe disabilities in the home, using the parents as the primary intervention agents. While this model varies from program to program, its basic intent is to teach parents how to use pedagogical techniques and procedures to educate and train their child in a one-to-one home setting. In most home-based models, a transdisciplinary team formulates and develops long-term goals for the infant, toddler, or young child. From these goals, precise weekly prescriptions are devised. Typically, the program facilitator meets with the family once a week to evaluate the child's progress and to provide additional instructional procedures. The parent is then observed working with the child to ensure that the prescribed behavior is being fostered. The following week a similar procedure is followed, with baseline data again collected at the beginning of the session.

While this structure is typical of the home-based model, there are many variations. Largely, variations have evolved from a basic desire to improve the services offered. The greatest criticism leveled against the home-based model is lack of interaction with nondisabled children. It is argued that a child with severe disabilities can acquire desirable, appropriate behavior more quickly and maintain it more easily by observing and imitating children without disabilities. An innovative program that solves this weakness is Project Telstar, which places children with severe disabilities in a "satellite" home with peers without disabilities. Located near each child's residence is the satellite worker

FIGURE 12.4

Children educated in the home-based service delivery model must have contact with children without disabilities.

(Courtesy of Angela Brimer.)

who cares for and programs for both children (Karnes & Zehrbach, 1977). Probably the second most common criticism was alluded to in chapter 11. Many parents are reluctant to teach their infant or child at home. This problem was addressed in Proyecto Casa, in which two specially trained high school students visited the home three times a week to provide stimulation and training to the infant or child with severe disabilities (Peterson, 1987). Between visits, others in the home are encouraged to continue with this training.

The transdisciplinary model works well with home-based service delivery. As depicted in figure 12.5, a facilitator has the primary responsibility for assisting the parents in implementing the program. Solid lines represent the flow of information from various specialists to the facilitator pertaining to the child's treatment and educational needs. The facilitator organizes this information into a comprehensive intervention program, which is primarily implemented by the parents. Broken lines represent additional contact by team members with the parents and child, such as initial assessment by a team member or monitoring of the progress made in the intervention program. The transdisciplinary model simplifies the lines of communication between parents (as the primary intervention agents) and the numerous specialists involved in

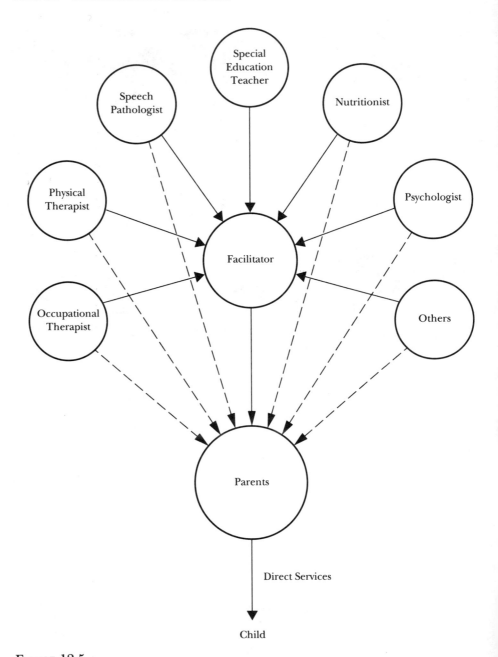

FIGURE 12.5

Transdisciplinary Model for Home-Based Service Delivery to Children with Severe Disabilities

(FROM: Sailor, Wayne, and Doug Guess. *Severely Handicapped Students: An Instructional Design.* Copyright © 1983 by Houghton Mifflin Company. Used with permission.)

early intervention. Parents communicate problems or areas of concern to the facilitator, who can access the appropriate team member. If, for instance, a feeding problem arises, the facilitator might contact both the occupational therapist and the nutritionist. These team members would then meet with the facilitator, parents, and infant to revise the feeding program or develop a new one.

Home-Based Followed by Center-Based Service Delivery Model

The **home-based followed by center-based service delivery** model, as its name suggests, serves infants, toddlers, and children with severe disabilities first in the home and later in a center, typically with other children with disabilities. The child usually spends one to three years in the home, with the parents as the primary intervention agents. Like the home-based paradigm, the basic intent of this approach is to teach parents how to use pedagogical techniques to educate their child in the home setting. A facilitator and a transdisciplinary team formulate long-term goals for the child, from which weekly objectives are generated. The first phase of this program is structurally very similar to the home-based model.

Generally when the child becomes 3 years old, the center assumes primary responsibility for intervention, extending and improving the skills developed by the parents. Contact with the parents does not end, however. In most programs, the facilitator analyzes the child's progress, determines the need for other transdisciplinary team members, and meets weekly with both trainers and parents to ensure that they are working toward the same objectives and are observing the same progress. Many programs offer a variety of other parental activities, ranging from group meetings and individual conferences to support groups and counseling services. Since the same treatment team works with the child from infancy, this model provides stability and continuity to both the parents and their child.

This structure is typical of the home-based followed by center-based model, but there are a number of variations. Probably the most common variation is in the child's age when the center-based training begins. Although most preschool programs begin at age 3, many begin shortly after birth. Another variation addresses the issue of contact with children without disabilities. Most programs in this model offer the child little or no such contact, but there are some programs in which one-third to one-half of the students are without disabilities. The amount of time spent in the center is also a common variable. Some children are at the center as little as three hours a day three days a week, others as much as six hours a day five days a week.

The transition from home-based to center-based service must first provide continuity for the children with severe disabilities and their parents. Continuity is enhanced if a member of the center-based team, not necessarily the teacher, serves as program facilitator during early intervention in the home. Services are then gradually shifted to the center program. This model has four advantages: (1) it provides continuous support to parents and to the child, (2) it extends the services of center-based programs into the home, (3) it moves the young child from the home to the center, and (4) it continues to assist the parents with home care problems and training programs.

Home-Based and Center-Based Service Delivery Model

Home-based and center-based service delivery educates children with severe disabilities in both the home and a center. Heavy reliance on this joint approach stems from the complementary benefits each setting offers. The home plays an important role in the child's early learning experiences, while the facilities of the center are needed for diagnosis, unique learning experiences, and modeling of desired behavior. Each setting can maintain and generalize skills taught by the other. For instance, parents can generalize eating skills taught by the staff at the center.

Following a comprehensive assessment, the transdisciplinary team formulates long-term goals from which weekly objectives for the student are developed. Unlike the home-based followed by center-based model, in which the parents provide instruction independent of the center, in this model the trainers at the center and the parents must be in harmony on every programming aspect. Since programming occurs simultaneously in the home and at the center, they must agree on instructional objectives, programming methods, reinforcement patterns, and prompting styles. While the most common parental activity is cooperative teaching, many programs offer a variety of other parental activities. For instance, in Project PEECH (Precise Early Education of Children with Handicaps) parental activities include large and small group meetings, individual conferences, classroom observation, and assisting with teaching, using the parent library and toy lending library, preparing the parent newsletter, and serving on the advisory board.

While the home-based and center-based service delivery model is the most popular way to educate young children with severe disabilities, there are numerous variations in how these programs are administered. Differences range from the age at which instruction is initiated to the diversity of services offered by the center and the instructional structure used. Two programs that illustrate structural diversity are the Central Institute of the Deaf, in which instruction occurs in large apartments that resemble middle class homes, and Project PEECH, in which instruction occurs in large, sophisticated playgrounds. Beyond the language component, there is also little agreement among programs about the curriculum. Some follow a traditional developmental approach, others the Piagetian philosophy, and still others a functional approach. But probably the greatest differences occur in the amount of integration with nondisabled children. Most programs are entirely composed of children with disabilities; some have a few peers without disabilities; others have a slightly larger contingency; and a few programs have about half students without disabilities.

The transition between home-based and center-based service delivery must provide continuity for the children and their parents. Continuity is enhanced if the members of the center-based team also provide service at home, consistent with the transdisciplinary model presented in figure 12.5. A member of the center-based team, not necessarily the teacher, should serve as program facilitator to work with the parents. The services for the child then shift gradually to the center.

Center-Based Service Delivery Model

Center-based service delivery programs provide educational, therapeutic, and individualized services to infants, toddlers, and children with severe disabilities in a school setting primarily serving others with disabilities. In this arrangement infants or children are brought to the center on a scheduled basis, usually five days a week, for all or part of the day. In most center-based programs, the first step is a comprehensive and functional assessment conducted by the transdisciplinary team. The program facilitator and the team then formulate long-term goals for the child, from which weekly objectives are derived. The teaching staff at the center provides the majority of the training to the child, although parents are encouraged to participate in training both at the center and at home.

As figure 12.6 illustrates, the center-based system uses the transdisciplinary model in a slightly different manner from home-based systems. First, the teacher and teaching aides at the center assume major responsibility for the direct delivery of services to the child. In this paradigm, the teacher is typically the program facilitator, who has access to the other team members when needed to resolve difficult or recurring problems. This model may be extended to the home where parents are taught how to provide additional training, maintenance, or generalization of acquired skills. This process is illustrated in the figure by the extra arrow going from the facilitator to the parents. In this model the parents are members of the transdisciplinary team as direct services are provided primarily by center staff members.

Center-based programs offer several advantages not available in home-based programs. One is greater access to a variety of specialists. The positive features of the transdisciplinary model are readily implemented in center-based programs. A second advantage is parent respite from the day-to-day responsibility of caring for their child. The fact that the child is out of the home for significant periods allows parents to engage in other employment, family, and household activities. A third advantage is an opportunity for parents to interact regularly with other parents of children with disabilities, to share information, concerns, and feelings about their roles, and to provide support to each other during trying times.

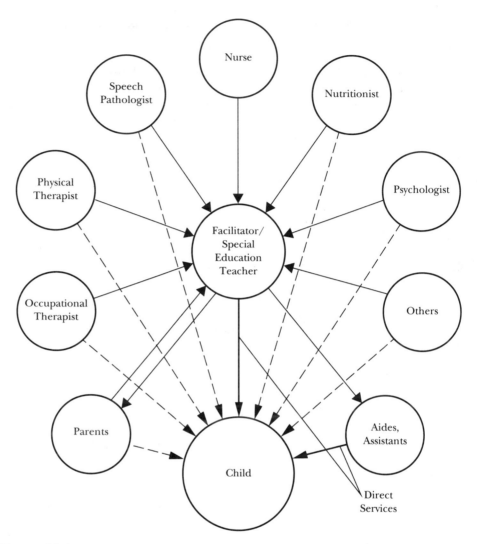

FIGURE 12.6

Transdisciplinary Model for Center-Based Service Delivery to Children with Severe Disabilities

(Adapted from Sailor, Wayne, and Doug Guess. *Severely Handicapped Students: An Instructional Design.* Copyright © 1983 by Houghton Mifflin Company. Used with permission.)

Integrated Center-Based Service Delivery Model

The integration of preschool children with severe disabilities in programs in which at least half of the other children are without disabilities has long been recommended as the most desirable way to serve such children (Bricker, 1978). While many reasons are given, the strongest arguments center around two points: complying with the child's human and civil rights and the effects of modeling on the development of appropriate behaviors. Most preschool integration efforts have concentrated on children with mild disabilities, ignoring children with severe disabilities. This restrictive philosophy has been described as the **doctrine of limitations** (Sontag, Certo, & Burton, 1979). Recent federal mandates, coupled with the trend toward normalization, have increased interest in **integrated center-based service delivery** for children with severe disabilities. Rather than emphasizing the differences between children with and without severe disabilities, these approaches focus on the commonalities all young children share. It is argued that there is no need to create a separate preschool program for children with severe disabilities; instead, the appropriate program for these children is the one that generally serves the nondisabled population.

While the proportion of children without disabilities varies from program to program, the recommended proportion is no less than 50 percent. Programs must attempt to maximize interaction between the children with severe disabilities and peers without disabilities through a variety of integrative approaches, most notably temporal, social, and instructional integration (Peterson, 1987). **Temporal integration** means that the child with severe disabilities spends a significant amount of time with nondisabled peers (e.g., spending the school day with such classmates). **Social integration** means that the child with severe disabilities interacts with nondisabled peers in a socially acceptable manner (e.g., appropriately playing with such classmates). **Instructional integration** means the child with severe disabilities is trained next to and in the same environment as peers without disabilities (e.g., learning with such classmates).

The integrated service delivery model is structurally similar to many of the models previously discussed. The first step is a comprehensive and functional assessment conducted by the transdisciplinary team. The program facilitator and the team then formulate long-term goals and weekly objectives for the child with severe disabilities. In this paradigm, however, goals and weekly objectives must also be developed for the children without disabilities, and the facilitator must systematically plan integrative activities among children with and without severe disabilities. For an integrative preschool program to be successful, it must facilitate peer-peer interactions as well as meeting the training and educational needs of both types of children (Guralnick, 1978).

Consultative Service Delivery Model

In the **consultative service delivery** model, the delivery of educational services to children with severe disabilities is indirect. Services typically take the form of technical assistance to the staff members in the child's educational programs, such as special instructional materials or equipment, a special methodology, or special diagnostic services. The first step again is a comprehensive and functional assessment conducted by the transdisciplinary team. The program facilitator and the team then formulate long-term goals and weekly objectives. But

FIGURE 12.7

Toddlers and children with severe disabilities should be educated alongside peers without disabilities.

(Courtesy of English Garden Toys.)

here the similarity to other models ends. In this model the child with severe disabilities is educated in a program in which all the other students are not disabled.

Since this is quite likely to be the teacher's initial contact with a child with severe disabilities, technical assistance takes on vital importance to the success of the program. The technical assistance has two components. The first is support from the transdisciplinary team in selecting instructional materials and a methodology or in preparing diagnostic analyses. The second is specialized training materials, techniques, and procedures to increase the competence of the inexperienced direct service provider. Some programs, such as the Wilkerson Hearing and Speech Center, conduct training through slides, movies, videotapes, printed materials, oral presentations, and group discussions.

One consultative service delivery model focuses on prevention. Termed the **prenatal model**, it promotes prenatal care, parenting skills, and interaction patterns in **high-risk potential mothers** who are enrolled in junior high and high schools. An added goal is to encourage these teenagers to recognize and respond to the social, emotional, cognitive, communicative, and physical needs of their children. An example of this model is Project FEED (Facilitative Environments Encouraging Development). The project population is drawn from areas where teenage pregnancy is high and environmental factors are significantly associated with high-risk births.

The rationale for Project FEED is essentially that a high-risk infant is the product of a high-risk mother, and that these mothers are usually teenagers. A large percentage have negative attitudes toward their unborn children, have inadequate medical care, lack male support, come from homes characterized by serious social and emotional problems, and give birth to premature babies who are frequently disabled. To broaden their background and change their attitudes, the potential mothers in this program are assigned work as aides in a model preschool class for children with disabilities and as attendants in a community hospital. The preschool class experience is intended to help the teenagers develop positive attitudes toward infants and children with disabilities and to understand their needs. The hospital experience is designed to promote a more positive attitude toward hospitals so that the teenagers will be willing to seek prenatal and postnatal care.

PHYSICAL FACILITIES AND ENVIRONMENTS

Infants and children with severe disabilities often experience difficulty interacting with their environment. This limits their development in a variety of ways and domains. The preschool teacher of such children must therefore create an environment that maximizes their overall development, one that offers opportunities for the children to explore actively and to assume a more passive role. The environment must provide activities that are inherently rewarding and noncompetitive. It must encourage both teacher-child and child-child interactions. The physical facility should be as flexible as possible, to foster social interactions and contact with the environment (Jones, 1977; Peterson, 1987). The preschool environment provides this vital first step in facilitating the child's overall development and growth.

Classroom design is likewise critical to successful intervention efforts. The design, equipment, and supplies should provide optimal educational opportunities for the children, an efficient service delivery system for teachers and staff, and careful attention to the health and safety needs of all. Obviously no two classrooms will be arranged in exactly the same way. Designs vary with the size and shape of the room, the needs of the children being served, the services being provided, the use of parents and volunteers, and the funds available for materials and equipment. However, certain features are essential to any classroom or facility serving children with severe disabilities.

Indoor Facilities

The interior space of a facility or classroom should provide for the varied and special needs of infants, toddlers, and children with severe disabilities. A properly designed preschool environment includes specialized equipment unique to those children and the equipment, materials, and supplies usually found in any preschool program (e.g., toys and mats). Typical of the specialized equipment are items for proper positioning and body alignment and adaptive materials for feeding, toilet training, and other self-care needs. Other useful items are a refrigerator and stove for food preparation, child-size tables and chairs for feeding and group instruction, and storage bins. Sand, water, and foam play areas may also be incorporated into the classroom.

Jones (1977) indicated that a preschool facility should have the following six components: (1) reception area, (2) instruction area, (3) bathroom area, (4) observation area, (5) storage area, and (6) conference area. The reception area is primarily designed for parents dropping off and picking up their children. It should be equipped and arranged for optimal interaction between parents and staff members. It can include a daily sign-up sheet, a health-check form, and a bulletin board to display important information for parents. The area should have shelves to store extra clothes, diapers, and other personal items for each child and places to store larger items such as wheelchairs and strollers.

The importance of the reception area cannot be overemphasized. Since many preschool children with severe disabilities are susceptible to illness and have chronic health problems that require continual monitoring, the reception area can be used by the staff to check the children as they arrive. Emergency and first-aid equipment should be kept in a convenient location in this area.

The instruction or training area should be flexible to permit and encourage a variety of activities. It should easily accommodate both individual and small group tasks. It must contain specialized equipment and materials appropriate for preschool children with severe disabilities, for instance, mats, standing tables, bolsters, wedges, parallel bars, walkers, therapy balls, and rolls. A small waterbed should be located there. To accommodate the instructional activities, the classroom should have movable cupboards and cabinets, which allow various divisions of the room as program needs change. A nap and rest area, with mats, mobiles, and musical toys, should be in a relatively quiet area of the classroom where traffic flow is kept to a minimum. One end of the room should have tables, chairs, storage space for instructional materials, a sink, a food storage cabinet, and a refrigerator. There should be desks for the teacher and teaching assistants and a filing cabinet, where the teaching staff can keep correspondence, progress analyses, and teaching files on each student. The classroom should also have space for speech, occupational, and physical therapy. A number of common sense health-related practices should be incorporated into the classroom, such as procedures for disinfecting materials and equipment and for maintaining a sanitary classroom. Disinfectant supplies should be stored throughout the classroom in areas out of reach of the children; there should be individual bins for storing each child's instructional materials; and the times and situations when staff members are required to wash their hands (Bauer & Shea, 1986). It is further recommended that all classroom personnel have first-aid training (including cardiopulmonary resuscitation), and each staff member should be familiar with the health problems of each child (Sailor & Guess, 1983). These simple and easily administered

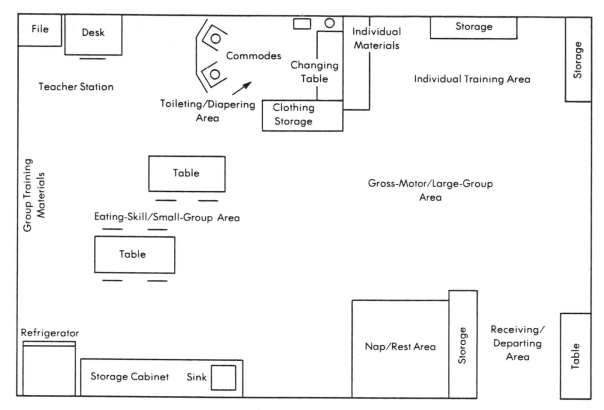

FIGURE 12.8

Floor Plan 1 for a Preschool Program for Children with Severe Disabilities

(From: Sailor, Wayne, and Doug Guess. *Severely Handicapped Students: An Instructional Design.* Copyright © 1983 by Houghton Mifflin Company. Used with permission.)

health precautions should reduce absenteeism among both children and staff members from illness.

Since instruction in functional toileting skills is an important part of the educational process, the bathroom should be adjacent to the therapy area of the classroom. It needs to have potty chairs, diapering tables, and toileting and diapering supplies. In this area children receive training in partial undressing and redressing and washing and drying their hands, as well as using the toilet.

An observation room or space should be provided in the facility so that parents and others can analyze a child's progress or learn new ways to educate the child. The facility should have storage space at strategic locations throughout the classroom. Finally, there should be space for transdisciplinary team meetings and meetings with parents.

The physical arrangements of classrooms and facilities vary. Any preschool environment, however, should allow a smooth flow of activities from one instructional area to another. Figures 12.8 and 12.9 present two physical

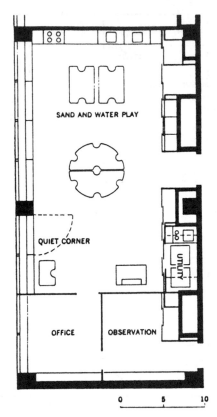

FIGURE 12.9

Floor Plan 2 for a Preschool Program for Children with Severe Disabilities

(FROM: "Pioneering Nursery School" by E. Berkely, 1969, *Architectural Forum.*)

configurations appropriate for the varied and special needs of preschool children with severe disabilities. Neither contains every area specified in this discussion, but they offer examples of workable designs for preschool facilities.

Outdoor Environments and Play Areas

Because the child with severe disabilities is often deprived of the opportunity to explore natural environments, the outdoor play area should provide grass, trees, water, plants, and other items typically found in outdoor settings. Two playgrounds are outstanding examples of attempts to meet the varied needs of children with severe disabilities. The first, the Stanton Developmental Playground, shown in figure 12.10, is divided into four areas, each offering varied experiences with natural materials: the bridge tree house, the foam and sand pits at ground level, the sand and water tables fed by an artificial waterfall, and the hill circle with embedded slide and periscope in the fence. This customized playground gives primary consideration to children using several types of locomotion. For instance, some activities offer multilevel viewing for children

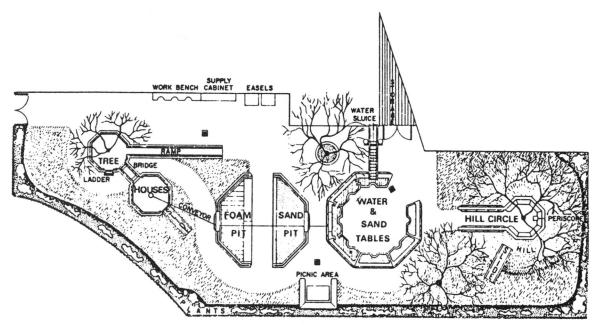

FIGURE 12.10

Stanton Developmental Playground for a Preschool for Children with Severe Disabilities

(FROM: "Physical Facilities and Environments" by M. Jones in *Early Childhood Education for Exceptional Children* by J. Jordon, A. Hayden, M. Karnes, and M. Woods (Eds.), 1977, Reston, VA: Council for Exceptional Children. Reprinted by permission.)

in wheelchairs, there are activities for children who cannot move about, and there are surface configurations in which children can develop gross motor skills.

The other exemplary playground, Project PEECH, shown in figure 12.11, was likewise designed by a landscape architect working closely with specialists in the motor development of preschool children with disabilities. The facilities are structured to provide activities that promote the development of children with severe disabilities. The playground is a total learning environment made up of interconnecting structures situated around a large open court. There are several climbing structures, with platforms, ladders, a sliding pole, and a slide; a winding, multilevel tricycle path; tunnels; tire swings; and a system of water troughs emptying into a wading pool surrounded by a sand play area. There is also a classroom area isolated from the remainder of the playground, so that instruction can occur outside.

According to its developers, the Project PEECH Learning Playground was designed to promote language, cognitive, social, and motor development in preschool children with disabilities. The colors, shapes, sizes, and textures of

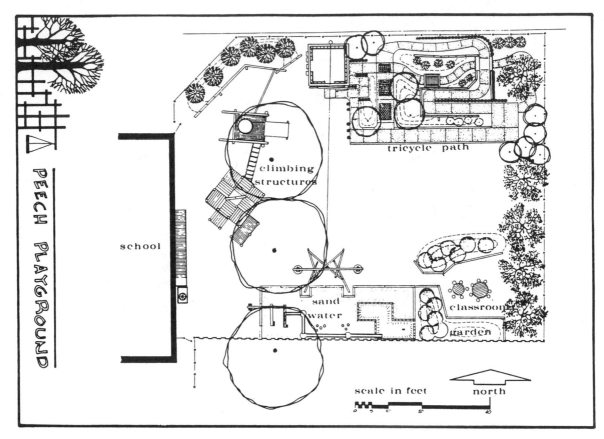

FIGURE 12.11

Project PEECH Learning Playground for a Preschool for Children with Severe Disabilities

(FROM: "Physical Facilities and Environments" by M. Jones in *Early Childhood Education for Exceptional Children* by J. Jordon, A. Hayden, M. Karnes, and M. Woods (Eds.), 1977, Reston, VA: Council for Exceptional Children. Reprinted by permission.)

the playground equipment are varied so that concepts about these qualities introduced in the classroom can be generalized to the playground. Structures such as tunnels, wide platforms on the climbers, and the very wide slide promote social development and language modeling. Equipment is designed so that children can practice a variety of motor skills at different developmental levels. For example, opportunities for walking on a balance beam range from using the wide railroad ties to walking on a narrow beam several feet above the ground (Jones, 1977).

Teachers may use these playgrounds in two ways. First, in periods of supervised free play, children are informally encouraged to practice basic motor skills as they interact with the playground environment. Language concepts such as up-down and slow-fast are introduced naturally by the teachers as opportunities arise. However, the development of preschool children with severe disabilities is too important to be left to chance, so teachers also devise lesson plans for use on the playground. These more formal activities typically have a game format. The games encourage each child to practice basic skills at his or her own level of development. They may motivate children to practice climbing, jumping, and throwing skills as well as promoting communication, socialization, and cognitive development (Jones, 1977). The developers of the Stanton Developmental Playground and the Project PEECH Learning Playground feel, as Piaget did, that play is the natural medium for the growth and development of young children with severe disabilities.

Conclusion

Early intervention for infants, toddlers, and children with severe disabilities has long been recognized as a vital cornerstone of integration and education. Yet this did not translate to the widespread creation of educational programs for children under age 5. Even today, only a small proportion of infants and young children with severe disabilities are being served in preschool educational programs. Recently enacted federal legislation mandates appropriate preschool services and encourages the development of new approaches for serving this previously underserved population. Teachers will become consultants, parents will become interventionists, therapists will become trainers, and professionals outside the educational system will become consultants in optimizing the development of the child. This long overdue attention to preschool education will give professionals the opportunity to reevaluate existing approaches to training infants and children with severe disabilities. The bottom line of this reexamination is to provide instructional strategies and services that maximize each child's growth and development.

SUMMARY

1. Previous federal mandates fell well short of providing appropriate intervention services for preschool children with disabilities. Now the Education of the Handicapped Amendments of 1986 require that children between 3 and 5 be adequately served by 1991. Somewhat later, infants and toddlers under 3 will receive appropriate intervention services.

2. Two curricula have been used for preschool children with severe disabilities: the developmental curriculum and the functional curriculum.

3. The basic assumption of the developmental curriculum is that the sequence of development in children without disabilities provides a logical structure for the educational goals of young children with severe disabilities.

4. The developmental approach may not provide a complete preschool curriculum because (1) it does not eliminate inappropriate behavior, (2) children with severe disabilities arrive at developmental milestones through atypical routes, and (3) it is not concerned with the acquisition of tool skills.

5. The functional curriculum focuses on the skills the young child needs to interact appropriately in his or her present environment or a future environment.

6. Four service treatment approaches are used with young children with severe disabilities: the unidisciplinary, multidisciplinary, interdisciplinary, and transdisciplinary models.

7. The most appropriate service system is the transdisciplinary team approach, in which professionals from a number of disciplines coordinate their services by pooling information, knowledge, and skills to set joint goals and objectives for the child.

8. The program facilitator in the transdisciplinary approach has primary responsibility for coordinating and integrating services from various team members.

9. Six preschool program models have been used to educate young children with severe disabilities: (1) home-based service delivery, (2) home-based followed by center-based service delivery, (3) home-based and center-based service delivery, (4) center-based service delivery, (5) integrated center-based service delivery, and (6) consultative service delivery.

10. In the home-based service delivery model, young children with severe disabilities are taught at home, with the parents being the primary intervention agents. Parents are taught pedagogical techniques and procedures by the transdisciplinary team.

11. In the home-based followed by center-based model, the children are first taught at the home by the parents and then at a center, typically with other children with disabilities.

12. The home-based and center-based service delivery model relies on the complementary benefits the home and the center offer in directly educating or assisting in the education of young children with severe disabilities.

13. The center-based service delivery model is primarily oriented toward providing educational services for young children with severe disabilities in a classroom setting.

14. In the integrated center-based service delivery system, young children with severe disabilities are educated alongside and in the same program with peers without disabilities.

15. In the consultative service delivery model, young children with severe disabilities are educated in a program designed for peers without disabilities.

Only one child with severe disabilities is enrolled in each program. The transdisciplinary team provides technical aid and assistance to program staff members.

16. The prenatal model is a unique consultative service delivery system that promotes prenatal care, parenting skills, and more positive parent-child inter-action patterns in high-risk potential mothers who are currently enrolled in junior high or high schools.

17. The preschool classroom must be designed for efficient service delivery by teachers and staff and optimal educational opportunities for children with severe disabilities. It should attend to the health and safety needs of both children and staff.

18. The preschool classroom should include the specialized equipment and materials unique to young children with severe disabilities and the equipment, materials, and supplies typically found in preschool programs for children without disabilities.

19. A preschool facility should have six components: (1) a reception area, (2) an instruction area, (3) a bathroom area, (4) an observation area, (5) a storage area, and (6) a conference area.

20. Many preschool programs for children with severe disabilities have play-ground facilities designed to promote communication, socialization, and cog-nitive development. Play is the natural medium for the growth and develop-ment of young children with severe disabilities.

CHAPTER 13

Instructional Modifications for Persons with Severe Disabilities

(Courtesy of Lynda Atherton.)

Why does a society spend time, energy, and resources to educate its citizens? What is the purpose of education? In a few cases, the answers are apparent. Medical students are educated to become competent doctors. Students majoring in special education are educated to become better teachers of students with disabilities. But what about public school students? Is the purpose of their education to increase their reading decoding and comprehension skills and to raise their competence in mathematical operations? Or is it to prepare them to live, work, and function as citizens in today's society? While it is not universally agreed, most people would say that the purpose of education is to prepare students to live and work in society (Kokaska & Brolin, 1985). This is true not only for persons with severe disabilities but also for university-bound valedictorians.

CHANGING GOALS OF EDUCATION FOR STUDENTS WITH SEVERE DISABILITIES

If persons with severe disabilities are going to be successfully integrated into society, they must develop the skills necessary for a rewarding and satisfactory life. Since the purpose of education is to prepare people to live and work in society, it is clearly the responsibility of the school program, from preschool on, to develop or assist in the development of skills that prepare students with severe disabilities to do this. This represents a dramatic change, because, instead of taking place solely in a classroom, the teaching of important daily living skills must also take place in community settings (Certo & Kohl, 1984; Horner, Sprague, & Wilcox, 1982). The public school, indeed the regular classroom, is the environment in which the student with severe disabilities must be prepared for eventual community living.

The goal of preparing students for independent living may be overambitious. Few, if any, of us live independently. We depend on a great many services and individuals for survival, from generic community services (e.g., mass transit, fire protection, grocery stores) to social service agencies (e.g., residential assistance, income support, daily guidance). Independence is a relative concept, measured by the range of activities and the proportion of time an individual can live without assistance. It is a direct function of environmental demands, changes in these demands, and the daily attempt to meet these demands.

The concept of independent living extends beyond simple self-reliance. The goal of preparing students for independent living is not simply to give them the same access to community services as persons without disabilities; it may also include reducing their dependence on community agencies (e.g., for income support). Successful preparation for independent living will allow persons with severe disabilities to live in less supported and less restrictive environments—in short, more normalized environments.

Independent living includes activities that reduce dependence on others and activities that give access to higher quality environments. Efforts to increase independent living may range from teaching people to be less dependent in group homes to teaching them to live completely independently in unsupervised apartments, from teaching them to work with less supervision to placing them in competitive employment; from teaching them skills that can

FIGURE 13.1

There is now greater recognition that students with severe disabilities must learn the skills that will prepare them for greater independence in home and community living.

(Courtesy of the Crestwood Company.)

be used in a segregated recreational environment to enabling them to participate in an integrated park district recreation program. The role of education, at the preschool, elementary, junior high, or high school level, should be to assist in the transition of students from the educational arena to the general community.

The goal of community integration and the focus on transition have, in recent years, redefined the scope and range of special education services for students with severe disabilities. Special educators now realize that these students must learn the skills that prepare them for greater independence at home, in the community, and in a vocation. The development of these varied skills requires content changes in instructional assessment, curriculum, methods, and settings.

ASSESSMENT OF STUDENTS WITH SEVERE DISABILITIES

The initial process in developing an instructional program for students with severe disabilities is to gather information about the student through assessment procedures. The intent is to determine the student's present skills and behaviors. Assessment enables parents, educators, and other professionals to determine the student's most pressing instructional needs. Once these are identified, they must be analyzed to ensure that they are functional, chronologically age-appropriate, and community referenced (Browder, 1987).

Student repertoires or **ecological inventories** assess whether the student's existing behaviors and skills are functional, age-appropriate, and community referenced. These inventories reflect the actual skills necessary to participate in natural community environments (Browder, 1987; Brown, Branston, Hamre-Nietupski, Pumpian, et al., 1979). Items are identified from an extensive inventory of skills performed by chronological-age peers without disabilities in the community in which the student will live after graduating from school. Student performance of these priority activities is then assessed.

There are four basic steps in conducting a student repertoire or ecological inventory. In the first step, the teacher identifies the skills required to participate in the selected priority activity, by observing and analyzing the performance of chronological-age peers without disabilities. In the second step, the teacher determines whether the student is able to perform the identified skills. In the third step, the teacher determines the discrepancy between the identified skills and the student's performance. If the student was unable to perform a skill, the teacher observes and analyzes the characteristics and aspects of that skill with which the student had difficulty. The fourth step is either to teach the skill to the student, to develop an adaptation or prosthesis that will assist the student in performing the skill, or to teach the student a similar skill that can be generalized to the skill required.

To illustrate, suppose that Mr. and Mrs. Mifflin, Robbie's parents, and Ms. Bradley, his teacher, selected crossing Maple Avenue at Twelfth Street as a priority activity for Robbie. In the first step, Ms. Bradley would identify all the skills 12-year-old boys without disabilities use when crossing Maple Avenue (e.g., pausing at the curb, looking to the right and to the left for oncoming vehicles, and walking across the street). In the second step, Ms. Bradley would observe and analyze Robbie's attempts to cross Maple Avenue. In the third step, Ms. Bradley would specify all the deficiencies Robbie exhibited in attempting to cross Maple Avenue. Specific knowledge of Robbie's inability to cross Maple Avenue gives Ms. Bradley critical information concerning instructional methods. In the fourth step, Ms. Bradley would determine whether it is more efficient to teach street crossing to Robbie, to develop an adaptation or prothesis to assist Robbie in performing the skill, or to teach Robbie a similar skill that could be generalized to crossing Maple Avenue. After analyzing and synthesizing this information, Ms. Bradley would generate short-term objectives while simultaneously determining what and how Robbie would be taught.

The student repertoire or ecological inventory is especially useful and appropriate when assessing a student's competence levels. If the purpose of education is to prepare students to participate in a variety of community environments to the maximum extent, student repertoires or ecological inventories are important tools, informing educators of the actual skills necessary for functioning in and meeting the demands of those community environments (Falvey, 1986).

CURRICULUM APPROACHES

The basic curriculum challenge to educators is determining the specific instructional activities that enhance community integration. Since there is seldom enough time to prepare the student adequately for total independence, the selection of items to include and items to exclude is particularly important.

Each selected instructional activity represents an explicit or implicit priority analysis based on the student's projected environment. But the priority analysis itself determines, to a considerable extent, the projected environment, since the student will likely not inhabit an environment after graduation that he or she was not prepared for in school.

The Criterion of Ultimate Functioning

The concentration of educational programs on community integration has been referred to as the **criterion of ultimate functioning** (Brown, Nietupski & Hamre-Nietupski, 1976). This concept means providing students with the skills perceived to be necessary for functioning in postschool environments. Central to this criterion is predicting, at the outset, where the student is likely to be located at the completion of schooling. The student is then prepared to adapt to the demands and expectations unique to that environment.

Distinct differences from community to community affect the life-styles of inhabitants. In small communities, for example, a public bus system may not be available, and students must be taught to use other forms of transportation. In larger communities numerous transportation modes, including public buses and rapid transit trains, may be available. In small communities, there may be few public recreational services and no arcade centers or miniature golf courses. Large communities may offer residents a large variety of public recreations, including arcade centers and miniature golf courses. Instruction in these activities is then not only appropriate but also necessary. The curriculum offered to persons residing in a small community would thus vary in several important dimensions from the curriculum provided to urban residents. Instructional activities must represent the environment in which the student is expected to live.

The Ecological Inventory

Because communities differ in a number of critical variables, no single curriculum is appropriate for every community. A recent trend in serving students with severe disabilities is to determine which instructional activities are functionally appropriate for a specific environment. This approach, called the *ecological inventory,* identifies functional skills and performance criteria directly referenced to the demands and expectations of the local community. Community referencing of the curricular content serves the dual role of validating and prioritizing the student's instructional objectives. Objectives are selected, not according to their position on a developmental sequence or according to prerequisite or readiness skills, but rather according to their frequency and importance in the specific environment the student will likely inhabit after graduating.

The ecological inventory focuses on discrepancies between the student's current abilities and the skills he or she must acquire to function in four domains of his or her present and future environments. Discrepancies in these four domains are the subjects for the instructional program. The student's present performance levels are compared to his or her present and future needs in the domestic domain, the leisure-recreational domain, the general community domain, and the vocational domain. Environmental features are then analyzed to delineate the performance demands, naturally occurring consequences, and environmental demands of each domain. In turn, this information is used to design the student's instructional program, identifying descrepancies between the student's present skills and those demanded in the different settings (e.g., Bellamy & Wilcox, 1980; Green, Canipe, Way, & Reid, 1986; Wilcox & Bellamy, 1982).

Domestic domain.   Skills in the **domestic domain** generally include those needed to reside in a community dwelling, to maintain a healthy life-style, and to present an acceptable personal appearance. For persons with severe disabilities the domestic domain is crucial for several reasons. First, these skills are mandatory for sustaining a healthy and vigorous life. Second, they are necessary for successful integration into the community (Schalock, Harper, & Carver, 1981). Competence in household responsibilities will practically guarantee successful living in a community residence. An acceptable personal appearance will greatly increase the student's chances of forming personal relationships with persons without disabilities.

A wide variety of program methods and materials have been used to teach domestic skills to students with severe disabilities. One approach, proposed by Cuvo (1978), uses a **task analysis** in conjunction with modeling by persons whose performance already meets standards of acceptability. A custodian, for instance, may be asked to model sweeping or mopping. A cook may be asked to model food preparation skills. Task analyses of these skills are then made and used to develop a training program. A second approach uses **pictorial instruction** (Spellman, DeBriere, Jarboe, Campbell, & Harris, 1978), reasoning that, "since persons with severe disabilities cannot use many of the existing symbol systems to obtain new information, picture books were developed as an instructional format" (p. 393). Various domestic skills can be taught through pictorial instruction manuals. In essence, pictures demonstrate the sequence in which certain tasks are completed. Pictorial instruction has been used for everything from food preparation to housekeeping and from shopping to clothing and linen care. Figure 13.2 shows picture book instructions for preparing a hot dog and chocolate milk.

Leisure-recreational domain.   All too often, persons with severe disabilities do not develop the skills required to use their free time creatively and constructively. Since nonpurposeful time dominates the life-style of persons with severe disabilities, many professionals argue that they must be taught recreational activities (Wehman, Renzaglia, & Bates, 1985). This is the theme of the

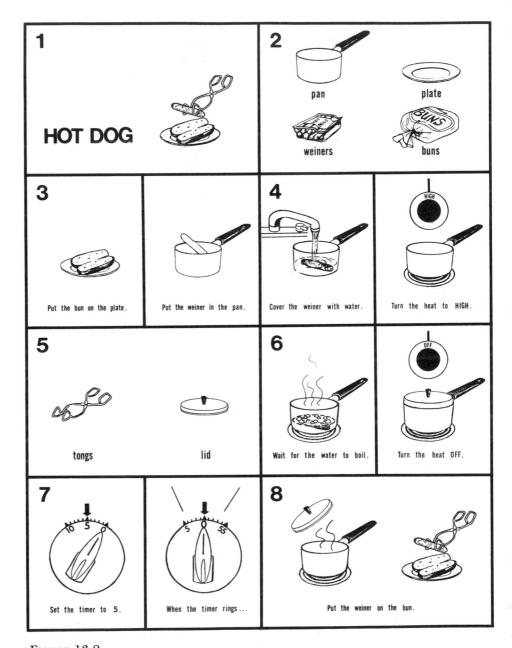

FIGURE 13.2

Picture Book Instructions for Preparing a Hot Dog and Chocolate Milk

(FROM: Spellman, C. R., DeBriere, T., Jarboe, D., Campbell, S., & Harris, C. (1978). "Pictorial instruction: Training daily living skills." In M. E. Snell (Ed.), *Systematic instruction of the moderately and severely handicapped* (pp. 391–411). Columbus, OH: C. E. Merrill Co.)

FIGURE 13.2 (continued)

leisure-recreational domain, specifically, to enable students with severe disabilities to engage in many of the same recreational activities as persons without disabilities. Undeniably, purposeful and constructive leisure activities play a key role in a person's social integration. Leisure and recreational activities, for instance, have been directly linked to developing physical fitness, physical coordination, physical attractiveness, social acceptability, interpersonal relationships, academic skills, community integration, and community normalization (Wehman, Renzaglia, Berry, Schutz, & Karan, 1978).

Leisure instruction is assuming increasing importance in the effort to foster independent living in students with severe disabilities. Professionals have designed instruction for developing leisure activities. For example, Wehman and Schleien (1980a, 1980b) have developed two comprehensive manuals that teachers can use to instruct their students in leisure-recreational activities. The first provides a structure for teaching a variety of hobby skills, such as camping, cooking, cycling, kite flying, painting, pet care, photography, and woodworking. The second manual pertains to teaching sport skills, such as badminton, basketball, bowling, croquet, fishing, golf, gymnastics, handball, horseshoes, shuffleboard, soccer, softball, swimming, tennis, volleyball, and weight training. Both manuals provide a task analysis of the skills, the teaching materials needed, instructional procedures, and criteria for successful performance of each activity. In a later article, Wehman and Schleien (1981) addressed the selection of leisure and recreational activities for persons with severe disabilities.

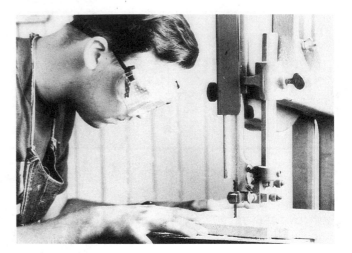

FIGURE 13.3

Purposeful and constructive leisure activities can play a key role in a person's future integration.

(FROM: Bancroft, serving people with developmental disabilities since 1883. Haddonfield, N. J., 08033.)

General community domain. The **general community domain** refers to a person's ability to participate independently in the myriad activities of community life, typically (1) using various community transit systems to move from one place to another, (2) shopping for groceries, clothing, personal care items, and household items, (3) using such community services as barber shops, telephones, and churches, and (4) eating in restaurants, cafeterias, and fast-food establishments.

The procurement of essential goods and services requires many varied behaviors. This domain includes consumer training on buying essential commodities and community-based instruction in the appropriate use of common services (e.g., barber shops and beauty salons). Obtaining a product or a service is only part of a complex process. It entails identifying the products or services a person needs for his or her life-style and survival, identifying where they may be obtained, and analyzing whether they are affordable. For persons with severe disabilities, those skills are a major avenue toward independent living and thus target behaviors for instruction at school. Teaching students with severe disabilities what and when to purchase is just as essential as teaching how to purchase.

An imaginative program that has become a classic clearly illustrates this point (Nietupski, Certo, Pumpian, & Belmore, 1976). In this instructional program, grocery shopping skills were directly tied to meal preparation. A prosthetic shopping aid was devised, consisting of removable tapes attached to grocery items at home. On each tape was a picture, icon, or logogram of that grocery item. As the items were used, the persons with severe disabilities would stick the tapes on a shopping list. When the new items were selected in the grocery store, students would remove the tapes from the list and put them on the newly purchased items. This technique combined meal preparation behavior with shopping behavior in a functional manner appropriate to students

FIGURE 13.4

Independent participation in the myriad activities of community life is an essential aspect of instruction for students with severe disabilities.

(Courtesy of Barbara Chatman.)

unable to read labels. Similar aids could be used in other areas, for instance, purchasing toiletries, household supplies, and clothing.

Vocational domain.   The development of **vocational domain** skills must receive primary emphasis in the educational program for students with severe disabilities. The extent to which students are prepared for remunerative employment will largely affect their community integration, the frequency of their recreational activities, and the range and sophistication of their life-style. There are several options for incorporating vocational training into an instructional program, depending on the availability of job-training programs in the community, the previous training provided to the student, and the vocational training resources in the public school.

Essentially, vocational training for students with severe disabilities falls into two approaches. In the most common type, the student is given prevocational training not specific to an employment site in the community. After graduation, the student typically enters sheltered employment. The second approach is similar to the vocational training program described in chapter 10. Potential remunerative employment sites are identified in the community, students with severe disabilities are assessed on the specific job skills demanded at a site, vocational objectives are established, the student is trained at the community site, and, after mastering the job requirements and criteria, the student is remuneratively placed in the community employment setting where he or she just completed training.

TRANSITIONAL CLUSTERING ACROSS DOMAINS

School programs that prepare students with severe disabilities for community living and work represent a significant departure from traditional educational services. Instead of concentrating on content, they emphasize processes. This orientation focuses directly on the outcomes of schooling—on the experiences that lead to a fulfilling and satisfying adult life. The central problem in this approach is how to select from the variety of adult behaviors the indices for integration into the community? The solution is exceedingly complex; it varies with the individual, the community, and the circumstances. Despite this elusiveness, the concept of quality in future adult life is the logical cornerstone around which school programs should be designed.

Instead of a single entity, the community-based instructional program should group the various transitional domains with each skill leading to more normalizing behavior. Successful integration into society depends on basic competence in the domains of leisure-recreational skills, domestic skills, general community skills, social-personal skills, communication skills, and career-vocational skills. Besides recognizing the importance of the four domains in the ecological inventories, this approach argues that communication and social skills play an essential role in community integration. Three transitional cluster areas have been proposed, leading to the development of normalized behaviors: (1) the home living skills cluster, (2) the community living skills cluster, and (3) the career development skills cluster. In the cluster approach, skills in one domain are taught simultaneously with skills in other domains through integrated activities, since skills do not develop in isolation in one domain. It is probable and logical for a domain to appear in more than one cluster area. The social-personal domain may be part of the career development skills cluster in some instructional activities and part of the community living skills cluster in others. In the former, instruction may center around developing a positive employer-employee relationship while in the latter it may concern appropriate social behavior during a recreational activity, such as getting along with other patrons at the Land of Oz video arcade.

Home Living Skills Cluster

In the elementary phase, the **home living skills cluster** tends to teach functional skills that enable the child with severe disabilities to adjust to living conditions at home. School instruction should aim at making it easier for the parents to maintain their child in the home. It is important to teach both generic and specific adaptive behaviors unique to the particular household. At the elementary level, the home living skills cluster may incorporate the domestic domain, the social-personal domain, the communication domain, and possibly the general community domain.

The secondary program necessarily places more emphasis on the skills required for independent living in a residence other than the parents' home. Instruction is provided in the domestic, general community, social-personal, leisure-recreational, and communication domains. The classroom teacher and the parents are jointly responsible for identifying skill deficiencies. Additional training in the deficit areas is then coordinated between school and home.

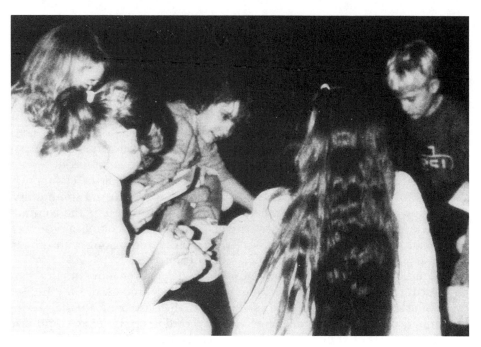

FIGURE 13.5

School programs for students with severe disabilities should teach them the specific skills they need for community living and career development.

(Courtesy of Lynda Atherton.)

Programs might, for example, provide instruction in shopping and meal planning, vacuuming and dusting, and sorting and washing clothes. If warranted, instruction could be provided in self-care needs and any other appropriate topic. Training is primarily oriented toward living in the community with a minimum of outside assistance.

It is vitally important that both assessment and training occur in natural settings. Conducting the discrepancy analysis in the natural environment permits the trainer to identify deficiencies that might not be considered in a training setting. To illustrate, instruction in sorting, washing, and drying laundry typically occurs in a utility room in or near the classroom. But the integrated adult with severe disabilities would use a community laundromat, in which skills other than measuring detergent, bleach, and fabric softener are required, such as associating and getting along with other customers. A deficit in these social-personal skills will not show up in a utility room assessment.

It must be emphasized that appropriate instruction in the home living skills cluster is also concerned with the content of the training provided. In many programs food preparation training is limited to making popcorn for a

Friday afternoon party. Since people must eat foods other than popcorn, training must cover preparation of the foods the students will eat as adults integrated in the community.

Community Living Skills Cluster

The **community living skills cluster** develops and enhances the skills necessary for using integrated community services. This cluster is primarily concerned with developing community mobility skills, environmental awareness, purchasing and shopping skills, skills in using public and commercial service facilities, and skills in using restaurants. The central thrust of the elementary grades is to create a basic awareness of and familiarity with the community. Instruction centers around awareness of the services offered by the community, getting around the community safely, learning about community service providers, using a variety of community services, getting along with others, expressing thoughts, and becoming cautious of strangers.

At the secondary level, the community becomes an even more integral part of the educational program. Certo and Kohl (1984) underscore the importance of teaching community living skills in both the classroom and the various community settings where the behavior is expected to occur. They emphasize that most skills should first be taught in the classroom, since structural components can be more quickly and readily arranged to produce successful training outcomes in the classroom than in the community (Guess & Noonan, 1982). But after initial acquisition the skill must be functionally maintained and generalized in the community. At the secondary level, instructional activities refine and generalize skills in the areas of community mobility, environmental awareness, shopping, using public and commercial service facilities, and using restaurants. This cluster incorporates the recreation-leisure domain, the general community domain, the social-personal domain, and the communication domain.

The community living skills cluster attempts to cover all the components that enhance independent participation in the various activities a community offers. There is a great deal of overlap between this and the other two clusters. For example, street-crossing skills (a community living skill), are related to career development when used to travel to and from work and are related to home living when used to travel to and from a laundromat. Earning money (a career development skill) is related to community living when used to pay for an afternoon of bowling and is related to home living when used to pay for groceries. In other words, skills such as riding a public bus, communicating to passersby, or purchasing food for a sack lunch may be used in the home living skills cluster, the community living skills cluster, and the career development skills cluster. This overlap mandates careful coordination of instruction to avoid unnecessary duplication and to promote skill generalization across environments.

Career Development Skills Cluster

The **career development skills cluster** is a multifaceted attempt to prepare students to engage in meaningful work as part of living (Hoyt, 1975). Unlike the earlier two clusters, in which more sophisticated skills are built on previously acquired skills, the career development skills cluster largely consists of four developmental stages, from the preschool level through the postschool level: (1) career awareness, (2) career exploration, (3) career preparation, and (4) career placement and follow-up. This arrangement is illustrated in figure 13.6.

Career awareness.   **Career awareness** receives its greatest emphasis during the elementary years. The major theme of the career awareness stage, according to Kokaska and Brolin (1985), is to develop the students' understanding that work is a positive and beneficial element that provides a major source of personal identification and satisfaction. Crucial to this theme are two interwoven philosophies. The first, which is essentially attitudinal, argues that vocational success depends on the formation of positive attitudes, most notably, attitudes of self-worth, self-confidence, and self-understanding. The second, essentially concerned with trait development, suggests that certain generic work traits (such as those found in table 10.1) are vital to future vocational success.

Career exploration.   **Career exploration** is emphasized during the junior high years, when students examine a number of integrated employment sites in the community. The strength of this stage depends directly on the number of employment settings students can experience. Ideally they should experience twenty diversified community job sites that have a high employment demand. Students are placed on each job site for a two-week period. Obviously, they will not become competent or skillful during two weeks; the period is intended to give them a taste of the job. During the placement, students are evaluated on their aptitudes, interests, and skills by the job supervisor, the teaching staff, and, to the extent possible, the students themselves. After a few years, a student could potentially have sixty job evaluations. At the same time, the teaching staff must design instructional experiences actively interwoven with the employment settings. Carefully planned and sequenced exploration activities and experiences make a relevant career preparation possible (Kokaska & Brolin, 1985).

Career preparation.   **Career preparation** receives greatest emphasis during high school. This stage has two central roles: First, a realistic career must be selected, and the student must receive additional training in that career. Selection begins with a review of the sixty or so evaluations collected during career exploration. From this review, a transdisciplinary team selects the four or five

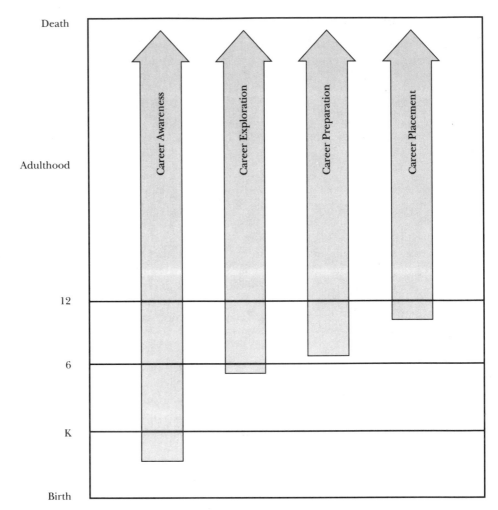

FIGURE 13.6

Stages of the Career Development Skills Cluster

(FROM: *Career Education for Handicapped Individuals* (2nd ed.) (p. 54) by C. Kokaska and D. Brolin, 1985, Columbus, OH: Charles E. Merrill. Copyright 1985 by Charles E. Merrill. Reprinted by permission of the publisher.)

jobs in which the student received the most favorable evaluations. If possible, the student should take an active role in selection. The student is then placed on these job sites for four weeks. Again, the supervisor, the teaching staff, and, to the extent possible, the student evaluate the performance. From this set of evaluations, the student, if possible, or the transdisciplinary team selects the optimum job for the student.

Career placement, follow-up, and continuing education.   Career placement takes place during the student's last year or possibly last two years of schooling. A placement is secured in the selected career field that can lead eventually to remunerative employment. The student is trained at that site until he or she has completely mastered the job requirements. For the remainder of the year, frequent **follow-up** evaluations are conducted to eliminate minor problems and ensure that the student is successful at that job site. The placement may be either full-time or part-time and may last longer than one year, depending on the student's ability level and needs. Many persons with severe disabilities, like other people, require **continuing education** and other postschool services. Therefore, follow-up, support, and retraining services should be incorporated into a lifelong program. This final stage in the career development skills cluster neatly interfaces with integration into society.

Successful community integration mandates that the classroom be converted from a training center to a staging area for community-based programming. As stated earlier, effective systems change requires that the curriculum specify the needs of students with severe disabilities in natural settings. To implement such an approach to curriculum development, teachers must deviate substantially from commonly used developmental scales and checklists to determine the skills that facilitate student integration into the least restrictive current and subsequent environments (Brown, Branston-McClean, et al., 1979). Educators must become proficient in identifying and analyzing innovative instructional targets for students with severe disabilities, and the curriculum must be individualized. In short, the standard curriculum, applicable to all students, has become a relic of the past.

INSTRUCTIONAL METHODS

Initially, an effective teacher must determine where to begin instruction and what skills to teach to the student. The "where" is specified by the results of the student repertoire or ecological inventory. The "what" is the curriculum; it is, in a sense, an instructional roadmap from which goals and objectives are generated. The where and what can direct instructional methods toward developing skills and reinforcing behaviors that are used in the student's natural community. Instruction must be aimed at meeting the student's present and future needs. It must be structured to develop, maintain, and generalize age-appropriate skills. Students must be exposed to a variety of instructional arrangements involving other students, including peers without disabilities. These techniques must facilitate learning and must be phased out systematically over time to increase the student's independence.

Students with severe disabilities must be taught not only to perform activities in the natural community but also to respond to the **natural cues and correction procedures** in that community. Natural cues and correction procedures are the **stimulus dimensions** typically available to persons in the natural community (Falvey, Brown, Lyon, Baumgart, & Schroeder, 1980). Students with severe disabilities must be taught to perform skills in response to cues and correction procedures equivalent in intensity, duration, and frequency to those in the community. For instance, the motor skills to cross Maple Avenue are only one set of the skills Robbie needs for street crossing; he must be systematically instructed to cross the street in response to the natural cues (e.g., Walk/Don't Walk signs, absence of traffic, presence of other pedestrians).

To teach students with severe disabilities to recognize the varied components of an activity in a community environment, materials natural to that environment must be used. For example, to teach James to eat a meal independently at Captain Jack's fast food restaurant, the actual utensils, condiment containers, and other materials must be used. To teach Janet to purchase coffee, milk, and cereal at Al's Buy-Rite Grocery, the actual grocery carts, store aisles, and cash registers must be used. To teach Fred to play the pinball machine in the Land of Oz arcade center, the actual pinball machine, music, comradeship, and background noise must be part of the training sessions. When teaching students to purchase items, real money must be used. If they do not actually use natural environments, teachers may overlook natural materials when training students with severe disabilities.

For students to acquire the skills necessary to interact with a variety of people, opportunities for interacting must be provided both inside and outside the school. Community environments offer numerous and varied opportunities. Students must learn to interact not just with family members, peers, and school personnel but also with grocery store clerks, fast food restaurant cashiers, and managers of arcade centers among others. Unless they are taught directly in a variety of community environments, students are unlikely to acquire such interaction skills.

INSTRUCTIONAL SETTINGS

Instructional settings for students with severe disabilities must have a variety of characteristics that facilitate the student's integration into the community. First and foremost, the school must be fully integrated. The classroom for students with severe disabilities must be located next to classrooms for students without disabilities of the same chronological age. By location and structure, these classrooms must accommodate and foster daily interaction between students with and without severe disabilities. Both groups must follow the same routines, share entrances/exits, and be scheduled for the same arrival/departure times. They must eat together in the cafeteria and share lunch tables. They must have opportunities to play together on the playground.

The setting must facilitate careful coordination of a variety of instructional activities both inside and outside the classroom. Many domestic skills required for independent living can first be taught in school, provided the equipment is available. Access to kitchen equipment, for instance, aids in teaching food preparation and cleanup skills, access to washing machines and dryers aids in teaching laundry skills, and access to a living room aids in teaching housekeeping skills. Later these skills can be maintained and generalized in the student's home. Unfortunately, many public schools are not adapted for teaching basic domestic skills. Other skills, such as use of vending machines, telephones, and water fountains, can and should be taught as they occur in the natural environment of the school building.

Some skills can be taught only in the community. Instruction in riding a bus, purchasing food, and shopping in a mall can occur in a wide variety of natural environments. But the number of students with severe disabilities receiving community instruction must reflect the natural proportion of the population. Rather than taking the class en masse into the community, teachers should take groups in which only one, two, or at most three are students with severe disabilities, and the rest are students without disabilities. For appropriate social integration, students with severe disabilities must have opportunities for interaction with persons without disabilities in the community environments (Certo & Kohl, 1984).

Some students with severe disabilities do not have all the skills required to participate in a variety of natural environments. Nevertheless, these students should not be excluded; rather they should be given opportunities to acquire the skills. If a student is unable to acquire a skill, the **principle of partial participation** should be followed (Baumgart et al., 1982). This calls for allowing a person access to environments and activities even if he or she is unable to perform all the necessary skills independently. Partial participation is more acceptable and appropriate than denying all access.

The Educational Experiences of Andrew Jackson Knibbs   EXAMPLE

Andrew Jackson Knibbs was born on a cloudy Saturday in June 1970 in a large midwestern city. Huck, Andy's father, indicated with a chuckle that they left for the hospital just as the "Baseball Game of the Week" came on television. "Wouldn't you know it," he added as he leaned back in his chair, "I missed the entire game, and it turned out to be a good one, too. It was the Yanks against Boston." He added after a long pause, "I kinda thought this was an omen, you know, like it was telling me something. I thought that one day I'll be watching him play big league ball but I guess that will never happen." His wife, Elizabeth, had dreams for the baby as well, but she also had concerns. For a long time, she had had a premonition that something was wrong, and, as her due date drew near, the premonition became stronger. For over a month she had had almost constant pain, and she was troubled with an eerie, indescribable feeling. The obstetrician reassured her that the pregnancy was progressing as expected. He believed that her premonition and strange feeling were nothing more than the jitters of a first pregnancy. He reportedly told her, "You first-time mothers are all alike—you worry about everything. Just relax, and your baby will be perfect." Nevertheless, the premonition persisted.

Andy's disabling condition was not immediately diagnosed. Despite what Elizabeth described as a "troubled pregnancy and a complicated delivery," both the obstetrician and the pediatrician assured her that Andy would be a normal intelligent, healthy child. But at 12 months, Andy was just learning to sit, was not yet crawling, and made what his mother described as "uncontrollable movements." During his pediatric checkup, the doctor agreed with Mr. and Mrs. Knibbs that Andy's lack of development warranted further testing. After testing, the pediatrician said the results were inconclusive and that Andy was probably "just a little slow, but definitely not retarded. In just a few months he will be like everyone else; there is no reason to be concerned. I've seen this type of thing hundreds of times." Nevertheless, Andy's lack of development was of concern, especially to Elizabeth.

Gradually, she began to suspect that Andy was mentally retarded. But Huck refused to accept this diagnosis and reiterated the doctor's opinion. Sooner or later, he believed, Andy's development would accelerate. Some morning they would awaken, as if from a bad dream, to find that Andy was the normal child they wanted, and they would live happily ever after.

With each passing day, Andy seemed to fall further behind. When he was about 2 the parents returned to the pediatrician to resolve their disagreement. Again Andy was tested. This time, the pediatrician informed them that Andy was mentally retarded and was functioning at the 12- to 18-month-old level. The pediatrician suggested that Andy be institutionalized and that the parents "get on with their lives." This recommendation escalated the rift surfacing between Huck and Elizabeth. Huck pushed for institutionalization; Elizabeth wanted Andy to remain at home. The arguments became more and more violent and the rift grew. Five days after Andy's 3rd birthday Huck moved out.

From then on, Elizabeth had primary responsibility for nurturing Andy. "That was probably the hardest time in my life. With the divorce and the trouble I was having with my job, I just couldn't seem to find enough time for Andy. And he seemed to know it too. And, for the first time, he began to hit me and bite me. The more these behaviors increased, the guiltier I felt. It was just a very bad time." Finding a baby-sitter for Andy was impossible; Elizabeth had over a dozen baby-sitters, who lasted from forty-five minutes to three months. Finally, she enlisted her mother. When Andy was 4, Elizabeth attempted to enroll him in a preschool program for low-income children. The program refused to accept him but the director recommended that Elizabeth try a group for "spastic" children on the east side of town. She promptly enrolled Andy in this program. To her chagrin, she learned that Andy could have attended this preschool since shortly after infancy.

The program was largely therapeutic for Andy, but he continued to hit and bite. Since the staff was unaccustomed to dealing with behavior problems, Andy was referred to a psychologist for evaluation. The major outcome of the evaluation was a recommendation that Andy's name be placed on a waiting list for the state school. Ms. Jackson, the director of the preschool program, indicated that institutionalization was the only hope for Andy. This recommendation only increased Elizabeth's frustration. The program had failed to give her concrete, useful information or advice. There was no mention of a prognosis, a behavior management program, or an alternative educational program more appropriate for Andy. "This was the only time that I wavered in my choice not to place him in an institution," Elizabeth explained, as if apologizing for the thought. Then, after a sip of coffee, she continued, "My social life was almost nonexistent, and I began to think that these experts knew more than I did. So I visited the state school." After seeing it, she vowed that Andy would always stay with her. "I just couldn't imagine him sitting in the dayroom for the next 30 years of his life." Despite numerous threats from Ms. Jackson to expel and institutionalize him, Andy continued at the program.

At age 5, Andy was eligible for placement in the public school system; nevertheless, the district director of special education determined that Andy could not be accepted. Elizabeth contended that he was less impaired than many of the children who were accepted, but the director countered that he could not be educated because of his self-injurious and externally directed hazardous behaviors. During that year, Elizabeth heard about a mothers' guild program at a local church. Andy entered that program, and in the course of the next two years became "a manageable child." Elizabeth again lobbied to have him placed in the local public school system. The following September, Andy was placed in a segregated school setting. According to the district director, this was the only placement available for Andy now and in the future. For the next five years, he remained in the segregated school; there was no mention of integration or the possibility of transferring him to a less restrictive educational setting.

In the spring of 1983 the school district decided to "promote" Andy to a segregated high school placement isolated in a rural area surrounded by farms. Elizabeth toured the school Andy would attend the following August and became concerned about what it could offer her son. All the students with disabilities were located in a separate wing of the building, with the words "Handicapped Programs" printed in big, bold letters above the entrance. They rode separate buses, ate in a separate lunchroom, and had separate extracurricular activities, including their own yearbook and prom. Weeks before school was to start, Elizabeth withdrew her consent for Andy to attend that school.

Elizabeth wanted Andy to attend an age-appropriate school in his own neighborhood so that he would be a part of the community and have contact with peers without disabilities on a regular basis. The director of special education rejected this option and instead proposed an interim placement in a junior high school several communities away. The director promised that some integration experiences would be arranged. In late August, Andy began to attend the junior high. The promised integrative activities were continuously postponed, and Andy remained segregated in a self-contained classroom. The teacher and the director contended that Andy had not yet developed the skills needed for integration. In May the school district recommended continued placement in this junior high school for Andy. Frustrated, Elizabeth requested a due process hearing. Just before school began the hearing officer concluded that the school district had failed to provide Andy with appropriate educational services in the least restrictive environment. He further indicated that Andy must attend his neighborhood school, Roosevelt High, in the fall.

Elizabeth was determined that Andy have an appropriate educational program at Roosevelt. She wanted a program that would enhance school integration while fostering Andy's prospects of community integration. The teacher proposed a three-part program consisting of home living skills, community living skills, and career development skills. Since then, Andy has made significant progress. He can get from place to place on the public bus, he can prepare a simple three-course meal, and, for all practical purposes, he is indistinguishable from his chronological-age peers. In the afternoon, he is enrolled in a grounds maintenance vocational program, and he has tentatively been hired at a local nursery and landscaping company this summer. According to Elizabeth, Andy now appears more mature, more self-assured, more competent, and a much happier person.

Andy has completed his third year at Roosevelt High. On his own and with the assistance of his special friend, he has formed numerous friendships at school. Throughout the day he is around peers without disabilities: in the hallways, in the cafeteria, on the school bus, at pep rallies, and in classes. When he is in the community shopping or out to dinner, schoolmates greet him and stop to chat, asking how he is, introducing him to their families, or complimenting him on his clothing. The admiration his schoolmates feel for him is reflected in an autograph in his yearbook by his friend Jay, "You are a wonderful person and a great friend. Take care of yourself, we all love you."

Recently, Elizabeth visited Ms. Jackson at the "spastic" program. She proudly gave a detailed listing of Andy's recent accomplishments. As she was leaving, Elizabeth said in her most serious voice: "You once told me to institutionalize Andy; and I almost did. If I would have done what you asked, then where do you think he would be today? What would have happened to him?" Elizabeth then turned and walked out.

CONCLUSION

"Where do you think he would be today? What would have happened to him?" The theme of this chapter centers around Elizabeth's questions. What type of life would Andy have had if he had not been educated? While it cannot be answered specifically, it is safe to conclude that he would not possess the skills that lead to community integration and a normalized life-style. Instead of being employed and living in the community, Andy might well have spent his life in a restrictive, segregated environment.

But beyond that inquiry, what life-style would Andy have had if he had been appropriately educated from age 3 or from shortly after birth? Again, those questions cannot be answered specifically but his prospects would clearly have been much brighter than they are today. At graduation, Andy would probably have a better job, have better community and domestic skills, and be an integral member of society. In the final analysis, isn't that the real purpose of education?

1. If the purpose of education is to prepare students for a satisfactory and rewarding life-style, then it is the school's responsibility to develop the skills necessary for successful entry into society.

SUMMARY

2. The intent of assessing students with severe disabilities is to determine the student's present level of skills accurately and to specify the skills he or she needs to develop.

3. The student repertoire or ecological inventory attempts to determine if the student's present skills are functional, chronologically age-appropriate, and community referenced.

4. The student repertoire or ecological inventory has four steps: (1) the teacher specifies the skills required to participate in a priority activity; (2) the student performs the priority activity; (3) the teacher analyzes any discrepancy between the student's performance and the required skills; (4) the teacher develops an instructional strategy for the priority activity.

5. Curricular activities for students with severe disabilities must relate to functional skills and performance criteria that meet the integrative demands of the local community.

6. The ecological curriculum attempts to identify community-referenced, functional, age-appropriate skills required for entry into society.

7. The domestic domain includes the skills required to reside in a community dwelling, pursue a healthy life-style, and maintain an acceptable personal appearance.

8. The leisure-recreational domain includes the skills that enable students with severe disabilities to engage in many of the same recreational activities as people without disabilities.

9. The general community domain includes the skills needed to participate independently in the activities associated with all aspects of community living.

10. Since remunerative employment largely affects the extent to which an individual is successfully integrated into the community, the vocational domain receives a major emphasis in educational programs for students with severe disabilities.

11. A curricular approach that is philosophically similar to the ecological curriculum is transitional clustering across domains. In this approach, domain skills are combined in clusters to optimize an individual's integration prospects. The three skill clusters are (1) the home living skills cluster, (2) the community living skills cluster, and (3) the career development skills cluster.

12. Across-domain skills are taught through integrated activities, recognizing that skills do not develop in isolation.

13. The home living skills cluster develops the direct and indirect skills required for functioning independently in a community-based residence.

14. The community living skills cluster develops the skills necessary for using integrated community activities and services.

15. The career development skills cluster prepares students for meaningful, remunerative employment. This cluster has four developmental stages, occurring from preschool to postschool levels: (1) career awareness, (2) career exploration, (3) career preparation, and (4) career placement, follow-up, and continuing education.

16. Students with severe disabilities must be taught not only to perform activities in the natural community but also to respond to natural cues and correction procedures. Materials natural to the environment must be used during training.

17. Instructional settings for students with severe disabilities must be totally integrated into the school program.

18. Instructional activities must occur in both the school and the natural community.

CHAPTER 14

Community and Adult
Programs for Persons with
Severe Disabilities

(Courtesy of Bancroft, serving people with developmental disabilities since 1883. Haddonfield, N. J., 08033.)

Special education for persons with severe disabilities is a progression of educational programs and services charged with preparing the students for post-school integration into community settings. Sadly, the time, energy, and resources used to educate students with severe disabilities have all too often been dissipated because community support systems were not present or were inadequate to maintain and enrich their lives after their departure from school. Indeed, recent graduates often are placed in institutions or other restrictive environments due to the absence of appropriate community support programs and services.

Clearly the goal of education for persons with severe disabilities is to develop the skills necessary for a rewarding and satisfactory life-style in the mainstream of society. The assimilation of persons with severe disabilities is deeply rooted in the moral and constitutional rights guaranteed to all citizens in our society. The principle of normalization suggests that the conditions, services, and opportunities provided to persons without disabilities must be provided to persons with severe disabilities. These adults must have vocational opportunities, adequate housing, medical services, recreational activities, and access to public transportation and buildings.

COMMUNITY INTEGRATION

Recently, the concept of **community integration** has received increased attention in special education journals, newsletters, and conferences. Most professionals accept community integration to mean the placement of persons with disabilities into community residences, facilities, and common activities in physical proximity to persons without disabilities (Novak & Heal, 1980). It includes activities ranging from living in a community residence to riding a public bus and from eating in a restaurant to purchasing clothes in a haberdashery.

Community services should augment rather than decrease a person's interactions with the community. Many professionals feel that services should reflect the full range of choices typically enjoyed by those without disabilities. Minimally, these include the right to live in a normalized, community-based apartment or home, the right to participate in any leisure-recreational activity, the right to patronize any business establishment, and the right to use any community service, public or private. True integration suggests that persons with severe disabilities would develop social relationships, that is, affection toward, interest in, and friendship with others.

Community Support System

It is doubtful that many adults with severe disabilities can be maintained in the community without a formal support system to identify and coordinate the services and programs they require. In an insightful study on community services, Vogelsberg, Williams, and Friedl (1980) found, surprisingly, that the greatest need was not for new services or programs but rather for more coordination and cooperation among agencies presently providing services. In an earlier study, Kenowitz, Gallagher, and Edgar (1977) indicated that **community action networks** should be established to help obtain and coordinate

FIGURE 14.1

Persons with severe disabilities must be allowed to participate fully in the community activities and facilities available to persons without disabilities.

(Courtesy of Karen Venstanberg.)

services for persons with severe disabilities. In particular, "the primary responsibility of this network would be to bring together families of the severely handicapped and all agencies responsible for delivering some type of service" (p. 38).

The concept of a community action network was strongly endorsed by Scheerenberger (1976). He advocated that every community have a central point of referral—a person or agency knowledgeable about community services and the criteria required for their use, because "without such a point of referral, programs may either not be used or not used in a timely manner" (p. 144). Although Scheerenberger was referring to persons with mental retardation, this concept is equally applicable to others with severe disabilities.

Activator of Support Services

The community support system model illustrated in figure 14.2 has an **activator** at the center—an individual who obtains and coordinates the necessary services for persons with severe disabilities.

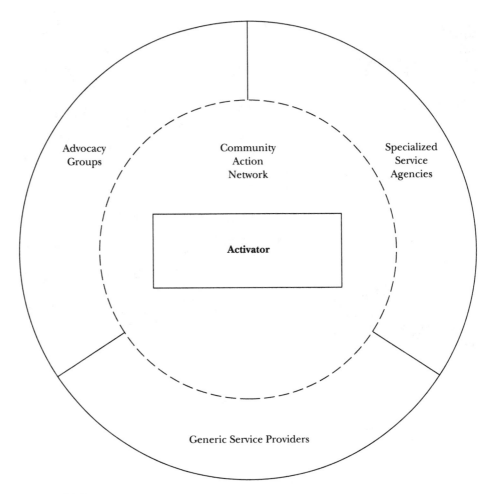

FIGURE 14.2

Community Support System Model for Serving Adults with Severe Disabilities

(FROM: Sailor, Wayne, and Doug Guess. *Severely Handicapped Students: An Instructional Design.* Copyright © 1983 by Houghton Mifflin Company. Used with permission.)

The activator is essential to the community action network. This person should be a compassionate professional formally trained in the educational needs of persons with severe disabilities and knowledgeable about the public and private services a community offers. The activator's responsibilities would vary somewhat from community to community, but Sailor and Guess (1983) suggest that he or she should assume four roles: (1) referral coordinator, (2) service coordinator, (3) information coordinator, and (4) support system coordinator.

Referral coordinator.   As a **referral coordinator**, the activator must be knowledgeable about and familiar with the various private and public programs and agencies serving adults with severe disabilities. The activator would typically concentrate on employment opportunities and residential options. He or she would maintain an up-to-date file of the programs, agencies, and persons to contact when a specific service is needed or when a problem arises.

Service coordinator.   As a **service coordinator**, the activator would develop and maintain a system to identify the services that each adult with severe disabilities presently requires and is receiving. The service coordinator would also maintain a record of each adult's current employment, residential arrangements, community integration, and recreational activities.

Information coordinator.   As an **information coordinator**, the activator would make the needs of adults with severe disabilities known to the general community and especially agencies that can assist in serving these adults. The activator must be an advocate and a lobbyist to safeguard the rights of adults with severe disabilities and ensure their complete community integration.

Support system coordinator.   As a **support system coordinator**, the activator would attempt to elicit support from community service clubs, service organizations, and other agencies so that needed services are provided in a timely and meaningful manner. The activator would coordinate the services provided by different agencies to ensure that training objectives are being met and that the individual is meaningfully integrated into the community.

Vocational Integration

Remunerative employment is viewed as the cornerstone of community integration because of the increased integrative opportunities it offers. Opportunities to serve consumers without disabilities, to work beside co-workers without disabilities, and to meet people without disabilities every day in chance encounters enhance the prospects of forming friendships with the nondisabled citizenry. Employment income increases the worker's range of recreational, shopping, and residential options. As Will (1984) stated, employment "expands the range of available choices, enhances independence, and creates personal status" (p. 2). Kiernan and Stark (1986) stress the importance of employment for adults with severe disabilities, stating that "work is viewed as the measure of one's worth to society. . . . To be denied the opportunity to work is to be denied the chance to belong and develop a sense of self in a positive and constructive fashion" (p. 103).

With the push for deinstitutionalization and normalization of adults with severe disabilities, it is not surprising that vocational skill development has

FIGURE 14.3

Remunerative employment offers increased integrative opportunities by putting the adult with severe disabilities in contact with nondisabled customers, co-workers, and other citizens.

(Courtesy of Partlow State School, Tuscaloosa, AL.)

become a focus for many service providers. Historically, most adults with severe disabilities have not been employed in either competitive settings or sheltered workshops (Rusch & Mithaug, 1980). In recent years, attempts have been made to obtain meaningful and gainful employment for them as a viable, attractive, and normalizing alternative to the more restrictive sheltered employment. Competitive employment provides wages and benefits in addition to integrative opportunities. It fosters friendships and the acquisition of appropriate social skills through observation and practice.

To succeed in community settings, it is increasingly recognized, adults with severe disabilities must be employed (Bellamy, Peterson, & Close, 1976; Bergeron, Perschbacher-Melia, & Kiernan, 1986). A recent framework based on this premise is the **Pathways to Employment Model**, illustrated in figure 14.4. It presents a concept of the role adults with severe disabilities play in the decision-making process and the outcomes achieved as a result. The Pathways Model presents a person-driven design. The individual is faced with a number of choices, all of which may enhance the **economic self-sufficiency** realized through employment. This outcome of self-sufficiency realized through employment is measured not by job placement but rather by its effects (Kiernan & Stark, 1986; Wehman, 1981). The key concept of the Pathways Model is its focus on expansion of the environments in which outcomes may occur. The

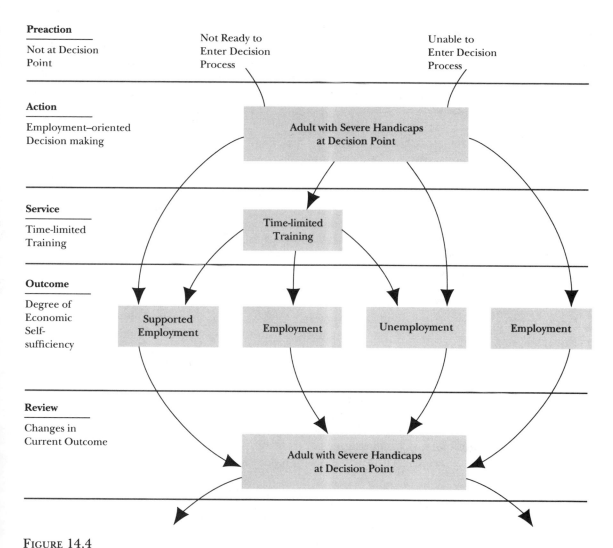

FIGURE 14.4

Pathways to Employment for Adults with Severe Handicaps: A Habilitation Model

(FROM: Kiernan, W. E., Stark, J. A. *Pathways to Employment for Adults with Developmental Disabilities.* Baltimore: Paul H. Brookes Publishing Co. (P.O. Box 10624, Baltimore, MD 21285-0624), © 1986.)

model is concerned with more than the creation of specific jobs; it attempts to determine what potential exists for workers with severe disabilities in their vocational and community settings. The design encourages exploration and establishment of new environments and new methods for these adults to attain employment (Kiernan & Stark, 1986).

As figure 14.4 illustrates, the Pathways Model has five stages: (1) preaction, (2) action, (3) service, (4) outcome, and (5) review. In the **preaction stage**, the adult with severe disabilities is not ready or is unable to decide on employment. At the **action stage**, the person makes a decision about the type of job he or she would like. It is at this stage that the person needs information about available options and the parameters of each. The options must be presented in a clear and detailed fashion so that the adult with severe disabilities can understand them. In the **service stage**, the individual makes a decision to obtain additional skill training before moving into employment. The adult usually has a general understanding of what he or she would like to do and the additional skills needed to attain this goal.

Once training is completed, movement into the **outcome stage** occurs. The Pathways Model defines the outcome as the degree of economic self-sufficiency realized through employment. The outcome can be either positive or negative. The positive outcome, employment, may be supported employment (i.e., benchwork, mobile crew, enclave, or supported jobs) or unassisted employment. The negative outcome, unemployment, includes placement in work activities and work adjustment programs. Whatever the outcome, it must reflect the individual's informed consent. In the **review stage**, the adult has the opportunity to reexamine and possibly modify his or her decision. Change should not be viewed as failure but rather as a maturing process (Kiernan & Stark, 1986). The stages of the Pathways Model are those persons without disabilities go through as they increase their economic self-sufficiency.

The Pathways Model focuses on the role of the adult with severe disabilities in the decision-making process. It views employment not as an end but as a means to increased economic self-sufficiency, the desired outcome. To put employment in its proper perspective, the Pathways Model explains occupational success with the following formula:

$$O = f[(P + Op + S) - D] \times DI$$

In this formula, *occupational success* (O) is a *function* (f) of five major variables: *preparation* (P) indicates that time-limited training may be necessary before entering into renumerative employment; *opportunity* (Op) indicates that environmental opportunities must be available; the *support system* (S) indicates that emotional support, guidance, and reinforcement from friends, parents, siblings, a job coach, and a citizen advocate are critical; negative *disincentives* (D) indicate that a number of barriers may hinder an adult with severe disabilities from even entering the job market or becoming successfully employed (e.g., loss of health care benefits upon employment, parental worries about the person's employability); and *degree of intensity* (DI) indicates that all the previous variables are multiplied by the level of effort that went into them (Stark, Schalock, & Berland, 1986).

Besides attempting to place occupational success in a clear perspective, the Pathways Model attempts to describe the positive integrative value of employ-

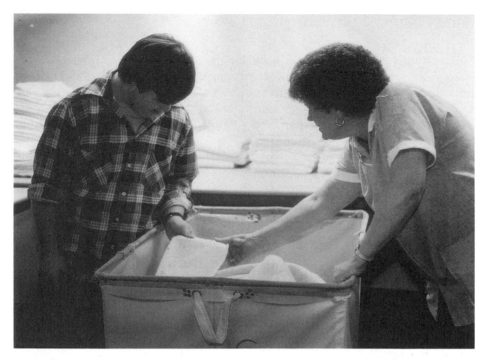

FIGURE 14.5
The outcome in the Pathways Model is not remunerative employment but rather the economic self-sufficiency realized through employment.

(Courtesy of Cahokia School District 187, Illinois.)

ment. This positive factor, called **habilitation**, is expressed in the following formula:

$$H = f(L + O + SI + R) \times EI$$

In this formula, *habilitation* (H) is the degree to which an adult with severe disabilities achieves his or her chosen level of economic independence. It is a function (f) of five variables: *living* (L) indicates how the person's residential arrangements contribute to economic independence and community integration; *occupation* (O) indicates the integrative aspects of the employment (e.g., serving consumers without disabilities and working beside co-workers without disabilities) and of traveling to and from work; *social integration* (SI) indicates the adult's integration in social environments and situations; *recreation* (R) indicates the activities that promote effective, enjoyable, and meaningful use of leisure; and *environmental intensity* (EI) indicates that all the previous variables are multiplied by a factor of effort that has five aspects: staff, equipment, finances, program facilities, and positive attitudes toward integrating the adult with severe disabilities (Stark, Schalock, & Berland, 1986).

ADULT DOMESTIC DEVELOPMENT

Most persons have oral and written language plus other standard symbol systems for processing information. But persons with severe disabilities must use other, more restrictive systems for processing information. Without some usable symbol system for obtaining information, persons with severe disabilities present a unique problem once their formal training has ended. Without a functional symbol system, adults with severe disabilities remain dependent on human trainers or on their limited memory. There are few published materials designed to teach domestic skills to adults with severe disabilities. Most instructional materials are designed to be read by the trainer, not the student, thus perpetuating dependence.

The Model Education for Severely Handicapped (MESH) Project has developed a unique alternative symbol system to teach domestic skills to integrated adults with severe disabilities living in the community. Since the amount of time used to teach domestic skills is minimal, the developers needed a symbol system that would convey information effectively. The system selected was pictures, and the programmatic approach is relatively straightforward and unencumbered. Since pictures are not always a sufficient cue to skill completion, the adults are taught to complete each task until they can easily translate the pictures into actions. Once the learners have acquired the skill, they keep the books of picture instructions as reference sources, much as a cook keeps the recipe for an often-baked cake. Using this basic format, adults with severe disabilities can be taught meal preparation, meal planning and shopping, and housekeeping duties (Spellman, DeBriere, Jarboe, Campbell, & Harris, 1978).

Meal Preparation

Meal preparation is a complex area of training because of the number and range of skills needed. Even a skilled cook without disabilities occasionally adds too much salt or leaves out a crucial ingredient. In meal preparation training, the adult with severe disabilities is required to use the picture recipe book and perform steps in a sequence specified by a **task analysis**. In the training sequence, the instructor begins by asking the adult to prepare a food item, for instance, "I would like you to make a hot dog, please." The first step is for the adult to open the book to the proper page. The next step is to obtain the necessary utensils for preparing the food item. For instance, to prepare a hot dog (see figure 13.2 earlier), the person initially needs a pan, a plate, a package of wieners, and a package of buns. The adult then performs the next five steps in the sequence leading to the final picture, putting the wiener on the bun. All the food preparation tasks are arranged in a left-to-right, top-to-bottom sequence, with each task serving as a stimulus or cue to the next task in the

<small>Figure 14.6</small>

Meal preparation is a complex area of training because of the number and range of skills it uses.

(Courtesy of Illinois School for the Visually Impaired.)

sequence. The picture recipe books are also personalized to the user's tastes and needs.

Picture recipe books help adults with severe disabilities the way cookbooks help persons without disabilities: they permit the individual to use more recipes without relying on memory. A slight alternative to the Project MESH materials was proposed by Robinson-Wilson (1977): pictures on five-by eight-inch cards joined with two rings at the top. The first card contains a large color picture of the final product; the next illustrates the equipment and food items to be set out; and subsequent cards illustrate the task, with three steps per card. Color coding is used for the stove burners and measuring utensils to simplify appliance use and measurement skills. The cards are plastic-coated and displayed on a wooden stand. Besides Robinson-Wilson, Johnson and Cuvo (1981) and Martin, Rusch, James, Decker, and Trytol (1982) have used similar procedures to teach a variety of sophisticated food preparation skills to adults with severe disabilities.

Meal Planning and Shopping

In meal planning and shopping, the adult with severe disabilities is first taught to follow a planned menu, typically a month-long menu providing a well-balanced, nutritious diet. In appearance, the menu resembles an appointment book divided into three daily meal sections. Each section illustrates the foods to be prepared at that meal. The pictures on the menu are the same as the pictures in the recipe book. The learner has to find the page in the recipe picture book for each food item on the menu and follow each recipe until all the menu items are prepared. After preparing an item, the adult is taught to mark an X beside its picture on the menu.

Although shopping for food is structurally independent of meal planning, the two skills are highly interwoven. In food shopping training, the adult is taught to prepare a shopping list from the picture recipes used to prepare the meals. The adult selects the recipes for the next week's menus. Then he or she determines whether the ingredients listed with each picture recipe are in stock. If they are, the card is returned to the picture book. If they are not, it is put in a "shopping list binder" for an upcoming grocery trip. At the grocery store, the adult with severe disabilities selects the items corresponding to the pictures in the shopping list binder. If the adult has difficulty selecting the appropriate brand or size or in differentiating between similar items, he or she can ask for assistance from a grocery clerk. After the shopping trip, the recipe cards are returned to the picture recipe book.

There are potential problems with this approach. What would happen, for instance, if the person had plenty of wieners but not enough buns? What if the adult likes mustard and relish on his or her hot dogs and these items are not clearly illustrated in the personalized picture book?

Housekeeping

A picture book is used for teaching housekeeping skills. The "how to" tasks are structurally arranged like the food preparation tasks. But, unlike food preparation, housekeeping tasks are completed at varying times. For instance, dusting may be required only twice a week, while bed making must be done daily. Thus, the housekeeping picture book must also include a "reminder" system indicating when tasks have to be performed. The system developed by Project MESH consists of a weekly schedule, somewhat like an appointment book, illustrating which tasks are to be done on which days of the week. As figures 14.7 and 14.8 show, the tasks are represented pictorially in a column at the left, while other columns list the days of the week. Each picture on the chart matches the front cover of an instruction book. A white square indicates that the housekeeping task needs to be completed that day. The person consults the chart daily to determine which tasks to do. After performing the task, he or she marks an X in the appropriate square.

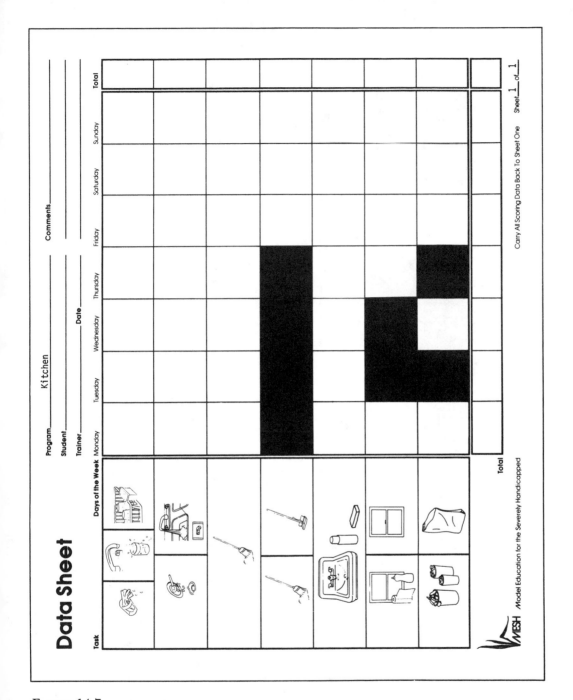

FIGURE 14.7

Picture Book Schedule for Housekeeping Duties in the Kitchen

(FROM: Spellman, C., DeBriere, T., Jarboe, D., Campbell, S., & Harris, C. (1978). Pictorial instruction: Training daily living skills. In M. E. Snell (Ed.), *Systematic Instruction of the Moderately and Severely Handicapped*, p. 404. Columbus, OH: Merrill Co. Reprinted by permission.)

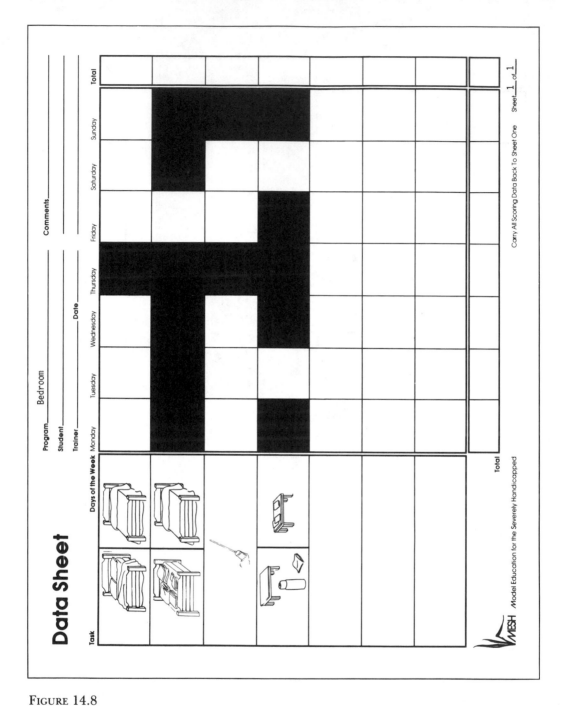

Figure 14.8

Picture Book Schedule for Housekeeping Duties in the Bedroom

(From: Spellman, C., DeBriere, T., Jarboe, D., Campbell, S., & Harris, C. (1978). Pictorial instruction: Training daily living skills. In M. E. Snell (Ed.), *Systematic Instruction of the Moderately and Severely Handicapped*, p. 405. Columbus, OH: Merrill Co. Reprinted by permission.)

The Transition Concept

Each year in the United States, approximately 300,000 persons drop out of, "age" out of, are elbowed out of, graduate from, or otherwise complete their eligibility for special education (Will, 1984).[1] The postschool employment status of school leavers with mild disabilities is not good. Their unemployment estimates range from 30 to 75 percent, and most studies report over 50 percent (U.S. Commission on Civil Rights, 1983). Coupled with this is an underemployment rate that exceeds 25 percent (Hasazi, Gordon, & Roe, 1985; Mithaug, Horiuchi, & Fanning, 1985). For persons with severe disabilities the prognosis is much worse. As a rule, they are not even considered for competitive employment or sheltered employment. Many are unserved, underserved, or inappropriately served in adult day training programs or work activity centers. The lack of appropriate services negates their opportunities to perform meaningful work and participate actively in their communities. Sadly, Edgar (1985) concludes that adults with severe disabilities "do not appear to be partaking of the fruits of our society" (p. 557).

Yet, several developments have recently converged to give a sense of urgency and national priority to the **transition** from secondary school to postschool settings. Follow-up studies clearly confirm that postschool outcomes are less than desirable (Edgar, 1985). With increasing regularity, these studies indicate that adults with severe disabilities are not remuneratively employed, do not use community services and resources effectively, face excessive if not interminable delays in getting access to adult services, and tend to be isolated from persons without disabilities (Brodsky, 1983; Hardman & McDonnell, 1987; Hasazi, Gordon, & Roe, 1985; Mithaug, Horiuchi, & Fanning, 1985; Wehman, Kregel, & Seyfarth, 1985). Over three-fourths of all persons with severe disabilities experience widespread financial instability coupled with dependence on family and societal resources (Hasazi, Gordon, & Roe, 1985; Mithaug, Horiuchi, & Fanning (1985).

Although the exact costs of unemployment and its resulting dependence on social service agencies are difficult to calculate, Hill, Hill, Wehman, and Banks (1985) have estimated that the direct costs of day-care programs and social security benefits are over $5,000 annually for each adult with severe disabilities. The indirect costs to society may be over four times that. Hill, Hill, Wehman, and Banks (1985) indicated that the average costs of serving a person with severe disabilities in day-care and associated programs was almost $7,000 per year for approximately forty years (i.e., $280,000 dollars). These expenditures are viewed as a necessary social responsibility resulting from unemployment and its effects. However, numerous studies clearly demonstrate that this money need not be spent, that persons with severe disabilities can be taught employment and community adjustment skills (Bates & Pancsofar, 1983; Edgar, 1985; McDonnell & Hardman, 1985; Wehman et. al., 1982).

Despite these impressive findings, reports over the past decade on persons with severe disabilities present a disappointing picture (Hasazi, Gordon, &

Roe, 1985; Mithaug, Horiuchi, & Fanning, 1985; Wehman, Kregel, & Seyfarth, 1985). They suggest that the extent to which these adults achieve the employment, community living, social and leisure opportunities, and quality of life they desire depends on the effectiveness of cooperative planning, coordination of services, and obtaining needed services. These studies stress the need to improve the scope and quality of transition services and planning efforts. They clearly demonstrate that postschool outcomes depend on the quality of the triad of transition: the sending agencies, the receiving agencies, and the handoff process.

The view that employment outcomes depend on the quality of secondary, postsecondary, and transitional services was recognized in the Education for All Handicapped Children Amendments of 1983, Public Law 98–199:

> The Subcommittee recognizes the overwhelming paucity of effective programming for these handicapped youth, which eventually accounts for unnecessarily large numbers of handicapped adults who become unemployed and therefore dependent on society. These youth historically have not been adequately prepared for the changes and demands of life after high school. In addition, few, if any, are able to access or appropriately use traditional transitional services. Few services have been designed to assist handicapped young people in their efforts to enter the labor force or attain their goals of becoming self-sufficient adults, and contributing members to our society [section 626].

Establishment of transitional "services designed to assist handicapped young people in their efforts to enter the labor market" was proposed by Madeline Will (1984), assistant secretary of the Office of Special Education and Rehabilitation Services, as a national priority, from the school years through the initial years of employment, for persons with severe disabilities. According to Will, "transition from school to working life is an outcome oriented process encompassing a broad array of services that lead to employment. Transition is a period that includes high school, the point of graduation, additional postsecondary education or adult services, and initial years of employment" (p.1). Wehman (1983) stresses that transition is "a carefully planned process which may be initiated either by school personnel or adult service providers, to establish and implement a plan for either employment or additional vocational training of handicapped students who leave school in three to five years; such a process must involve special educators, parents and/or the student, and adult service system representatives, and possibly an employer" (p. 2).

Although employment has been viewed as the most important outcome of the transitional process, other components are vitally important to a person's community integration (Halpern, 1985). A comprehensive transition planning program needs to consider all these variables: leisure-recreational skills, domestic skills, general community skills, social-personal skills, and communication skills. The components are highly interdependent and directly proportional to each other. Edgar (1985), for instance, indicates that "earning less than minimum wage does not permit one to live independently. Unless

FIGURE 14.9

Transition is a dynamic partnership between the student, the school system, and the community services the student will likely use after leaving school.

(Courtesy of Crestwood Company.)

employment offers the opportunity to be promoted above these [subminimum wage] levels, I contend that the current employment status of special education graduates is a classic case of progressive *status quoism*" (p. 556).

Transition is conceptualized as a dynamic process involving a partnership of consumers, school and postschool service agencies, and local community elements to optimize an adult's employment, independent living, integration, and community participation. In this definition, the key concept is partnership. To be an **outcome-oriented process**, transition must involve thorough planning and coordination of secondary and postsecondary resources. The Office of Special Education and Rehabilitative Services defined the critical elements of transition planning as: (1) effective high school programs that prepare students to work and live in the community; (2) a broad range of adult service programs that meet the needs of persons with disabilities in employment and community settings, and (3) comprehensive and cooperative transition planning between educational and community service agencies to develop the needed services (Will, 1984). The intent of transition is to bring the daily life of the adult with severe disabilities close to that of a person without disabilities.

Unlike special education, in which a public agency has clear responsibility for service delivery, adult transition services are presently administered by a number of agencies. By both statute and administration, these agencies have different, sometimes even conflicting, goals and objectives. Agencies typically provide a particular spectrum of services to designated individuals. Program goals include providing basic financial and medical support for those unable to work, assisting persons to enter the work force, maintaining a community residence, and simply meeting the social service needs defined by local and state authorities. No single agency is responsible for coordinating adult services. This often results in a lack of systematic information on the effectiveness and efficiency of services.

Fragmentation and lack of coordination make transition planning difficult. Services established for any individual are likely to form an incomplete mosaic of programs and support systems. Constructing the optimum mosaic requires information about the diverse programs for which the individual may be eligible and details of how those programs actually operate in the particular community. Fragmentation also creates difficulty in lobbying for expansion or improvement of services, since there are usually many targets for advocacy efforts.

TRANSITION: AN EXEMPLARY PROGRAM

It is somewhat ironic that persons with severe disabilities are experiencing disturbing postschool integrative conditions at a time when reports describe many effective transition models that illustrate community integrative experiences for students with severe disabilities (Bates, Suter, & Poelvoorde, 1987; Bellamy, Sheenhan, Horner, & Boles, 1980; Hardman & McDonnell, 1987; Wehman, Kregel, & Barcus, 1985). These studies have found correlations between transition services and tremendous reductions in the costs of dependence. Instead of spending an average of $280,000 per person over forty years, if society invests slightly over $5,000 in transition services, persons with severe disabilities can be placed in remunerative employment that earns them an average income in excess of $6,000 a year plus fringe benefits (Hill, Hill, Wehman, & Banks, 1985).

Because of the potential benefits transition offers to persons with severe disabilities, a variety of transition programs are now being developed. While they vary in some important dimensions, they all share the factor of a partnership between consumers and direct service agencies. One exemplary transition program, the Illinois Transition Project,[2] can illustrate this dynamic process.

The Illinois Transition Project is built around three interdependent concepts (Bates, Suter, & Poelvoorde, 1987). Its conceptual structure attempts to ensure a longitudinal commitment to the improvement of existing services and the development of more effective transitional resources for persons with severe disabilities. While it offers no short-term cure for the present lack of services, it clearly recognizes that delays in providing these services are inhumane and hinder postschool integration.

The first major concept of the project is creation of a **Transition Assistance Committee (TAC)**. The primary assignment of the TAC is to operationalize and coordinate interagency resources for improving school and postschool transition (Bates, Suter, & Poelvoorde, 1987). The importance of this committee cannot be overemphasized. Several reviews of transition programs indicate that cooperative planning between school and adult service agencies at the state and local level is virtually nonexistent (Brodsky, 1983; Hasazi, Gordon, & Roe, 1985; McDonnell & Hardman, 1985; Wehman, Kregel, & Barcus, 1985). The TAC should also identify the skills a student with severe disabilities will need well in advance of graduation to enhance integration into society and should facilitate increases in the availability and effectiveness of transition services. While transition services concentrate on remunerative employment, other postsecondary needs such as residential arrangements and daily living skills are addressed as well.

The second major concept of the Illinois Transition Project is evaluation of the effectiveness of present services, conducted largely by following up persons who have graduated from or left special education programs (Bates, Suter, & Poelvoorde, 1987). Absence of data is a major obstacle in the effort to develop more effective transition policy and services. Hasazi (1985), for instance, emphasizes the need for follow-up information to evaluate the appropriateness of present programs. McDonnell, Wilcox, and Boles (1986) suggest that lack of data prevents a systems change to establish an array of transition services that may enhance postschool outcomes for consumers with severe disabilities. By requiring a follow-up of all school leavers with severe disabilities, the TAC develops an information base for continual evaluation of the postschool status of persons with severe disabilities and the programs that educate them.

The third major concept of the Illinois Transition Project is development of a formal transition plan for the student. This mulifaceted **Individualized Transition Program (ITP)** projects the student's vocational, residential, and continuing education goals and identifies the secondary school services required to accomplish them (Bates, Suter, & Poelvoorde, 1987). McDonnell and Hardman (1985) suggest that the initial planning process be conducted early enough so that potential service options and support needs are identified and addressed prior to graduation. In the Illinois Project, the ITP is first developed shortly after the student turns 14. Ideally, the ITP is developed in conjunction with the student's **Individualized Education Program (IEP)**. Then many of the goals identified in the ITP can become educational goals in the IEP.

Conclusion

Transition represents a Promethean attempt to enhance the integration prospects of adults with severe disabilities. Supported employment, supported living, and community integration are reasonable expectations, given the demonstrated potential of persons with severe disabilities. Many recent school leavers, however, are inappropriately served, underserved, or unserved. The lack of appropriate services negates the opportunities for these persons to participate meaningfully and actively in their communities. The long waiting lists and meager services that are available fail to take advantage of the potential for employment and integration repeatedly demonstrated by students with severe disabilities. Selecting the best from existing services will seldom result in a desirable transition outcome. Instead, advocates need to change the objectives and methods of existing adult services.

The emerging process of transition is more active and demanding than the popular notion of assessment and placement in an adult service delivery system. Those participating in the transition process must first determine the life-style the person desires and then identify the services and support systems that would enable it. Next the process ensures that these services and support systems will actually be available through existing or new organizations. Recent concepts, such as supported employment and supported living, offer important chances to develop needed local services. But note that they offer an opportunity, not a mandate. Their implementation in any community depends on local effort. An integrated, productive life for all students with severe disabilities following special education need not be a mirage; it can and should become a reality.

SUMMARY

1. For successful community assimilation and integration, adults with severe disabilities must be provided the same vocational opportunities, residential arrangements, recreational opportunities, and community services as persons without disabilities.

2. To enhance integration prospects, many professionals recommend that a community action network be established, with an activator to obtain and coordinate necessary services for persons with severe disabilities.

3. An activator performs the roles of referral coordinator, service coordinator, information coordinator, and support system coordinator.

4. Remunerative employment is the cornerstone of integration because of the increased integration opportunities it offers.

5. The Pathways to Employment Model is an employment paradigm that takes into account the choices of adults with severe disabilities. In this model, the outcome is the degree of economic self-sufficiency realized through employment.

6. The Pathways Model has five stages: (1) in the preaction stage the person with severe disabilities is not ready or able to decide on employment; (2) in the action stage the adult makes a decision about the type of job he or she would like; (3) in the service stage the adult determines whether additional training is needed; (4) in the outcome stage the degree of economic self-sufficiency realized through employment is evaluated; (5) in the review stage the adult can reexamine and modify his or her decision.

7. To put employment in proper perspective, the Pathways Model explains occupational success with the formula $O = f[(P + Op + S) - D] \times DI$. Occupational success (O) is thought to be a function (f) of preparation (P), opportunity (Op), the support system (S), and the negative impact of disincentives (D). These variables are multiplied by a factor reflecting the degree of intensity (DI).

8. The Pathways Model also attempts to describe the positive integrative value of employment. This integrative factor, habilitation, is expressed in the formula $H = f(L + O + SI + R) \times EI$. Habilitation (H) is thought to be a function (f) of living arrangements (L), occupation (O), social integration (SI), and recreation (R). These variables are multiplied by environmental intensity (EI).

9. To assist adults with severe disabilities in acquiring domestic skills, Project MESH has developed pictorial instructional materials.

10. In meal preparation training, the adult performs steps in a sequence specified by a picture recipe book.

11. In meal planning, the adult follows a planned menu that identifies, through pictures, the foods to be prepared and the steps in preparing them.

12. In food shopping, the adult checks the picture recipe book to determine whether the ingredients on next week's menu are in stock. If not, the picture recipe is placed in a "shopping list binder" for an upcoming grocery trip.

13. In housekeeping, the adult performs "how to" steps in a sequence specified by a housekeeping picture book and uses a picture reminder system to indicate when certain tasks should be performed.

14. To improve community integration, many states are developing school-to-postschool transition programs. Transition outcomes appear to depend on three factors: the sending agencies, the receiving agencies, and the handoff process.

15. While employment is viewed as the most important outcome of the transition process, other vitally important integration skills are leisure-recreational skills, domestic skills, general community skills, social-personal skills, and communication skills.

16. Transition is a dynamic process involving a partnership of consumers, school and postschool service agencies, and local community elements to optimize an adult's employment, independent living, integration, and community participation.

17. Adult transition services are presently administered by a number of agencies each responsible for a particular spectrum of services. Because services are fragmented, uncoordinated, and often conflicting, transition planning is difficult.

18. A major concept of the Illinois Transition Project is creation of a Transition Assistance Committee (TAC) to coordinate and operationalize interagency resources for improving transition services.

19. The second major concept of the Illinois Transition Project is to evaluate the effectiveness of present services by following up adults who are no longer served in public school special education programs.

20.   The third major concept of the Illinois Transition Project is development of a formal plan, the Individualized Transition Program (ITP), by a planning committee, to establish vocational, residential, and continuing education objectives for each person with severe disabilities.

NOTES   [1]Although this chapter primarily analyzes the effects of transition on persons with severe disabilities, transition typically applies to persons with mild disabilities as well.

[2]Presently fewer than a dozen states have transition projects that attempt to enhance the postschool integration of persons with disabilities. The Illinois Transition Project is codirected by Dr. Paul Bates and Mr. Carl Suter.

CHAPTER 15

Advocacy and Advocate Services for Persons with Severe Disabilities

(Courtesy of Cahokia School District 187, Illinois.)

Paul Donelson is employed as a baker's helper in a small "mom and pop" donut shop. Although his hours are erratic and his income is minimum wage, he derives great pleasure from his job and has never missed a day in six years. Paul rents a room from the Rickers in a house two blocks from the donut shop. He eats his meals with the Rickers and generally can do whatever he wants in the other rooms of the house. Recently, his major source of recreation has been watching the neighborhood boys play baseball in the park across the street. While he feels he is too "big" to participate, he enjoys the sunshine and the noisy chatter of the boys. When he returns to his room one Friday evening, Mr. Ricker informs him that he has to move immediately. Neighbors have complained about Paul's hanging around the smaller boys. They hinted at fears of molestation and generally complained that Paul's watching the boys was "unnatural." Paul believes that he must indeed move the next day. He is not sure where to turn or what to do.

On his way home from work one evening, Jefferson Schrage stopped at the local drugstore for a soda. He had been living in the community for slightly over three years, but he hadn't learned to be very cautious. He began talking to three teenage boys while he drank his soda, and they induced Jefferson to invite them to his room on the pretext of listening to his radio. Once inside his room, they beat him and stole his money and some of his things. A short time later, Jefferson was found by the houseparents of the group home in which he lived. After listening to his story, the houseparents called the police, who conducted a short investigation. The police report concluded that the incident was probably a "falling-out among homosexuals" and noted that Jefferson "looked and acted kind of funny."

For the past two years, Erwin Jacobson has been working in an extended employment sheltered workshop. Even though his salary is marginal (between $4 and $6 a week), he likes the work and the camaraderie of the workshop. Recently, he has been trained to operate industrial laundry equipment and has achieved a high degree of proficiency. The workshop staff has expressed a desire to place Erwin in a hospital job, where he would operate the same type of laundry equipment. While he would earn competitive wages and is excited about the prospects of working in this normalized environment, Erwin has serious reservations about accepting the job. He is worried that if he fails in the hospital laundry room he will be placed on a waiting list for readmission to the workshop and might not be readmitted for two years or more. He has seen this happen to several of his friends. Erwin is confused and upset; he just does not know whom to ask for advice.

The personal difficulties expressed in these episodes may be resolved, at least to a certain degree, by a **citizen advocate**. As more and more persons with severe disabilities are integrated into community settings, it is increasingly evident that they may need to relate to, associate with, and depend on other citizens in the community at times. Wolfensberger (1973) describes a citizen advocate as a mature, competent volunteer representing the interests of a child or adult who has a difficulty solving practical day-to-day problems of living and who has a major need for emotional support. These needs are presently unmet and will likely remain unmet without special intervention. According to Wolfensberger, a citizen advocate essentially views the rights, interests, welfare, and needs of a person with severe disabilities as if they were his or her own. Citizen advocacy is not an agency representation or representation by professionals acting in professional roles; rather it is a representation by competent and suitable citizens. Conceivably, advocates can function singly or in groups and can represent the interest of either an individual or a group. Advocacy is an important complement to the training programs that prepare persons to live in community settings.

Advocacy and Advocate Services: An Overview

Central to the principle of normalization are reduction of conditions that impede integration and enhancement of the person's functional skills. Advocacy, or speaking for and acting on behalf of a person with severe disabilities, in many instances enables the person to function in the mainstream of society rather than outside of it. Advocacy protects the rights, interests, and welfare of persons with disabilities. Copeland, Addison, and McCann (1974) define advocacy as

> a one-to-one relationship between a capable volunteer ("advocate") and a mentally retarded person ("protege") in which the advocate defends the rights and interests of the protege and provides practical or emotional reinforcement (or a combination of both) for him. All this occurs within the framework of a structured advocacy system [p. 8].

The central concept of this definition is the **advocate-protege relationship**. Typically, advocates play one or both of two roles. The first is to solve practical day-to-day problems of the protege. In this role, the advocate may be a spokesperson for the individual who is unable to speak or may provide practical guidance, advice, and instruction in daily activities. The second role is to provide emotional support and reinforcement for the protege. The advocate may act as a friend, providing attention, offering affection, and letting the protege know that someone cares. The intent of both advocacy roles is to increase the independence and community integration of the protege.

A slightly different definition is offered by Biklen (1979), who views advocacy "as an independent movement of consumers (e.g., parents, people with disabilities, children) and their allies to monitor and change human service agencies" (p. 310). Biklen's definition is outcome-oriented and emphasizes **self-advocacy**. While fully capitalizing on the advocate-protege relationship, self-advocacy is predicated on the notion that the person should be taught to make decisions and speak out for himself or herself (Shoultz, 1986). In general, self-advocacy proposes that persons with severe disabilities have the right to self-determination and to live as fully and independently as possible.

To outline the parameters of his definition, Biklen proposes four principles of advocate services. These principles promote quality human services and recognize that persons with severe disabilities are guaranteed basic human and civil rights. The first principle is that advocates should attempt to eliminate the conditions that create a dependent status in persons with disabilities. Biklen strongly asserts that an advocate should help people with severe disabilities to be as independent as possible. The second principle is that advocates should attempt to understand their proteges' feelings, desires, and needs and should perform only those services desired by the proteges. The third principle is that advocates should identify and eliminate conditions and attitudes in society that dehumanize persons with disabilities. Dehumanizing attitudes often impede normal integration. The fourth principle is that advocates should obtain services to which their proteges are legally entitled regardless of any criticisms directed toward the advocates. Through these principles, Biklen attempts to ensure that persons with severe disabilities attain optimum self-determination and independence.

Central to Biklen's four principles are two underlying themes. The first is identification and protection of the protege's human and civil rights. **Human rights** allow an individual to develop to his or her fullest potential. They are interwoven with the right of self-determination in a truly integrated society. **Civil rights** are the powers, privileges, or guarantees granted to people under the law. In general, civil rights attempt to ensure that every citizen is treated with justice and reason.

The second underlying theme is the relationship of advocacy to normalization. Normalization stresses the essential similarity of all people and the need for persons with severe disabilities to acquire skills relevant to the community in which they live, work, and play. Advocates play an essential role in ensuring that the necessary services are provided to proteges. Advocates may also facilitate normalization by assisting proteges to develop friendships with other people without disabilities.

A third slightly different perspective was proposed by Weinrich (1987), who defines advocacy as a two-phase continuous process that seeks to ensure the basic human and civil rights of persons with severe disabilities and an ever-improving quality of life for them. Central to Weinrich's concept are four issues of advocacy. First, advocacy should ascertain that service providers are using the latest approaches, opportunities, and techniques to benefit persons with severe disabilities. Second, advocacy should assure that services are accessible and properly delivered. Third, advocacy should ensure that services are delivered through a cooperative effort by public and private providers. Fourth, advocacy should guarantee that all community resources, services, and activities are physically accessible to persons with severe disabilities. Weinrich, like Biklen, recommends that advocates promote as much self-determination and independence as possible for persons with severe disabilities.

While the concept of advocacy varies somewhat in different analyses, it generally refers to advancing or securing the rights and interest of persons with severe disabilities, individually and collectively. This goes far beyond traditional volunteer activities. In some instances, advocacy-directed protection could translate into informal instruction in vocational development, grooming skills, and physical appearance; at other times, the advocate could use techniques of behavioral support and guidance ranging from delicate and subtle to frank and blunt; at still other times, the advocate and protege could simply "hang out" together or jointly participate in recreational activities. Reduced to its lowest common denominator, advocacy is mainly aimed at enhancing interactions between persons with severe disabilities and persons without disabilities.

Purposes of Advocate Services

Advocacy is as much an attitude as a form of concerted action. In a broad sense, every effort on behalf of a person with disabilities is advocacy. It involves social, political, and legal efforts and strategies to bring about more favorable conditions for children and adults with severe disabilities.

According to Crowner (1979), there are four major purposes of advocacy. The first is to eliminate or reduce any restrictive features of a service or facility in the community. Advocate services attempt to integrate persons with severe disabilities totally whether they are students being integrated into school programs or adults being integrated into community programs. The second purpose is to ensure that programs and services are appropriate to the needs of the person. The **criterion of need** should be the yardstick for evaluating programs and services in both school and community. The third purpose is to coordinate the mosaic services offered by community agencies. Services should be tied directly to the person's individualized education program, individualized transition program, or individualized habilitation program. The fourth purpose is to lobby for school and postschool services so that each graduate can have a rewarding and fulfilling life.

Advocate services should be directed toward meeting the diverse and unique needs of persons with severe disabilities. Presently, unmet needs are addressed by a number of professionals. These educators, social workers, psychologists, and other social service professionals are often essential to solve the various crises that persons with severe disabilities face from time to time. But many of these crises might be averted by an advocate. Although professionals may attempt to provide advocacy, all too often, their efforts are cumbersome and inadequate.

When public-minded citizens provide advocate services, they tend to give not only their time, energy, and material resources but also their hearts and minds. The value of their efforts may equal or surpass the costs of services that social service agencies would otherwise have to provide. For example, a family that adopts a child with Down syndrome might save the public the cost of lifelong institutionalization; an advocate might give a protege advice about housing that otherwise would have required intervention by a social worker;

FIGURE 15.1

Advocacy is designed to facilitate integration while meeting the diverse and unique needs of persons with severe disabilities.

(Courtesy of Ruthanna Bryant.)

and the friendship and emotional support provided by an advocate might prevent behaviors that otherwise would have resulted in police or legal action. As the need for services from social agencies is increasing and funding is scrutinized more and more closely, advocacy can simultaneously meet human needs and reduce costs.

In some cases, advocates must play the role of adversaries to social service agencies in order to protect the interests and welfare of proteges. In other instances, advocates can combine their services with those of agencies to increase an agency's probability of success. To illustrate, community integration of adults with severe disabilities has not been particularly successful because of the lack of adequate follow-up and supervision. The track record of community agencies in this area has been dismal, but public-minded citizens appear to be better suited for such one-to-one supervision. They tend to be more accommodating than agency personnel in helping proteges deal with failure or disappointing experiences and thus can be highly effective.

Both voluntary citizen advocates and social service agencies have strengths and weaknesses, and both have a place in serving children and adults with severe disabilities. Agencies provide a variety of professional services, training, supervision, and follow-up. Advocates offer flexibility, enthusiasm, inspiration, friendship, and dependability. Advocate services are unencumbered by the typical rigidities of public agencies; however, some advocates can be undisciplined, incompetent, and nonsupportive. Possibly the major strength of advocacy is that it brings previously uninvolved citizens into the ranks. Consumer, special interest, and self-help action groups may find in advocacy programs a major means for recruiting members interested in serving persons with severe disabilities. In the advocate movement in mental retardation, parents and professionals found others willing to provide the intimate support and action they had previously provided only by themselves.

Goals of Advocate Services

Advocacy is based on the premise that persons with severe disabilities will encounter many unanticipated problems that can be greatly alleviated by advocate services. Active efforts at advocacy are important for several reasons. First, there are not enough social service professionals to accommodate all persons with disabilities. Therefore, the first goal of advocacy is to provide the necessary services. Second, advocates can facilitate social relationships. By the nature of their role, advocates enlarge the protege's circle of friends and acquaintances. Third, persons with severe disabilities need to know that persons without disabilities care about and accept them. These feelings cannot possibly emerge in an isolated instructional or residential setting. These three goals will be more closely examined in the following section.

Providing social services.   Although the primary purpose of education is to foster functional integration in the community, many school leavers with severe disabilities enter the community inadequately prepared for the pressures of integration and the changes that occur with time. Postschool transition services ease some of these pressures, but they fall far short of eliminating them. Many adults must have additional training and preparation. To make community integration more enjoyable and rewarding, they need to develop friendships and social relationships with persons without disabilities. It is doubtful that a single or even several social service professionals can provide the training, preparation, and social relationships needed for the vast array of community experiences that make integration rewarding and successful. Some special education professionals (viz., Blatt, 1987) even suggest that knowledgeable and dedicated citizens can provide friendship, social relationships, and community training better than the mosaic pattern of services offered by community agencies.

Facilitating social relationships.   Friendships bring satisfaction and security to life. They are the basis for personal growth, community integration, and the prospect of normalization. They represent the "fit" between persons, an ongoing reciprocal liking and mutual involvement between them (Epstein, 1986;

FIGURE 15.2

A knowledgeable and dedicated advocate may provide friendship, social relationships, and community training better than different community agencies.

(Courtesy of Barbara Chatman.)

Stainback & Stainback, 1987). Persons with severe disabilities have difficulties "fitting" with other persons. According to a study by Gollary, Freedman, Wyngarden, and Kurtz (1978), 80 percent of community residents with mental retardation are without any friends. The other 20 percent indicated they had one or two friends. Over 90 percent of all community-integrated persons with severe disabilities have indicated that they lead meaningless and lonely lives (Baker, Seltzer, & Seltzer, 1977; Matson & DiLorenzo, 1986). Many also felt that there was no one in the community they could trust or depend on. A number of researchers (Asher & Renshaw, 1981; Richardson, 1981; Strully & Strully, 1985) have concluded that the social relationship success of community residents with severe disabilities is directly dependent on having adequate advocate services.

Offering acceptance by persons without disabilities.   People obtain a sense of personal well-being when their basic needs for love, esteem, and acceptance are satisfied (Maslow, 1970). Cobb (1971), working from Maslow's hypothesis, noted that love, esteem, and acceptance are largely determined by an individual's relationship with his or her environment and the people within that environment. Cobb observed that an environment can contribute to an individual's sense of well-being by providing mutually satisfying contact with other persons. For many persons with severe disabilities, integrated community living offers access to a whole range of new activities and experiences—options for recreation, for meeting new people, and for going to different places. Yet, persons with severe disabilities often assume a dependent behavioral stance. They seldom if ever initiate contact with others and may remain in quiescent boredom unless someone takes the initiative to integrate them. Advocates can solve this dilemma. Not only can they provide mutually satisfying interpersonal experiences but, probably of greater importance, they also can help their proteges develop friendships with other persons without disabilities based on love, esteem, and acceptance.

BASIS FOR ADVOCATE SERVICES

The concept of advocate services did not evolve independently. Rather it is based on a number of premises and principles, in particular, three: a legal basis, a moral basis, and a philosophical basis. In unison, these principles preserve and protect the rights, interests, and welfare of persons with severe disabilities.

The Legal Basis

The legal basis of advocacy consists of three legal principles or rights granted by statutory and constitutional law to all citizens: (1) positive presumption, (2) due process, and (3) instrumental protection. While they have often been denied to persons with severe disabilities, their importance is indisputable. Since these rights are universally guaranteed, it is untenable that they should be denied to persons classified as severely disabled.

The **principle of positive presumption** was clearly enunciated by Thomas Jefferson in the phrase in the Declaration of Independence that all people "are endowed by their Creator with certain unalienable rights, that among these are life, liberty and the pursuit of happiness." An individual, regardless of any disabling condition, is entitled to basic and universal rights that cannot legally or morally be denied. Nevertheless, in Western culture this principle is seldom extended to persons with severe disabilities. While the principle of positive presumption is a legal concept, it also rests firmly on moral grounds. The underlying moral philosophy centers around the intrinsic, inherent value of being a person. By simply being a person, a human being enjoys the fundamental right to express his or her unique human qualities. Cobb (1973) contends that denial of this right is the equivalent of "moral genocide."

The **principle of due process**, an extension of the principle of positive presumption, states that a legally established procedure must be followed before any substantive right of a person is abridged. The established procedures include the right to prior notice, the right to representation by counsel, the right to a fair and impartial hearing, and the right to appeal. There are two important corollaries that have a direct relevance to persons with severe disabilities. First, before denying a person a substantive right, sufficient cause must be given. A disability classification is not sufficient cause for denying a person substantive rights. Second, an individual's rights must be restored when their denial is no longer justifiable. This corollary assumes that any human condition is subject to change. Thus, an individual who once had rights abridged may reclaim those rights when there no longer is evidence to confirm abridgment.

The **principle of instrumental protection** refers to the laws and institutions (e.g., the court system, the police department) established to protect an individual's unalienable rights or to encourage an individual to express his or her rights more fully. Persons with severe disabilities, in the past and today, have suffered from social ostracism, excessive restrictions, and dehumanizing treatment. Many have endured physical, sexual, and verbal abuse; ridicule, baiting, and loss of dignity; social isolation, loneliness, and lack of contact with persons without disabilities. Rather than halting or hindering these practices, many social service agencies have fostered them. Society has the duty to provide instrumental protection for individuals to exercise their rights.

There is a basic distinction between the rights of adults and those of children. As legal dependents, children have rights to protection, nurturance, and education. While children with severe disabilities may require special services, they have the same legal status as other children. If a child is abused or neglected, his or her rights are violated regardless of any disabling condition. A child who is adjudged to be improperly nurtured in his or her home is entitled to a legal remedy irrespective of a disabling condition, even though that condition may be a factor underlying the improper care. When a person moves from the status of dependent minor to adult, he or she acquires a new set of rights. This is true of persons without disabilities, but in many instances these rights are denied to persons with severe disabilities because of predictions made largely on the basis of IQ scores or observed conditions.

The Moral Basis

The moral basis of advocacy focuses on the intrinsic value of being a person. By simply being human, a person has the fundamental right to express his or her unique human qualities regardless of how others feel about the propriety of his or her contribution. This concept of human dignity has long formed the basis of religious and social principles in modern society. The moral basis of advocacy rests on a number of traditional precepts. However, various issues are raised when these moral precepts are directly applied to advocate services. What one moral principle may condone, another may condemn, and a moral "truth" accepted by some may be repudiated by others.

Refocusing on the recipient of advocate services raises a troublesome question: what is in the best interests of the person with severe disabilities? Haille (1981), analyzing the nature of cruelty in the Nazi death camps, argues that it does not consist solely of physical pain. True cruelty "involves the maiming of a person's dignity, the crushing of a person's self-respect" (p. 23). An act of cruelty may or may not inflict physical pain, but it always inflicts humiliation. The most insidious cruelty of all, says Haille, is institutional cruelty—the kind that over the years instills in its victims the belief that they somehow deserve ill treatment and humiliation. It is this that allows society to blame victims for their problems and that seduces victims into believing that the blamers are correct.

Advocacy cannot be examined without looking at the religious and ethical fiber of the society, in particular, the Christian perspective, the Judaic perspective, and the utilitarian perspective.

The **Christian perspective** centers around enabling persons to be or act more like God. This ideal is best expressed in terms of love between persons. It is evinced in such Christian doctrines as "Love your neighbor as yourself" (Luke 6:31) and "Do unto others as you would have them do unto you" (Matthew 7:12). These are the linchpins of the **doctrine of empathic reciprocity**. Applying this doctrine to advocate services, advocates must develop empathic relationships with their proteges. That is, if the advocates were in similar circumstances, how would they want to be treated? The Christian doctrine of empathic reciprocity emphasizes the humanness of the individual as reflected by the basic needs of human beings. The empathic reciprocity of advocacy, therefore, neatly dovetails into the Christian doctrine of love your neighbor (Turnbull & Guess [with Backus et al.], 1986).

The **Judaic perspective** requires that services be provided that uphold the dignity of the individual. Dignity is conceptualized as life enhancement. It is achieved by increasing a person's capacities for enjoying and learning from life. Underscoring this belief is the doctrine of empathic reciprocity, which asks advocates how they would like to be treated, if their circumstances were similar to their proteges'. Advocate services are appropriate only if they advance the dignity of the individual's life, if they make it more like that of persons without disabilities. Does advocacy advance the dignity of an individual's life? The answer is yes; its long-term result appears to be durable, generalizable, and increased community integration. Therefore, the Judaic perspective would favor advocacy (Turnbull & Guess [with Backus et al.], 1986).

A secular doctrine that applies to the moral basis of advocacy is the **utilitarian perspective**, which holds that the purpose of all action should be to bring the greatest happiness to the largest number in society. Every action must be analyzed to determine if it represents the "true good" by this standard. Applied utilitarianism assesses the economic, social, political, and personal impact of every action on both the individual and society. Do advocate services produce more good than harm for more people? If so, then advocacy is "moral" under utilitarian principles. Without question, advocacy benefits some people, but does it benefit more people than it harms? Brandt (1983) indicated that preferable activities from the perspective of classical utilitarian ethics increase an individual's functional autonomy (make a person freer). The utilitarian principle would favor any actions that reduce the effects of disability, since they would result in greater functionality, greater autonomy, greater happiness, and therefore increased productivity. Thus, advocacy appears to be "moral" from a utilitarian perspective.

The Philosophical Basis

Pinker (1973) has provided a systematic and extremely useful philosophical analysis that can be applied to advocacy. Building on the work of Mauss (1954) and Titmuss (1971), Pinker begins with the position that social services are social exchanges in which it is possible to distinguish between givers and receivers. These exchanges tend, by nature, to be unequal. If the giver bestows a gift, the receiver can never make up for it completely, even if the receiver were to present the giver with an item of equivalent value. While the giver gave voluntarily from a sense of generosity, the receiver experiences a sense of gratitude accompanied by a sense of obligation. Pinker distinguishes between non-social-service transactions and social service transactions. Using borrowing money as an example of the former, he suggests that the borrower experiences dependence on the lender, but the dependence is temporary and ends with repayment of the principal plus interest. When a person receives social services, in contrast, the dependence is permanent: it cannot be repaid with interest. Moreover, argues Pinker, the exchange may make the receiver feel his or her dependence acutely.

Reviewing the works of anthropologists studying preindustrial societies, Pinker concludes that a sense of obligation and reciprocity along kinship lines and among neighbors appeared to permeate relationships in those societies. The issue of dependence, however, did not seem to be critical; interdependence was a way of life. Neighbors could depend on neighbors. Systems of exchange were largely based on norms of reciprocity between equals. In modern, industrial societies, Pinker argues, obligations usually begin and end with the nuclear family, or at best the extended family. While simpler societies tend to be egalitarian, complex societies are characterized by social inequalities. The issue, then, does not seem to be dependence, since it has existed in all societies in one form or another.

Pinker suggests that the critical factor is the **nature of the dependence**, whether the exchange is between people who perceive themselves to be equal or unequal and the degree to which receivers are able to reciprocate. In preindustrial societies, receivers were more likely to believe that they would reciprocate if necessary, and givers gave with this understanding. In complex societies, reciprocity appears to be more elusive. While neighborliness continues to exist, neighbors often do not have the skills or the time to assist each other. Because of this, modern societies have created highly specialized social institutions. Nursing homes were built to share in the care of the elderly and sick; public service departments were established, in part, to provide safe and well-maintained streets; and other agencies were founded to meet other social and economic needs of the citizenry (Moroney, 1986). In practice, this may create nonreciprocal relationships in which receivers feel their dependence acutely.

How does this affect advocacy for persons with severe disabilities? To a large extent, the answer revolves around the manner in which advocacy is provided. If it is offered as a social service, as a gift from a social agency, it will likely create an unequal, nonreciprocal relationship that makes the receiver acutely aware of his or her dependence. The advocate-protege relationship will then deteriorate, and advocacy will never become viable in the integration process. Conversely, if advocacy is viewed as a reciprocal exchange between individuals who are equals as human beings, it can be a rewarding experience for both the advocate and the protege. Such advocacy could greatly enhance the protege's full integration into society and the advocate's sense of accomplishing a worthwhile goal.

Advocacy Service Delivery Systems

Although an advocate is generally perceived as a citizen who protects, supports, and argues for the interests and welfare of another, advocacy can take other forms. Parents, by role and function, are advocates on behalf of their children. Although seldom addressed specifically, the role of teachers as advocates is not new. They have long been involved in advocacy to obtain services for children with disabilities. Persons with disabilities can also serve as their own advocates. Self-advocacy, as this is called, means that an individual looks out for his or her rights, interests, and welfare. These three advocate systems are further examined next.

Citizen Advocacy

Wolfensberger (1972) describes a citizen advocate as a mature, competent volunteer representing the short-term and long-term interests of a child or adult who has difficulty solving practical day-to-day problems of living and who has a major need for emotional support. The range of citizen advocate services depends on the needs of the protege. The intent of the advocate-protege relationship, according to Wolfensberger and Brown (1973), is to improve the protege's quality of life, social acceptance, dignity, status, and citizenship rights. The time shared by the advocate and the protege might be used, for instance, to attend recreational activities, go shopping, or nurture a friendship. Wolfensberger (1973) and Turnbull (1983) suggest that citizen advocacy is somewhat analogous to Big Brother and Big Sister programs.

Citizen advocacy can also adopt a more formal, directed structure. An advocate may assume the role of job coach or job advocate, for instance, providing one-to-one training in job duties or work-related skills at the protege's job site. As the potential employee becomes more proficient in doing the job to the employer's standards, job assistance from the citizen advocate is reduced. A citizen advocate may assume the role of guidance counselor to ensure a smooth and orderly transition from school to community. After transition, the citizen advocate may assume specific responsibilities, such as assisting the protege to develop friendships, use recreational resources, or get around in the community. These advocate services help bridge the gap between the protege's existing skills and those required to function in the environment. Gap-bridging takes the strengths of the person into account while fostering maximum independence. The citizen advocate can prevent service "overkill" by providing the minimum training necessary for successful community integration.

A unique form of citizen advocacy is **student-to-student advocacy,** in which a student without disabilities looks out for the interests, welfare, and needs of a schoolmate with severe disabilities (Fenrick & McDonnell, 1980; McCarthy & Stodden, 1979; Poorman, 1980). While the primary purpose of student-to-student advocacy is to increase interactions between students with and without severe disabilities, student advocates may take other roles and responsibilities. For instance, they may teach specific skills to, chart the performance of, and modify certain behaviors of their proteges; assist proteges around the school building; accompany them on field trips; help them to board the school bus; or simply become their friends. It is hoped that many student advocates will "graduate" into citizen advocacy for their proteges upon completing school.

Parent-Professional Advocacy

Often referred to as **legal advocacy, parent-professional advocacy** can enhance the coping strategies and social acceptance of persons with severe disabilities. The parental role is an advocate role, overtly or covertly protecting, defending, and supporting the interests and welfare of the children. Many parents have long been involved in obtaining necessary educational and community services for their children.

The duties and responsibilities of teachers likewise often compel them to function as advocates. Since teachers foster skill acquisition for functioning more effectively in the natural environment, they are covert advocates for their students. Scandary and Bigge (1982) suggest that teachers need to perform three other advocate roles. First, they should develop the skills that will facilitate the students' functional integration into their communities. Second, they should protect the students' civil and human rights. Third, they should actively participate in local, state, and national organizations to develop appropriate services for persons with disabilities.

One of the primary purposes of legal advocacy is to provide formal and informal support systems for persons with severe disabilities. This may take the form of instituting a lawsuit, lobbying for legislation, or participating in a due process hearing. Parent-professional coalitions have been vital to successful coping and community integration (Richardson, 1981). This advocacy has been extremely effective in advancing the quality of life for persons with severe disabilities in educational, vocational, and personal terms. Parent-professional advocacy reinforces the principles of Public Law 94–142, and provides a meaningful forum in which parents and professionals can interact harmoniously and work jointly.

Self-Advocacy

The age of "doing for" persons with disabilities is rapidly retreating. Increasingly, persons with disabilities are asserting themselves and serving as their own advocates (Scandary & Bigge, 1982). For persons with disabilities, self-advocacy means speaking up about their own rights, interests, welfare, and needs (Shoultz, 1986). While speaking out can be risky, its importance cannot be denied. Citizen advocates may be competent but they are not always available when needed. Therefore persons with disabilities must be taught to defend their own rights and interests. For someone who cannot speak, the best spokesperson is probably another person with a disability who can speak. Because of similar experiences, such a person clearly understands the views and feelings of the protege.

The central premise of self-advocacy is freedom to make choices. Typically, persons with severe disabilities are told what to do: when to eat, where to live, and how to get ready for work. They have few choices about doing things or going places. People with severe disabilities who live in the community should have the right to make decisions, just as anyone else does. The choices are endless—choosing friends, deciding when friends can visit, picking which church to attend or deciding not to go to church at all, determining which specialized services to obtain or deciding not to participate in any (Shoultz, 1986; Williams & Shoultz, 1982). The freedom to make choices is emphasized in transition planning. Persons with severe disabilities should, to the extent possible, assume a major role in planning the programs and services that will be provided to them. They should be empowered to make decisions that affect their lives (Bates, Suter, & Poelvoorde, 1987).

Problems Associated with Advocacy

There is little question that advocate services have resulted in changes and opportunities for children and adults with severe disabilities. A citizen advocate can enhance the skills and abilities a protege needs for successful community integration. Nirje (1969) indicates that the central message of normalization is that citizens in the community recognize and consider the basic human needs of persons with disabilities. While this appears to be a clear endorsement of advocacy, other professionals argue that advocacy hinders normalization and thus integration. They raise three basic issues.

The first argument concerns what Blatt (1987) calls the **Golden Rule of Advocacy**, referring to Wolfensberger's (1972) definition of the citizen advocate as "a mature, competent citizen volunteer representing, *as if they were his own* [italics added], the interests of another citizen who is impaired in his instrumental competency, or who has major expressive needs which are unmet and which are likely to remain unmet without special intervention" (p. 11). This means that advocates are expected to put themselves in the place of persons with disabilities. To truly represent the interests of proteges as if they were the advocates' own, advocates must protect and supervise the daily behavior of proteges. This, in effect, places advocates in the position of "parent" and proteges in the position of "child" irrespective of chronological age. This may not only hinder the protege's ultimate integration in society but also reduce his or her self-respect, dignity, and personal pride.

The second argument against advocacy concerns potential disagreements between the advocate, the protege, and the protege's family. It would be folly to believe that parents, siblings, and friends will agree with every decision the advocate makes. From time to time, they will have different ideas or thoughts, and the protege's best interests may be open to interpretation. The advocate is then in conflict with family members who also have the best interests of the protege at heart.

Another possible conflict is disagreement between the advocate and the protege. If they reach different conclusions about a given situation, no one is then advocating for the rights of the protege. Suppose the protege wants to do something that the advocate fears may be potentially dangerous. Is it in the protege's best interests for the advocate to prevent the activity or to support the protege's choice and wishes? Neither the citizen advocate nor the protege is provided with a means of solving such disagreements in present advocacy structures.

A third concern is practical. An advocate must, by definition, be a mature, competent, committed, motivated, inspired, and stable individual. He or she must have continuity in the community, must be willing to undergo orientation, must understand the advocacy mission, must have a good moral character, must have time to carry on the advocate-protege relationship, and must have sincere humanitarian reasons for wanting to be an advocate. Advocates are expected to know something about persons with severe disabilities, about law, and about the structure and function of bureaucratic organizations. Unquestionably, these criteria are stiff. How many individuals fit them? Even if enough altruistically oriented people are available, how many would have the enormous amount of time needed to monitor the daily needs of another person? Such an investment is expected of people with particular roles in society, such as parents and siblings, and, in limited ways, clergy, social workers, and teachers, but it seems naive to expect a large number of others to volunteer to reorganize their daily lives around the human and civil rights of another person, especially if they understand the lifetime commitment that seems inherent in advocacy for persons with severe disabilities (Blatt, 1987; Weinrich, 1987).

CONCLUSION

It is increasingly apparent that integration is more than the absence of segregation. Students with severe disabilities are isolated from schoolmates in hallways, cafeterias, and playgrounds in integrated schools across the country. Adults with severe disabilities lead lonely and isolated lives in group homes in their communities. Excursions into the community often mean that the special education class or residents of the group home are transported by separate bus or van to the zoo, ball stadium, or community park. Even though they are educated and live in integrated settings, many experience frustration, ostracism, and failure. A possible solution is the use of advocates. Peer tutors, peer buddies, and special friends could greatly aid in the integration of students with severe disabilities in educational settings. Citizen advocates could greatly aid in their integration into community and recreational activities. Advocates could transform segregated interactions into truly integrated, normalized situations.

Is advocacy really necessary? Not if society provided adequate opportunities for children and adults with severe disabilities; not if society openly and warmly received persons with severe disabilities; not if society practiced the belief that all persons are created equal. Sadly we do not live in such a society, but maybe someday we will. Then, advocacy would not be necessary and should be discarded.

SUMMARY

1. Three definitions of advocacy have received widespread professional acceptance. The first defines advocacy as a one-to-one relationship in which a capable volunteer provides practical and emotional support to a person with disabilities. The second defines advocacy as an independent movement of consumers and their allies to monitor and improve human services agencies. The third defines advocacy as a continuous two-phase process to protect a person's basic human and civil rights and to improve his or her quality of life.

2. Advocacy has four purposes: to eliminate restrictive social and physical features; to ensure that services are appropriate to the needs of persons with severe disabilities; to coordinate the mosaic pattern of services offered by community agencies; and to lobby for school and community services that enable persons with severe disabilities to lead rewarding and satisfying lives.

3. There are three goals of advocacy: to provide the services to which persons with severe disabilities are rightfully entitled; to increase proteges' circles of friends and acquaintances; and to demonstrate to proteges that they are liked and respected by persons without disabilities.

4. Advocacy is based on legal, moral, and philosophical precepts.

5. Underlying the legal basis of advocacy are the principles of positive presumption, due process, and instrumental protection.

6. The principle of positive presumption states than an individual is entitled to certain unalienable rights (i.e., life, liberty, and the pursuit of happiness) that cannot legally or morally be denied.

7. The principle of due process states that legally established procedures must be followed before any substantive right is abridged.

8. The principle of instrumental protection recognizes that society establishes

institutions and laws to protect individuals and to enable them to exercise their rights.

9.   The moral basis of advocacy may be examined from three perspectives: the Christian, the Judaic, and the utilitarian.

10.   The Christian perspective asks: How would the advocate wish to be treated if he or she were in the same circumstances as the protege?

11.   The Judaic perspective requires that advocacy uphold the protege's inherent dignity. In this perspective, dignity means life enhancement. It is achieved by increasing the person's capacity for enjoying and learning from life.

12.   The utilitarian perspective argues that preferable activities are ones that increase a person's functionality, autonomy, happiness, and productivity.

13.   The philosophical basis of advocacy examines the giver-receiver relationship. This relationship may be either positive or negative depending on the equality, dependence, and reciprocity of the parties to it.

14.   The citizen advocate is a mature, competent volunteer representing the interests of a child or adult who has difficulty solving practical day-to-day problems of living and who has a major need for emotional support.

15.   A unique form of citizen advocacy is student-to-student advocacy, in which students without disabilities look out for the interests, welfare, and needs of schoolmates with severe disabilities.

16.   Parents and teachers, by the nature of their role and function, often serve as advocates. Parents have long lobbied for educational and community services for their children. Teachers foster the acquisition of skills that permit their students to function more effectively in their environment.

17.   Self-advocacy means speaking up about one's own rights, interests, welfare, and needs.

18.   While advocacy appears to have a positive influence on normalization and integration, many professionals insist that it hinders the integration of persons with severe disabilities.

19.   One argument against advocacy suggests that it forces the advocate and the protege into a parent-child relationship. The dependence in this relationship may reduce the protege's self-respect, dignity, and pride, thereby hindering his or her integration into society.

20.   A second argument against advocacy is that it does not offer ways to resolve potential disagreements between the advocate, the protege, and the protege's family.

21.   A third argument against advocacy is that few altruistically oriented people have the time to monitor the daily needs of another person.

CHAPTER 16

Perspectives in Serving Persons with Severe Disabilities: Today and Tomorrow

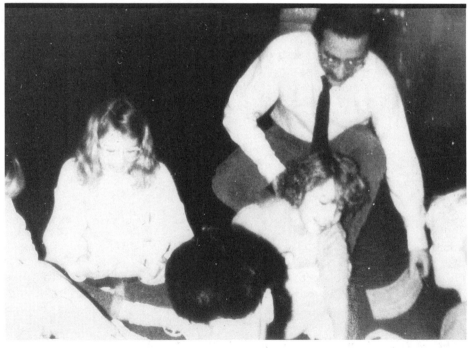

(Courtesy of Lynda Atherton.)

Any attempt to predict the future of a complex process such as the education of students with severe disabilities is presumptuous. Nevertheless, predicting can identify crucial factors and trends in the field. Paradoxically, by identifying developments that can be expected in the future, predictions may lead to their occurrence.

Some events are predictable, even though they result from interactions of considerable complexity. Since Newton, for instance, astronomers have been able to predict the positions of parts of the solar system—not just planets and moons but also asteroids, comets, and spaceships. If a portion of the object's orbit can be determined, scientists can predict the entire orbit within the accuracy limits of their instruments. For years, people have extrapolated this success to other fields, reasoning that if one can determine the progression of a trend over a short period of time, one should be able to predict the future of that trend.

The paradox is that the predictor must know, at the time of the prediction, the knowledge, philosophy, thoughts, and political events of the future. This is like asking a composer to hum the aria she will compose next spring. Future trends in serving persons with severe disabilities depend largely on contingencies that are outside the field of education. To be sure, we can fill in the details of what is already known, spot the latest trends, identify methodologies and procedures that appear the most promising, describe and give preliminary evaluations of developments already under way. But this is not the content of the future in serving persons with severe disabilities. To know the future, we must know its breakthroughs. Breakthroughs mean new kinds of observations, ideas, and approaches. Breakthroughs cannot be predicted.

What we most want to know about the future is thus securely sealed from us. This is high among the reasons why predicting is one of the most fascinating activities for the spectator, what Jacques Barzun once called "the glorious entertainment." Yet, if we can be content with less, predictions not about the content but rather about the shape of services to come for persons with severe disabilities may be of great value. Several powerful trends now operate, which can be grouped into five clusters: changing services, changing sites, changing staff, changing approaches, and changing times.

CHANGING SERVICES: HOW WILL THEY BE EDUCATED?

Over the past decade, special educators have begun to reexamine the programmatic methods and techniques for educating students with severe disabilities. Traditional methods have proved dramatically less than satisfactory. The employment rate of persons with severe disabilities is dismal at best (Bates, Suter, & Poelvoorde, 1987). Their community integration desperately needs improvement (Laski, 1980). Their residential arrangements are definitely insufficient (Heal, Sigelman, & Switzky, 1980). Educational programs for students with severe disabilities are often conducted in segregated environments that isolate them from schoolmates without disabilities. The skills and knowledge they acquire are often not referenced to the community, so that many students graduate with a marked disparity between their skills and those required for successful entry into the community (Donder & York, 1984). Perhaps the greatest concern in our present educational system is use of procedures and techniques that have been described as morally, ethically, and pedagogically unsound (Guess & Turnbull, 1987; Turnbull & Guess [with Backus et al.], 1986).

Clearly "how" we educate persons with severe disabilities has not proved successful. Many professionals now agree that present practices are fundamentally flawed. An increasing awareness of the abuses, deficits, and basic inhumanity of various techniques has convinced many service providers to initiate humane programs more conducive to the students' optimal development. Awareness of present flaws also delineates how educational methods are likely to change in the future. Two major changes seem likely.

Ethical, moral, and legal issues are likely to alter instructional techniques dramatically. Recently, many professionals have expressed serious reservations about the use of certain behavioral control procedures to elicit, shape, and direct behaviors, about the widespread use of psychotropic drugs to alter an individual's mood and behavior, about the appropriateness of certain goals and objectives, about the adequacy of some treatment procedures, about lack of confidentiality, about deprivation of food and water, and about the painful nature of some approaches. These are unacceptable in light of the long-term benefits to the student, they contend. Sadly, laws designed to protect the individual are often not considered when these procedures and techniques are applied to students with severe disabilities (Guess & Turnbull, 1987; Matson & DiLorenzo, 1984; Turnbull & Guess [with Backus et al.], 1986).

It seems fair to conclude that interventions of the future will use humane, empathic, considerate, and benevolent methods. Humane programs maximize an individual's integration into the community and must be effective, durable, generalizable, and functional. The specific factors that make intervention techniques "humane" differ among service providers, but justification of a program solely on the basis of alleged effectiveness without considering competing interests has all too often resulted in inhumane and ineffective programming. One procedure to unravel the various conflicting interests is the **interest analysis**. As Turnbull (1981) noted, interest analysis carefully dissects each party's stakes (interests) in a given situation and assists in weighing the competing interests and resolving conflicts among them. It is a useful tool for making difficult programmatic choices. As programs become more humane, effective, durable, generalizable, and functional, it is likely that interest analysis will be used increasingly.

Natural contexts will receive increased attention in programming. Historically, most children and adolescents with severe disabilities have been excluded from integrated school services on the assumption that training them to function effectively in their home communities was both unrealistic and unnecessary (Donder, Hamre-Nietupski, Nietupski, & Fortschneider, 1981; Donder & York, 1984). There appeared little or no justification for giving such students the skills and experiences they needed to interact with community counterparts without disabilities. Despite the continuation of segregation, several studies have substantiated the effectiveness and positive results of integration for students with severe disabilities.

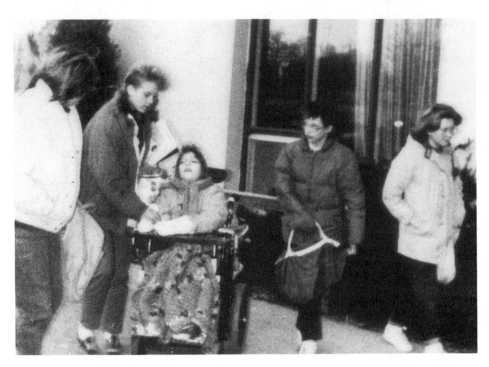

FIGURE 16.1

Placing students with severe disabilities into integrated school settings provides them with a normalized, natural environment in which to develop the skills they need to function as independently as possible as adults in the community.

(Courtesy of Lynda Atherton.)

A major reason for placing students in integrated school settings is to provide them with a normalized, natural environment in which to develop the skills they need to function as independently as possible as adults in the community (Voeltz, 1984). It seems logical that such skills are best taught and practiced in "criterion" situations (Falvey, Brown, Lyon, Baumgart, & Schroeder, 1980). Integrating classrooms for students with severe disabilities into the elementary and secondary schools exposes students with disabilities to the natural cues, correction procedures, and contingencies available in the "real world" as opposed to the various manipulations and simulations of artificial instructional environments. Highly structured, discrete trial instruction in isolated classroom settings may indeed result in the acquisition of behaviors in the classroom. But it is readily apparent that such skills are not useful outside the instructional environment, are typically not generalizable, and even when maintained often become maladaptive or inappropriate. Thus, it seems fair to conclude that functional and generalizable skills will be taught in integrated elementary and secondary school environments. Classroom models and strategies, in the future, will reflect meaningful instruction in which the student with severe disabilities acquire normalized behaviors in natural environments reinforced by natural cues and contingencies.

CHANGING SITES: WHERE WILL THEY BE EDUCATED?

A current popular view is that the needs of students with severe disabilities are so unique that they require specialized services that cannot be provided in the regular education program. It is generally assumed that neither students with severe disabilities nor students without disabilities could benefit from a shared public school education. Few have considered the possibility that these students might coexist and interact positively with each other (Brown, Branston, Hamre-Nietupski, Pumpian, et al., 1979). A philosophy that stresses the essential similarity of all human beings and their need to acquire skills that are functional in the communities in which they live comes into unavoidable conflict with the current practices of segregation. Such a philosophy mandates educational environments for children that provide the necessary preparation. In other words, educational settings must provide daily and longitudinal interactions between students with severe disabilities and their counterparts without disabilities (Brown et al., 1981).

Segregation of students with severe disabilities impedes their acquisition and generalization of functional, age-appropriate interaction skills that facilitate community integration. Students can hardly learn to interact appropriately with nondisabled peers without being exposed to them. Of course, exposure alone does not ensure interactions, but lack of exposure can guarantee lack of interactions (Brown, Branston, Hamre-Nietupski, Pumpian, et al., 1979). Despite notable improvements, the restrictive segregationist point of view is still prevalent in schools and communities. Educational services for students with severe disabilities often do not promote interactions with community members in schools, social activities, or employment. The segregated educational model continues to predominate even though many professionals conclude that it is ideologically unsound, educationally counterproductive, and ridiculously cost-inefficient (Donder & York, 1984).

The dominant attitude mandates that students with severe disabilities be educated in environments that serve only other students with severe disabilities. This segregation dramatically limits student interaction to classmates with severe disabilities or teachers, therapists, aides, psychologists, cafeteria workers, and other "helpers" (Landesman-Dwyer, Berkson, & Romer, 1979; Certo & Kohl, 1984). In almost all interactions with caregivers and professionals, the student with severe disabilities is the recipient. He or she is helped to do something by a professional who sets the rules and generally requires rather rigid adherence to expectations. This limited range of social experiences cannot promote social competence or develop rewarding social relationships.

A small but growing number of parents and educators now advocate active integration of students with severe disabilities into mainstream education (Stainback & Stainback, 1987). This means placement of students with severe disabilities into chronologically age-appropriate regular classes in neighborhood schools. In these settings interactions between them and peers without disabilities are possible. Interactions may be structured and facilitated initially by the program, but eventually they should occur spontaneously. Nearly all children with severe disabilities can be included in regular classrooms for selected activities and programs and go to special education classrooms for other activities and programs.

Regular education is not at present structured or equipped to meet the needs of all students with severe disabilities. This does not mean, however, that integration is inappropriate or impractical. It only indicates that integration must proceed carefully as the regular educational system is modified and expanded to meet the needs of all students. It seems fair to conclude that, in the future, students with severe disabilities will be educated in regular classrooms alongside schoolmates without disabilities for some activities and in special education classrooms and the general community for others. This opportunity is important to them, since being educated in the mainstream is the only realistic way to prepare them for living in the mainstream in their postschool years (Stainback & Stainback, 1987; Voeltz, 1984). After all, there are no "special" worlds. There are no "special" sections of theaters, grocery stores, banks, or churches. There are no "special" ticket takers, cashiers, or tellers. In short, the two separate worlds in the public schools do not exist in the community. In the future, the "special" world at school will end.

Many professionals also suggest that students with severe disabilities be educated in their home communities. Since the fundamental goal of their schooling is to prepare them to become competent community members, the educational experience must foster community competence. Despite this, schools erect barriers to community interaction. The secondary level curriculum, for instance, often emphasizes academic skills or developmental progressions, ignoring tasks vital to employment and community success. Instruction is usually provided in segregated classrooms on the assumption that the students are not yet "ready" to go into the community (Wilcox, 1987).

Developing community competence in persons with severe disabilities requires more than an occasional field trip. Students can and should be taught to shop for groceries, to cash checks, to dine in local restaurants, and to get around in the community. Above all else, instruction must take place in the community. Wilcox (1987) noted that persons with severe disabilities cannot possibly get ready for the complexity of the community in the sterility of a classroom. She suggests that students with severe disabilities spend the majority of their school day learning and generalizing functional skills in the community. At a minimum, she indicates, beginning high school students should spend a fourth of their school day and older students a third of their day in the community. It seems fair to conclude that students with severe disabilities will

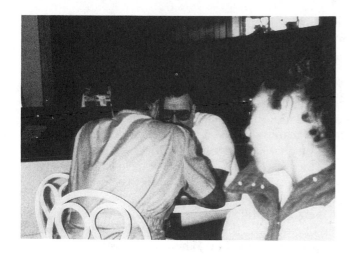

FIGURE 16.2

Since the goal of schooling for students with severe disabilities is to prepare them to become competent community members, it is imperative that their educational experience foster community competence.

(Courtesy of Barbara Chatman.)

spend a greater amount of time being taught functional skills in the community where they expect to use those skills after graduation.

CHANGING STAFF: WHO WILL EDUCATE THEM?

School integration is a multifaceted process involving much more than the physical removal of students from segregated environments and their placement in normalized settings. To facilitate the integration of students with severe disabilities into public school programs, present services must be restructured to meet the students' longitudinal needs. Changes in the location of services have far-reaching implications for both direct and indirect service professionals. For some, integration will require restructuring and rearranging their responsibilities; for others, it may bring dramatically new and altered responsibilities. Service delivery personnel who have been excluded from serving students with severe disabilities will now be assigned to direct service positions.

Probably the greatest changes will occur in the special and regular education teaching staffs. The regular classroom teacher will likely have major responsibility for training students with severe disabilities, that is, providing instruction, reinforcing behaviors, monitoring progress, and facilitating learning. In short, regular classroom teachers will be just as accountable for students with severe disabilities as for students without disabilities.

The responsibilities of special education teachers also will be quite different, probably more varied and diverse. The special educator of the future will join other staff members in a transdisciplinary team of teachers. The team will foster integration by planning cooperative activities, selecting instructional materials, implementing joint instructional programs, and planning the instructional schedule, in short, by purposefully structuring integration into school activities. Besides facilitating integration, the special education teacher will be responsible for direct instruction, provided at times in the regular classroom (with the special educator serving as an itinerant teacher), or in the special education classroom (with the special educator serving as the primary teacher), or in the community (with the special educator facilitating the maintenance and generalization of acquired skills). Finally, the special educator will act as a transdisciplinary coordinator, scheduling services by physical therapists, speech pathologists, other specialists, and classroom teachers to ensure that all school personnel are following the goals and objectives specified in the student's IEP.

A number of auxiliary personnel will also have direct instructional responsibilities. Within their areas of expertise, these specialists will identify deficiencies and remediate them through instruction. Whenever possible instruction will take place in the student's community. For instance, if the physical therapist determines that Janet has poor equilibrium reactions, this specialist will remediate the deficiency by teaching Janet to climb the steps of the Metro bus. After teaching Janet the communication skills required to shop at Burton's Grocery and to play at the Midtown Bowling Lanes, the speech pathologist will document Janet's proficiency by evaluating her in these settings. Besides teaching Janet the skills required at her potential job site, her job coach will determine if she has the skills required to travel from school to the job site and from the job site to home. If she has deficits in these areas, the job coach will instruct her until she acquires the skills.

While the importance of the professional staff cannot be denied, it must also be recognized that schoolmates without disabilities can significantly influence the future education and integration of students with severe disabilities. Age-appropriate public school placements will foster formal and informal integrative activities. While peer tutors, peer buddies, and special friends can formally enhance the integration process, over time, informal relationships will develop between students with and without severe disabilities both inside and outside school.

In the future, parents will take a more active role in the education of their children with severe disabilities. While it sounds almost trite, parents will become true partners in the education of their children. This partnership will evolve around an informal contract in which parents will specify the instructional objectives for their child, and the professional staff will teach the skills needed to meet those objectives. Once the skills are acquired, the parents will provide opportunities for the child to maintain and generalize them in natural settings. This cooperative approach will capitalize on the strengths of both parents and professional staff, while ensuring that the student is taught functional, community-referenced skills. Although this concept was clearly mandated in Public Law 94–142, it has not yet been translated into practice. In the future, it will be common practice.

FIGURE 16.3

In the future, special educators will analyze the community to determine the functional daily living skills a student with severe disabilities will need for postschool survival.

(Courtesy of Barbara Chatman.)

CHANGING APPROACHES: WHEN WILL WE EDUCATE THEM?

Efforts to develop and implement quality educational programs for children and adolescents with severe disabilities have received increased attention in recent years. Various models detail the crucial program components that enable community integration (Brown et al., 1981; Halpern, 1985; Wehman, Kregel, & Barcus, 1985). As a result, recent programs have dramatically changed how students with severe disabilities are educated and trained. Teachers now analyze the functional daily living skills required for postschool survival in the person's community, they teach clusters of skills that tend to occur simultaneously, they use natural contingencies to ensure maintenance of recently acquired skills, and they present multiple examples during training to increase the probability of generalization.

While these efforts have changed training methods, they have not yet changed the schooling process. The levels of schooling specified in Public Law 94–142 encouraged school programs for students with severe disabilities from ages 3 through 21. Nevertheless, most public school programs are more restrictive, typically serving students between 5 and 18. Sometime within the next decade and a half, because of Public Law 99–457, infants, toddlers, and children under 5 will receive special education services. In the near future, services will probably be provided to persons with severe disabilities from birth or shortly after birth through age 21.

Eventually, it is likely that special education services will be even more extensive, following a womb-to-tomb approach. At the "womb" end, prenatal services will be provided to potential mothers of high-risk children. This assistance can take forms such as prenatal medical care, dietary care, and instruction on the coming child's social, emotional, cognitive, communicative, and physical needs. At-risk mothers can be assigned work that will refine their parenting skills, for instance, serving as aides in model preschool programs or assisting nurses or nutritionists in community hospitals.

The "tomb" end will begin at graduation. Even if well prepared for a meaningful adult life, adults with severe disabilities may from time to time experience failure and frustration. Like persons without disabilities, some may become unemployed or underemployed, may be evicted from their homes, or may encounter legal difficulties. Technological advances may create problems for them in the areas of meaningful employment, community integration, and living opportunities. These problems can easily fester, grow, and hinder future integrative attempts, in some cases leading to segregated or restricted living patterns. To prevent minor problems from "snowballing" into major ones, citizen advocates, case managers, ombudsmen, and social service agencies must continuously be available for assistance.

CHANGING TIMES: WHAT WILL TOMORROW BRING?

What will tomorrow bring? Soothsayers and fortune-tellers in the past usually answered with a variant of society's oldest drama, "Us versus Them." The first of these productions, written in antiquity by Mephistopheles, starred Cain and Abel. That ancient theme has resurfaced throughout history cast with various players—Rich and Poor, Black and White, Old and Young, Catholic and Protestant. Current stars are the Nondisabled and the Disabled. The script for this production revolves around the energy and expenditures used to educate and integrate students and adults with severe disabilities. The Us camp argues that expenditures are too great and society would be better served if persons with disabilities were segregated and isolated. If this drama continues until the final act, there will be years of struggle, heartache, and broken dreams.

Instead, tomorrow could bring a revolution in effective and ethical service delivery systems for students and adults with severe disabilities. Then, it is expected, persons with severe disabilities would be accepted by others and thoroughly integrated into society. These expectations are based largely on the developments and improvements in service delivery over the past decade and a half. Free educational programs have been provided to all students with severe disabilities. Training programs are now being located in normalized settings. Instructional methods and technologies to teach a wide range of functional skills have been developed. A cadre of professional personnel has now been trained to educate students with severe disabilities. Thus, the outlook for this population can be viewed as promising and optimistic.

An enlightened society has recently proposed changes in the education of students with severe disabilities. The changes made and those to come will enhance the quality of life for these persons. In addition, there is promise of breakthroughs and discoveries in the coming years. Although developments in the past decade and a half have been impressive, if growth and improvement of services are to continue there must be further breakthroughs in research and in service delivery systems.

Conclusion

The Pleiades, in Greek mythology, were the seven daughters of Atlas, a Titan, and Pleione, a minor goddess. The first six Pleiades: Maia, Taygete, Electra, Alcyone, Celaeno, and Sterope, were mistresses to either Zeus, Poseidon, or Ares. The seventh daughter, Merope, had to be content with the love of a mere mortal. Myth has it that the Pleiades were being pursued across the mountains of Boeotia by the hunter Orion, who interestingly was the grandson of the Pleiad, Alcyone. When they were about to fall into his clutches, they cried to Zeus for help. He rescued them, turned them into stars, and placed them into the constellation of Taurus. The six Pleiades who were loved by the gods shine brightly in the summer sky; Merope, since she was married to a mortal, is hidden by interstellar dust and is largely invisible. She is often referred to as the "Lost Pleiad."

In many ways, persons with severe disabilities are analogous to Merope— they have gone unnoticed by most citizens. But recently cosmologists and astronomers have examined celestial bodies with ultraviolet, infrared, and radio spectrography and with orbiting telescopes, finding new and fascinating details. Merope has become as important and interesting as her sisters. Likewise, the life-styles of persons with severe disabilities have gained interest. Special educators and other professionals have developed methods for enhancing the functional skills of these students, and numerous studies have substantiated the benefits derived from their full participation in integrated public school and community settings.

Advertisements for the Army urge, "Be all that you can be." This is exactly what is requested by persons with severe disabilities: the chance to be all that they can be. Anything less is unfair not only to them but also to society.

1. Trends in serving persons with severe disabilities may be grouped into five clusters: changing services, changing sites, changing staff, changing approaches, and changing times.   **SUMMARY**

2. How will persons with severe disabilities be educated? The program approaches of the future will likely have two basic themes: (1) intervention practices will emphasize the use of humane, empathic, and benevolent techniques, and (2) functional and generalizable skills will be taught in integrated schools and natural environments, so that students acquire normalized behaviors reinforced by natural cues and contingencies.

3. Where will they be educated? Students with severe disabilities will likely be educated in regular classrooms alongside schoolmates without disabilities. The students will also spend more time in the community maintaining and generalizing the skills they are expected to use after graduation.

4. Who will educate them? In the schools of tomorrow a variety of personnel will provide direct services. Besides the special educator, the regular classroom teacher and auxiliary personnel will have major responsibilities for educating students with severe disabilities. Special educators will have responsibility for planning integration activities, coordinating instructional tasks, and fostering active involvement by schoolmates and parents.

5. When will we educate them? In the future, education will likely follow a womb-to-tomb approach, from prenatal services for high-risk mothers to follow-up services for persons integrated into the community to prevent minor problems from "snowballing" into major ones.

6. What will tomorrow bring? It is hoped that, in the twenty-first century, effective and ethical services will be provided to all students with severe disabilities and that these persons will be totally accepted and integrated into the schools and society.

GLOSSARY

aberrant chromosomes Chromosomes with abnormal numbers or structures. Aberrant chromosomes typically occur through either nondisjunction or translocation.

acceptance and accommodation (stage of parental adjustment) The parents accept the child and begin to plan a course of action for their child. This is the tenth and final stage.

action stage (of Pathways to Employment Model) This stage is marked by adults with disabilities selecting the type of job in which they would like to be employed. (*see Pathways to Employment Model*)

activator A professional trained in the educational needs of persons with severe disabilities. The activator should assume four roles: (1) referral coordinator; (2) service coordinator; (3) information coordinator; and (4) support system coordinator.

advocacy The process of representing the rights and interests of a person with disability. It may take the form of self-advocacy, citizen advocacy, or parent-professional advocacy.

advocate-protege relationship A one-to-one relationship between a capable volunteer (advocate) and a person with disabilities (protege) in which the advocate defends the rights and interests of the protege and provides practical and emotional reinforcement for him or her.

akinetic seizure disorder One of the petit mal triad disorders characterized by a sudden loss of muscle tone. (*see petit mal triad disorders*)

alarm reaction The initial reaction to a stressful situation; it is marked with excitation and resistance. If this does not satisfactorily address the stressful situation, countershock occurs. (*see countershock*)

American Sign Language The most common manual language used in America. It is a nongenerative system with its own syntax, semantics, and grammar. It is primarily used by persons with hearing impairments. (*see manual communication*)

anger (stage of parental adjustment) As the impact of their child's disability becomes more evident, the parents become angry about it. This is the sixth stage.

antecedent events A Piagetian concept in which events are structured to produce disequilibrium in the child. (*see Piagetian curriculum*)

arthrogryposis multiplex congenita A condition characterized by stiff joints, weak muscles, and spinal cord deformities.

assessment-linked curriculum An approach in which assessment and curriculum are closely intertwined. The present skills of a student with disabilities are compared to a sequential developmental profile. The first few items the student failed in each content domain of the developmental profile becomes targeted as the curriculum for that student.

associative integration Students without disabilities socially interact inside and outside the school with students with severe disabilities.

ataxic cerebral palsy (ataxia) A physiological classification characterized by poor muscle coordination, a lack of balance, and a poor conception of position in space.

athetosis cerebral palsy A physiological classification characterized by contorted, wormlike, purposeless movements of the limbs.

augmentative expressive systems Non-oral expressive communication systems designed to convey information through manual, picture, or representational symbol systems. (*see manual communication, picture systems, rebuses, and Blissymbols*)

augmentative techniques   Structural and physical components designed to convey the information (from the symbols) in an effective and efficient manner. (*see communication board*)

aura   An unusual perception or sensation occurring moments before a seizure.

autonomic seizure disorder   A disorder characterized by abdominal cramping, postictal lethargy, episodic headaches, skin flushing, pupillary dilation, and olfactory sensations. Autonomic seizure disorders are sometimes called psychomotor seizure disorders.

autosomes   Any of the first 22 pairs of chromosomes in the living human cell; all chromosomes are autosomes except the two sex chromosomes.

bargaining (stage of parental adjustment)   The parents bargain with their Deity offering to reform or to exchange something if their Deity will make their child nondisabled. This is the eighth stage.

behavior disorders   A category of persons who frequently exhibit a number of abnormal behavior patterns such as temper tantrums, hyperaggressive behavior, and withdrawn behavior. These behavior patterns may be caused by an underlying emotional problem.

behavioral-analytic model (of social-personal skill development)   Specific social behaviors of persons without disabilities are analyzed and prioritized; the highest priority skill is taught to the person with severe disabilities. There are three phases in this model: situational analysis, response enumeration, and response evaluation. (*see situational analysis, response enumeration, and response evaluation*)

benchwork supported employment model   Approximately 15 employees with severe disabilities work with a small number of staff who provide intensive training and supervision on contract tasks. This model is the most restrictive of the supported employment models. (*see supported employment*)

Blissymbols   A generative symbol system with each symbol corresponding to a concept. Blissymbols can be combined in a number of ways to generate thousands of concept symbols.

cardiac impairments   A collection of disorders in which there is some type of structural defect of the heart, arteries, veins, or capillaries.

cardiopulmonary impairments   An impairment of the heart, lungs, and associated networks.

career awareness   A stage in the career education continuum concerned with developing and understanding the beneficial nature of work. This stage begins in the preschool level, but receives its greatest emphasis in the elementary grades.

career development skills cluster   A multifaceted attempt to teach persons with disabilities the skills needed for meaningful work and community integration.

career exploration   A stage in the career education continuum marked with the student examining a variety of job opportunities to aid him or her in selecting a career. This stage begins in the elementary grades but receives its greatest emphasis in the junior high school years.

career follow-up   Evaluating an employee's success at a worksite after he or she has been employed on a job.

career placement   A stage in the career education continuum primarily concerned with the student being placed on the job of his or her choice at an integrated, competitive site. This stage occurs in the student's last year or last two years of schooling.

career preparation   A stage in the career education continuum concerned with the student making a realistic career choice and receiving additional training in this career. This stage begins in the junior high school years, but receives its greatest emphasis in the high school years.

cascade model of community integration   Depicted as an inverted pyramid, this model projects an array of community residential options tailoring these arrangements to the skills and needs of persons with severe disabilities.

cascade model of school integration   Depicted as an inverted pyramid, this model projects an array of school and instructional integration opportunities for students with severe disabilities.

case management   A case manager who identifies the needs, coordinates the services, maintains records, and monitors the services to ensure that persons with severe disabilities are receiving the services they need.

casual recognition (stage of parental adjustment) The nature of the child's problem and its consequences are explained to the parents. This is the fourth stage.

cell The basic unit of life.

center-based service delivery model The individualized educational and therapeutic services are provided to children with severe disabilities in a school-like setting.

cerebral palsy A nonprogressive disorder of movement, coordination, and posture caused by damage to motor areas of the brain. Some of the symptoms include muscle flaccidity, excessive involuntary motion, postural imbalance, and spasticity.

cervical vertebrae The first seven vertebrae; roughly, the upper third of the back. (*see figure 4.1*)

childhood psychosis A childhood disorder characterized by a profound disturbance in social relations, abnormal behavior patterns, and unusual cognitive functioning. (It includes the disorders of childhood schizophrenia and early infantile autism.)

childhood schizophrenia (schizophreniform) A childhood disorder characterized by disturbances in social adjustment, little contact with reality, abnormal language structures, and unusual behavior patterns. This disorder typically occurs after a period of normal development. (*see childhood psychosis*)

Christian perspective (on advocacy) This perspective emphasizes the doctrine of emphatic reciprocity: how would the advocate want to be treated if he or she were in similar circumstances? (*see doctrine of emphatic reciprocity*)

chromatin The genetic material in the nucleus of the living cell.

chromosomes The strands in the chromatin that carry the genes. They are composed of a DNA core and are responsible for hereditary transmission. Found in pairs, they represent genes from both the father and the mother. In humans the body cells contain 46 chromosomes arranged in 23 pairs.

citizen advocacy A mature, competent volunteer representing the interests of a child or adult who has a difficulty in solving the practical day-to-day problems of living and who has a major need for emotional support. These needs are presently unmet and will likely remain unmet without special intervention.

civil rights The powers, privileges, or guarantees granted to children or adults under the law; these guarantees attempt to ensure that every citizen is treated with justice and reasonableness.

classroom helper program An aspect of the parent training program in which parents assist and imitate the teacher in educating their child with disabilities.

cocaine A stimulant made from the coco plant that produces feelings of euphoria.

cogwheel cerebral palsy *See rigid cerebral palsy.*

communication The transmission of information through verbal or nonverbal means involving a sender, a message, and a receiver.

communication board (conversation board) A method of transmitting information through a series of symbols (i.e., photographs, line drawings, rebuses).

community action network An agency which coordinates services and fosters cooperation among the community agencies providing services to persons with disabilities.

community integration The placement of persons with disabilities into community residences, facilities, and activities which are simultaneously used by persons without disabilities.

community living skills cluster This cluster refers to developing and enhancing skills that are necessary for utilizing integrated community activities and services.

competitive integrated employment A community worksite composed mainly of persons without disabilities and which earns a salary at or near minimum wage.

conscious recognition (stage of parental adjustment) The child's problem and its consequences are explained to the parents. This is the third stage.

consequence approach (to social-personal skill development) Direct intervention with reinforcing consequences following the episodic expression of social-personal behaviors.

consultative service delivery model   A consultant works directly with the teachers and other service providers who, in turn, educate and train infants and children with severe disabilities.

content domains   Generic categories of similar behaviors such as the communication, cognition, self-care, motor, and social-personal categories.

contractual-employed workshops   An extended employment sheltered workshop which has a contract to manufacture, fashion, or assemble a product for a local business or industry. (*see extended employment program*)

countershock   The second reaction to a stressful situation; it is marked with adaptation and defense. (*see alarm reaction*)

criterion of need   A method of evaluating programs and services by determining if a service fulfills the identified needs of persons with severe disabilities.

criterion of the next educational environment   A philosophy which recommends that future educational settings should be taken into consideration when establishing goals for students with severe disabilities.

criterion of ultimate functioning   A philosophy which focuses on the skills needed by an adult with severe disabilities to live as a productive, independent member of the community.

critical skills   Skills that are deemed essential to the development of other skills.

cystic fibrosis   An inherited disease characterized by chronic respiratory and digestive problems.

deinstitutionalization   The policy of removing persons with disabilities from institutions and integrating them into the community. This treatment policy stems from a recognition of the debilitating effects of long-term institutionalization.

denial (stage of parental adjustment)   The parents deny that their child is disabled and find "growth" in their child to discount that classification. This is the fifth stage.

depression (stage of parental adjustment)   The parents realize that their child is disabled and will likely remain that way for the rest of his or her life. This is the ninth stage.

developmental approach (to language intervention)   The sequence in which children without disabilities learn and master language is the basis for language intervention in students with severe disabilities.

developmental curriculum model   This curriculum model assumes that the normal sequence of development provides a logical structure around which the educational objectives and goals of children with severe disabilities may be arranged.

development of a better relationship with others   Explores the skills needed to establish and maintain successful forms of interpersonal relationships.

diplegia   A topographical classification in cerebral palsy marked by major involvement of the legs and minor involvement of the arms.

disequilibrium   A Piagetian concept referring to a child's response to newly assimilated information that is not in agreement with past knowledge. (*see Piagetian curriculum and equilibrium*)

doctrine of emphatic reciprocity   This doctrine holds that persons without disabilities should treat persons with severe disabilities in a manner that they would like to be treated if they were in similar circumstances.

doctrine of limitations   A philosophy which emphasizes the differences between children with and without severe disabilities. This doctrine suggests that students with severe disabilities should be educated in separated facilities away from students without disabilities.

domestic domain   This domain includes the competencies required to reside in a community dwelling, as well as those skills needed to maintain a healthy lifestyle and an acceptable personal appearance.

dominant gene   A gene that manifests itself (e.g., eye color) regardless of its partner gene.

double hemiplegia   A topographical classification in cerebral palsy marked by major involvement of the arms and minor involvement of the legs.

Down syndrome   A syndrome resulting in moderate to severe mental retardation usually caused by a trisomy of chromosome 21. The most apparent clinical manifestations of Down syndrome include epicanthic folds, a large tongue, broad, flat bridge of the nose, and poor muscle tone. (*see trisomy*)

Duchenne muscular dystrophy The most common form of muscular dystrophy which is marked by a progressive diffuse weakness of all muscle groups characterized by a degeneration of muscle cells and their replacement by fat cells and fibrous tissues. (Duchenne muscular dystrophy is sometimes referred to as progressive muscular dystrophy or pseudohypertrophic muscular dystrophy.)

early infantile autism A severe childhood disorder characterized by the child's inability to relate to people, speech disturbances, and abnormal behavior patterns. Onset generally occurs before 30 months of age. (*see childhood psychosis*)

echolalia The repetition of words or phrases spoken without trying to communicate. Passages are spoken in a high-pitched, parrotlike, squeaky monotone.

ecological inventory An individualized functional, community-referenced assessment for determining the skills which students with severe disabilities need for integration into the community.

ecological model (of social-personal skill development) The identification of acceptable behavioral standards for persons with severe disabilities by comparing his or her present skills to the skills exhibited by his or her chronological age peers without disabilities in similar circumstances.

economic self-sufficiency The degree to which an individual supports himself or herself. Employment success makes no distinction between sheltered employment or supported employment. (*see Pathways to Employment Model*)

enclave supported employment model A supported employment approach in which employees with severe disabilities are trained and supervised by a model worker without disabilities who is already employed in a similar position in that industry or business.

encopresis An involuntary loss of bladder control.

enuresis An involuntary emission of urine.

environmental approach (to social-personal skill development) Planned activities in the natural environment that can influence the acquisition of social-personal skills in persons with severe disabilities.

environmental theory This theory affirms that severe behavior disorders are triggered by a stressful environmental event.

equilibrium A Piagetian concept which perceives higher cognitive skills as a reconciliation between new experiences and past experiences involving the mutual processes of assimilation and accommodation. (*see Piagetian curriculum, disequilibrium*)

etiology The cause or origin of a condition, syndrome, or disease.

exemplars Items or situations that are present in both the treatment and the untrained settings to facilitate generalization. (*see train sufficient exemplars*)

extended employment program Long-term sheltered employment with little or no chance of progressing beyond the workshop setting in the immediate future. There are two types of extended employment workshops: self-employed and contractual-employed.

external locus of control Looking to authority figures and others to tell a person how and when to perform certain skills. Persons with severe disabilities have an external locus of control.

externalizing syndrome A behavior pattern in children which is at variance with the expectations of schools and other social institutions; typical behaviors include aggressive, disruptive, defiant, and disobedient behaviors.

externally administered reinforcers Events or items delivered by others contingent on the occurrence of targeted behaviors.

externally directed hazardous behaviors Behaviors which are potentially dangerous or harmful to other persons or to their property. Common behaviors include head-banging, hair-pulling, eye-gouging, hitting, biting, and scratching.

extralinguistic behaviors Behaviors which interfere with the process of learning to communicate.

extreme visual impairment An individual with this level of impairment cannot rely on his or her vision; he or she must rely on the other senses.

familial hypercholesterolemia A genetic defect in which the child exhibits an extremely high level of blood cholesterol.

feedback Information provided directly to the person with severe disabilities on the adequacy of his or her behavior.

focal seizure disorder A disorder characterized by a stiffening and jerking of one arm or leg (usually the ipsilateral arm and leg). Focal seizure disorders are sometimes referred to as "march" or "Jackson" seizure disorders.

fortuitous communication The process of accidentally or incidentally imparting a message to a receiver.

functional approach (to language intervention) The language skills necessary for a person to control, modify, and interact with the environment receive the highest priority.

functional curriculum model The skills necessary for a person to control, modify, and interact with the community receive the highest instructional priorities.

functional integration Persons with severe disabilities utilize the day-to-day activities and services which are typically found in his or her community and used by persons without disabilities.

general community domain The myriad activities associated with all aspects of community life.

generalization Applying prior knowledge to new settings or situations.

generalization across behaviors A change in a behavior not specifically targeted for change.

generalization across settings A behavior change in a setting other than the specific environment in which treatment occurred. The presence or absence of salient discriminative stimuli is the criterion for determining if the situation is new or different.

generalization across subjects A behavior change in the nontargeted person that is similar to the behavior change in the targeted person.

generalization across time A continuation of the behavior change that endures after the training contingencies have been withdrawn. (Generalization across time is another term for maintenance.)

generalization gradient A three dimension transfer and retroaction surface indicating the probable success of generalization as treatment and untrained conditions vary.

gene therapy A treatment approach in which physicians treat a congenital disability by replacing a "defective" gene with a normal gene in the cells of a patient.

genes The portion of the chromosomes that contain the chemical codes for a specific sequence of amino acids which determines every aspect of the human body.

Golden Rule of Advocacy Persons without disabilities should treat persons with severe disabilities in the manner that they would like to be treated if they were in similar circumstances.

grand mal seizure disorder A disorder characterized by a loss of consciousness, lack of body control, possibly incontinence and which may be followed by a deep sleep. Typically the person falls to the ground quivering, shaking, with the arms and legs jerking synchronously.

grooming, hygiene, and personal appearance skills The components involved in looking after and caring for oneself as well as caring for one's dress and appearance.

group training program A type of parent intervention program in which the parents, as a group, are taught certain child rearing skills such as behavior modification.

habilitation The integration of persons with severe disabilities into society. According to the Pathways to Employment Model habilitation is dependent on living, working, recreating, and socializing in the community.

habilitation services Services designed to provide the adult with training in the skills he or she needs for integration into the community.

hemiplegia A topographical classification in cerebral palsy in which the lateral half of the body is involved.

heterozygote A union of gametes from the mother and father to form the zygote, or a developing embryo.

high risk potential mothers Teenage pregnant girls who typically are poorly nourished, come from the lower socioeconomic environments, and are not prepared for the demands of parenthood.

holophrastic The use of one manual sign or symbol to refer to an entire sentence or thought.

home-based and center-based service delivery model Infants and children are jointly taught in the home and the center, utilizing the strengths of both the home and the school.

home-based followed by center-based service delivery model Infants and children are first served in the home and later in a center, typically with other children with disabilities.

home-based service delivery model Infants and children are served in the home with the parents being the primary intervention agents.

home living skills cluster This cluster is concerned with the functional skills required to make integrated home living more enjoyable, fulfilling, and satisfying.

homemaker services Instruction to adults with severe disabilities in routine domestic duties by trained homemakers.

home teacher A professional who works in a home training program. (*see home training program*)

home training program A teacher who works with both the parent and child in the home, as well as observing the parent interacting with and teaching their child.

human rights The basic right which every individual has to develop to his or her fullest potential in an enabling, integrated society.

hydrocephaly A condition caused by an abnormal accumulation of the cerebrospinal fluid in and around the brain which pressures the brain and causes the head to be enlarged. Moderate to profound mental retardation and myelomeningocele is common.

immature sensory impairments Individuals with both a visual and hearing impairment, but who are presently too young or immature to profit from a formal educational program.

individualized curriculum sequencing model An instructional strategy in which the generaliza-

tion of recently taught skills immediately follows the acquisition of those skills.

Individualized Education Program (IEP) A program written for every student with disabilities receiving specialized services. It describes the student's current performance and goals for the school year, the particular special education services to be delivered, and the procedures by which outcomes are evaluated.

Individualized Transition Program (ITP) A multifacet document which requires the student's transition planning committee to project the student's vocational, residential, and educational goals.

infantile seizure disorders A disorder characterized by synchronous muscle contractions in which the infant's arms, neck, and trunk flex forward and backward. This seizure pattern is usually seen in the first few years of life and is associated with immature brain development.

information coordinator A professional who ensures that the needs of adults with severe disabilities are known by those agencies that provide services or assist in providing services. (*see activator*)

instructional integration Students with severe disabilities are trained and educated next to, and in the same environment as, his or her peers without disabilities.

integrated center-based service delivery model Educational and therapeutic services are provided to children with severe disabilities in a school setting with at least half the children in the program being without disabilities.

integrative skills Behaviors which are viewed as socially appropriate by one's peers and which maximize social interactions with others.

intentional communication The intentional and purposeful process of imparting a specific message to a specific receiver.

interaction theory A stressful environmental event may "set off" the behavior disorders in a vulnerable individual. (The interaction theory is sometimes called the diathesis-stress theory.)

interdisciplinary model Professionals work with other professionals in the development of jointly planned programs for students with severe disabilities.

interest analysis A process that dissects everyone's interests in a given situation, assists in balancing the various interests, then weights and resolves the conflicts among those interests.

internalizing syndrome A behavior pattern which implies a retreat from the environment. Typical behaviors include disordered speech and language patterns, distorted motor movements, and inappropriate responses to environmental events.

Itard, Jean Mark Gaspard He educated Victor, the wild boy of Aveyron, over a five year period. His efforts stimulated the instruction of persons with disabilities throughout Europe and the United States.

joint team effort A concept embodied in the transdisciplinary team approach in which a group of professionals are jointly responsible for program planning and program delivery. *(see transdisciplinary team model)*

judaic perspective (of advocacy) Advocate services should fulfill or complement the dignity of the individual; persons with severe disabilities should be able to lead a life similar to that of a person without disabilities.

juvenile rheumatoid arthritis A chronic syndrome which strikes only children and adolescents. It is marked by extreme inflammation of a joint, damage to that joint, and eventually permanent crippling of the joint.

karyotype A photograph of a cell nucleus in which chromosome pairs are arranged systematically according to their decreasing size and structural characteristics.

language The process of sending a message through a formal symbol system. *(see communication and speech)*

lead pipe cerebral palsy *See rigid cerebral palsy.*

legal basis of advocacy Three principles underlie the legal basis of advocacy: (1) principle of positive presumption; (2) principle of due process; and (3) principle of instrumental protection.

leisure-recreational domain Persons with severe disabilities should participate in the same purposeful and constructive leisure and recreational activities as do persons without disabilities.

lumbar vertebrae The last five vertebrae; roughly the lower fourth of the back. *(see figure 4.1.)*

mainstreaming The placement of children with disabilities in an educational setting alongside, and in the same classrooms, as children without disabilities.

maintenance *See generalization across time.*

manual communication A nongenerative communication system which produces a word through hand and arm configurations or movements. *(see augmentative expressive systems)*

marked extreme visual impairment The most severe visual impaired classification; the individual is totally without sight. He or she must rely exclusively on his or her other senses.

marked hearing impairment The individual will require hearing aids, auditory training, and speech and language training of an intensive nature.

means-end behavior An infant may use a person to obtain an object or uses an object to get a person's attention.

mediator A trained response used to facilitate generalization. *(see train to mediate generalization)*

meningocele A form of spina bifida caused by a malformation of the spinal column with a cystic swelling around the spine; the covering bulges out in a sac with no defect of the nerve fibers. *(see spina bifida and figure 4.2)*

microcephaly A condition characterized by a small head and mental retardation ranging in degree from moderate to profound.

mild hearing impairment The least hearing impaired classification; the individual may have difficulty with distant sounds and may require some speech and language training.

mild sensory impairment The least visually impaired hearing impaired classification; the individual should be totally integrated into school and society. The individual may require speech, language, and other consultant services from time to time.

mixed cerebral palsy A physiological classification in which two or more movement disorders of cerebral palsy are found in the same individual.

mixed seizure disorder A disorder in which two or more seizures are found in the same individual.

mixed syndrome A behavior pattern in children which is symptomatic of both the internalizing and externalizing syndromes. Frequently cited behaviors include immaturity, hyperactivity, anxiety, withdrawal, and a negative self-concept.

mobile crew supported employment model A crew of about five persons with disabilities spends its working day performing contracted grounds-keeping and janitorial work in the community.

modeling Observing another person perform a targeted behavior with the expectation that the observer will imitate the model.

moderate hearing impairment The individual will have trouble with conversational speech; he or she may miss class discussions, will require a hearing aid, and will need speech and language therapy.

moderate sensory impairment The student should be educated in a regular classroom; he or she will require intensive speech and language therapy as well as any other ancillary services.

moderate visual impairment The least visually impaired classification; the individual will need special aids to perform most everyday tasks.

monoplegia A topographical classification in cerebral palsy in which one limb is involved.

Moral Management A therapeutic approach in which persons with disabilities were treated in quiet and supportive religious settings where they could talk out their problems, work, walk, pray, rest, and receive wholesome and dignified care. This therapy was largely developed by Phillippe Pinel and William Tuke.

mosaicism A condition in which two or more "lines" of cells (one line of normal cells and one line of trisomy 21 cells) are present in the same individual.

multidisciplinary model The various professionals recognize that other disciplines have important contributions to the habilitation of children with disabilities, but each professional provides its service in isolation.

multiple disabilities An individual who exhibits two or more disabilities simultaneously.

muscular dystrophy A progressive, diffuse musculoskeletal weakness characterized by a degeneration of muscle cells and their replacement of fat cells and fibrous tissues.

musculoskeletal impairments An impairment involving the muscles and skeleton.

myelomeningocele A form of spina bifida caused by a malformation of the spinal column with the nerve fibers and spinal cord lining protruding through an opening in the lower back. (*see spina bifida and figure 4.2*)

myoclonic seizure disorder A petit mal triad disorder marked by a brief contraction of a muscle or group of muscles. There is usually a brief sudden neck flexion, the arms may jerk upward, and the trunk may bend sharply. (*see petit mal triad disorders*)

natural cues and correction procedures The use of naturally occurring cues to maintain and generalize behaviors.

nature of dependence The extent to which an exchange is perceived to be equal or unequal. Relative to advocate services, if the exchange is perceived to be between equals then it can be a rewarding experience; if the exchange is perceived as unequal then the relationship will deteriorate.

neurological impairment An abnormal performance arising from the transmission of information from the brain, feedback to the brain, or uncontrolled burst of instructions from the brain.

neuropsychopharmacological theory A form of the organic theory which holds that persons with severe behavior disorders experience a chemical imbalance which can be eliminated through antipsychotic drugs in the hope of restoring the proper chemical balance in the body. (*see organic theory*)

nondisjunction aberrations An error caused by improper cell division resulting in a cell with an excess of one chromosome (three 21 chromosomes) and another cell without that chromosome. This error accounts for the most common form of Down syndrome.

normalization A principle stating that services and treatment for persons with disabilities be provided that enable them to live in a manner as close as possible to what everyone else experiences.

normative analysis model (of social-personal skill development) An analysis of the appropriateness of social-personal skills in persons with severe disabilities in terms of frequency, duration, time, place, and chronological age.

nucleus The central portion of all living cells.

nuisance behaviors Nondangerous behaviors which result in the person being less acceptable to others. Common nuisance behaviors include drooling, slobbering, flatulence, inappropriate verbalization, and throwing food.

nursing care The teaching of self-care and health care skills to persons with severe disabilities.

object permanence The concept that objects still exist even though they may be out of sight.

occupational success Occupational success is determined by the level of self-support which can be obtained through a job. It is thought to be a function of job preparation, job opportunity, and the support given to the person during employment.

organic theory The theory that severe behavior disorders are caused by physical or organic determinants.

organizational community integration The use by persons with severe disabilities of the generic public services typically used by and available to persons without disabilities.

orthomolecular theory A form of the organic theory which holds that severe behavior disorders are caused by allergies or allergic reactions. (*see organic theory*)

osteogenesis imperfecta A defect of the protein matrix in the bone resulting in brittle, easily broken, bones. Sometimes called the brittle bone disease.

outcome-oriented process An approach to measure the success of transition services. While employment is the most predominant outcome measurement, other outcomes include the community integration and use of generic community facilities (i.e., leisure-recreational, general community, domestic components).

outcome stage (of Pathways to Employment Model) The degree of economic self-sufficiency realized through employment. (*see Pathways to Employment Model*)

paraplegia A topographical classification in cerebral palsy marked by an involvement of the lower half of the body.

parent-professional advocacy Attempts to enhance the coping strategies and social acceptance of persons with severe disabilities by protecting, defending, and supporting the interests and welfare of the child.

parent training A variety of methods designed to help the primary care-giver develop certain competencies, participate in parent training programs, or become familiar with pedagogical techniques by assisting the classroom teacher.

partial reinforcement A schedule in which a behavior is occasionally or intermittently rewarded. Partial reinforcement is typically used to maintain a behavior.

participatory integration Students without disabilities provide direct instruction and assistance in service activities to students with severe disabilities.

Pathways to Employment Model A conceptual framework describing the role an adult with severe disabilities plays in the decision-making process, while projecting the outcomes which may be achieved as a result of this process.

pauciarticular juvenile rheumatoid arthritis A child with this form of arthritis experiences four or fewer inflamed joints; probably the most serious is an inflammation of the iris and the controlling muscle of the lens. This form affects about 30% of all children with arthritis. (*See polyarticular, systemic, and juvenile rheumatoid arthritis*)

peer buddies Students without disabilities socially interact with students with severe disabilities outside the classroom. Typical tasks include escorting them to the cafeteria, assisting them around school buildings, accompanying them on field trips, or helping them to board the bus.

peer integrative approach Activities designed to systematically increase the interactions between students with severe disabilities and students without disabilities. The most common peer integrative approaches include peer tutors, peer buddies, and special friends.

peer tutors Students without disabilities tutor students with severe disabilities in a role similar to a classroom aide. Besides tutoring, the peer tutor may chart performance, modify certain behaviors, or generalize behaviors.

personal integration Opportunities to have a satisfactory and meaningful private life with friends, siblings, parents, relatives, spouse, or a close friend of the same or opposite sex.

petit mal triad disorders Three different seizure disorders that are similar in patterns and treatment. This triad consists of the typical petit mal, myoclonic, and akinetic seizure disorders. This triad is sometimes called the Lennox-Gastaut syndrome.

physical component (of communication) The method of transmitting the symbols to a receiver.

physical integration Persons with severe disabilities are in close structural proximity to students without disabilities.

physiological classification system (of cerebral palsy) A classification system based on movement limitations. This system is used in combination with the topographical classification system.

Piagetian curriculum According to this curriculum, a person progresses from one developmental level to the next level by analyzing new concepts (disequilibrium) and incorporating this new information with his or her previous experiences (equilibrium). Piaget divides this developmental progression into four distinct periods: sensorimotor (birth to 2 years); preoperational thought (2 years to 7 years); concrete operations (7 years to 11 years); and formal operations (11 years and beyond).

pictorial instruction Illustrations, line drawings, or photographs that are used to demonstrate the sequential order in which certain tasks are completed.

picture systems Communication through the use of illustrations, line drawings, or photographs.

pity and self-pity (stage of adjustment) The parents feel sorry for themselves because of the "death of their idealized child" and the unfulfilled dreams the parent had for that child. This is the seventh stage.

polyarticular juvenile rheumatoid arthritis In this form of arthritis, the child experiences inflamed joints in the knees, ankles, wrists, fingers, elbows, shoulders, hip, and jaw which causes great pain and difficulties in almost any daily activity. This is the most common form of juvenile rheumatoid arthritis affecting over half of all children with arthritis. (*see pauciarticular, systemic, and juvenile rheumatoid arthritis*)

practice in the natural environment Performing a targeted skill in the community after it has been acquired.

pragmatics The testing of rules which govern early language and communication development.

preaction stage (of Pathways to Employment Model) The individual is either not ready to make an employment decision or is unable to enter into the decision making process. (*see Pathways to Employment Model*)

prelinguistic behaviors The foundations of language development which are largely established through the early interactions between the infant and his or her social and physical environment.

prenatal model A unique consultative program that promotes prenatal care, parenting skills, and interaction patterns in high risk potential mothers. The goal is to make these potential mothers recognize the social, emotional, cognitive, communicative, and physical needs of her child. (*see high risk potential mothers*)

principle of due process Legally established procedures must be followed prior to the abridgment of any procedural or substantive right.

principle of instrumental protection Laws and institutions that have been established to protect an individual's rights or to encourage an individual to more fully utilize his or her rights.

principle of partial participation Participation in activities and access to environments even if the student with severe disabilities is unable to independently perform all the skills required.

principle of positive presumption An individual regardless of his or her disability is entitled to certain basic, human, and universal rights which cannot legally or morally be denied.

profound hearing impairment The most severe hearing impaired classification; the individual may be aware of very loud sounds; he or she must rely on vision rather than hearing for processing information.

profound sensory impairment   The most severe sensory impaired classification; the individual will require special methods, training, and education. An individual with this classification should be able to develop social, communication, self-care, daily living skills, and limited academic growth.

profound visual impairment   The individual has difficulty performing most detailed visual tasks.

program facilitator   A member of the transdisciplinary team who has the responsibility for coordinating and integrating the delivery of services from the various team members. (*see transdisciplinary team model*)

proto-word   The one-word stage of communication development in which the child's linguistic utterances operate effectively to regulate the environment.

quadriplegia   A topographical classification in cerebral palsy marked by an involvement of both arms and legs.

rebuses   Nongenerative, iconic, pictorial symbols which represent a word. Because of their pictorial nature, rebuses are easy to understand and use.

recessive inheritance   A pattern of inheritance in which a trait is manifested only if both members of a chromosome pair carry the gene for that trait.

reciprocal integration   Students without disabilities socially interact in the school with students with severe disabilities.

referral coordinator   A professional who is familiar with the various private and public programs and agencies serving adults with severe disabilities. (*see activator*)

rehearsal   Practicing a desirable response that was initially acquired through modeling.

respite care   A method of providing temporary relief to the primary care givers from the constant physical and emotional demands of caring for a person with severe disabilities.

response approach (to social-personal skills development)   A multicomponent process focused on making the person with severe disabilities aware of how to respond, what to perform, and when to exhibit the desirable behaviors.

response enumeration   A listing of potential responses to specific social-personal situations which

a person with severe disabilities experiences. This is the second step of the behavioral-analytic model. (*see behavioral-analytic model*)

response evaluation   A ranking of the responses to specific social-personal situations which a person with severe disabilities experiences. The most effective response is then taught to the person with severe disabilities. (*see behavioral-analytic model*)

reverse-role tutors   Students with severe disabilities tutor students without disabilities in a skill such as sign language.

review stage (of Pathways to Employment Model)   In this stage, the individual has the opportunity to reexamine his or her decision and if desired to modify that decision. (*see Pathways to Employment Model*)

rheumatoid arthritis   A chronic syndrome characterized by inflammation of the joints, damage to that joint, and eventually permanent crippling of the joint.

rigid cerebral palsy (rigidity)   A physiological classification in cerebral palsy characterized by a constant resistance to movement or a resistance to movement which lacks constancy.

role release   A characteristic of the transdisciplinary model in which the parents and professionals teach others to implement training procedures and skills which, by tradition, have been considered to be the responsibility of a particular profession. (*see transdisciplinary team model*)

school integration   Systematic efforts designed to maximize the opportunities in which students with severe disabilities can interact in the school setting with students without disabilities.

secondary characteristics   Society's reaction to children with severe disabilities or to the parents of children with severe disabilities. Typical characteristics include stress, pressure, segregation, and restricted opportunities.

seizure disorders   Spontaneous, transitory disturbances in the state of consciousness, motor activity, and sensory experiences caused by an uncontrolled electrical discharge in the brain.

self-administered reinforcers   Events or items that a person gives to himself or herself for performing a targeted personal objective.

self-advocacy Persons with disabilities making decisions and speaking out for himself or herself. Self-advocacy proposes that persons with severe disabilities have the right to self-determination and to live as fully and as independently as possible.

self-care development Any skill or behavior needed for integration into the mainstream of school or society.

self-development The skills necessary for personal achievement and a satisfactory relationship with other people.

self-dressing skills Tasks concerned with putting on and taking off one's clothing, including such tasks as buttoning, zipping, and clothing selection and laundering.

self-employed workshops An extended employment sheltered workshop facility that produces a service or commodity sold directly to the public. (*see extended employment program*)

self-esteem An aspect of self-development, self-esteem nurtures the individual's abilities, interests, needs, and wants. (*see self-development*)

self-feeding skills Tasks concerned with independent eating and drinking, including such skills as food preparation, meal cleanup, and mealtime behavior.

self-hygienics skills Tasks concerned with toileting, grooming, and bathing, as well as oral and nasal hygiene, health care, first aid, and skin and nail care.

self-injurious behaviors Behaviors that harm or injure part of one's body through his or her own actions.

self-management skills The elimination of inappropriate behaviors and the acquisition of appropriate community living skills.

self-related behaviors A component of social interaction and social involvement. This category ranges from accepting criticism to developing manners and from accepting authority to displaying self-control.

self-regulatory model (of social-personal skill development) This model is dependent on the ability to think critically, to determine relevant information, and to act independently. It consists of the interrelated stages of defining the task, arriving at alternative ways to complete the task, implementing an alternative, and assessing the outcome of the alternative. There are five competencies in self-regulation: self-monitoring, self-standard setting, self-evaluation, self-reward, and self-delaying of gratification.

self-understanding An aspect of self-development, self-understanding is concerned with learning how to constructively and appropriately interact with others. (*see self-development*)

sensory impairment and immaturity Children with visual impairments and hearing impairments who are too young or immature to profit from formal education. They should be provided with a program of stimulation coupled with training in communication, self-care, socialization, daily living, and orientation and mobility.

service coordinator A professional who identifies the services that each adult with severe disabilities presently requires and the services he or she is presently receiving. (*see activator*)

service delivery team A group of professionals who, with the parents, determine the kind of services that will be provided to the child and his or her family, and the manner in which it will be provided.

service stage (of Pathways to Employment Model) In this stage the individual has a general awareness of what he or she would like to do and an understanding of the additional skills that are necessary to attain this goal. (*see Pathways to Employment Model*)

severe hearing impairment The individual can only hear very loud sounds close up. He or she needs intensive special education, hearing aids, auditory training, and speech and language training.

severe sensory impairment The individual will require special and unique educational and instructional services. The individual can acquire academic skills to the sixth grade level and he or she should be competitively employed and live independently.

severe visual impairment The individual can perform a visual task at a reduced level of speed, endurance, and precision with the use of special aids.

sexual awareness skills This skill area includes

such components as human reproduction, fertility regulation, awareness of self, and appropriate social/sexual behaviors with the same or the opposite sex.

sheltered workshops A generic term referring to programs in which persons with disabilities work in noncompetitive employment sites. Shelter work settings may be categorized into four types: (1) work activities; (2) work adjustment; (3) extended employment; (4) transitional employment.

situational analysis Identification of the social-personal situations in which a person with severe disabilities is presently experiencing or may experience in the future. This is the first step of the behavioral-analytic model. (*see behavioral-analytic model*)

social community integration The natural development of social relationships between persons without disabilities and people with severe disabilities throughout the community.

social integration Integration of children with severe disabilities with their nondisabled peers in a socially acceptable manner.

social interaction and involvement skills Skills which improve the integration prospects for persons with severe disabilities; typical skills range from manners and greeting skills to the elimination of stereotypic behavior and accepting criticism.

social-personal behavior The competencies which maximize social interactions with others and are perceived as socially appropriate by one's peers and significant others.

social-personal skills Those competencies or behaviors which would maximize social interactions with others and be perceived as socially appropriate by one's peers and significant others.

social validity The frequency and duration of specific social-personal responses in relation to specific social contexts.

societal integration Persons with severe disabilities are responsible for their own opportunities of growth, maturity, and self-fulfillment.

spastic cerebral palsy (spasticity) A physiological classification in which the tight limb muscles are immobilized by muscular contractions.

special friends Students without disabilities develop meaningful social relationships with students with severe disabilities. These relationships endure over time and extend outside of and beyond the school careers of these individuals.

speech The oral transmission of language. (*see communication and language*)

spina bifida Three congenital anomalies characterized by a defect in the bony encasement of the spinal cord. In these conditions the lower end of the spinal cord fails to close. The three anomalies are: spina bifida occulta, meningocele, and myelomeningocele.

spina bifida occulta One of the forms of spina bifida in which the skin may be intact and the spinal cord undamaged; the bony defect is covered with skin. (*see spina bifida and figure 4.2*)

spinal cord impairment An injury to the spinal cord pathways; the messages are transmitted but never received. Individuals with spinal cord impairments may suffer from respiratory, urinary, skin infections, and lower body paralysis.

spinal muscular atrophy A progressive degeneration of the spinal cord and the cranial nerves of the brain stem. Symptoms range from a chronic, minimally disabling weakness to a rapid degeneration with complete incapacitation, dependent existence, and early death.

staff development approach A characteristic of the transdisciplinary model in which the parents and professionals train one another drawing on each other's particular areas of expertise, information, and background of experience. (*see transdisciplinary team model*)

Standard Rebus Glossary A glossary which contains 818 different rebuses plus over 1200 combinations of rebuses. Rebuses from this glossary are the ones typically used on persons with severe disabilities.

stereotypic behaviors A pattern of repetitive, nonfunctional behaviors that may be self-stimulating. Typical stereotypic behaviors include rocking, object twirling, masturbating, rumination, random verbalizations, eye rubbing, and finger waving.

stimulus dimensions Important factors of dimensions which represent the environment the student is projected to inhabit.

stranger trainer An approach used to teach persons with severe disabilities acceptable, responsible, and cautious interaction patterns with unfamiliar persons.

structural component (of communication) The manner in which symbols are combined or arranged so that they are interpretable and understood by the receiver.

student repertoire inventory *See ecological inventory.*

student-to-student advocacy Students without disabilities looking out for the interests, welfare, and needs of a schoolmate with severe disabilities.

support system coordinator A professional who elicits timely and meaningful support to any service agency. (*see activator*)

supported employment A remunerative, competitive job located in an integrated community environment. It must earn a salary at approximately minimum wage, the worksite must be primarily composed of persons without disabilities, and the employees must receive ongoing support and supervision.

supported jobs employment model Persons with severe disabilities are placed on competitive employment sites in the community, trained at that site, then follow-up on a regular basis to ensure success on the worksite.

symbol component (of communication) Characters (i.e., rebuses, pictures) used to represent ideas, thoughts, and feelings.

systematic school integration An interactive approach in which students without disabilities provide direct instruction or assistance to students with severe disabilities.

systemic juvenile rheumatoid arthritis In this form of arthritis, the child experiences high fevers, enlarged lymph nodes, generalized illness, and fatigue. This is the least common form of juvenile rheumatoid arthritis. (*see pauciarticular, polyarticular, and juvenile rheumatoid arthritis*)

task analysis procedure A method that breaks down complex tasks into simpler component parts; each component part is taught separately until mastered, then the component parts are taught together.

temporal integration Children with severe disabilities spend a significant and meaningful amount of time with his or her peers without disabilities.

teratogen An agent that causes malformations in the developing embryo.

tetraplegia A topographical classification in cerebral palsy in which all four limbs are involved.

thoracic vertebrae The eighth through twentieth vertebrae; the middle back. (*see figure 4.1*)

tool skills Skills which are critical for learning more sophisticated skills.

topographical classification system (of cerebral palsy) A classification based on the location and the number of limbs impaired. This classification system is used in combination with the physiological classification system.

total task teaching method The entire job sequence is taught to the student as a unified task instead of dividing it into its component parts and teaching each component part separately.

train and hope After treatment and behavior change is effected, generalization is hoped for and passively planned but not actively pursued.

train common stimuli The training program contains the same conditions and stimuli that are present in the natural environment.

train general case After being trained to use a particular set of items, the individual is asked to generalize this learned skill to untrained members of that set.

train in the natural settings After treatment in the natural environment, generalization is hoped for and passively planned for but not actively pursued.

train loosely The time, settings, and behaviors are intentionally varied from treatment period to treatment period to create a greater similarity between the treatment settings and the generalization setting.

train multiple case After being trained to use a particular subcategorical subset, the individual is asked to generalize to untrained members of that subcategory.

train sufficient exemplars Generalization to untrained conditions may be maximized by an indefinite number of exemplars which are present in both the treatment and the untrained settings.

train to generalization Generalization from one untrained, generalized condition to another untrained condition.

train to indiscriminable contingencies The settings or conditions that would be reinforced cannot be discriminated from the settings or the conditions which would not be reinforced.

train to instructional generalization Specific verbal instructions to generalize from one untrained, generalized condition or situation to another untrained condition or situation.

train to mediate generalization Establishing a trained response, or a mediator, who could then be used to constitute a sufficient commonality between treatment and untrained conditions.

train to natural maintaining contingencies Generalization from the treatment setting to the natural environment is maintained by the natural reinforcers in that environment.

train to sequential modification After treatment and behavior change is effected, generalization is planned for but not actively pursued. The adequacy of generalization is, then, assessed. If generalization is absent or deficient, then additional training and generalization are initiated.

training to criterion Training on a task is continued until criterion has been met.

transdisciplinary team model An approach in which the goals and objectives are jointly developed and prioritized by the parents and a team of professionals.

transfer The effect of a learned task on a subsequent task by varying either the stimulus conditions or the response conditions.

transition A dynamic partnership of consumers, school service agencies, postschool service agencies, and local community elements which is designed to optimize a student's postschool integration into the community while maximizing his or her levels of employment, independent living, recreational activities, and community participation.

Transition Assistance Committee (TAC) A committee that identifies well in advance of graduation the specific competencies that a student with severe disabilities will need that enhance that person's prospects of successful integration into society. A primary responsibility of the TAC is to coordinate the interagency resources between school and postschool services.

transitional employment program Short-term placement in a sheltered facility to refine the specific vocational skills needed for competitive, remunerative employment in an integrated setting.

translocation aberrations A condition resulting from improper cell division, with all or a portion of one chromosome attaching itself onto another chromosome.

tremor cerebral palsy A physiological classification in cerebral palsy marked by involuntary quivering or shaking.

triaxial model An analysis of the longitudinal and structural nature of the family in terms of subgroups.

triplegia A topographical classification in cerebral palsy in which three limbs are involved, usually one arm and both legs.

trisomy Improper cell division resulting in a cell with an excess chromosome, normally the twenty-first chromosome. This error accounts for the most common form of Down syndrome. (*see Down syndrome*)

typical petit mal seizure disorder One of the petit mal triad disorders marked by a momentary suspension of all activities. (*see petit mal triad disorders*)

unawareness (stage of adjustment) The family is unaware that their child is disabled and treats him or her like they would any new baby. This is the first stage.

uneasiness (stage of adjustment) The family is generally uncomfortable about their child's lack of progress and search for a possible explanation. This is the second stage.

unidisciplinary model Each professional works independently and without consulting the other specialists.

utilitarian perspective (of advocacy) Advocacy should attempt to increase an individual's functional autonomy.

vitamin theory A form of the organic theory which holds that severe behavior disorders are caused by vitamin and mineral deficiencies. (*see organic theory*)

vocational domain This domain is concerned with the development of skills that will prepare a student for competitive, remunerative employment in the community.

work activity program Long-term placement of individuals who have numerous behavior and skill deficits and are viewed as being unable to qualify for work adjustment programs.

work adjustment program Long-term placement of individuals who are considered incapable of acquiring the skills necessary for obtaining extended sheltered employment.

REFERENCES

Abraham, L. (1988, July 22). Pregnant women face AIDS dilemma. *American Medical News, 3,* 34–35.

Abramowicz, H., & Richardson, S. (1975). Epidemiology of severe mental retardation in children: Community studies. *American Journal of Mental Deficiency, 80,* 18–39.

Abt Associates. (1974). *Assessments of selected resources for severely handicapped children and youth. Vol. I: A state-of-the-art paper.* Cambridge, MA: Author. (ERIC Document Reproduction Service No. ED 134 614).

Achenbach, T. (1982a). Assessment and taxonomy of children's behavior disorders. In B. Lahey & A. Kazdin (Eds.), *Advances in clinical and child psychology.* New York: Plenum.

Achenbach, T. (1982b). *Developmental psychopathology* (2nd ed.). New York: Ronald Press.

Achenbach, T., & Edelbrock, C. (1978). The classification of child psychopathology: A review and analysis of empirical efforts. *Psychology Bulletin, 85,* 1275–1301.

Achenbach, T., & Edelbrock, C. (1981). Behavior problems and competencies reported by parents of normal and disturbed children aged four through sixteen. *Monographs of the Society for Research in Child Development, 46*(1, Serial No. 188).

Achenbach, T., & Edelbrock, C. (1983). Taxonomic issues in child psychopathology. In T. Ollendick & M. Hersen (Eds.), *Handbook of child psychopathology.* New York: Plenum.

Adams, E., & Durell, J. (1984). Cocaine: A growing public health problem in America. In J. Grabowski (Ed.), *Cocaine pharmocology, effects, and treatment of abuse* (National Institute on Drug Abuse, Research Monograph No. 50). Washington, DC: U.S. Government Printing Office.

Adelson, E., & Fraiberg, S. (1974). Gross motor development in infants from birth. *Child Development, 45,* 114–120.

Adkins, J., & Matson, J. (1980). Teaching institutionalized mentally retarded adults socially appropriate leisure skills. *Mental Retardation, 18,* 249–252.

Agosta, J., Bradley, V., Rugg, A., Spence, R., & Covert, S. (1985). *Designing programs to support family care for persons with developmental disabilities: Concepts to practice.* Boston: Human Services Research Institute.

Alberto, P., Garrett, E., Briggs, T., & Umberger, F. (1983). Selection and initiation of a nonverbal communication program for severely handicapped students. *Focus on Exceptional Children, 15*(7), 1–15.

Albin, R., & Horner, R. (1988). Generalization with precision. In R. Horner, G. Dunlap, & R. Koegel (Eds.), *Generalization and maintenance: Life-style changes in applied settings.* Baltimore: Paul H. Brookes.

Allen, E. (1978). Early intervention for young severely and profoundly handicapped children: The preschool imperative. *AAESPH Review, 3,* 34–41.

Almond, P., Rodgers, S., & Krug, A. (1979). Mainstreaming: A model for including elementary students in the severely handicapped classroom. *Teaching Exceptional Children, 11,* 135–139.

Alper, J. (1986). Depression at an early age. *Science 86, 7*(4), 44–50.

Altshuler, K. (1975). Identifying and programming for the emotionally handicapped deaf child. In D. Naiman (Ed.), *Needs of emotionally disturbed hearing impaired children.* New York: School of Education, New York University.

American Academy of Pediatrics, Committee on Nutrition. (1976). Megavitamin therapy for childhood psychosis and learning disabilities. *Pediatrics, 58,* 910–911.

Anastasiow, N. (1978). Strategies and models for early childhood intervention programs in integrated settings. In M. Guralnick (Ed.), *Early intervention and the integration of handicapped and nonhandicapped children.* Baltimore: University Park Press.

Anderson, W. (1985). Beating nature's odds: Gene therapy may right some inherited wrongs. *Science 85, 6*(9), 49–50.

Apgar, V., & James, L. (1962). Further observations on the newborn scoring system. *American Journal of Diseases of Children, 104,* 419–428.

Asher, T., & Renshaw, B. (1981). Citizen advocacy for handicapped children. *Education and Training of the Mentally Retarded, 16,* 124–129.

Ashman, A. (1982). Coding, strategic behavior, and language performance of institutionalized mentally retarded young adults. *American Journal of Mental Deficiency, 86,* 627–636.

Aveno, A. (1987). A survey of leisure activities engaged in by adults who are severely retarded living in different residence and community types. *Education and Training in Mental Retardation, 22,* 121–127.

Baker, B., Seltzer, G., & Seltzer, M. (1977). *As close as possible.* Boston: Little, Brown.

Baker, D. (1978). *Project LEARN parent training manual.* Lawrence, KA: Bureau of Child Research.

Baltes, P., & Reese, H. (1984). The life-span perspective in developmental psychology. In M. Bornstein & M. Lamb (Eds.), *Developmental psychology: An advanced textbook.* Hillsdale, NJ: Lawrence Erlbaum.

Balthazar, E., & Stevens, H. (1975). *The emotionally disturbed, mentally retarded.* Englewood Cliffs, NJ: Prentice-Hall.

Banerdt, B., & Bricker, D. (1978). A training program for selected self-feeding skills for the motorically impaired. *AAESPH Review, 3,* 222–310.

Bank-Mikkelsen, N. (1969). A metropolitan area in Denmark: Copenhagen. In R. Kugel & W. Wolfensberger (Eds.), *Changing patterns in residential services for the mentally retarded.* Washington, DC: President's Committee on Mental Retardation.

Bank-Mikkelsen, N. (1980). Denmark. In R. Flynn & K. Nitsch (Eds.), *Normalization, social integration and community services.* Austin, TX: PRO-ED.

Barney L., & Landis, C. (1988). Developmental differences in communication. In J. Neisworth & S. Bagnato (Eds.), *The young exceptional child: Early development and education.* New York: Macmillan.

Baroff, G. (1986). *Mental retardation: Nature, cause, and management* (2nd ed.). New York: Hemisphere.

Barol, B. (1986, July 28). Cocaine babies: Hooked at birth. *Newsweek,* pp. 55–57.

Barthel, M. (1985). Family-professional interactions. In R. Bruininks & K. Lakin (Eds.), *Living and learning in the least restrictive environment.* Baltimore: Paul H. Brookes.

Baskin, Y. (1984). Doctoring the genes. *Science 84, 5*(10), 52–60.

Bates, E., Benigni, L., Bretherton, I., Camaioni, L., & Volterra, V. (1979). *The emergence of symbols: Cognition and communication in infancy.* New York: Academic Press.

Bates, E., Benigni, L., Camaioni, L., & Volterra, V. (1977). *Cognition and communication from 9-13 months: A correlational study* (Program on Cognitive and Perceptual Factors in Human Development Report No. 12). Boulder, CO: Institute for the Study of Intellectual Behavior, University of Colorado.

Bates, P., & Pancsofar, E. (1983). Project EARN (Employment and Rehabilitation-Normalization): A competitive employment training program for severely disabled youth in the public schools. *British Journal of Mental Subnormality, 29*(2, Part 2), 97–103.

Bates, P., Suter, C., & Poelvoorde, R. (1987). *Illinois transition project: Transition plan development for special education students in Illinois public schools.* Springfield, IL: Governor's Planning Council on Developmental Disabilities.

Bateson, G., Jackson, D., Haley, J., & Weakland, J. (1956). Toward a theory of schizophrenia. *Behavioral Science, 1,* 251–264.

Bateson, M. (1975). Mother-infant exchanges: The epigenesis of conversational interaction. In D. Aaronson & R. Rieber (Eds.), *Developmental psycolinguistics and communication disorders.* New York: Academy of Sciences.

Batshaw, M., & Perret, Y. (1986). *Children with handicaps: A medical primer* (2nd ed.). Baltimore: Paul H. Brookes.

Bauer, A., & Shea, T. (1986). Hepatitis B: An occupational hazard for special educators. *Journal of the Association for Persons with Severe Handicaps, 11,* 171–175.

Baumgart, D., Brown, L., Pumpian, I., Nisbet, J., Ford, A., Sweet, M., Messina, R., & Schroeder, J. (1982). Principle of partial participation and individualized adaptations in educational programs for severely handicapped students. *Journal of the Association for Persons with Severe Handicaps, 7,* 17–27.

Beattie v. Board of Education of Antigo, 172 N.W. 153 (Wis. 1919).

Beckman-Bell, P. (1981). Child-related stress in families of handicapped children. *Topics in Early Childhood Special Education, 1*(3), 45–53.

Bellamy, G., & Buckley, J. (1985). National survey of day and vocational programs for adults with severe disabilities: A 1984 profile. In P. Ferguson (Ed.), *Issues in transition research: Economic and social outcomes.* Eugene, OR: Specialized Training Program, University of Oregon.

Bellamy, G., Peterson, L., & Close, D. (1976). Habilitation of the severely and profoundly retarded: Illustrations of competence. *Education and Training of the Mentally Retarded, 10,* 174–186.

Bellamy, G., Rhodes, L., & Albin, J. (1986). Supported employment. In W. Kiernan & J. Stark (Eds.), *Pathways to employment for adults with developmental disabilities.* Baltimore: Paul H. Brookes.

Bellamy, G., Sheehan, M., Horner, R., & Boles, S. (1980). Community programs for severely handicapped adults: An analysis. *Journal of the Association for the Severely Handicapped, 5,* 307–324.

Bellamy, G., & Wilcox, B. (1980). Secondary education for severely handicapped students: Guidelines for quality services. In B. Wilcox & A. Thompson (Eds.), *Critical issues in the education of autistic children and youth* (U.S. Office of Education). Washington, DC: U.S. Government Printing Office.

Bender, L. (1947). Childhood schizophrenia. *American Journal of Orthopsychiatry, 17,* 40–56.

Berg, B. (1975). Convulsive disorders. In E. Bleck & D. Nagel (Eds.), *Physically handicapped children: A medical atlas for teachers.* New York: Grune & Stratton.

Bergeron, T., Perschbacher-Melia, S., & Kiernan, W. (1986). Supporting the employment initiative. In W. Kiernan & J. Stark (Eds.), *Pathways to employment for adults with developmental disabilities.* Baltimore: Paul H. Brookes.

Berkson, G. (1983). Repetitive stereotyped behaviors. *American Journal of Mental Deficiency, 88,* 239–246.

Best, G. (1978). *Individuals with physical disabilities: An introduction for educators.* St. Louis: C. V. Mosby.

Bettelheim, B. (1967). *The empty fortress.* New York: Free Press.

Bigge, J. (1982). *Teaching individuals with physical and multiple disabilities* (2nd ed.). Columbus, OH: Charles E. Merrill.

Biklen, D. (1979). The community imperative. *Institutions, 2*(8), 1–8.

Billingsley, F. (1984). Where are the generalized outcomes? (An examination of instructional objectives). *Journal of the Association for the Severely Handicapped, 9,* 186–192.

Bingol, N., Fuchs, M., Stone, R., & Gromisch, D. (1987). Teratogenicity of cocaine in humans. *Journal of Pediatrics, 78,* 93–96.

Birch, H., & Gussow, J. (1970). *Disadvantaged children.* New York: Harcourt Brace Jovanovich.

Blackard, M., & Barsh, E. (1982). Parent's and professional's perceptions of the handicapped child's impact on the family. *Journal of the Association for Persons with Severe Handicaps, 7,* 62–70.

Blackstone, E. (Ed.). (1987). *Augmentative communication: An introduction.* Madison, WI: Trace Research & Development.

Blatt, B. (1987). *The conquest of mental retardation.* Austin, TX: PRO-ED.

Bleck, E. (1975a). Cerebral palsy. In E. Bleck & D. Nagel (Eds.), *Physically handicapped children: A medical atlas for teachers.* New York: Grune & Stratton.

Bleck, E. (1975b). Muscular dystrophy—Duchenne type. In E. Bleck & D. Nagel (Eds.), *Physically handicapped children: A medical atlas for teachers.* New York: Grune & Stratton.

Bleck. E. (1975c). Myelomeningocele, meningocele, spina bifida. In E. Bleck & D. Nagel (Eds.), *Physically handicapped children: A medical atlas for teachers.* New York: Grune & Stratton.

Bleck, E. (1975d). Osteogenesis imperfecta. In E. Bleck & D. Nagel (Eds.), *Physically handicapped children: A medical atlas for teachers.* New York: Grune & Stratton.

Bliss, C. (1965). *Sematography.* Sidney, Australia: Sematography Publications.

Bobath, B., & Bobath, K. (1972). Cerebral palsy. In P. Pearson & C. Williams (Eds.), *Physical therapy services in developmental disabilities.* Springfield, IL: Charles C Thomas.

Boles, S., Bellamy, G., Horner, R., & Mank, D. (1984). Specialized training program: The structured employment model. In S. Pain, G. Bellamy, & B. Wilcox (Eds.), *Human services that work: From innovation to standard practice.* Baltimore: Paul H. Brookes.

Borden, P., & Vanderheiden, G. (Eds.). (1988). *Communication, control, and computer access for disabled and elderly individuals. Resource book 4: Update to books 1, 2, and 3.* Madison, WI: Trace Research and Development Center.

Borkowski, J., & Varnhagen, C. (1984). Transfer of learning strategies: Contrast of self-instructional and traditional training formats with EMR children. *American Journal of Mental Deficiency, 88,* 369–379.

Bower, E. (1960). *Early identification of emotionally handicapped children in school.* Springfield, IL: Charles C Thomas.

Bower, E. (1982). Defining emotional disturbances: Public policy and research. *Psychology in the Schools, 19,* 55–60.

Boyd, D. (1950). The three stages. Reported in J. Fotheringham & D. Creal, Handicapped children and handicapped families. *International Review of Education, 20,* 355–371.

Brandenburg, S., & Vanderhelden, G. (Eds.). (1987a). *Communication, control, and computer access for disabled and elderly individuals: Communication aids. Resource book 1.* Boston: College-Hill Press.

Brandenburg, S., & Vanderheiden, G. (Eds.). (1987b). *Communication, control, and computer access for disabled and elderly individuals: Hardware and software. Resource book 3.* Boston: College-Hill Press.

Brandenburg, S., & Vanderheiden, G. (Eds.). (1987c). *Communication, control, and computer access for disabled and elderly individuals: Switches and environmental controls. Resource book 2.* Boston: College-Hill Press.

Brandt, R. (1983). The real and alleged problems of utilitarianism. *Hastings Center Report, 13*(2), 37–43.

Breen, C., Haring, T., Pitts-Conway, V., & Gaylord-Ross, R. (1985). The training and generalization of social interaction during breaktime at two job sites in the natural environment. *Journal of the Association for Persons with Severe Handicaps, 10,* 41–50.

Brenton, I. (1974). History of treating the mentally retarded. In M. Mahoney & C. Thoresen (Eds.), *Self-control: Power to the person.* Monterey, CA: Brooks/Cole.

Breslau, N. (1982). Siblings of disabled children: Birth order and age-spacing effects. *Journal of Abnormal Child Psychology, 10,* 85–96.

Breslau, N., Weitzman, M., & Messenger, K. (1981). Psychologic functioning of siblings of disabled children. *Pediatrics, 67,* 344–353.

Bricker, D. (1978). A rationale for the integration of handicapped and non-handicapped preschool children. In M. Guralnick (Ed.), *Early intervention and the handicapped and non-handicapped children.* Baltimore: University Park Press.

Bricker, D., Bricker, W., Iacino, R., & Dennison, L. (1976). Intervention strategies for the severely profoundly handicapped child. In N. Haring & L. Brown (Eds.), *Teaching the severely handicapped* (Vol. 1). New York: Grune & Stratton.

Bricker, W., & Bricker, D. (1970). A program of language training for the severely language handicapped child. *Exceptional Children, 37,* 101–111.

Brimer, R. (1985). *Improving self-concept and school achievement in children through specific self-regulatory activities.* Paper presented at the meeting of the Illinois chapter of the Association for Persons with Severe Handicaps, Chicago.

Brimer, R., & Barudin, S. (1981). Due process, right to education and the exceptional child: The road to equality in education. *Exceptional People Quarterly, 1,* 40–70.

Bristol, M., & Gallagher, J. (1986). Research on fathers of young handicapped children: Evolution, review, and some future directions. In J. Gallagher & P. Vietze (Eds.), *Families of handicapped persons: Research, programs, and policy issues.* Baltimore: Paul H. Brookes.

Brodsky, M. (1983). *Post high school experiences of graduates with severe handicaps.* Unpublished doctoral dissertation, University of Oregon, Eugene, OR.

Brody, G., & Stoneman, Z. (1983). Children with atypical siblings: Socialization outcomes and clinical participation. In B. Lakes & A. Kazdin (Eds.), *Advances in Clinical Child Psychology, Vol. 6.* New York: Plenum.

Brofenbrenner, U. (1974). *A report on longitudinal evaluations of preschool programs: Is early intervention effective?* (Vol. 11) (Department of Health, Education, and Welfare Publication No. 74–25). Washington, DC: U.S. Government Printing Office.

Brolin, D. (1976). *Vocational preparation of retarded citizens.* Columbus, OH: Charles E. Merrill.

Bronicki, G., & Turnbull, A. (1987). Family-professional interactions. In M. Snell (Ed.), *Systematic instruction of persons with severe handicaps* (3rd ed.). Columbus, OH: Charles E. Merrill.

Browder, D. (1987). *Assessment of individuals with severe handicaps: An applied behavior approach to life skills assessment.* Baltimore: Paul H. Brookes.

Browder, E., & Shapiro, E. (1985). Applications of self-management to individuals with severe handicaps: A review. *Journal of the Association for Persons with Severe Handicaps, 10,* 200–208.

Brown, L., Branston, M., Hamre-Nietupski, S., Johnson, F., Wilcox, B., & Gruenewald, L. (1979). A rationale for comprehensive longitudinal interactions between severely handicapped and non-handicapped students and other citizens. *AAESPH Review, 4,* 3–14.

Brown, L., Branston, M., Hamre-Nietupski, S., Pumpian, I., Certo, N., & Gruenewald, L. (1979). A strategy for developing chronological-age appropriate and functional curricular content for severely handicapped adolescents and young adults. *Journal of Special Education, 13,* 81–90.

Brown, L., Branston-McClean, M., Baumgart, D., Vincent, L., Falvey, M., & Schroeder, J. (1979). Utilizing the characteristics of a variety of current and subsequent least restrictive environments as factors in the development of curricula content for severely handicapped students. *AAESPH Review, 4,* 407–424.

Brown, L., Ford, A., Nisbet, J., Sweet, M., Donnellan, A., & Gruenewald, L. (1979). Opportunities available when severely handicapped students attend chronological age appropriate regular schools in accordance with the natural population. In L. Brown, J. Nisbet, A. Ford, M. Sweet, B. Shiraga, & L. Gruenewald (Eds.), *Educational programs for severely handicapped students* (Vol. 12). Madison, WI: University of Wisconsin and the Madison Metropolitan Schools.

Brown, L., Ford, A., Nisbet, J., Sweet, M., Donnellan, A., & Gruenewald, L. (1983). Opportunities available when severely handicapped students attend chronological age appropriate regular schools. *Journal of the Association for Persons with Severe Handicaps, 8,* 16–24.

Brown, L., Nietupski, J., & Hamre-Nietupski, S. (1976). The criterion of ultimate functioning. In M. Thomas (Ed.), *Hey, don't forget about me! Education's investment in the severely and profoundly handicapped.* Reston, VA: Council for Exceptional Children.

Brown, L., Pumpian, I., Baumgart, D., Van Deventer, P., Ford, A., Nisbet, J., Schroeder, J., & Gruenewald, L. (1981). Longitudinal transition plans in programs for severely handicapped students. *Exceptional Children, 47,* 624–630.

Brown, L., Wilcox, B., Sontag, E., Vincent, B., Dodd, N., & Gruenwald, L. (1977). Toward the realization of the least restrictive educational environments for severely handicapped students. *AAESPH Review, 2,* 195–201.

Bruner, J. (1975). From communication to language: A psychological perspective. *Cognition, 3,* 225–287.

Bruner, J., Roy, C., & Ratner, N. (1978). The beginnings of request. In K. Nelson (Ed.), *Children's language* (Vol. 1). New York: Gardner Press.

Bullis, M., Rowland, C., Schweigert, P., & Stremel-Campbell, K. (1986). *Communication skills center for young children with deaf-blindness.* Monmouth, OR: Teaching Research Publications.

Bureau of Education for the Handicapped. (1975). 40 C.F.R., 45 Federal Register 127.

Buss, A. (1966). *Psychopathology.* New York: John Wiley.

Byasee, J., & Murrell, S. (1975). Interaction patterns in families of autistic, disturbed, and normal children. *American Journal of Orthopsychiatry, 45,* 473–478.

Calhoun, J., Acocella, J., & Goldstein, L. (1977). *Abnormal psychology: Current perspectives* (2nd ed.). New York: Random House.

Carr, E., & Kologinsky, E. (1983). Acquisition of sign language by autistic children II: Spontaneity and generalization effects. *Journal of Applied Behavior Analysis, 16,* 297–314.

Certo, N., & Kohl, F. (1984). A strategy for developing interpersonal interaction content for severely handicapped students. In N. Certo, N. Haring, & R. York (Eds.), *Public school integration of severely handicapped students: Rational issues and progressive alternatives.* Baltimore: Paul H. Brookes.

Chaffin, J. (1975). Will the real "mainstreaming" program please stand up! (or . . . should Dunn have done it?). In E. Meyen, G. Vergason, & R. Whelan (Eds.), *Alternatives for teaching exceptional children.* Denver: Love.

Chapman, R. (1981). Exploring children's communicative intents. In J. Miller (Ed.), *Assessing language production in children: Experimental procedures.* Austin, TX: PRO-ED.

Chapman, R., & Miller, J. (1980). Analyzing language and communication in the child. In R. Schiefelbusch (Ed.), *Nonspeech language and communication: Acquisition and intervention.* Baltimore: University Park Press.

Chasnoff, I. (1987). Perinatal effects of cocaine. *Contemporary Obstetrics and Gynecology, 29,* 163–179.

Chasnoff, I., Burns, W., Schnoll, S., & Burns, K. (1985). Cocaine use in pregnancy. *New England Journal of Medicine, 393,* 666–669.

Chasnoff, I., Bussey, M., Savich, R., & Stack, C. (1986). Perinatal cerebral infarction and maternal cocaine use. *Journal of Pediatrics, 108,* 456–459.

Chinitz, S. (1981). A sibling group for brothers and sisters of handicapped children. *Children Today, 6,* 21–23.

Clark, C. (1981). Learning words using traditional orthography and the symbols of rebus, Bliss, and carrier. *Journal of Speech and Hearing Disorders, 46,* 191–196.

Clark, C. (1984). A close look at the standard rebus system and Blissymbolics. *Journal of the Association for Persons with Severe Handicaps, 9,* 37–48.

Clark, C., Davies, C., & Woodcock, R. (1974). *Standard rebus glossary.* Circle Pines, MN: American Guidance Service.

Clark, C., Moores, D., & Woodcock, R. (1976). *Minnesota early language developmental sequence.* Minneapolis, MN: Research, Developmental, and Demonstration Center, University of Minnesota.

Clements, P., Bost, L., DuBois, Y., & Turpin, W. (1980). Adaptive behavior scale, part two: Relative severity of maladaptive behavior. *American Journal of Mental Deficiency, 84,* 465–469.

Close, D., O'Connor, G., & Peterson, S. (1981). Utilization of habilation services by developmentally disabled persons in community residential facilities. In H. Haywood & J. Newbrough (Eds.), *Living environments for developmentally retarded persons.* Baltimore: University Park Press.

Cobb, H. (1971). *The forecast of fulfillment: A review of research on predictive assessment of adult retarded for social and vocational adjustment.* New York: Teachers College Press, Columbia University.

Cobb, H. (1973). Citizen advocacy and rights of the handicapped. In W. Wolfensberger & H. Zauha (Eds.), *Citizen advocacy and protective services for the impaired and handicapped.* Toronto: National Institute on Mental Retardation.

Cobb, S. (1971). *A community level model for depression.* (Working Paper No. 3). Unpublished manuscript, Center for Community Studies, George Peabody College for Teachers, Nashville, TN.

Cohen, S., & Warren, R. (1985). *Respite care: Principles, programs, and policies.* Austin, TX: PRO-ED.

Cole, M., & Cole, J. (1981). *Effective intervention with the language impaired child.* Rockville, MD: Aspen Systems.

Colenbrander, A. (1977). Dimensions of visual performance. *Archives of the American Academy of Ophthalmology, 83,* 332–337.

Collis, G., & Schaffer, H. (1975). Synchronization of visual attention in mother-infant pairs. *Journal of Child Psychology and Psychiatry, 16,* 315–324.

Comptroller General of the United States. (1977). *Preventing mental retardation—more can be done.* (HRD No. 77–37). Washington, DC: U.S. Government Printing Office.

Cone, J., Bourland, G., & Wood-Shuman, S. (1986). Template matching: An objective approach to placing clients in appropriate residential services. *Journal of the Association for Persons with Severe Handicaps, 11,* 110–117.

Connor, F., Williamson, G., & Siepp, J. (Eds.). (1978). *Program guide for infants and toddlers and neuromotor and other developmental disabilities.* New York: Teachers College Press, Columbia University.

Conroy, J. (1982). Trends in deinstitutionalization of the mentally retarded. *Mental Retardation, 15,* 44–46.

Conroy, J., Efthimiou, J., & Lemanowicz, J. (1982). A matched comparison of the developmental growth of institutionalized and deinstitutionalized mentally retarded clients. *American Journal of Mental Deficiency, 86,* 581–587.

Cooper, R., & Zubek, J. (1958). Effects of enriched and restricted early environments on the learning ability of bright and dull rats. *Canadian Journal of Psychology, 12,* 159–164.

Copeland, S., Addison, M., & McCann, B. (1974). *Avenues to change* (Books I–IV). Dallas: National Association of Retarded Citizens.

Creak. E. (1963). Childhood psychosis: A review of 100 cases. *British Journal of Psychiatry, 109,* 84–89.

Creak, M. (1952). Discussion: Psychoses in childhood. *Social Medicine, 45,* 797–800.

Cregler, L., & Mark, H. (1986). Cardiovascular dangers of cocaine abuse. *American Journal of Cardiology, 57,* 1185–1186.

Crittenden, P., & Bonvillian, J. (1984). The relationship between maternal risk status and maternal sensitivity. *American Journal of Orthopsychiatry, 54,* 250–262.

Crowder, R. (1976). *Principles of learning and memory.* Hillsdale, NJ: Lawrence Erlbaum.

Crowner, T. (1979). Developing and administering programs for severely and profoundly handicapped students in public school systems. In R. York & E. Edgar (Eds.), *Teaching the severely handicapped* (Vol. IV). Seattle: American Association for the Education of the Severely/Profoundly Handicapped.

Cuvo, A. (1978). Validating task analysis of community living skills. *Vocational and Work Adjustment Bulletin, 11*(3), 13–21.

Dain, N. (1964). *Concepts of sanity in the United States, 1789–1895.* New Brunswick, NJ: Rutgers University Press.

Dattilo, J. (1987). Computerized assessment of leisure preferences: A replication. *Education and Training in Mental Retardation, 22,* 128–133.

Dattilo, J., & Mirenda, P. (1987). An application of a leisure preference assessment protocol for persons with severe handicaps. *Journal of the Association for Persons with Severe Handicaps, 12,* 306–311.

DeMyer, M., Barton, S., DeMyer, W., Norton, J., & Steele, R. (1973). Prognosis in autism: A follow-up study. *Journal of Autism and Childhood Schizophrenia, 3,* 199–246.

DeMyer, M., Hingtgen, J., & Jackson, R. (1981). Infantile autism reviewed: A decade of research. *Schizophrenia Bulletin, 7,* 388–451.

Dennis, W. (1951). A further analysis of reports of wild children. *Child Development, 22,* 153–158.

Deno, E. (1970). Special education as developmental capital. *Exceptional Children, 37,* 229–237.

Desforges, J. (1983). AIDS and preventive treatment in hemophilia. *New England Journal of Medicine, 308,* 94–95.

Deutsch, A. (1949). *The mentally ill in America* (2nd ed.). New York: Teachers College Press, Columbia University.

Developmental Disabilities Act of 1984, Report No. 98–1074, §102(11)(F) (1984).

Diamond, S. (1981). Growing up with parents of a handicapped child: A handicapped person's perspective. In J. Paul (Ed.), *Understanding and working with parents of children with special needs.* New York: Holt, Rinehart & Winston.

Dilley, J., Ochitill, H., Perl, M., & Vollberding, P. (1985). Findings in psychiatric consultations with patients with acquired immune deficiency syndrome. *American Journal of Psychiatry, 142,* 82–85.

Dixon, S., Coen, R., & Crutchfield, S. (1987). Visual dysfunction in cocaine-exposed infants. *Pediatric Research, 21,* 359–369.

Doll, E. (1962). A historical survey of research and management of mental retardation in the United States. In E. Trap & P. Himmelstein (Eds.), *Readings on the exceptional child: Research and theory.* New York: Appleton-Century-Crofts.

Dollar, S., & Brooks, C. (1980). Assessment of severely and profoundly handicapped individuals. *Measurement of Exceptionality, 12,* 87–101.

Donder, D., Hamre-Nietupski, S., Nietupski, J., & Fortschneider, J. (1981). Problem solving and strategy development. In R. York, W. Schofield, D. Donder, & D. Ryndak (Eds.), *Organizing and implementing services for students with severe and multiple handicaps.* Springfield, IL: Illinois State Board of Education.

Donder, D., & York, R. (1984). Integration of students with severe handicaps. In N. Certo, N. Haring, & R. York (Eds.), *Public school integration of severely handicapped students.* Baltimore: Paul H. Brookes.

Donnellan, A., LaVigna, G., Zambito, J., & Thvedt, J. (1985). A time-limited intervention program model to support community placement for persons with severe behavioral problems. *Journal of the Association for Persons with Severe Handicaps, 10,* 123–131.

Donnellan, A., Mirenda, P., Mesaros, R., & Fassbender, L. (1984). Analyzing the communicative functions of aberrant behavior. *Journal of the Association for Persons with Severe Handicaps, 9,* 201–212.

Dore, J. (1975). Holophrases, speech acts and language universals. *Journal of Child Language, 2,* 21–40.

Drabman, R., Hammer, D., & Rosenbaum, M. (1979). Assessing generalization in behavior modification with children: The generalization map. *Behavioral Assessment, 1,* 203–209.

Drage, J., Berendes, H., & Fisher, P. (1969). The APGAR score and four year psychological examination performance. In *Perinatal factors affecting human development* (Scientific Publication No. 185). New York: Pan American Health Organization.

Dunlap, G., Koegel, R., & Burke, J. (1981). Educational implications of stimulus overselectivity in autistic children. *Exceptional Education Quarterly, 2*(3), 37–50.

Dunlap, G. & Plienis, A. (1988). Generalization and maintenance of unsupervised responding via remote contingencies. In R. Horner, G. Dunlap, & R. Koegel (Eds.), *Generalization and maintenance: Life-style changes in applied settings.* Baltimore: Paul H. Brookes.

Dunn, L. (1973). *Exceptional children in the schools.* New York: Holt, Rinehart & Winston.

Durant, W. (1944). *Caesar and Christ.* New York: Simon & Schuster.

Durant, W. (1966). *The life of Greece.* New York: Simon & Schuster.

Eason, L., White, M., & Newson, C. (1982). Generalized reduction of self-stimulatory behavior: An effect of teaching appropriate play to autistic children. *Analysis and Intervention in Developmental Disabilities, 2,* 157–169.

Edelbrock, C., & Achenbach, T. (1984). The teacher version of the child behavior profile: I. Boys aged 6–11. *Journal of Consulting and Clinical Psychology, 52,* 207–217.

Edgar, E. (1985). How do special education students fare after they leave school? A response to Hasazi, Gordon, and Roe. *Exceptional Children, 51,* 470–473.

Education for All Handicapped Children Act of 1975, Public Law 94–142 (S.6). 94th Cong., 1st Sess. (1975).

Education for All Handicapped Children Amendments of 1983, Public Law 98–199.

Education of the Handicapped Amendments of 1986, Public Law 99–457.

Egan, I., Fredericks, H., Peters, J., Hendrickson, K., Toews, J., & Buckley, J. (1984). *Associated work skills: A manual.* Monmouth, OR: Teaching Research Publications.

Epilepsy Foundation of America. (1982). *Questions and answers about epilepsy.* Landover, MD: Author.

Epstein, L. (1986). Community placement and parental misgivings. In C. Salisbury & J. Intagliata (Eds.), *Respite care: Support for persons with developmental disabilities and their families.* Baltimore: Paul H. Brookes.

Eyman, R., & Call, T. (1977). Maladaptive behavior and community placement of mentally retarded persons. *American Journal of Mental Deficiency, 82,* 137–144.

Falvey, M. (1986). *Community-based curriculum: Instructional strategies for students with severe handicaps.* Baltimore: Paul H. Brookes.

Falvey, M., Brown, L., Lyon, S., Baumgart, D., & Schroeder, J. (1980). Strategies for using cues and correction procedures. In W. Sailor, B. Wilcox, & L. Brown (Eds.), *Methods of instruction for severely handicapped students.* Baltimore: Paul H. Brookes.

Farber, B. (1960). Family organization and crisis: Maintenance of integration in families with a severely mentally retarded child. *Monographs of the Society for Research in Child Development, 25* (No. 1).

Farber, B. (1968). *Mental retardation: Its social context and social consequences.* New York: Houghton Mifflin.

Feagans, L., & McKinney, J. (1981). The pattern of exceptionality across domains in learning disabled children. *Journal of Applied Developmental Psychology, 1,* 313–328.

Fedum, J., Kiely, R., & Krugman, A. (1969). Educational and social characteristics of crippled children. *Archives of Diseases in Childhood, 44,* 118–122.

Feldman, D. (1986). *Pet therapy as a leisure activity for persons with severe handicaps.* Paper presented at the meeting of the Association for Severe Handicaps, Boston.

Fenerick, N., & McDonnell, J. (1980). Junior high school students as teachers of the severely retarded: Training and generalization. *Education and Training of the Mentally Retarded, 15,* 187–194.

Ferrari, M. (1982). Chronic illness: Psychosocial effects on siblings–I. Chronically ill boys. *Journal of Child Psychology and Psychiatry, 25,* 459–476.

Flandermeyher, A. (1987). A comparison of the effects of heroin and cocaine abuse upon the neonate. *Natal Network, 6*(3), 42–48.

Flexer, R., & Martin, A. (1978). Sheltered workshops and vocational training settings. In M. Snell (Ed.), *Systematic instruction of the moderately and severely handicapped.* Columbus, OH: Charles E. Merrill.

Fotheringham, J., Skelton, M., & Hoddinott, B. (1971). *The retarded child and his family: The effects of home and institution.* Monograph Series No. 11. Toronto, Canada: Ontario Institute for Studies in Education.

Fotheringham, J., Skelton, M., & Hoddinott, B. (1972). The effects on the family of the presence of a mentally retarded child. *Canadian Psychiatric Association Journal, 17,* 283–290.

Foucault, M. (1965). *Madness and civilization.* New York: Random House.

Fowler, S. (1988). The effects of peer-mediated interventions on establishing, maintaining, and generalizating children's behavior changes. In R. Horner, G. Dunlap, & R. Koegel (Eds.), *Generalization and maintenance: Life-style changes in applied settings.* Baltimore: Paul H. Brookes.

Fowler, S., Johnson, M., Whitman, T., & Zukotynski, G. (1978). Teaching a parent in the home to train self-help skills and increase compliance in her profoundly retarded adult daughter. *AAESPH Review, 9,* 151–161.

Frankel, F., Simmons, J., Fichter, M., & Freeman, B. (1984). Stimulus overselectivity in autistic and mentally retarded children—a research note. *Journal of Child Psychology and Psychiatry, 25,* 147–155.

Fredericks, H., Covey, C., Hendrickson, K., Deane, K., Gallagher, J., & Schwindt, A. (1986). Part-time work for high school students. *Teaching Research Infant and Child Center Newsletter* (Teaching Research, Monmouth, OR), *15*(1), 1–7.

Fredericks, H., Covey, C., Hendrickson, K., Deane, K., Schwindt, A, & Perkins, C. (1989). *Vocational transition training for students with severe handicaps.* Austin, TX: PRO-ED.

Freeman, J., & Lietman, P. (1973). A basic approach to the understanding of seizures and the metabolism of anti-convulsants. *Advances in Pediatrics, 20,* 291.

Friedman, R., & MacQueen, J. (1971). Psychoeducative considerations of physical handicapping conditions in children. *Exceptional Children, 37,* 538–539.

Frierson, R., & Lippman, S. (1987). Psychological implications of AIDS. *American Family Physician, 35,* 109–116.

Fristoe, M., & Lloyd, L. (1978). A survey in the use of non-speech systems with the severely communication impaired. *Mental Retardation, 16,* 99–103.

Froomkin, J. (1972). *Estimates and projections of special target group populations in elementary and secondary schools* (Report prepared for the President's Commission on School Finance). Washington, DC: U.S. Government Printing Office.

Fulton, G., Metress, E., & Price, J. (1987). AIDS: Resource materials for school personnel. *Journal of School Health, 57,* 14–18.

Gallagher, J. (1975). *Teaching the gifted child* (2nd ed.). Boston: Allyn & Bacon.

Gallagher, J., Forsythe, P., Ringelheim, D., & Weintraub, F. (1975). Federal and state funding patterns for programs for the handicapped. In N. Hobbs (Ed.), *Issues in the classification of children* (Vol. 2). San Francisco: Jossey-Bass.

Garcia, E., & DeHaven, E. (1974). Use of operant techniques in the establishment and generalization of language: A review and analysis. *American Journal of Mental Deficiency, 79,* 169–178.

Gardner, W., Clees, T., & Cole, C. (1983). Self-management of disruptive verbal ruminations by a mentally retarded adult. *Applied Research in Mental Retardation, 4,* 41–58.

Gastaut, H. (1970). Clinical and electroencephalographic classification of epileptic seizures. *Epilepsia, 11,* 102–103.

Gearheart, B. (1980). *The handicapped student in the regular classroom* (2nd ed.). St. Louis: C. V. Mosby.

Gentry, D., & Adams, G. (1978). A curriculum-based direct intervention approach to the education of handicapped infants. In N. Haring & D. Bricker (Eds.), *Teaching the severely handicapped* (Vol. 3). Seattle: American Association for the Education of the Severely/Profoundly Handicapped.

Giangreco, M. (1986). Delivery of therapeutic services in special education programs for learners with severe handicaps. *Physical and Occupational Therapy in Pediatrics, 6*(2), 5–25.

Glidden, L. (1986). Families who adopt mentally retarded children: Who, why and what happens. In J. Gallagher & P. Vietze (Eds.), *Families of handicapped persons: Research, programs, and policy issues.* Baltimore: Paul H. Brookes.

Goetz, L., Gee, K., & Sailor, W. (1985). Using a behavior chain interruption strategy to teach communication skills to students with severe disabilities. *Journal of the Association for Persons with Severe Handicaps, 10,* 21–30.

Gold, M. (1980). *Try another way: Training manual.* Champaign, IL: Research Press.

Goldfarb, W., Yudkovitz, E., & Goldfarb, N. (1973). Verbal symbols to designate objects: An experimental study of communications in mothers of schizophrenic children. *Journal of Autism and Childhood Schizophrenia, 3,* 281–298.

Goldfried, R., & D'Zurilla, R. (1969). A behavioral-analytic model for assessing competence. In C. Spielberger (Ed.), *Current topics in clinical and community psychology.* New York: Academic Press.

Goldstein, A. (1983). United States: Causes, controls, and alternatives to aggression. In A. Goldstein & M. Segall (Eds.), *Aggression in global perspective.* New York: Pergamon Press.

Goldstein, H., & Wickstrom, S. (1986). Peer intervention effects on communicative interaction among handicapped and nonhandicapped preschoolers. *Journal of Applied Behavior Analysis, 19,* 209–214.

Goldstein, M., Baker, B., & Jamison, K. (1980). *Abnormal psychology: Experiences, origins, and interventions.* Boston: Little, Brown.

Gollary, E., Freedman, R., Wyngarden, M., & Kurtz, N. (1978). *Coming back: The community experience of deinstitutionalized mentally retarded people.* Cambridge, MA: Abt Associates.

Gopnik, A., & Meltzoff, A. (1984). Semantic and cognitive development in 15- to 21-month old children. *Journal of Child Development, 11,* 405–413.

Gottesman, I., & Schields, J. (1972). *Schizophrenia and genetics.* New York: Academic Press.

Green, C., Canipe, V., Way, P., & Reid, D. (1986). Improving the functional utility and effectiveness of classroom services for students with profound multiple handicaps. *Journal of the Association for Persons with Severe Handicaps, 11,* 162–170.

Greenfeld, J. (1972). *A child called Noah.* New York: Holt, Rinehart & Winston.

Greenfeld, J. (1978). *A place for Noah.* New York: Holt, Rinehart & Winston.

Greenleigh Associates. (1975). *The role of the sheltered workshop in the rehabilitation of the severely handicapped* (Report to the U.S. Department of Health, Education, and Welfare, Rehabilitation Services Administration). Washington, DC: U.S. Government Printing Office.

Greenspan, S., & Budd, K. (1986). Research on mentally retarded parents. In J. Gallagher & P. Vietze (Eds.), *Families of handicapped persons: Research, programs, and policy issues*. Baltimore: Paul H. Brookes.

Greer, B. (1975). On being the parent of a handicapped child. *Exceptional Children, 41,* 519.

Grossman, F. (1972). Brothers and sisters of retarded children. *Psychology Today, 5*(11), 102–104.

Grossman, H. (Ed.) (1973). *Manual on terminology and classification in mental retardation.* Washington, DC: American Association on Mental Deficiency.

Grossman, H. (Ed.). (1983). *Classification in mental retardation.* Washington, DC: American Association on Mental Deficiency.

Group for the Advancement of Psychiatry, Committee on Child Psychiatry. (1966). *Psychopathological disorders in children: Theoretical considerations and a proposed classification* (GAP Report No. 62). New York: Author.

Guess, D., & Horner, D. (1979). The severely and profoundly handicapped. In E. Meyen (Ed.), *Basic readings in the study of exceptional children and youth.* Denver: Love.

Guess, D., & Noonan, M. (1982). Curricula and instructional procedures for severely handicapped students. *Focus on Exceptional Children, 14*(4), 1–12.

Guess, D., & Rutherford, D. (1967). Experimental attempts to reduce stereotyping among blind retardates. *American Journal of Mental Deficiency, 71,* 984–986.

Guess, D., & Turnbull, H. (1987). The application of aversive procedures: Technological abuse or responsibility? *TASH Newsletter, 13*(7), 1, 11.

Guevremont, D., Osnes, P., & Stokes, T. (1988). The functional role of preschoolers' verbalizations in the generalization of self-instructional training. *Journal of Applied Behavior Analysis, 11,* 225–241.

Guralnick, M. (1976). The value of integrating handicapped and nonhandicapped preschool children. *American Journal of Orthopsychiatry, 46,* 236–245.

Guralnick, M. (1978). *Early intervention and the integration of handicapped and nonhandicapped children.* Baltimore: University Park Press.

Gurdin, P., & Anderson, G. (1987). Quality care for ill children: AIDS-specialized foster family homes. *Child Welfare, 66,* 291–302.

Haille, P. (1981). From cruelty to goodness—the personal voyage of a student of ethics. *Hastings Center Report, 11*(3), 23–28.

Halliday, M. (1975). Learning how to mean. In E. Lenneberg & H. Lenneberg (Eds.), *Foundations of language development: A Multi-disciplinary approach* (Vol. 1). New York: Academic Press.

Halpern, A. (1985). Transition: A look at the foundations. *Exceptional Children, 51,* 479–486.

Handicapped Children's Early Education Assistance Act of 1968. Public Law 90–538 (HR 17,090/S 3,446), 90th Congress, 2nd Session.

Hansen, C. (1980). History of vocational habilitation of the handicapped. In C. Hansen (Ed.), *Expanding opportunities: Vocational education for the handicapped*. Seattle: University of Washington.

Harder, L., & Bowditch, B. (1982). Siblings of children with cystic fibrosis perceptions of the impact of disease. *Children's Health Care, 10,* 116–120.

Hardman, M., Drew, C., & Egan, M. (1987). *Human exceptionality: Society, school, and family* (2nd ed.). Boston: Allyn & Bacon.

Hardman, M., & McDonnell, J. (1987). Implementing federal transition initiatives for youths with severe handicaps: The Utah community-based transition project. *Exceptional Children, 53,* 493–498.

Harris-Vanderheiden, D., Brown, W., MacKenzie, P., Reiner, S., & Scheibel, C. (1975). Symbol communication for the mentally handicapped. *Mental Retardation, 13,* 34–37.

Harvey, B. (1975). Cystic Fibrosis. In E. Bleck & D. Nagel (Eds.), *Physically handicapped children: A medical atlas for teachers*. New York: Grune & Stratton.

Harvey, D., & Greenway, A. (1984). The self-concept of physically handicapped siblings: An empirical investigation. *Journal of Child Psychology and Psychiatry, 25,* 273–284.

Hasazi, S. (1985). Facilitating transition from high school: Policy and practices. *American Rehabilitation, 11,* 9–11.

Hasazi, S., Gordon. L., & Roe, C. (1985). Factors associated with the employment status of handicapped youth exiting high school from 1979 to 1983. *Exceptional Children, 51,* 455–469.

Hay, W. (1951). Mental retardation problems in different age groups. *American Journal of Mental Deficiency, 55,* 191–197.

Hayden, A., McGinnes, G., & Dmitriev, V. (1976). Early and continuous intervention strategies for severely handicapped infants and very young children. In N. Haring & L. Brown (Eds.), *Teaching the severely handicapped* (Vol. 1). New York: Grune & Stratton.

Head, D. (1979). A comparison of self-concept scores for visually impaired adolescents in several class settings. *Education of the Visually Handicapped, 10,* 51–55.

Heal, L., Sigelman, C., & Switzky, H. (1980). Research on community residential alternatives for the mentally retarded. In R. Flynn & K. Nitsch (Eds.), *Normalization, social integration, and community services*. Austin, TX: PRO-ED.

Healey, W., & Karp-Nortman, D. (1975). *The hearing impaired, mentally retarded: Recommendations for action*. Washington, DC: American Speech and Hearing Association.

Heber, R. (Ed.). (1961). *A manual on terminology and classification in mental retardation* (Monograph No. 66, Supplement 64). Washington, DC: American Journal of Mental Deficiency.

Hermalin, B., & O'Connor, N. (1970). *Psychological experiments with autistic children*. London: Pergamon Press.

Hewett, F., & Forness, S. (1977). *Education of exceptional learners* (2nd ed.). Boston: Allyn & Bacon.

Hewett, F., & Taylor, F. (1980). *The emotionally disturbed child in the classroom. The orchestration of success*. Boston: Allyn & Bacon.

Hill, B., & Bruininks, R. (1984). Maladaptive behavior of mentally retarded individuals in residential facilities. *American Journal of Mental Deficiency, 88,* 380–387.

Hill, J., Wehman, P., & Horst, G. (1982). Toward generalization of appropriate leisure and social behavior in severely handicapped youth: Pinball machine use. *Journal of the Association for Persons with Severe Handicaps, 6,* 38–44.

Hill, M., Hill, J., Wehman, P., & Banks, P. (1985). An analysis of monetary and nonmonetary outcomes associated with competitive employment of mentally retarded persons (Monograph, Vol. 1). In *Competitive employment for persons with mental retardation: From research to practice.* Richmond, VA: Virginia Commonwealth University.

Hingtgen, J., & Bryson, C. (1972). Recent developments in the study of early childhood psychoses: Infantile autism, childhood schizophrenia and related disorders. *Schizophrenia Bulletin, 5,* 8–54.

Hingtgen, J., & Churchill, D. (1971). Differential effects of behavioral modification in four mute autistic boys. In D. Churchill, G. Alpern, & M. DeMyer (Eds.), *Infantile autism.* Springfield, IL: Charles C Thomas.

Holland, D. Cocaine use and toxicity. *Journal of Emergency Nursing, 8,* 166–169.

Hoorweg, J., & Stanfeld, P. (1972). The influence of malnutrition on psychological and neurological development: Preliminary communication. In *Nutrition, the nervous system and behavior.* Conference proceedings, Panamerican Health Organization.

Horner, R., Bellamy, G., & Colvin, G. (1984). Responding in the presence of nontrained stimuli: Implications of generalization error patterns. *Journal of the Association for Persons with Severe Handicaps, 9,* 287–296.

Horner, R., & Billingsley, F. (1988). The effect of competing behavior on the generalization and maintenance of adaptive behavior in applied settings. In R. Horner, G. Dunlap, & R. Koegel (Eds.), *Generalization and maintenance: Life-style changes in applied settings.* Baltimore: Paul H. Brookes.

Horner, R., & Budd, C. (1983). *Teaching manual sign language to a nonverbal student: Generalization of sign use and collateral behavior.* Eugene, OR: Center on Human Development, University of Oregon.

Horner, R., Eberhard, J., & Sheehan, M. (1986). Teaching generalized table busing: The importance of negative teaching examples. *Behavior Modification, 10,* 457–471.

Horner, R., Jones, D., & Williams, J. (1985). A functional approach to teaching generalized street crossing. *Journal of the Association for Persons with Severe Handicaps, 10,* 71–78.

Horner, R., Sprague, J., & Wilcox, B. (1982). General case programming for community activities. In B. Wilcox & G. Bellamy (Eds.), *Design of high school programs for severely handicapped students.* Baltimore: Paul H. Brookes.

Horowitz, F. (1980). Intervention and its effects on early development: What model of development is appropriate? In R. Turner & H. Reese (Eds.), *Life-span developmental psychology: Intervention.* New York: Academic Press.

Houston, J. (1976). *Fundamentals of learning.* New York: Academic Press.

Hoyt, K. (1975). *An introduction to career education: A policy paper.* Washington, DC: U.S. Government Printing Office.

Hunt, N. (1967). *The world of Nigel Hunt: The diary of a mongoloid.* New York: Garrett Publications.

Hurlbut, B., Iwata, B., & Green, J. (1982). Nonvocal language acquisition in adolescents with severe physical disabilities: Blissymbol versus iconic stimulus formats. *Journal of Applied Behavior Analysis, 15,* 241–258.

Hutchings, J. (1988). Pediatric AIDS: An overview. *Children Today, 17*(3), 4–7.

Hutchinson, D. (1974). *A model for transdisciplinary staff development.* New York: United Cerebral Palsy Association.

Hutt, C., & Ounsted, C. (1966). The biological significance of gaze aversion with particular reference to the syndrome of infantile autism. *Behavioral Science, 11,* 342–356.

Inhelder, B. (1968). *The diagnosis of reasoning in the mentally retarded.* New York: John Day.

Irwin, J. (1982). Human language and communication. In G. Shames & E. Wiig (Eds.), *Human communication disorders: An introduction.* Columbus, OH: Charles E. Merrill.

Itard, J. (1932). *The wild boy of Aveyron.* (G. Humphrey & M. Humphrey, Trans.). New York: Appleton-Century-Crofts.

Jenkins, J., & Jenkins, L. (1985). Peer tutoring in elementary and secondary programs. *Focus on Exceptional Children, 17*(6), 1–12.

Jensema, C. (1980). A profile of deaf-blind children with various types of educational facilities. *American Annals of the Deaf, 125,* 896–900.

Johnson, B., & Cuvo, A. (1981). Teaching mentally retarded adults to cook. *Behavior Modification, 5,* 187–202.

Jones, M. (1977). Physical facilities and environments. In J. Jordan, A. Hayden, M. Karnes, & M. Woods (Eds.), *Early childhood education for exceptional children: A handbook of ideas and exemplary practices.* Reston, VA: Council for Exceptional Children.

Justen, J. (1976). Who are the severely handicapped? A problem in definition. *AAESPH Review, 1*(5), 1–11.

Kagan, J. (1978). Resilience and continuity in psychological development. In A. Clarke & A. Clarke (Eds.), *Early experience: Myth and evidence.* New York: Free Press.

Kaiser, A., Alpert, C., & Warren, S. (1987). Teaching functional language: Strategies for language intervention. In M. Snell (Ed.), *Systematic instruction of persons with severe handicaps.* Columbus, OH: Charles E. Merrill.

Kaiser, A., & Fox, J. (1986). Ecological analysis of families of handicapped children. In J. Gallagher & P. Vietze (Eds.), *Families of handicapped persons: Research, programs, and policy issues.* Baltimore: Paul H. Brookes.

Kanner, L. (1943). Autistic disturbance of affective contact. *Nervous Child, 2,* 217–250.

Karnes, M., & Teska, J. (1980). Toward successful parent involvement in programs for handicapped children. In J. Gallagher (Ed.), *New directions in exceptional children: Parents and families of handicapped children.* San Francisco: Jossey-Bass.

Karnes, M., & Zehrbach, R. (1977). Alternative models for delivery services to young handicapped children. In J. Jordan, A. Hayden, M. Karnes, & M. Woods (Eds.), *Early childhood education for exceptional children: A handbook of ideas and exemplary practices.* Reston, VA: Council for Exceptional Children.

Katz, E. (1968). *The retarded adult in the community.* Springfield, IL: Charles C Thomas.

Kauffman, J. (1980). Where special education for disturbed children is going: A personal view. *Exceptional Children, 48,* 522–527.

Kauffman, J. (1985). *Characteristics of children's behavior disorders* (3rd ed.). Columbus, OH: Charles E. Merrill.

Kaufman, B. (1976). *Son-rise*. New York: Harper & Row.

Kazdin, A. (1980). Acceptability of alternative treatments for deviant child behavior. *Journal of Applied Behavior Analysis, 13,* 259–273.

Keller, H. (1955). *Teacher: Anne Sullivan Macy--a tribute by the foster-child of her mind*. Garden City, NY: Doubleday.

Kelly, T., Bullock, L., & Dykes, M. (1977). Behavior disorders: Teachers' perceptions. *Exceptional Children, 43,* 316–318.

Kennedy, C., Drage, J., & Schwartz, B. (1963). Preliminary data with respect to the relationships between APGAR score at one and five minutes and fetal outcome. In N. Peterson, *Early intervention for handicapped and at-risk children*. Denver: Love.

Kenowitz, L., Gallagher, J., & Edgar, E. (1977). Generic services for the severely handicapped and their families: What's available? In E. Sontag, J. Smith, & N. Certo (Eds.), *Educational programming for the severely and profoundly handicapped*. Reston, VA: Division on Mental Retardation, Council for Exceptional Children.

Keogh, W., & Reichle, J. (1985). Communication intervention for the "difficult-to-teach" severely handicapped. In S. Warren & A. Rogers-Warren (Eds.), *Teaching functional language: Generalization and maintenance of language skills*. Baltimore: University Park Press.

Kiernan, W., & Stark, J. (1986). Comprehensive design for the future. In W. Kiernan & J. Stark (Eds.), *Pathways to employment for adults with developmental disabilities*. Baltimore: Paul H. Brookes.

Killilea, M. (1962). *Karen*. New York: Prentice-Hall.

Kirk, S., & Gallagher, J. (1986). *Educating exceptional children* (5th ed.). Boston: Houghton Mifflin.

Kirk, S., & Johnson, G. (1951). *Educating the retarded child*. Cambridge, MA: Riverside Press.

Kirkland, B., & Caughlin-Carver, E. (1982). The assessment of behavioral interrelationships in child behavior therapy. *Behavioral Assessments, 4,* 131–165.

Kirtley, D. (1975). *The psychology of blindness*. Chicago: Nelson-Hall.

Kissel, R., & Whitman, T. (1977). An examination of the direct and generalized effects of a play-training and overcorrection procedure upon the self-stimulatory behavior of a profoundly retarded boy. *AAESPH Review, 2,* 131–146.

Klein, C. (1977). Coping patterns of parents of deaf-blind children. *American Annals of the Deaf, 122,* 310–312.

Knoblock, P. (1983). *Teaching emotionally disturbed children*. Boston: Houghton Mifflin.

Koegel, R., Firestone, R., Kramme, K., & Dunlap, G. (1974). Increasing spontaneous play by suppressing self-stimulation in autistic children. *Journal of Applied Behavior Analysis, 7,* 521–528.

Koegel, R., & Koegel, L. (1988). Generalized responsivity and pivotal behaviors. In R. Horner, G. Dunlap, & R. Koegel (Eds.), *Generalization and maintenance: Life-style changes in applied settings*. Baltimore: Paul H. Brookes.

Koegel, R., & Mentis, M. (1985). Motivation in childhood autism: Can they or won't they? *Journal of Child Psychology and Psychiatry, 26,* 185–191.

Koegel, R., Rincover, A., & Egel, A. (1982). *Educating and understanding autistic children*. San Diego, CA: College-Hill Press.

Kokaska, C., & Brolin, D. (1985). *Career education for handicapped individuals* (2nd ed.). Columbus, OH: Charles E. Merrill.

Koocher, L. (1976). *Deinstitutionalization: An analytical review and sociological perspective.* Rockville, MD: National Institute of Mental Health.

Koop, C. (1987). *Report of the surgeon general's workshop on children with HIV infection and their families* (DHHS Publication No. HRS–D–MC 87–1). Washington, DC: Department of Health and Human Services.

Korn, S., Chess, S., & Fernandez, P. (1980). The impact of children's physical handicaps on marital quality and family interaction. In R. Lerner & G. Spanier (Eds.), *Child influences on marital and family interaction.* New York: Academic Press.

Kraemer, K., Cusick, B., & Bigge, J. (1982). Motor development, deviations, and physical rehabilitation. In J. Bigge (Ed.), *Teaching individuals with physical and multiple disabilities* (2nd ed.). Columbus, OH: Charles E. Merrill.

Kubler-Ross, E. (1969). *On death and dying.* New York: Macmillan.

Kvaraceus, W., & Hayes, E. (1969). *If your child is handicapped.* Boston: Porter Sargent.

Lack, A. (Producer & Director). (1989). *Cocaine babies on West 57th Street* [Television program 212–227]. New York: CBS News Division, CBS, Inc.

Landesman-Dwyer, S., Berkson, G., & Romer, D. (1979). Affiliation and friendship of mentally retarded residents in group homes. *American Journal of Mental Deficiency, 83,* 571–580.

Landesman-Dwyer, S., Ragozin, A., & Little, R. (1981). Behavioral correlates of prenatal alcohol exposure: A four-year follow-up study. *Neurobehavioral Toxicology and Teratology, 3,* 187–193.

Laski, F. (1980). The right to live in the community: The legal foundation. In P. Roos, R. McCann, & M. Addison (Eds.), *Shaping the future: Community-based residential services and facilities for mentally retarded people.* Baltimore: University Park Press.

Lavigne, J., & Ryan, M. (1978). Psychologic adjustment of siblings of children with chronic illness. *Pediatrics, 63,* 616–622.

Lazar, I., & Darlington, R. (Eds.). (1982). Lasting effects of early education: A report from the Consortium for Longitudinal Studies. *Monographs of the Society for Research in Child Development, 47*(2–3, Serial No. 195). (Summary report, DHEW Publication No. OHDS 80–30179).

Lelord, G., Muh, J., Barthelemy, C., Martineau, J., Garreau, B., & Callaway, E. (1981). Effects of pyridoxine and magnesium on autistic symptoms. Initial observations. *Journal of Autism and Developmental Disorders, 11,* 219–230.

Leonard, L. (1981). An invited article facilitating linguistic skills in children with specific language impairment. *Applied Psycholiguistics, 1,* 89–118.

Liberty, K. (1984). Self-monitoring and skill generalization: A review of current research. In M. Boer (Ed.), *Investigating the problem of skill generalization: Literature review I* (Institute for the Education of Severely Handicapped Children, Washington Research Organization, U. S. Department of Education, Contract No. 300–82–0364). Seattle: College of Education, University of Washington.

Lister, A. (1970). Future for children with spina bifida. *Lancet, 2,* 982–983.

Locket, T., & Rudolph, J. (1980). Deaf-blind children with maternal rubella: Implications for adult services. *American Annals of the Deaf, 125,* 1000–1006.

Look, T., Dahl, E., & Gale, A. (1977). *Improving productivity and the quality of work life.* New York: Praeger.

Lovaas, O., Koegel, R., & Schriebman, L. (1979). Stimulus overselectivity in autism: A review of research. *Psychological Bulletin, 86,* 1236–1254.

Lovaas, O., Litrownik, A., & Mann, R. (1971). Response latencies to auditory stimuli in self-stimulatory behavior. *Behavior Research and Therapy, 2,* 39–49.

Lovaas, O., Schreibman, L., Koegel, R., & Rehm, R. (1971). Selective responding by autistic children to multiple sensory input. *Journal of Abnormal Psychology, 77,* 211–222.

Luftig, R. (1984). An analysis of initial sign lexicons as a function of eight learnability variables. *Journal of the Association for Persons with Severe Handicaps, 9,* 193–200.

Lyon, S., & Lyon, G. (1980). Team functioning and staff development: A role release approach to providing integrated educational services to severely handicapped students. *Journal of the Association for the Severely Handicapped, 5,* 250–263.

Lyons, D., & Powers, V. (1963). Study of children exempted from Los Angeles schools. *Exceptional Schools, 30,* 155–162.

MacGregor, S., Kieth, L., Chasnoff, I., Rosner, M., Shaw, P., & Minogue, J. (1987). Cocaine use during pregnancy: Adverse perinatal outcomes. *American Journal of Obstetrics and Gynecology, 157,* 686–690.

MacMillan, D. (1982). *Mental retardation in school and society* (2nd ed.). Boston: Little, Brown.

Mank, D., & Horner, R. (1987). Self-recruited feedback: A cost-effective procedure for maintaining behavior. *Research in Developmental Disabilities, 8,* 91–112.

Mank, D., Rhodes, L., & Bellamy, G. (1986). Four supported employment alternatives. In W. Kiernan & J. Stark (Eds.), *Pathways to employment for adults with developmental disabilities.* Baltimore: Paul H. Brookes.

Manning, D., & Balson, P. (1987). Policy issues surrounding children with AIDS in schools. *Clearing House, 61,* 101–104.

Martchetti, A., McCartney, J., Drain, S., Hooper, M., & Dix, J. (1983). Pedestrian skills training for mentally retarded adults: Comparison of training in two settings. *Mental Retardation, 21,* 107–110.

Martin, J. (1980). A longitudinal study of the consequences of early mother-infant interaction: A microanalytic approach. *Monographs of the Research in Child Development, 46*(3, Serial No. 190).

Martin, J., Rusch, F., James, V., Decker, P., & Trytol, K. (1982). The use of picture cues in the preparation of complex meals. *Applied Research in Mental Retardation, 3,* 105–119.

Maslow, A. (1970). Some educational implications of the humanistic psychologies. *Harvard Educational Review, 38,* 685–696.

Mates, T. (1982). *Siblings of autistic children: Their adjustment and performance at home and in school as a function of sex and family size.* Unpublished doctoral dissertation, University of North Carolina, Chapel Hill, NC.

Matson, J. (1980). A controlled group study of pedestrian-skill training for the mentally retarded. *Behavior Research and Therapy, 18,* 99–106.

Matson, J., & Barrett, R. (1982). *Psychopathology in the mentally retarded.* New York: Grune & Stratton.

Matson, J., & DiLorenzo, T. (1984). *Punishment and its alternatives: A new perspective for behavior modification.* New York: Springer.

Matson, J., & DiLorenzo, T. (1986). Social skills training and mental handicap and organic impairment. In C. Hollin & P. Trower (Eds.), *Handbook of social skills training: Clinical applications and new directions* (Vol. 2). New York: Pergamon Press.

Mauss, M. (1954). *The gift.* London: Allen & Unwin.

McCarthy, R., & Stodden, R. (1979). Mainstreaming secondary students: A peer tutoring model. *Teaching Exceptional Children, 11,* 162–163.

McDonald, E. (1980). *Teaching and using Blissymbolics.* Toronto: Blissymbolics Institute.

McDonnell, J., & Hardman, M. (1985). Planning the transition of severely handicapped youth from school to adult services: A framework for high school programs. *Education and Training of the Mentally Retarded, 20,* 275–286.

McDonnell, J., Wilcox, B., & Boles, S. (1986). *Do we know enough to plan for transition? A national survey of state agencies responsible for service to persons with severe handicaps.* Unpublished manuscript, University of Oregon, Eugene, OR.

McHale, S., & Simeonsson, R. (1980). Effects of interactions on nonhandicapped children's attitudes towards autistic children. *American Journal of Mental Deficiency, 85,* 18–24.

McHale, S., Simeonsson, R., & Sloan, J. (1983). Children with handicapped brothers and sisters. In E. Schopler & G. Mesibov (Eds.), *Issues in autism: Vol. 2. The effects of autism on the family.* New York: Plenum.

McNaughton, S., & Kates, B. (1974). The application of Blissymbolics. In R. Schiefelbusch (Ed.), *Nonspeech language and communication: Analysis and interventions.* Baltimore: University Park Press.

Meighan, T. (1971). *An investigation of the self-concept of blind and visually handicapped adolescents.* New York: American Foundation for the Blind.

Menchetti, B., Rusch, F., & Lamson, D. (1981). Social validation of behavioral training techniques: Assessing the normalizing qualities of competitive employment training procedures. *Journal of the Association for Persons with Severe Handicaps, 6,* 6–16.

Mercer, J. (1970). Sociological perspectives on mild mental retardation. In H. Haywood (Ed.), *Social-cultural aspects of mental retardation.* New York: Appleton-Century-Crofts.

Mercer, J. (1973). *Labeling the mentally retarded.* Berkeley, CA: University of California Press.

Meyer, L., & Evans, I. (1986). Modification of excessive behavior: An adaptive and functional approach for educational and community contexts. In R. Horner & H. Fredericks (Eds.), *Education of learners with severe handicaps: Exemplary service strategies.* Baltimore: Paul H. Brookes.

Miller, J. (1975). Juvenile rheumatoid arthritis. In E. Bleck & D. Nagel (Eds.), *Physically handicapped children: A medical atlas for teachers.* New York: Grune & Stratton.

Miller, M. (1987, November 23). Drug use: Down but not in the ghetto. *Newsweek,* p. 33.

Mills v. Board of Education of District of Columbia, 348 F. Supp. 866 (D.D.C. 1972).

Minear, W. (1956). A classification of cerebral palsy. *Pediatrics, 18,* 841.

Minnesota Developmental Disabilities Program. (1982). *Annual Report—Minnesota Council on Developmental Disabilities.* Minneapolis, MN: Minnesota Council on Developmental Disabilities.

Mithaug, D., Horiuchi, C., & Fanning, P. (1985). A report on the Colorado statewide follow-up survey of special education students. *Exceptional Children, 51,* 394–404.

Mittleman, H., Mittleman, R., & Elser, B. (1984). Cocaine. *American Journal of Nursing, 43,* 1092–1095.

Moerk, E. (1977). Processes and products of imitation: Additional evidence that imitation is progressive. *Journal of Psycholinguistics Research, 6,* 219–230.

Monmaney, T. (1987, September 7). Kids with AIDS. *Newsweek,* pp. 51–59.

Moon, M., & Bunker, L. (1987). Recreation and motor skills programming. In M. Snell (Ed.), *Systematic instruction of persons with severe handicaps* (3rd ed.). Columbus, OH: Charles E. Merrill.

Morgan, S. (1981). *The unreachable child: An introduction to early childhood autism.* Memphis: Memphis State University Press.

Moroney, R. (1986). Family care: Toward a responsive society. In P. Dokecki & R. Zaner (Eds.), *Ethics of dealing with persons with severe handicaps: Toward a research agenda.* Baltimore: Paul H. Brookes.

Morrow, L., & Presswood, S. (1984). The effects of self-control technique on eliminating three stereotypic behaviors in a multiply-handicapped institutionalized adolescent. *Behavior Disorders, 9,* 247–253.

Morse, W. (1975). The education of socially maladjusted and emotionally disturbed children. In W. Cruickshank & G. Johnson (Eds.), *Education of exceptional children and youth* (3rd ed.). Englewood Cliffs, NJ: Prentice-Hall.

Morse, W., & Coopchik, H. (1979). Socioemotional impairment. In W. Morse (Ed.), *Humanistic teaching for exceptional children: An introduction to special education.* Syracuse, NY: Syracuse University Press.

Musselwhite, C.,, & St. Louis, K. (1982). *Communication programming for the severely handicapped: Vocal and non-vocal strategies.* San Diego: College-Hill Press.

Mussen, P., Conger, J., Kagan, J., & Huston, A. (1984). *Child development and personality* (6th ed.). New York: Harper & Row.

National Information Center for Handicapped Children and Youth. (1986). *News Digest* (April). Washington, DC: Author.

National Institute on Drug Abuse. (1987). *Data from the Drug Abuse Warning Network (DAWN)* (Series 1, No. 6) (DHHS Publication No. 87–1530). Washington, DC: U.S. Government Printing Office.

National Society for Crippled Children and Adults. (1967). *Trends affecting program planning in Easter Seal societies.* Chicago: Author.

Nietupski, J., & Williams, W. (1974). Teaching severely handicapped students recreational activities and to respond appropriately to telephone requests to engage in selected recreation activities. In L. Brown, T. Crowner, W. Williams, & R. York (Eds.), *A collection of papers and programs related to public school services for severely handicapped students* (Vol. IV). Madison, WI: Madison Public Schools.

Nietupski, R., Certo, N., Pumpian, I., & Belmore, K. (1976). Supermarket shopping: Teaching severely handicapped students to generate a shopping list and make purchases functionally linked with meal preparation. In L. Brown, N. Certo, K. Belmore, & T. Crowner (Eds.), *Madison alternative for zero exclusion: Papers and programs related to public school services for secondary age severely handicapped students* (Vol. VI, Part 1). Madison, WI: Madison Public Schools.

Nihira, L., & Nihira, K. (1975). Jeopardy in community placement. *American Journal of Mental Deficiency, 79,* 538–544.

Nirje, B. (1969). The normalization principle and its human management implications. In R. Kugel & W. Wolfensberger (Eds.), *Changing patterns in residential services for the mentally retarded.* Washington, DC: President's Committee on Mental Retardation.

Nirje, B. (1980). The normalization principle. In R. Flynn & K. Nitsch (Eds.), *Normalization, social integration, and community services.* Austin, TX: PRO-ED.

Nordquist, V., & Wahler, R. (1973). Naturalistic treatment of an autistic child. *Journal of Applied Behavior Analysis, 6,* 79–87.

Novak, A., & Heal, L. (1980). *Integration of developmentally disabled individuals into the community.* Baltimore: Paul H. Brookes.

Olson, S. (1988). Pediatric HIV. More than a health problem. *Children Today, 17*(3), 8–9.

Osguthorpe, R., Top, B., Eiserman, W., Scruggs, T., & Shisler, L. (1988). Students with handicaps as tutors. *Counterpoint, 8*(3), 6–7.

Osterholm, M., & MacDonald, K. (1987). Facing the complex issues of pediatric AIDS: A public health perspective. *Journal of the American Medical Association, 258,* 2736–2737.

Owens, R. (1988). *Language development: An introduction* (2nd ed.). Columbus, OH: Charles E. Merrill.

Paluszny, M. (1979). *Autism: A practical guide for parents and professionals.* Syracuse, NY: Syracuse University Press.

Pancsofar, E., & Bates, P. (1985). The impact of the acquisition of successive training exemplars on generalization. *Journal of the Association for Persons with Severe Handicaps, 10,* 95–104.

Parke, R. (1986). Fathers, families, and support systems: Their role in the development of at-risk and retarded infants and children. In J. Gallagher & P. Vietze (Eds.), *Families of handicapped persons: Research, programs, and policy issues.* Baltimore: Paul H. Brookes.

Parmenter, T. (1980). *Vocational training for independent living.* New York: World Rehabilitation Fund.

Pea, R. (1980). The development of negation in early child language. In D. Olson (Ed.), *The social foundations of language and thought: Essays in honor of Jerome S. Bruner.* New York: W. W. Norton.

Pennsylvania Association for Retarded Children (PARC) v. Pennsylvania, 343 F. Supp. 279 (E.D. Pa. 1972).

Peterson, L. (1963). Immediate memory: Data and theory. In C. Cofer & B. Musgrave (Eds.), *Verbal behavior and learning.* New York: McGraw-Hill.

Peterson, N. (1987). *Early intervention for handicapped and at-risk children: An introduction to early childhood-special education.* Denver: Love.

Peterson, N., & Haralick, J. (1977). Integration of handicapped and nonhandicapped pre-schoolers: An analysis of play behavior and social integration. *Education and Training of the Mentally Retarded, 12,* 235–245.

Pinker, R. (1973). *Social theory and social policy.* London: Heinemann Educational Books.

Pittman, V. (Producer and director). (1989). *Cocaine babies on Health Talk* [radio program 89–217]. New York: CBS Radio News Division, CBS Inc.

Plomin, R., DeFries, J., & McClearn, G. (1980). *Behavioral genetics: A primer.* San Francisco: W. H. Freeman.

Pollin, W. (1972). The pathogenesis of schizophrenia. *Archives of General Psychology, 27,* 29–37.

Pollin, W. (1985). The danger of cocaine. *Journal of the American Medical Association, 254,* 98.

Polloway, E., Epstein, M., & Cullinan, D. (1985). Prevalence of behavior problems among educable mentally retarded students. *Education and Training of the Mentally Retarded, 20,* 3–13.

Poorman, C. (1980). Mainstreaming in reverse with a special friend. *Teaching Exceptional Children, 12,* 136–142.

Powell, T., & Ogle, P. (1985). *Brothers and sisters: A special part of exceptional families.* Baltimore: Paul H. Brookes.

President's Committee on Mental Retardation. (1975). *Changing patterns in residential services for the mentally retarded.* Washington, DC: U.S. Government Printing Office.

Pritchard, D. (1963). *Education and the handicapped: 1760–1960.* London: Routledge & Kegan Paul.

Ramey, C., & Baker-Ward, L. (1982). Psychosocial retardation and the early experience paradigm. In D. Bricker (Ed.), *Intervention with at-risk and handicapped infants: From research to application.* Baltimore: University Park Press.

Ramey, C., & MacPhee, D. (1985). Developmental retardation among the poor: A systems theory perspective on risk and prevention. In D. Farran & J. McKinney (Eds.), *Risk in intellectual and psychosocial development.* New York: Academic Press.

Ramey, C., Yeates, K., & Short, E. (1984). The plasticity of intellectual development: Insights from prevention intervention. *Child Development, 55,* 1913–1925.

Ranier, J. (1975). Severely emotionally handicapped hearing impaired children. In D. Naiman (Ed.), *Needs of emotionally disturbed hearing impaired children.* New York: School of Education, New York University.

Reich, R. (1978). Gestural facilitation of expressive language in moderately/severely retarded preschoolers. *Mental Retardation, 16,* 113–117.

Reichle, J., & Karlan, G. (1985). The selection of an augmentative system in communication intervention: A critique of decision rules. *Journal of the Association for Persons with Severe Handicaps, 10,* 146–156.

Reichle, J., Rogers, N., & Barrett, C. (1984). Establishing pragmatic discriminations among the communicative functions of requesting, rejecting, and commenting in an adolescent. *Journal of the Association for Persons with Severe Handicaps, 9,* 31–36.

Reiss, S., Levitan, G., & Szyszko, J. (1982). Emotional disturbance and mental retardation: Diagnostic overshadowing. *American Journal of Mental Deficiency, 86,* 567–574.

Rensberger, B. (1984). Cancer: A new synthesis: cause. *Science 84, 5*(7), 28–33.

Restak, R. (1982). Islands of genius. *Science, 193,* 62–67.

Rhode, G., Morgan, D., & Young, K. (1983). Generalization and maintenance of treatment gains of behaviorally handicapped students from resource rooms to regular classrooms using self-evaluation procedures. *Journal of Applied Behavior Analysis, 16,* 171–188.

Rice, M. (1984). Cognitive aspects of communication development. In R. Schiefelbusch & J. Pickar (Eds.), *The acquisition of communicative competence.* Baltimore: University Park Press.

Richardson, S. (1981). Living environments: An ecological perspective. In H. Hayworth & J. Newbrough (Eds.), *Living environments for developmentally retarded persons.* Baltimore: University Park Press.

Richardson, S., Birch, H., Grabic, E., & Yoder, K. (1972). The behavior of children in school who were severely malnourished in the first two years of life. *Journal of Health and Social Behavior, 13,* 276–284.

Richmond, H., & Tarjan, G. (1977). Mental retardation and the normal distribution curve. *American Journal of Mental Retardation, 81,* 991–994.

Rie, G., & Rie, J. (1980). Students' and teachers' perceptions of the mentally retarded child. In J. Gottlieb (Ed.), *Educating mentally retarded persons in the mainstream.* Baltimore: University Park Press.

Rimland, B. (1964). *Infantile autism.* New York: Appleton-Century-Crofts.

Rimland, B. (1971). The differentiation of childhood psychoses: An analysis of checklists for 2,218 psychotic children. *Journal of Autism and Childhood Schizophrenia, 2,* 161–174.

Rimland, B., Callaway, B., & Dreyfus, P. (1978). The effect of high doses of vitamin B6 on autistic children: A double blind crossover study. *American Journal of Psychiatry, 135,* 472–475.

Rimland, B., & Meyer, D. (1967). *Malabsorption and the celiac syndrome as possible causes of childhood psychosis: A brief discussion of evidence and need for research.* San Diego: Institute for Child Behavior Research.

Ritvo, E., & Brothers, A. (1982). Genetic and immunohematologic factors in autism. *Journal of Autism and Developmental Disorders, 12,* 109–110.

Ritvo, E., & Freeman, B. (1977). *Definition of the syndrome of autism.* Washington, DC: National Society of Autistic Children.

Ritvo, E., & Freeman, B. (1978). National Society for Autistic Children definition of autism. *Journal of Autism and Developmental Disorders, 8,* 162–167.

Robbins, R., Mercer, J., & Meyers, C. (1967). The school as a selecting-labeling system. *Journal of School Psychology, 5,* 270–279.

Robinson-Wilson, M. (1977). Picture recipe cards as an approach to teaching severely and profoundly retarded adults to cook. *Education and Training of the Mentally Retarded, 12,* 69–73.

Rodin, E., Shapiro, H., & Lennox, K. (1976). *Epilepsy and life performance.* Detroit: Lafayette Clinic.

Roe, R. (1987). Should persons with contagious diseases be barred from school? *Social Education, 37,* 238–241.

Rosenfeld, A. (1981). The heartbreak gene. *Science 81, 2*(10), 46–50.

Rosenhan, D., & Seligman, M. (1984). *Abnormal Psychology.* New York: W. W. Norton.

Rosenthal, D. (1968). The heredity-environment issue in schizophrenia: Summary of the conference and present status of our knowledge. In D. Rosenthal & S. Kety (Eds.), *The transmission of schizophrenia.* London: Pergamon Press.

Rusch, F., & Mithaug, D. (1980). *Vocational training for mentally retarded adults: A behavior analytic approach.* Champaign, IL: Research Press.

Rusch, F., & Schutz, R. (1986). Vocational and social work behavior research: An evaluative review. In J. Matson & J. McCartney (Eds.), *Handbook of behavior modification with the mentally retarded.* New York: Plenum.

Rutter, M. (1978). Diagnosis and definition of childhood autism. *Journal of Autism and Childhood Schizophrenia, 8,* 139–161.

Rutter, M., Graham, P., & Yule, W. (1970). Neuropsychiatric study in childhood. *Clinics in developmental medicine.* Philadelphia: Lippincott.

Rutter, M., Lebovic, S., Eisenberg, L., Sneznevsky, A., Sadoun, R., Brooke, E., & Lin, T. (1969). A tri-axial classification of mental disorder in childhood. *Journal of Child Psychology and Psychiatry, 10,* 41–61.

Rutter, M., Tizard, J., Yule, P., Graham, P., & Whitmore, K. (1974). Isle of Wight studies. *Psychological Medicine, 6,* 313–332.

Sailor, W., & Guess, D. (1983). *Severely handicapped students: An instructional design.* Boston: Houghton Mifflin.

Sailor, W., & Haring, N. (1977). Some current directions in the education of the severely/multiply handicapped. *AAESPH Review, 2,* 67–86.

Salisbury, C., & Griggs, R. (1983). Developing respite care services for families of handicapped persons. *Journal of the Association for Persons with Severe Handicaps, 8,* 50–57.

Salvia, J., Schultz, E., & Chapin, N. (1974). Reliability of Bower Scale for screening of children with emotional handicaps. *Exceptional Children, 41,* 117–118.

Salzberg, C., & Villani, T. (1983). Speech training by parents of Down syndrome toddlers: Generalization across settings and instructional contexts. *American Journal of Mental Deficiency, 87,* 403–413.

Sameroff, A., & Chandler, M. (1975). Reproductive risk and the continuum of child-taking casualty. In F. Horowitz (Ed.), *Review of child developmental research* (Vol. 4). Chicago: University of Chicago Press.

Sameroff, A., & Seifer, R. (1983). Familial risk and child competence. *Child Development, 54,* 1254–1268.

Sameroff, A., Seifer, R., & Zax, M. (1982). Early development of children at risk for emotional disorder. *Monographs of the Society for Research in Child Development, 47*(7, Serial No. 199).

Scandary, J., & Bigge, J. (1982). Advocacy. In J. Bigge (Ed.), *Teaching individuals with physical and multiple disabilities* (2nd ed.). Columbus, OH: Charles E. Merrill.

Schalock, R., Harper, R., & Carver, G. (1981). Independent living placement: Five years later. *American Journal of Mental Deficiency, 86,* 170–177.

Schalock, R., & Jensen, M. (1986). Assessing the goodness-of-fit between persons and their environment. *Journal of the Association for Persons with Severe Handicaps, 11,* 103–109.

Scheerenberger, R. (1976). A study of public residential facilities. *Mental Retardation, 14,* 32–35.

Schleien, S., Wehman, P., & Kiernan, J. (1981). Teaching leisure skills to severely handicapped individuals: An age-appropriate dart game. *Journal of Applied Behavior Analysis, 14,* 513–519.

Schneider, J., & Chasnoff, I. (1987). Cocaine abuse during pregnancy: Its effects on infant motor development—a clinical perspective. *Trauma Rehabilitation, 2,* 59–69.

Schopler, E., & Reichler, R. (1971). Psychobiological referents for the treatment of autism. In D. Churchill, G. Alpern, & M. DeMyer (Eds.), *Infantile autism.* Springfield, IL: Charles C Thomas.

Schreibman, L., Charlop, M., & Britten, K. (1983). Childhood autism. In R. Morris & T. Kratochwill (Eds.), *The practice of child therapy.* New York: Pergamon Press.

Schreibman, L., Kohlenberg, B., & Britten, K. (1986). Differential responding to content and intonation components of a complex auditory stimulus by nonverbal and echolalic autistic children. *Analysis and Intervention in Developmental Disabilities, 6,* 109–125.

Schreibman, L., & Mills, J. (1983). Infantile autism. In T. Ollendick & M. Hensen (Eds.), *Handbook of child psychopathology.* New York: Plenum.

Schroeder, S., & Schroeder, C. (1982). Organic theories. In J. Paul & B. Epanchin (Eds.), *Emotional disturbances in children.* Columbus, OH: Charles E. Merrill.

Schutz, R., Vogelsberg, T., & Rusch, F. (1980). A behavioral approach to integrating individuals in the community. In A. Novak & L. Heal (Eds.), *Integration of developmentally disabled individuals in the community.* Baltimore: Paul H. Brookes.

Schutz, R., Williams, W., Iverson, G., & Duncan, D. (1984). Social integration of severely handicapped students. In N. Certo, N. Haring, & R. York (Eds.), *Public school integration of severely handicapped students.* Baltimore: Paul H. Brookes.

Schwarz, M., & Hawkins, R. (1970). Application of delayed reinforcement procedures to the behavior of an elementary school child. *Journal of Applied Behavior Analysis, 3,* 85–96.

Sedlak, R., Doyle, M., & Schloss, P. (1982). Video games: A training and generalization demonstration with severely retarded adolescents. *Education and Training of the Mentally Retarded, 17,* 332–336.

Seligmann, J., Katz, S., Hutchinson, S., & Huck, J. (1986, September 22). Babies born with AIDS. *Newsweek,* pp. 70–71.

Selling, L. (1940). *Men against madness.* New York: Greenberg Publishing.

Sells, C., & Bennett, F. (1977). Prevention of mental retardation: The role of medicine. *American Journal of Mental Deficiency, 82,* 117–129.

Selye, H. (1975). Confusion and controversy in the stress field. *Journal of Human Stress, 1,* 37–44.

Senatore, V., Matson, J., & Kazdin, A. (1985). An inventory to assess psychopathology of mentally retarded adults. *American Journal of Mental Deficiency, 82,* 459–466.

Sever, J. (1970). Infectious agents and fetal disease. In H. Weissman & G. Kerr (Eds.), *Fetal growth and development.* New York: McGraw-Hill.

Shane, H. (1980). Approaches to assessing the communication of nonoral persons. In R. Schiefelbusch (Ed.), *Nonspeech language and communication: Analysis and intervention.* Baltimore: University Park Press.

Shane, H., & Bashir, A. (1980). Election criteria for the adoption of an augmentative communication system: Preliminary considerations. *Journal of Speech and Hearing Disorders, 5,* 408–414.

Shane, H., Reynolds, A., & Geary, D. (1977). The elicitation of latent oral communicative potential in a severely handicapped adult: Procedures and implications. *AAESPH Review, 2,* 202–209.

Shearer, D., & Shearer, M. (1972). The Portage Project: A model for early childhood intervention. In T. Tjossem (Ed.), *Intervention strategies for high risk infants and young children.* Baltimore: University Park Press.

Shestakofsky, S., Van Gelder, M., & Kiernan, W. (1986). Employment strategies and service system. In W. Kiernan & J. Stark (Eds.), *Pathways to employment for adults with developmental disabilities.* Baltimore: Paul H. Brookes.

Shonkoff, J. (1972). Biological and social factors contributing to mild mental retardation. In K. Heller (Ed.), *Selection and placement of students in programs for the mentally retarded.* Washington, DC: Committee on Child Development Research and Public Policy, National Academy of Sciences.

Shoultz, B. (1986). Self-advocacy: Speaking for yourself. *TASH Newsletter, 12*(10), 8–9.

Shoultz, B., & Kalyanpur, M. (1987a). *Families for all children.* Syracuse, NY: Center on Human Policy, Syracuse University.

Shoultz, B., & Kalyanpur, R. (1987b). *Respite care for parents of children with disabilities.* Syracuse, NY: Center on Human Policy, Syracuse University.

Silverman, H., McNaughton, S., & Kates, B. (1978). *Handbook of Blissymbolics for instructors, users, parents, and administrators.* Toronto: Blissymbolics Communication Institute.

Simeonsson, R., & Bailey, D. (1986). Siblings of handicapped children. In J. Gallagher & P. Vietz (Eds.), *Families of handicapped persons: Research, programs, and policy issues.* Baltimore: Paul H. Brookes.

Simeonsson, R., & McHale, S. (1981). Research on handicapped children: Siblings relationship. *Child Care, Health, and Development, 7,* 153–171.

Smith, J. (1988). The dangers of prenatal cocaine use. *American Journal of Maternal Child Nursing, 13,* 174–179.

Smith, J., & Deitch, K. (1987). Cocaine: A maternal, fetal, and neonatal risk. *Journal of Pediatric Health Care, 1,* 120–124.

Smith, M. (1985). Managing the aggressive and self-injurious behavior of adults disabled by autism. *Journal of the Association for Persons with Severe Handicaps, 10,* 228–232.

Smith, M., & Belcher, R. (1985). Teaching life skills to adults disabled by autism. *Journal of Autism and Developmental Disorders, 15,* 163–175.

Snell, M. (1987). *Systematic instruction of persons with severe handicaps* (3rd ed.). Columbus, OH: Charles E. Merrill.

Snell, M., & Beckman-Brindley, S. (1984). Family involvement in intervention with children having severe handicaps. *Journal of the Association for Persons with Severe Handicaps, 9,* 213–230.

Snell, M., & Browder, D. (1986). Community-referenced instruction: Research and issues. *Journal of the Association for Persons with Severe Handicaps, 11,* 1–11.

Snyder, L., Apolloni, T., & Cooke, T. (1976). Integrated settings at the early childhood level: The role of nonretarded peers. *Exceptional Children, 43,* 262–266.

Song, A. (1979). Acquisition and use of Blissymbols by severely mentally retarded adolescents. *Mental Retardation, 17,* 253–255.

Sontag, E., Certo, N., & Button, J. (1979). On a distinction between the education of the severely and profoundly handicapped and a doctrine of limitations. *Exceptional Children, 45,* 604–616.

Spellman, C., DeBriere, T., Jarboe, D., Campbell, S., & Harris, C. (1978). Pictorial instruction: Training daily living skills. In M. Snell (Ed.), *Systematic instruction of the moderately and severely handicapped.* Columbus, OH: Charles E. Merrill.

Spreat, S., & Isett, R. (1981). Behavioral effects of intra-institutional relocation. *Applied Research in Mental Retardation, 2,* 229–237.

Stainback, W., & Stainback, S. (1987). Educating all students in regular education. *TASH Newsletter, 13*(4), 1, 7.

Stein, J. (1963). Motor function and physical fitness of the mentally retarded: A critical review. *Rehabilitation Literature, 24,* 230–242.

Stein, L., Palmer, L., & Weinberg, B. (1980). *Characteristics of a young deaf-blind population* (Siegel Report No. 18). Chicago: Siegel Institute.

Stephens, W. (1971). The appraisal of cognitive development. In W. Stephens (Ed.), *Training the developmentally young.* New York: John Day.

Stephens, W. (1977). A Piagetian approach to curriculum development. In E. Sontag (Ed.), *Educational programming for the severely and profoundly handicapped.* Reston, VA: Council for Exceptional Children.

Stevenson, M., & Lamb, M. (1981). The effects of social experience. In M. Lamb (Ed.), *Infant social cognition: Theoretical and empirical considerations.* Hillside, NJ: Lawrence Erlbaum.

Stewart, J. (1981). The deaf-blind: Their nature and needs. In P. Valletutti & B. Sims-Tucker (Eds.), *Severely and profoundly handicapped students: Their nature and needs.* Baltimore: Paul H. Brookes.

Stillman, R., Alymer, J., & Vandivort, J. (1983). *The functions of signaling behaviors in profoundly impaired deaf-blind children and adolescents.* Paper presented at the 107th annual meeting of the American Association on Mental Deficiency, Dallas.

Stokes, T., & Baer, D. (1977). An implicit technology of generalization. *Journal of Applied Behavioral Analysis, 10,* 349–367.

Stokes, T., Baer, D., & Jackson, R. (1974). Programming the generalization of a greeting response in four retarded children. *Journal of Applied Behavior Analysis, 7,* 559–601.

Stokes, T., & Osnes, P. (1986). Programming the generalization of children's social behavior. In P. Strain, M. Guralnick, & H. Walker (Eds.), *Children's social behavior: Development, assessment and modification.* Orlando, FL: Academic Press.

Stokes, T., & Osnes, P. (1988). The developing applied technology of generalization and maintenance. In R. Horner, G. Dunlap, & R. Koegel (Eds.), *Generalization and maintenance: Life-style changes in applied settings.* Baltimore: Paul H. Brookes.

Storey, K., Bates, P., & Hanson, H. (1984). Acquisition and generalization of coffee purchase skills by adults with severe disabilities. *Journal of the Association for Persons with Severe Handicaps, 9,* 178–185.

Strain, P., Odom, S., & McConnell, S. (1984). Promoting social reciprocity of exceptional children: Identification, target behavior selection and intervention. *Remedial and Special Education, 5,* 21–28.

Strully, J., & Strully, C. (1985). Friendship and our children. *Journal of the Association for Persons with Severe Handicaps, 10,* 224–227.

Sugarman, S. (1978). Some organization aspects of pre-verbal communication. In I. Markova (Ed.), *Social context of language.* London: John Wiley.

Tarjan, G., Wright, S., Eyman, R., & Keeran, C. (1973). Natural history of mental retardation: Some aspects of epidemiology. *American Journal of Mental Deficiency, 77,* 369–379.

Taylor, S. (1980). The effect of chronic childhood illness upon well siblings. *Maternal-Child Nursing Journal, 9,* 109–116.

Telsey, A., Merrit, T., & Dixon, S. (1988). Cocaine exposure in a term neonate: Necrotizing enterocolitis as a complication. *Clinical Pediatrics, 27,* 547–549.

Templeman, D., Gage, M., & Fredericks, H. (1982). Cost effectiveness of the group home. *Journal of the Association for Persons with Severe Handicaps, 6,* 11–16.

Thomason, J., & Arkell, C. (1980). Educating the severely/profoundly handicapped in the public schools: A side-by-side approach. *Exceptional Children, 47,* 114–122.

Tinbergen, N. (1974). Etiology and stress disease. *Science, 185,* 20–27.

Titmuss, R. (1971). *The gift relationship.* London: Allen & Unwin.

Tronick, E. (1981). *Social interchange in infancy.* Baltimore: University Park Press.

Tseng, W., & McDermott, J. (1979). Triaxial family classification: A proposal. *Journal of the American Academy of Child Psychiatry, 18,* 22–43.

Turnbull, A. (1983). Parent professional interactions. In M. Snell (Ed.), *Systematic instruction of the moderately and severely handicapped* (2nd ed.). Columbus, OH: Charles E. Merrill.

Turnbull, H. (1981). Two legal analysis techniques and public policy analysis. In R. Haskins & J. Gallagher (Eds.), *Models for social policy analysis.* Norwood, NJ: Ablex.

Turnbull, H., & Guess, D. (with Backus, L., Barber, P., Fiedler, C., Helmstetter, E., & Summers, J.). (1986). A model for analyzing the moral aspects of special education and behavioral interventions: The moral aspects of aversive procedures. In P. Dokecki & R. Zaner (Eds.), *Ethics of dealing with persons with severe handicaps: Toward a research agenda.* Baltimore: Paul H. Brookes.

Tuttle, D. (1984). *Self-esteem and adjusting with blindness.* Springfield, IL: Charles C Thomas.

Ullmann, C. (1952). *Identification of maladjusted school children* (Public Health No. 7). Washington, DC: U.S. Government Printing Office.

U.S. Commission on Civil Rights. (1983). *Accommodating the spectrum of disabilities.* Washington, DC: U.S. Government Printing Office.

U.S. Department of Education. (1984). *Sixth annual report to Congress on the implementation of Public Law 94–142: The Education for All Handicapped Children Act.* Washington, DC: U.S. Government Printing Office.

U.S. Department of Education. (1985a). *New services for deaf-blind children* (SEP Memorandum). Washington, DC: U.S. Government Printing Office.

U.S. Department of Education. (1985b). *Seventh annual report to Congress on the implementation of Public Law 94–142: The Education for All Handicapped Children Act.* Washington, DC: U.S. Government Printing Office.

U.S. Department of Health, Education, and Welfare. (1971). *Children and youth. Selected health characteristics, United States, 1958 and 1968: Vital and health statistics.* Washington, DC: U.S. Government Printing Office.

U.S. Department of Labor. (1977). *Sheltered workshop study, workshop survey* (Vol. 1). Washington, DC: U.S. Government Printing Office.

U.S. Department of Labor. (1979). *Sheltered workshop study, workshop survey* (Vol. 2). Washington, DC: U.S. Government Printing Office.

Utley, B. (1982). Motor skills and adaptations. In L. Sternberg & G. Adams (Eds.), *Educating severely and profoundly handicapped students.* Rockville, MD: Aspen Publishers.

Uzgiris, I. (1981). Experience in the social context, imitation, and play. In R. Schiefelbusch & D. Bricker (Eds.), *Early language: Acquisition and intervention.* Baltimore: University Park Press.

Vicker, B. (1974). *Non-oral communication system project 1964/1973.* Iowa City: University of Iowa.

Vincent, L., Salisbury, C., Walter, G., Brown, P., Gruenewald, L., & Powers, M. (1980). Program development and curriculum development in early childhood/special education: Criteria of the next environment. In W. Sailor, B. Wilcox, & L. Brown (Eds.), *Methods of instruction for severely handicapped students.* Baltimore: Paul H. Brookes.

Voeltz, L. (1984). Program and curriculum innovations to prepare children for integration. In N. Certo, N. Haring, & R. York (Eds.), *Public school integration of severely handicapped students: Rational issues and progressive alternatives.* Baltimore: Paul H. Brookes.

Voeltz, L., Johnson, R., & McQuarter, R. (1983). The integration of school-aged children and youth with severe disabilities. In S. Maurer (Ed.), *Integration strategies for students with moderate and severe handicaps.* Des Moines, IA: Iowa Department of Public Instruction.

Vogelsberg, R., Williams, W., & Friedl, M. (1980). Facilitating systems change for the severely handicapped: Secondary and adult services. *Journal of the Association for the Severely Handicapped, 5,* 73–85.

Wallin, J. (1955). *Education of mentally retarded children.* New York: Harper & Row.

Wallis, C. (1986, January 20). Cocaine babies: Addicts bear ailing infants. *Time,* p. 50.

Warren, D. (1984). *Blindness and early childhood development.* New York: American Foundation for the Blind.

Warren, R., & Dickman, I. (1981). *For this respite, much thanks: Concepts, guidelines, and issues in the development of community respite services for families of persons with developmental disabilities.* New York: United Cerebral Palsy Association.

Wehman, P. (1979). Teaching recreational skills to severely and profoundly handicapped persons. In E. Edgar & R. York (Eds.), *Teaching the severely handicapped* (Vol. IV). Seattle: AAESPH.

Wehman, P. (1981). *Competitive employment: New horizons for severely disabled individuals.* Baltimore: Paul H. Brookes.

Wehman, P. (1983). Toward the employability of severely handicapped children and youth. *Teaching Exceptional Children, 16,* 220–225.

Wehman, P., & Hill, J. (1979a). *Vocational training and placement for severely disabled individuals* (Vol. 1). Richmond, VA: Virginia Commonwealth University.

Wehman, P., & Hill, J. (1979b). *Vocational training and placement for severely disabled individuals: Project employability* (Vol. 2). Richmond, VA: Virginia Commonwealth University.

Wehman, P., & Hill, M. (1982). *Vocational training and placement for severely disabled individuals: Project employability* (Vol. 3). Richmond, VA: Virginia Commonwealth University.

Wehman, P., Hill, M., Goodall, P., Cleveland, P., Brookes, V., & Pentecost, J. (1982). Job placement and follow-up of moderately and severely handicapped individuals after three years. *Journal of the Association for the Severely Handicapped, 7,* 5–16.

Wehman, P., Kregel, J., & Barcus, J. (1985). School to work: Vocational transition model for handicapped youth. In P. Wehman & J. Hewett (Eds.), *Competitive employment for persons with mental retardation: From research to practice.* Richmond, VA: Virginia Commonwealth University.

Wehman, P., Kregel, J., Barcus, J., & Schalock, R. (1986). Vocational transition for students with developmental disabilities. In W. Kiernan & J. Stark (Eds.), *Pathways to employment for adults with developmental disabilities.* Baltimore: Paul H. Brookes.

Wehman, P., Kregel, J., & Seyfarth, J. (1985). Employment outlook for young adults with mental retardation. *Rehabilitation Counseling Bulletin, 12,* 90–99.

Wehman, P., Kregel, J., & Zoller, K. (1984). *A follow-up of mentally retarded graduates' vocational and independent living in Virginia.* Unpublished manuscript. Virginia Commonwealth University, Richmond, VA.

Wehman, P., & McLaughlin, P. (1979). Teacher's perceptions of problem behavior in severely and profoundly handicapped students. *Mental Retardation, 17,* 20–21.

Wehman, P., & McLaughlin, P. (1981). *Program development in special education.* New York: McGraw-Hill.

Wehman, P., Moon, M., Everson, J., Wood, W., & Barcus, J. (1988). *Transition from school to work: New challenges for youth with severe disabilities.* Baltimore: Paul H. Brookes.

Wehman, P., Renzaglia, A., & Bates, P. (1985). *Functional living skills for moderately and severely handicapped individuals.* Austin, TX: PRO-ED.

Wehman, P., Renzaglia, A., Berry, G., Schutz, R., & Karan, O. (1978). Developing a leisure skill repertoire in severely and profoundly handicapped adolescents and adults. *AAESPH Review, 3,* 162–172.

Wehman, P., & Schleien, S. (1980a). Assessment and selection of leisure skills for severely and profoundly handicapped persons. *Education and Training of the Mentally Retarded, 14,* 50–58.

Wehman, P., & Schleien, S. (1980b). Leisure skills programming for severely handicapped children. In G. Cartlege & S. Cartwright (Eds.), *Teaching social skills to exceptional children.* New York: Pergamon Press.

Wehman, P., & Schleien, S. (1981). *Leisure programs for handicapped persons: Adaptations, techniques, and curriculum.* Austin, TX: PRO-ED.

Weinrich, K. (1987). Advocates as a vocational training resource. *Rehabilitation Literature, 50,* 26–34.

Weintraub, F., & Abeson, A. (1974). New education policies for the handicapped: A quiet revolution. *Phi Delta Kappa, 55,* 526–529, 569.

White, O. (1983). *Research in facilitating generalized responding.* Paper presented to the meeting of the Association for Persons with Severe Handicaps, San Francisco.

White, O. (1985). Aim star wars (setting aims that compete), episodes II and III. *Journal of Precision Teaching, 5,* 86–94.

Whitehead, C. (1979). Sheltered workshops in the decade ahead: Work and wages or welfare. In G. Bellamy, G. O'Connor, & O. Karan (Eds.), *Vocational rehabilitation of severely handicapped persons.* Baltimore: University Park Press.

Whitman, T., Hurley, J., Johnson, M., & Christian, J. (1978). Direct and generalized reduction of inappropriate behavior in a severely retarded child through a parent-administered behavior modification program. *AAESPH Review, 3,* 67–77.

Whitman, T., & Sciback, J. (1979). Behavior modification research with severely and profoundly retarded. In N. Ellis (Ed.), *Handbook of mental deficiency, psychological theory, and research* (2nd ed.). New York: Lawrence Erlbaum.

Wiegerink, R., & Parrish, V. (1976). A parent-implemented preschool program. In D. Lillie & P. Trohanis (Eds.), *Teaching parents to teach.* New York: Walker.

Wikler, L. (1986). Family stress theory and research on families of children with mental retardation. In J. Gallagher & P. Vietze (Eds.), *Families of handicapped persons: Research, programs, and policy issues.* Baltimore: Paul H. Brookes.

Wilcox, B. (1987). What should parents expect? *TASH Newsletter, 13*(3), 1, 3.

Wilcox, B., & Bellamy, G. (1982). *Design of high school programs for severely handicapped students.* Baltimore: Paul H. Brookes.

Will, M. (1984). *OSERS programming for the transition of youth with disabilities: Bridges from school to working life* (Policy paper of the Office of Special Education and Rehabilitative Services). Washington, DC: U.S. Government Printing Office.

Williams, P., & Shoultz, B. (1982). *We can speak for ourselves: Self-advocacy by mentally handicapped people.* Bloomington, IN: Indiana University Press.

Williams, W., Brown, L., & Certo, N. (1975). Basic components of instructional programs. *Theory into Practice, 14,* 123–136.

Williams, W., Hamre-Nietupski, S., Pumpian, I., McDaniel-Marks, J., & Wheeler, J. (1978). Teaching social skills, In M. Snell (Ed.), *Systematic instruction of the moderately and severely handicapped.* Columbus, OH: Charles E. Merrill.

Wilson, J. (1973). *Environment and birth defects.* New York: Academic Press.

Wing, L. (1972). *Autistic children: A guide for parents and professionals.* New York: Brunner/Mazel.

Wing, L. (1976). *Early childhood autism.* Elmsford, NY: Pergamon Press.

Wing, L. (1985). *Autistic children: A guide for parents and professionals* (2nd ed.). New York: Brunner/Mazel.

Winton, P., & Turnbull, A. (1981). Parent involvement as viewed by parents of preschool handicapped children. *Topics in Early Childhood Special Education, 1*(3), 11–19.

Wolf, J., & McAloniue, M. (1977). A multimodality language program for retarded preschoolers. *Education and Training of the Mentally Retarded, 12,* 197–202.

Wolf, M. (1978). Social validity: The case for subjective measurement, or how behavior analysis is finding its heart. *Journal of Applied Behavior Analysis, 11,* 203–214.

Wolfensberger, W. (1972). *The principle of normalization in human services*. Toronto: National Institute on Mental Retardation.

Wolfensberger, W. (1973). Citizen advocacy for the handicapped, impaired, and disadvantaged: An overview. In W. Wolfensberger & H. Zauha (Eds.), *Citizen advocacy and protective services for the impaired and handicapped*. Toronto: National Institute on Mental Retardation.

Wolfensberger, W. (1980). A brief overview of the principle of normalization. In R. Flynn & K. Nitsch (Eds.), *Normalization, social integration, and community services*. Austin, TX: PRO-ED.

Wolfensberger, W., & Brown, B. (1973). Youth advocacy. In W. Wolfensberger & H. Zauha (Eds.), *Citizen advocacy and protective services for the impaired and handicapped*. Toronto: National Institute on Mental Retardation.

Wolfensberger, W., Nirje, B., Olshansky, S., Perske, R., & Roos, P. (1972). *The principle of normalization in human service systems*. Toronto: National Institute on Mental Retardation.

Wood, F., & Zabel, R. (1978). Making sense of reports on the incidence of behavior disorders/emotional disturbances in school-aged children. *Psychology in the Schools, 15*, 45–51.

Woods, J., Plessinger, M., & Clark, K. (1987). Effect of cocaine on uterine blood flow and fetal oxygenation. *Journal of the American Medical Association, 257*, 957–961.

Woodward, M. (1963). The application of Piaget's theory to research in mental deficiency. In N. Ellis (Ed.), *Handbook of mental deficiency*. New York: McGraw-Hill.

Woodward, M. (1979). Piaget's theory and the study of mental retardation. In. N. Ellis (Ed.), *Handbook of mental deficiency* (2nd ed.). Hillsdale, NJ: Lawrence Erlbaum.

Wyatt v. Aderhold, 503 F.2d 1305, 712634 (5th Cir. 1974).

Wyatt v. Ireland, 430 F.2d 2208 (5th Cir. 1979).

Wyatt v. Stickney, 344 F. Supp. 373, 387 (M.D. Ala. 1972).

Zaslow, R., & Breger, A. (1969). A theory and treatment of autism. In L. Breger (Ed), *Clinical cognitive psychology*. Englewood Cliffs, NJ: Prentice-Hall.

Zeaman, D., & House, B. (1963). The role of retardate discrimination learning. In N. Ellis (Ed.), *Handbook of mental deficiency*. New York: McGraw-Hill.

Ziegler, S., & Hambleton, D. (1976). Integration of young TMR children into regular elementary school. *Exceptional Children, 42*, 459–461.

Zifferblatt, S., Burton, S., Horner, R., & White, T. (1977). Establishing generalization effects among autistic children. *Journal of Autism and Childhood Schizophrenia, 4*, 337–346.

Zilboorg, G., & Henry, G. (1941). *A history of medical psychology*. New York: W. W. Norton.

Index